Downward Causation

Downward Causation

Minds, Bodies and Matter

Edited by
Peter Bøgh Andersen
Claus Emmeche
Niels Ole Finnemann
Peder Voetmann Christiansen

AARHUS UNIVERSITY PRESS

Copyright: Aarhus University Press, 2000
Word-processed by Peter Bøgh Andersen
Printed in England at the Alden Press, Oxford
ISBN 87 7288 814 1

AARHUS UNIVERSITY PRESS
Langelandsgade 177
DK-8200 Aarhus N
Fax 8942 5380

73 Lime Walk
Headington, Oxford OX3 7AD
Fax (01865) 75 00 79

Box 511
Oakville, Connecticut 06779
Fax (860) 945 9468

ww.au.dk/unipress

∞
ANSI/NISO
Z39.48-1992

Preface

The past two decades have witnessed a growing change in the way we view and understand the world. One of the insights fueling this change is very simple and can be succinctly stated as follows:

- Complex behavior can be generated by many simple interacting components.

This simple idea has cropped up in many different fields (cf. Casti 1997): chemistry (e.g. Prigogine's theory of dissipative structures), biology (the ALife research programme launched by Christopher Langton in 1987, the seminal paper by Aristid Lindenmayer from 1968), geometry (e.g., the Mandelbrot set discovered by Benoit Mandelbrot in 1979), meteorology (Ed Lorenz' discovery of the 'butterfly effect' around 1960), computer science (McClelland et al's influential book on parallel distributed processing from 1986, and the current interest in autonomous agents), and sociology (Gilberg & Doran 1994). Computer-simulations played an important role in verifying this simple idea.

On the one hand, this insight seems to be a fulfillment of the classical positivistic dream of reducing the teeming complexity of life and society to the micro-moments of myriads of elementary physical particles, and being able to predict the progress of the universe by simple physical laws. But, by an irony of history, the same insight that created this hope, undermined it completely by two unfortunate side-effects:

- In complex chemical processes, time, chance, irreversibility, and — as a consequence — *history* entered hard science.
- In complex chaotic systems, predictability was severely limited, not for practical but for theoretical reasons.

Thus, although it could be proven that complexity could arise from the interaction of many simple processes, it could unfortunately also be proven that some of these processes were irreversible, making repetitions of experiments problematic, and that in addition they were extremely sensitive to initial conditions, making predictions from measurements with errors unreliable.

In the classical tradition of science that saw the world as a deterministic clockwork, *prediction* and *control* were highly valued, and with good reason. In the new universe, determinism has been divorced from predictability and repeatability has shrunk to a small island, surrounded by a vast sea of unpredictability and irreversibility, and we are only beginning to develop reliable methods for navigating this ocean.

The new points of view put many new kinds of problems on the scientific agenda. One of these is the topic of this book. It was termed *downward causation* by the late social psychologist and philosopher D.T. Campbell (Campbell 1974) and can be defined as follows: if many small-scale interactions can create emergent large-scale patterns

• can large-scale patterns re-influence the small-scale interactions that generated them?

Does the cell as a system reorganize the biochemical processes inside it in a new way? So that, once established, capacity for DNA-replication and cellular self-reproduction begins to act as constraining conditions for the metabolic interactions via the genetic code that — out of a huge space of possible proteins — selects or controls which small set of highly specific proteins can be realized.

Do psychosomatic illnesses exist? Can the psyche, conceived as an emergent phenomenon of biological processes, influence the same processes that created it? And if so, how is this done? Similarly, although it is clear that groups consist of individuals, and that the psyches of the individuals influence the group's global behavior, is it possible that the group can re-influence the individuals. Is mass-psychology a reality?

Is the so-called hermeneutic circle real? When we read a book (whole), we start by assigning provisional meanings to the words (parts). After having interpreted a sentence, the temporary interpretations of the words are revised, which again modifies the interpretation of the sentence. This kind of mutual modifications does not stop at the sentence level but continues the whole text through. In the beginning, the word 'rose' may mean a flower, but in the ending it may have got an elaborate non-standard metaphorical meaning due to the global theme of the book. In the hermeneutic circle, parts determine the whole and the whole determines the parts.

Should we interpret these higher-level phenomena as indicating a new ontolo-gical layer, with its own units and laws? Are there special substances of life, mind and meaning? If so, can these new entities change the behavior of the lower-level entities? Can life change biochemical laws? Can mind change the body? Can meaning and culture change our animal behavior beyond recognition? If these substances do not exist, then how do we explain the improbable fact that ontogenesis nearly always manages to harness biochemical processes so that they produce well-formed babies? How can we explain the fact that our intentions, ideas and ideologies continually inspire the way we change our social and physical environment? Which forces, if not meaning and communication, have endowed human society with the combination of stability and restlessness that has increased its causal and functional complexity tremendously, compared to animal social organizations.

The present collection of papers address these questions from the viewpoints of different disciplines. Part 1 contains a classification of positions with respect to the concept of 'Downward Causation' to which many of the papers relate. The emphasis in Part 2 is on physics, and Part 3 discusses biology and psychology. Part 4 deals with social and communicative systems, and the last part contains two general philosophical papers. Most of the authors participated in a small two-day seminar in Denmark where drafts were discussed. After the seminar the papers were revised.

We are grateful for financial support from the Aarhus University Research Foundation and from the Danish Research Councils.

Aarhus, December, 1999

Peter Bøgh Andersen
Claus Emmeche
Niels Ole Finnemann
Peder Voetmann Christiansen

References

CAMPBELL, D.T. 1974. 'Downward causation' in hierarchically organised biological systems. In F. Ayala & T. Dobzhansky (eds.), *Studies in the Philosophy of Biology*. Berkeley: University of California Press, 179-86.

CASTI, J.L. 1997. *Would-Be Worlds*. New York: Wiley & Sons.

GILBERG, N. & J. DORAN (eds.) 1994. *Simulating Societies*. London: UCL Press.

LANGTON, C.G. (ed.) 1989. *Artificial Life*. Redwood City: Addison-Wesley.

LINDENMAYER, A. 1968. Mathematical models for cellular interaction in development, Parts I and II. *Journal of Theoretical Biology* 18: 280-315.

MCCLELLAND, J. et al. (eds.) 1986. *Parallel Distibuted Processing*. Cambridge, Mass: MIT Press.

PEITGEN, H.O, H. JÜRGENS & D. SAUPE 1992. *Chaos and fractals*. Berlin: Springer-Verlag.

PRIGOGINE, I. & I. STENGERS 1984. *Order out of Chaos. Man's new dialogue with nature*. New York: Bantam Books.

Contents

Part I
Introduction

1

Levels, Emergence, and Three Versions of Downward Causation

CLAUS EMMECHE, SIMO KØPPE & FREDERIK STJERNFELT

Abstract

The idea of a higher level phenomenon having a downwardly causal influence on a lower level process or entity has taken a variety of forms. In order to discuss the relation between emergence and downward causation, the specific variety of the thesis of downward causation (DC) must be identified. Based on some ontological theses about inter-level relations, types of causation and the possibility of reduction, three versions of DC are distinguished. Of these, the 'Strong' form of DC is held to be in conflict with contemporary science; the 'Medium' version of DC may for instance describe thoughts constraining neurophysiological states, while the 'Weak' form of DC is physically acceptable but may not in practice be a feasible description of the mind/brain or the cell/molecule relation. All forms have their specific problems, but the Medium and the Weak version seems to be most promising.

Introduction

The concept of Downward Causation has a rather diffuse origin and it is difficult to ascertain the first use of the concept.[1] In any case, downward causation must presuppose the assumption that several levels of reality co-exist, be it merely as levels of description or as levels of description as well as of ontology. Together with level theories, the concept of emergence is very often used as a designation for the relation between the new or unpredictable property on the higher level

---

[1] In his 1923 treatise, Lloyd Morgan used the term supervenience (which later acquired a different meaning) for the return action of emergents upon the lower level events from which they arose. Campbell (1974) uses the term explicitly, as does Sperry (see below). For comments, see Blitz (1992).

and its basis in the lower level. As a kind of immediate extrapolation of this idea, downward causation is used as a designation for an alleged downward effect which emanates from the emergentically defined higher level onto its constituents in the lower level. Thus, as Jaegwon Kim has put it, '... downward causation is much of the point of the emergentist program' (Kim 1993: 350). Thus, to maintain a theory of ontological levels and emergence, a rational interpretation of the concept of Downward Causation must be given. This shall be our aim in this paper. The sections 1 and 2 will contain some remarks on the concepts of level, causation, form, and substance, which we shall use for discussing the distinct versions of the downward causation concept.

Inclusivity of levels

Several attempts have been made to formulate emergence theories of levels of organization, description, systems, or reality. In many ontological versions of these theories, the entities of each level are considered as being irreducible to those at the level below. The vitalism/reductionism debate in the life sciences shows that a concept of emergence as something inexplicable in principle will often be falsified by the history of science. Nevertheless, the concept of emergence keeps reappearing in various sciences (most recently in complex systems research and artificial life), and it seems that it cannot easily be dispensed with.

We have elsewhere[2] argued for an ontological non-reductionist theory of levels of reality which includes a concept of emergence, and which can support an evolutionary account of the origin of levels. Though the interpretation of *emergence* as 'the creation of new properties' involves several philosophical problems (such as specification of the vague terms 'new' and 'creation'), the intuition involved in the basic idea does not refer to anything mysterious. The concept can be defined formally[3] so as to conform to a more careful standard interpretation of emergence, according to which 'a property of a complex system is said to be 'emergent' just in case, although it arises out of the properties and relations characterizing simpler constituents, it is neither predictable from, nor reducible to, these lower-level characteristics.'[4] The ontology of levels we attempted to give was framed in a materialist and evolutionary perspective that implied that the relation between levels was considered to be *inclusive*, permitting the 'local' existence of different ontologies, all included within the physical level and non-violating physical laws. We identified, as a working hypothesis, four primary levels — the physical, the biological,

---

2   Emmeche, Køppe & Stjernfelt (1997). Our argument in the present paper is a separate one, but the
     notions of local ontology and inclusiveness are discussed in greater detail in the previous paper.
3   Baas (1994); Baas & Emmeche (1997)
4   Kim (1995). Of course, there are problems with this interpretation too. See also Beckermann, Flohr &
     Kim (1992).

the psychic and the social level, these having non-homomorphic inter-level relations. *Inclusiveness* entails the two theses that (a) the evolutionary emergence of a new higher level from the physical (all-inclusive) level does not violate or change any physical laws in spite of the appearance of a new irreducible level of organization (and generally, that lower-level principles of organization are not altered by the emergence of higher levels); (b) the biological ontology is *local* to the extent that different biologies, different organizing principles of life, may emerge on other planets (who knows if life universally takes shape as the natural selection of DNA-coded genotypes?).[5] Furthermore, the inter-level relations are *nonhomomorphic* in the sense that the emergence of the biological from the physical level does not have the same complex of inter-level relations of dependence as the emergence of the social and psychic levels from the biological one, due to the continuous mutual conditioning and interdependence between emergent psyche and sociality. The processes that lead to the first-time emergence of the biological level differ not only materially but also in a formal ontological way from the processes that constitute the psychological and the sociological level: for the latter two, involving the emergence of self-consciousness and institutions, these level-constituting processes are interwoven and depend on both intersubjectivity and language; while for the biological level, they depend upon specific conditions at one single level, the physical one (leading to the evolution of the first cells). But the different cases of emergent phenomena must share some formal features that distinguish them as emergent in comparison with non-emergent phenomena.

One can argue at length about the number of (and demarcations between) the primary levels. Our choice of the four levels mentioned was in part pragmatical (thus, multicellular life and non-self-conscious psyche are serious candidates for further primary levels), but what is ontologically important is that such levels of reality can in fact be rationally distinguished. Our methods for making such distinctions are of course dependent on the historical development of scientific theories and disciplines; thus, one may conceive of arriving at an even more fine-grained theory of levels. By scientific we mean the natural sciences, which deal primarily with phenomena at the physical and biological level, as well as the humanities and the social sciences, which deal with phenomena at the other levels.

Recent research in self-organizing non-linear dynamical systems represents a revival of the scientific study of emergence, and it can be argued that these developments are the final 'devitalisation' or demystification of emergence and thus may also help to clarify the concept of downward causation.

---

5   If truly different local ontologies exist in the universe, inclusiveness and locality imply that the historically contingent form of a given, say, biological, level may influence the further emergence of higher levels. Thus, if self-consciousness and institutions are characteristic for the primary entities at the psychological and sociological level locally known on Earth, we cannot be sure that these characteristics are universally found. Though this is speculative, the general theory of levels conforms to the principles of contemporary science.

Form, substance, causality

We shall try to discern three different conceptions of downward causation and exemplify them by concrete descriptions of alleged emergence, that is, biochemical system —> (emergence of) cell, and nervous system —> (emergence of) psychic system, two of the most classic level borders in the various level theories. Before doing so, we shall formulate two postulates or hypotheses, each of which is given in its inverse variant, to function as an axis in the discussion.

In level theories, the concept of *entity* is used as a designation for the unit that is constitutive for a given level. A level is thus characterized by a certain primary entity possessing the emergent property defining the level. Hence, the specific conception of this entity is crucial as regards the kind of level theory for which one opts.

1 a   *Constitutive reductionism.* Ontologically or materially, a higher level entity (for instance a biological cell) consists of entities belonging to the lower level (the cell consists of molecules). These lower level entities are constituents of the higher level and are organized in a certain way that yields the higher level entity (the cell). This does not mean that the higher level can be reduced to the lower (in which case no levels would be relevant), but that the higher level does not add any substance to the entities of the lower level.

1 b   *Constitutive irreductionism.* Ontologically or materially, a higher level entity is constituted by the lower level, but even if the lower level entities are a necessary condition for the higher level, this higher level cannot be reduced to the form or organization of the constituents. Thus, the higher level must be said to constitute its own substance and not merely to consist of its lower level constituents.

2 a   *Formal realism of levels.* The structure, organisation or form of an entity is an objectively existent and irreducible feature of it. The specific form characterizing a higher level entity (organizing its lower level constituents) cannot be reduced to lower level forms or substances.

2 b   *Substantial realism of levels.* A higher level entity is defined by a substantial difference from lower level entities. The morphological or organizational aspect is a necessary but not sufficient condition of a higher level entity. Through emergence, an ontological change in substance takes place.

These hypotheses are related in such a way that 1a and 2a are often connected in a given argument, as are 1b and 2b. Most theories of downward causation can be placed under one of these two headlines, depending on whether it is the first or the second set of assumptions which (most often implicitly) founded the theory.

Finally, we shall use a reinterpretation of the traditional four Aristotelian types of causality (which of course are not exclusive), and thus distinguish between the following:

(i)   *Efficient causality* is a temporal cause-effect relation involving an interactional exchange of energy pertaining to the entities of a given level. It results in a temporal sequence of states being causally interrelated. In everyday language it is often described in terms like 'implies', 'effects', 'entails', 'causes', 'inflicts', 'bring about', etc.

(ii)   *Material causality* refers to immanent properties in the entities of a given level (which may themselves be composed of the entities of a lower level). Material causality is often described by concepts such as 'consisting of', 'made of', etc.[6]

(iii)   *Formal causality* refers to the form of a given entity or process insofar as it is not reducible to effective or material causality. It is often described by concepts like 'the structure of', 'organizes', etc.

(iv)   *Functional causality* refers to the role played by a part within an integrated processual whole, or the purpose of a behavior seen from the perspective of a system's chance of remaining stable (or 'surviving') over time. Terms such as 'govern', 'control', 'regulate', 'role' and, of course, 'functions' are applied here.

Our reason for using the Aristotelian framework will appear in detail below, but can briefly be stated here: there is a place for a rational concept of downward causation (in some version) in science and philosophy, but only within a broader framework of causal explanation. Very often 'causality' is implicitly equated with the usual notion of efficient causality, but if downward causation is regarded as an instance of efficient causality it will form a 'strong version' of the concept, which, as we shall see, is not a plausible one. The notion of causality should therefore be enlarged to make sense of downward causation. Even in everyday language the dominance of the 'efficient' sense of causality is well known, as can be noticed, for instance, in the apparent oddity of expressions such as 'the wood is the cause of the table', which refers to the material cause and makes perfect sense when translated to the proposition 'the table is made of wood.' The notion of functional causality, our reinterpretation of the Aristotelian 'final cause' (often misunderstood as implying the paradox of a future state (a goal) influencing a present state) does not play any substantial role in the present argument and is only included here to emphasize the general necessity of a set of multiple causal explanatory

---

6   Depending on the specific entity and frame of description, the properties may include potential energy, or specific energy states of particles, field strength, etc.

tools in science, and to posit that this notion can be interpreted in a scientifically legitimate way as well (regardless of whether it is reinterpretation as functional causality, as above, or as intentional causality, which is an alternative possibility).

Now, our idea is that theories of downward causation fall in three types: strong, medium, and weak downward causation, respectively. Before discussing these three types, it is necessary to point out the relation of downward causation to what may be termed *upward causation*. The assumption of downward causation most often rests on the idea of 'bottom-up' processes involving upward causation, and it is possible that, in turn, upward causation always rests on a certain interpretation of the concept of emergence.[7]

The idea behind *upward causation* can be termed as follows: the emergence of a higher entity from a lower one is characterized by a certain causal process leading from the lower level entities to the higher ones, so that the lower level can be seen as the cause and the higher level as the effect. Now, this interpretation of upward causation — to which we shall return in our discussion of the three alternatives — has a tendency to leave the higher level as a fairly impotent construction, seriously threatened to be but an epiphenomenon of the lower one. Thus, supplying this first assumption of upward causation with a complementary one of a downward causation type, thereby restoring the higher level's ontological prominence, seems unavoidable. The idea is that once constituted, the higher level is equipped with causal powers of its own, so that it is then able to inflict effects on the lower level having caused it. Consequently, the biological cell is able to control the single molecules of which it consists, or thought processes are able to guide their neurophysiological substrate in the brain. In this way, every time downward causation is assumed, this is a supplementary gesture to counterweight the threatening reductionism inherent in a previous upward causation. Of course, once both are at work, they work in exactly opposite directions, which is rather hard to imagine; sometimes the notion of 'dialectics' is invoked to picture this process.

Now, given the fact that some kind of downward causation is a necessary supplement to every supposition of an upward causation, the downward causations tend to group in the following three categories.

Strong downward causation

The idea of strong downward causality may be briefly described as follows: a given entity or process on a given level may causally inflict changes or effects on entities or processes on a lower level.

---

7   Cf. Küppers (1992).

This idea requires that the levels in question are sharply distinguished and autonomous, and it can thus be seen as associated with the theses 1b and 2b above. In the history of science, representatives of this theory may be found in the classical vitalists of early biology, who supposed the existence of a creative or formative power outside the range of scientific description. When the vital power has done its work and created the higher level entity, this entity functions autonomously and independently of the lower level. The best examples of such theories are probably found in psychology and philosophy among the classical dualists, who assumed the existence of an immaterial soul that inhabits the body and is able to control it due to its special causal powers.

The theory of strong downward causation is thus based on a constitutive irreductionism (1b): higher level entities do not (only) consist of lower level entities; they possess a substantial existence qualitatively different from lower level entities.

The main arguments against strong downward causation theories are the following. (a) Faced with vital power or the powers of the soul, scientific description is by definition ruled out. Entities like these are simply outside the realm of science (an idea which betrays the theological heritage in this position). (b) Even if a possible and sufficient scientific description of vital power and the soul were imagined, the theory would still be unacceptable because it entails a direct change in the laws of the lower level (or at least a change in lawful regularities at this level) effected from above. If, for instance, gravity could be influenced by secret means belonging to the soul — and a higher level phenomenon thus could inflict a direct causal influence on the lawfulness of processes at a lower level — then the hypothesis of *the inclusivity of levels* does not hold (that is, the idea that higher levels are based on certain complicated subsets from the lower levels and do not violate lower level laws).

The theory of strong downward causation is based on hypotheses 1b and 2b, it introduces a non-scientific, that is, irrational principle, and violates the assumption of the inclusivity of levels. By considering a cell as an emergent entity on the biological level and its physical basis, this criticism of strong downward causation may be exemplified. In describing this emergent entity, we are very often tempted to use downward causation-like concepts in the strong sense; as if, for instance, the emergence of the cell as a living substance efficiently causes changes in the molecules, making them somehow specifically 'biological', i.e. substantially different from molecules of the non-living world,[8] or, alternatively, as if the cell as such

---

8   As if 'organic chemistry' needed other laws of chemistry than inorganic chemistry, as once believed. (By the early 1840s, organic chemistry had become a chemistry of carbon compounds, not a chemistry of living systems as such). Of course, proteins in living cells are indeed characterized by their bio-functional specificity, but this is exactly related to the their functional role in the metabolism of the cell and the property of being (partly) specified by the sequence information in the DNA and produced by the cell's complex molecular machinery. However, this feature of being produced this way and having such

(efficiently) causes changes in the biochemical reactions among its constituents. But if we imagine a microscopic view of this alleged causal process, we will be unable to find any effective causality in the scenario. First, the process does not take place in time; second, the two events in question do not even possess the ability of causing each other. Of course, it is evident that the biological cell 'governs' or 'influences' the biochemical processes taking place in it — but at the same time the cell remains in itself a biochemical construct. So on the biochemical level we see nothing but individual biochemical reactions causing one another. There is simply no identifiable process through which the cell ('as such', i.e., non-biochemically conceived) inflicts a cause on biochemistry. The cell consists of biochemical processes, we could say, but this is a non-temporal (mereological) relation and therefore non-causal in the efficient-causality use of the word. So even the idea of an upward efficient cause (or 'strong' upward causation) from biochemistry to cell is wrong because of this; what we could say instead is that the molecules and the biochemical relations in question *constitute* the cell, that is, they are the material and formal causes of the cell. (Therefore, the cell is — to anticipate the notion of weak DC — like a stable (pseudo)-cyclical attractor in a biochemical phase space and thus it attracts the trajectories for the biochemical processes, but this 'attraction' is a tendency in phase space, a property in the biochemical system in question and not a cause in the efficient use of the word. This attractor description is explained in the section on weak DC).

The concept of strong downward causation may be the result of too radical and substantial a divorce between levels, making it impossible for them to influence each other at all. When I kick a ball, it is the physics of my body which by means of efficient causality influences another physical object; it is not an autonomous psychical poseur incarnating itself in physics. On the other hand, the physics of my body is of a certain, very complicated kind, yielding emergent properties of a biological as well as of a psychical kind. The physics possessing these complicated psychical properties is able to kick the ball.[9]

---

and such a functional role does not change the chemical properties of a given molecule. A biological protein such as a cytochrome C enzyme is not qualitatively different from other non-natural (artificially produced) proteins in its substance, and differs only in chemical properties (e.g., its reaction kinetics) from such non-natural proteins for the same reason that two biological proteins (with different three-dimensional structures) differ in their chemical properties. In other words: the biological specificity of naturally occurring proteins is their ability to catalyze a particular chemical reaction that is functional for the living cell; the fact that the cell contains DNA that specify (or 'code') the primary structure of these proteins (a tiny amount out of a huge space of combinatorically possible proteins of a given size) is a consequence of the whole evolutionary history of the cell. In this sense, the chemical properties of biological proteins are perfectly chemically explainable, but their functional role in the cell and their evolutionary origin involve kinds of explanation (functional-cybernetic and evolutionary) different from pure biochemistry.

9   Pattee (in a comment on a version of this paper) remarked that this is a good illustration of why 'the universal cause' (see Pattee's paper in this volume) does not explain anything, as we seem to be 'begging the question of what makes a good model of measurement and control processes (...). Why is not the psychical state of John's brain that ardently desires a goal as efficient a cause (or useful or acceptable an explanation) as the physics of collisions?' Pattee suggest that we should 'try telling a soccer

For this reason, strong downward causation seems to be in danger of re-importing ideas about causation that pose the same unsolvable problems as vitalism did in biology. Before going on to — what we consider — the two more plausible versions of downward causation, it might be worthwhile to attempt to understand the reason behind the recurrent and faulty assumption of strong downward causation. What in fact is the intuition behind the very idea of a (strong) upward causation?

The naive scenario leading to this idea is probably the following: 'first' we gather a range of complicated organic molecules on the lower, physical level and 'then' this structure 'causes' a biological organism to 'be created.' When 'first' constituted, its metabolism functions as a stable and tightly regulated system, so that as a whole it emits 'causes downwards' onto the chemical-physical level, which consequently is now governed by a downward cause. (The example of physics/biology may easily be substituted by brain/psyche or any other prominent distinction between levels).

The fault in this scenario or thought experiment is first of all the temporal, processual rhetoric structuring it — here emphasized by quotation marks — making it appear as if the process of the thought experiment corresponds to a real, existent chain of efficient causes, a regularity in time involving the exchange of energy. But contrary to what seems to be demonstrated by the experiment, the upward- and downward causes are not temporally distinct (the lower level does not cease to make up the higher one while this is assumed to 'cause back'). Given this situation, the same phenomena are at the same time cause and effect for each other (which, it will be recalled, is Kant's definition of the organism in *Kritik der Urteilskraft*).[10] It is not easy (within the restricted framework of efficient causality) to understand how this should be possible except in cases where the interchangeable causes and effects do in fact belong to the same level — unless one

---

player who had just made the winning kick that it was not he, an excited 'psychical poseur', who caused the goal, but only the most probable sum-over-histories of collisions of innumerable quarks and gluons. It is just because the latter is an *in principle* universal cause-less model for all conceivable events that it is not in practice useful, appropriate, or explanatory for events where there is a simple causal model.' We agree with Pattee's emphasis on the pragmatics of explanation in any given situation, as well as with his realism concerning mental causation (so the desire of the player to score is in this sense an efficient cause). We do not claim to have answered the ontological question about the causal relations between the different modes of existence of various parts of the physical universe. The intention of a person may be enough as explanation in some contexts, but when physical, biological, psychological and social science enters the scene, each with different kinds of explanations of the same act, the ontological question remains. When Pattee (this volume) writes that 'concepts of causation are subjective *in so far as* they cannot be separated from the observer's choice of observables and the choice of measuring devices' (our emphasis) he is quite right, but causation is objective *in so far as* the causal powers of nature exist even though our conceptual representations of these powers are observer-relative.

10 Kant, 1790 [1951], §66, second part: 'This principle, which is at the same time a definition, is as follows: *An organized product of nature is one in which every part is reciprocally purpose [end] and means. In it nothing is vain, without purpose, or to be ascribed to a blind mechanism of nature.*' One can easily interpret this as an instance of our modified Aristotelian concept of functional causality.

tries to wrap the problem up in pseudo-explanations like 'dialectics'.[11] An additional fault in the experiment is that it is even interpreted as a real process. The biological system is not 'first' realized physically-chemically, causing in turn the appearance of the biological system. The biological system *is constituted* by a certain constellation of the physical-chemical level. Of course, the coming into being of this constellation, arrangement, organisation, or whatever is the reason why the physical system is now also biological. But since the system remains physical *at the same time* as being biological (it is not *first* physical and *then* biological; it is our language from the thought experiment which erroneously leads us to introduce this temporality), it is mysticism to say that the physical level exerts an upward causality on the biological level. We may say that *when* we have a physical-chemical system in a certain arrangement, *then* it is also biological, but the words 'when' and 'then' in this context refer to a logical sequence, not a temporal one.

Even if we regard talking about physical causes as unproblematic, talking about *upward causes* in a strong sense is already problematic, as it is unclear what the ramifications are of assuming that a physical cause could have an effect which was not physical (and, moreover, with which it is simultaneous, in contrast to the conception of efficient cause as a temporal regularity). A phenomenological experience which leads us to accept this fallacious idea is probably an intuition like the following: if we inflict a small physical cause on our biological organism, then it might be amplified and cause severe biological changes, in some cases death, that is, effects on the biological level. But what fools us here is the fact that the 'little physical cause' is only a releasing cause and not the whole physical cause of the development in question; this cause or complex network of causes is constituted by the physical description of the whole organism in addition to the small spectacular change, which just seems peculiarly cause-like seen from our point of view because of our possibility to inflict it or remove it (whilst we cannot remove crucial parts of our body ...).

Thus, the naive assumption of even strong upward causality must be discarded. Consequently, even more problematic, if possible, is the idea of a strong downward causation — the idea that the biological level *as such* should be able to inflict purely physical effects. A physical effect may only be the result of a physical cause which eo ipso does not exist on the higher level, unless the higher level is interpreted as a peculiarly complex and stable organisation of entities of the lower level. But then the cause is no longer biological in any strict, level use of the word. This whole difficulty is in our opinion purely conceptual and has its background

---

11   Within a broader framework, however, one could interpret 'being cause and effect for each other' as an instance of functional causation, and then give some standard account of 1) the occurrence of natural functional relations in organisms by referring to the operation of evolutionary adaptation by Darwinian natural selection, or 2) the occurrence of artificially created functional relations in tools and machines by referring to intentional construction by human beings.

in the artificial isolation of physics, and the assumption that physics as we know it in its present state is already a complete and mainly microphysical science. When this is assumed, higher organizations of physical matter may of course seem mystical and strange. But the fact that physical systems of far more complicated and self-organizing kinds exist — organisms, for instance — may suggest that this complexity is in itself a property in certain arrangements of matter and, as such, a physical property. Earthly DNA-life is, as is well-known, deeply dependent on carbon chemistry — without it being the case that carbon should be the cause and life its effect. The fact that carbon life is possible is rather a physical property in carbon, even if it may not be deduced from the observation of a single carbon atom.

Quite a different question from the one raised in our — logical, not temporal — thought experiment is the truly temporal question of how the actual origin of biology in its earthly version came about, that is, what complicated and extraordinary but still purely physical processes took place in the primordial soup leading to life. This historical and exciting question of efficient causality must not be mixed up with the purely logical question of which levels are constituted — not caused — by processes and entities on other levels. It simply does not make sense to say that any efficient cause should go from the lower towards the higher level or vice versa. The levels are not objects for causes, they are not real in the sense of the saying, all is real that has causal powers. In our view, the very source of the vitalist fallacy is the identification between this temporal chain and the constitutive relation.

Now, given the rejection of the vitalism (and substance dualism) inherent in strong downward causation, two more possibilities exist, according to whether we ascribe the purely formal cause on the higher level any power to constrain lower level processes or not — these we will coin medium downward causation and weak downward causation, respectively.

Medium downward causation

The distinctive feature of medium DC in contrast to strong DC is that it does not allow higher level phenomena to have a direct influence on lower level laws. The medium DC defends 1b (in which a higher level entity, such as a cell or a psyche, is a real substantial phenomenon in its own right), but can exist with both 2a and 2b.

As an example of this position, the neuropsychologist Roger W. Sperry (1980, 1986) and his 'emergent interactionism' may be mentioned. For most of his professional life Sperry was reductionist in a way we do not discuss here — everything could be reduced to physics, also the psychic. It was rather late that he started defending so-called emergent interactionism — after his investigation of split-brain patients and the duality of the brain.

One of the central examples given by Sperry (1969) is quite simple: a wheel running downhill. None of the single molecules constituting the wheel or gravity's pull on them are sufficient to explain the rolling movement. To explain this one must recur to the higher level at which the form of the wheel becomes conceivable. On the one hand, Sperry rejects any law-changing strong downward causation as well as the idea of a substantial dualism (or pluralism, for that matter). On the other, he maintains — as is evident from the concept of 'interactionism' — that the higher level performs a function irreducible to the lower. If we take a neuropsychological example and try to explain the origin of some state of consciousness from the state of the nervous system, then the only consistent interpretation of Sperry's point of view is that a given state of consciousness is *chosen* among a series of states of consciousness made possible by the nervous system at a certain moment. The decisive point in this *choice* of state of consciousness lies on the higher level, in this case the psychical level. It is the previous states of consciousness which determine or select which one of the possible states of consciousness should be realized. Hence the interactionism; the interaction between the manifested states of consciousness decides which possibility is to be realized.

Medium downward causation can be defined as follows: an entity on a higher level comes into being through a realization of one amongst several possible states on the lower level — with the previous states of the higher level as the factor of selection. This idea can be made more precise with the aid of an interpretation of the concept of 'boundary condition.'

This concept is primarily used in physics and mathematics. Mathematically, the boundary condition is the set of selection criteria by which one can choose one among several solutions to a set of differential equations describing the dynamics of a system.[12] In classical mechanics, a system's initial conditions are defined as the set of parameters describing the starting point of a system at a certain moment and which — measured with sufficient precision — may form the basis for the calculation of an, in principle, unlimited prediction of the system's behavior. In complex physical phenomena it is supposed that certain changes in initial conditions make central properties in the dynamics change; these are named boundary conditions because they delimit the set of initial conditions within which the properties in questions will be found. In this context the concept does not entail the assumption of levels.

---

12 E.g., if the solution contains *r* arbitrary constants, these constants may be eliminated to give a unique solution to a problem if there are *r* given *conditions* that the solution must satisfy. *Boundary* conditions, which may be for the function and/or its derivatives at certain boundary points, may be used to obtain a solution which is valid for the region specified by the conditions.

In relation to level theories, boundary conditions are conceived as the conditions which select and delimit various types of the system's several possible developments. The realization of the system implies that one of these typical developments is selected, and the set of initial conditions yielding the type of possibility chosen are thus a certain type of boundary condition which has been called *constraining conditions*. They only exist in complex multi-level phenomena on a level higher than the focal level, and are the conditions by which entities on a high level constrain the activity on the lower focal level.[13]

On this basis, *medium downward causation* can be reformulated as follows: *higher level entities are constraining conditions for the emergent activity of lower levels*. And — hence the Sperry example — in a process, the already realized higher level states are constraining conditions for the coming states.

How are we to understand the nature of this constraint? One interpretation is to say that the higher level is characterized by *organizational principles* — lawlike regularities — that have an effect ('downward', as it were) on the distribution of lower level events and substances. Thus, if, for instance, evolution by natural selection is such a lawlike regularity, we can only understand the physical distribution of energy and matter in a ecosystem if we consider the effect of natural selection on frequencies of genotypes, and thus on the phenotypes of the various existing organisms, which themselves influence the cycles of matter and energy in the system. This interpretation of medium DC is close to the view of Campbell (1974).

In contrast to weak downward causation, medium downward causation is characterized by this claim; even if no law-breaking influence top down is admitted, the higher level *constrains* which higher level phenomenon will result from a given lower level state. Thus, the radical forms of dualism or vitalism of strong downward causation is avoided at the expense of a less radical idea that the same lower level constituents may correspond to a series of different higher level phenomena.

In contrast to strong DC, medium DC does not involve the idea of a strict 'efficient' temporal causality from an independent higher level to a lower one, rather, the entities at various levels may enter part-whole relations (e.g., mental phenomena control their component neural and biophysical sub-elements), in which the control of the part by the whole can be seen as a kind of functional (teleological) causation, which is based on efficient, material as well as formal causation in a multinested system of constraints. The kind of determinative relation between part and whole is not quite clear, and the term 'interaction' is according

13 In Salthe's (1985) triadic structure, an entity must be considered at its own (focal) level, the level above and the level below. Lower level constraints act on the emergent process as possibilities or *initiating conditions*, higher level constraints or *constraining conditions* may act as the boundary conditions of the environment or other such constraints. Salthe has since (1993) modified his model.

to Sperry (1987) not the best for the kind of relationship envisaged.[14] Thus, 'Mind is conceived to move matter in the brain and to govern, rule, and direct neural and chemical events without interacting with the components at the component level, just as an organism may move and govern the time-space course of its atoms and tissues without interacting with them' (Sperry 1987).

We have to differentiate between the following two assumptions. (a) Higher level entities function as criteria for the selection of lower level emergent processes. The higher level entities constrain the development of lower level processes in accordance with the history of the level. (b) One set of entities at a lower level can be the starting point for different entities at the higher level. This is a sort of inverse supervenience. One can, for the sake of the argument, assume that two organisms consist of the same amount of different substance — but are very different organisms. This conclusion rests on the premise that the levels already exist — they cannot be used to describe or explain the development of levels.

Weak downward causation

The theory of weak downward causation admits neither of the two claims just mentioned and instead interprets the concept in the light of theses 1a and 2a. Thus, the higher level is conceived as an organizational level, characterized by the organization, the whole, the pattern, the structure, in short *the form* into which the constituents are arranged. Even if it subscribes to the constitutive reductionism of 1a, it must not be identified with physical or mechanical reductionism; the forms of the higher level are supposed to be non-reducible. In contrast to medium downward causation it is characterized by not admitting the special interpretation of boundary conditions as constraining conditions, and hence it does not allow the possibility that several higher level phenomena correspond to one and the same lower level phenomenon.[15] One possible way of describing weak downward causation is by using the phase-space terminology invented by qualitative dynamics.[16] Phase space maps all the possible states of a system into a space defined by a

---

14 'Mental phenomena are described as primarily supervening rather than intervening, in the physiological process' (Sperry 1987). For further discussion of Sperry's interactionism, see Kim's paper, this volume.

15 Of course, it is easy to imagine, for instance, that a brain cell in a certain state may partake in several different thought or emotion processes. But advocates of weak downward causation will argue that the range of observation is mistakenly chosen here: constitutive reductionism requires the lower level process to be envisaged in the right proportions, that is, the same proportions as the higher level process (the thought) in question. On the level of whole connected series of thoughts, then, it cannot be the case that identical lower level (neurological) processes give rise to different higher level (psychological) processes. It is the stable forms of the higher levels which determine the scope of observation.

16 A phase space is a multiple space in which the coordinates represent the variable required to specify the states of the system (e.g., a six-dimensional space incorporating three dimensions of positions and three of the momentum of a single particle, or a $6N$ state space in which a single point characterizes the positions and momentums of a gas of N particles). For a popular introduction to this concept and qualitative dynamics, see Gleick (1987).

set of dimensions, each of them corresponding to a parameter of the system. Through a continuous change in these parameters, any change in the system will be modelled by a trajectory in the phase space. Classical conservative mechanical systems will result in one distinct trajectory through the phase space, but various dampened, thermodynamic systems lose energy all along and may approach the same behavior as systems with other initial conditions. An *attractor* is the name of a set of points in the phase space in which trajectories with many different initial conditions end. Attractors may vary in kind from points (corresponding to no change in the system), to orbits (corresponding to cyclically recurrent states), to pseudo-cycles (corresponding to overall but not precisely recurrent behavior), and the strange attractors of chaos theory (with unpredictable behavior due to exponentially divergent trajectories from nearby points — but still with pattern properties). Attractors are of course not unique to emergent behavior (unless all thermodynamic micro-macro distinctions involve emergent behavior), but it seems to be the case that emergent higher levels are regulated by stable and complicated attractors for the dynamics of the lower level, often characterized by cyclical mechanisms of regulation.

Hence, in the biological case, organisms can analogically be regarded as consisting of highly complicated attractors for the behavior of organic molecules in a biochemical space — an attractor with stable part-cycles (metabolism, reproduction, etc.). Given the relevant organic molecules, these attractors exist in a certain (Platonic) sense before the particular living organism. As argued in detail by the theoretical biologists Kauffman and Goodwin, the fact that a biological species consists of stable organisms is neither a wonder nor solely a product of selection, as traditionally held by neo-Darwinism.[17] The stability is the result of internal, formal properties in the organisation of the organism, and the job of natural selection is only to sort the possible stable organisms and find those most fit for the given milieu; in this sense, the genes selected by natural selection set the parameters that specify the initial conditions for emergent development.

As a formal tool the attractor description may be applied to various cases of biological complexity. A relatively simple example is provided by our body, which consists of about 250 different *cell types*, each cell (except red blood cells) has approximately 75,000 different genes. Nearly all contain the same genes, but they differ in their type-specific set of genes that is 'turned on' or 'off.' Thus a liver cell may be modelled as a stable point in the whole state space of the human cells characterized by the configuration of n active and 75,000-n inactive genes (n may typically be in the range of 10,000 to 15,000). Though an eye cell and a liver cell might have the same n, the eye cell has genes (e.g., for pigment) turned on that are inactive in the liver, etc. Now this description allows us to see developmental cell

---

17 Kauffman (1993); Goodwin (1994).

differentiation as the establishment of a historical tree of trajectories (representing cell divisions and cell diversification during embryogenesis) moving towards about 250 different basins of attraction, where each attractor represents a stable cell type in the adult organism, and where a point on that attractor represents, for example, a possible configuration of the active and inactive genes in which a liver cell can be. If it is a point attractor, there is only one such configuration, but cells usually have many genetic states and may thus cycle along a cyclic attractor (see Kauffman (1993) for a detailed model).

An attractor conception of the higher level as characterized by formal causes of the self-organization of constituents on a lower level does not yet constitute a detailed explanatory theory, but merely gives a framework for description. Yet it makes clearer some crucial implications of the idea of levels. The fact that the attractor resulting in the higher level entities is highly complicated and presupposes a specific historical process of generation means that it is localized in a strongly delimited part of the biochemical phase space. The boundary conditions for its stability (and origin) are many and specific (even if they may occur generically in certain realms of the phase space). Thus it is rather small and delimited areas in the phase space which constitute the basin of attraction of this attractor; and the feeling that life is 'rare' in relation to other parts of physics confers the idea that systems must pass through a very narrow bottleneck for higher levels to show up (Gell-Mann 1994). On the other hand there are two local properties which might counterweight the overall rarity of this attractor: first it can be imagined that areas exist (still relatively rare, globally conceived) where the occurrence of stable attractors is generic, that is, where a movement of the trajectory outside the basin of attraction does not lead to a non-species (or, a non-higher level entity), but instead to *another* species (or higher level entity). Second, any attractor is the center of a basin of attraction, that is, even if it is very rare on the global level, it is locally generic; stable and insensitive to perturbations. This insensibility might be the reason for the assumption of downward causation: even if you give an organism a disease, a small push, a little distress, in a large number of cases it will be able to push off the change, that is, stay inside the basin of attraction and hence return to the stable attractor after having rejected the perturbation for some time. The relative stability of the attractor is, then, identical to the 'governing' of the behavior of the entity, which is so easy to interpret as a case of downward causation: the physical perturbation is regulated by the biological attractor. The attractor functions as a 'whole' at a higher level than the processes that constitute it — hence the frequent talk of holism in connection with the discussions of level and emergence.[18]

---

18 One should remember that the attractor is a set of points in a phase space, and a single point represents a complete (micro) state description of the entire system.

This gestalt holism is natural, insofar as the bundle of processes described by the attractor constitutes a pattern which necessarily comprises a plurality of entities from the lower level — but the attractor model is totally deprived of vitalism. The attractor does not 'take care' to sustain itself in any spiritual use of the word, and any attractor of the kind described possesses its own limit of tolerance for perturbations. Beyond this limit, the dynamics enter another basin of attraction and the organism ceases to exist.[19]

The attractor also functions, however, as a whole in another sense of the word. Because the attractor is the drain of a basin of different initial conditions (which is small globally but very large locally in comparison with the attractor itself), the attractor automatically becomes a sign for all the initial conditions attracted by it: the attractor thus subsumes these states. This implies that the attractor is a general *type*, of which the single phase-space points in its basin will be *tokens*. Put in another way: the entity on the higher level may be instantiated by a long range of (tightly related) constellations of entities from the lower level. The entity on the higher level is thus necessarily *more general* than the particular constellation of entities from the lower one. This general 'governing' of particular lower level constellations is phenomenologically very striking and one more reason for the widespread interpretations of it as teleological and too strongly downwardly causal — seen from a weak downward causation point of view. A tiger is a tiger, even if it may be so in a very wide range of physical ways and may appear in a lot of different states; a thought is a thought even if it may be bio-physically instantiated differently in different brains.

Consequently, the organizing pattern which the weak downward causation point of view may interpret in the attractor language of qualitative dynamics has the character of potentiality. In a certain sense,[20] it existed before it was realized, just as water — given the properties of oxygen and hydrogen — existed as a potentiality, as an attractor, before the single empirical water molecule was realized. It is possible to try to use Occam's razor against potentialities of this type, arguing that the phase space in which these attractors dwell is so enormous that we have no practical or even theoretical possibility to map it. It must contain attractors (in the biochemical case) not only for any single species, extinct or alive, but also for any possible species in any possible world (with our biochemistry). What is lost by an Occam cut here, however, is *the conception of higher level entities as attractors for the dynamics of lower levels*. In that case, the stronger down-

---

19 This presupposes that the organism can be specified as a set of states [within such an attractor–or within a cluster of 'healthy' as well as 'diseased' attractors] amenable to a (physical) dynamical systems description. For some systems that are 'self-modifying' this presupposition may not be met (Kampis 1991).

20 At least in the mathematical sense of some real forms (a mathematical description of an attractor) that may or may not correspond to actual 'empirical,' existent things. According to modern cosmology, no molecules and very few kinds of elements existed in the very early universe, except (according to a potentialistic interpretation of natural laws) as a mere possibility of the organization of elementary particles.

ward causation versions threaten to replace these potentialities with actualities, with certain yet unknown causal powers, and this very easily borders on seeing the formation of higher level entities as a mystical and para-religious act of creation.[21] Even 'weaker' points of view than weak downward causation, on the other hand, will try to explain away higher level entities, either as mere contingent facts of specific phenomena, or as targets for physicalist reductionist programs not yet, if ever, possible. Nobody, of course, will shave so close with Occam's razor that also rather well-described cases of higher level entities as attractors for lower level dynamics disappear — as, for instance, the water molecule. But where should the limit be fixed, how close must the shave be? It would in this respect be appropriate to recall that already at the pre-biological level of organic macromolecules, the amount of possible chemical compounds is completely unknown and in principle probably ungraspable. That is, even if we restrict the content of our biochemical phase space to only organic macromolecules, we have no precise idea of the geography of the attractors of this phase space. But this fact does not logically force us to accept the notion of strong downward causation in this case, or to believe in claims that these molecules are just 'created' in some mystical process.

On the other hand, accepting the pattern/attractor model of weak downward causation invariably entails certain important consequences. First off, we will find these phenomena in a much larger variety of cases than in the few famed emergent transitions between large levels. *Patterns* are already crucial in macrophysics, solid state physics, hydrodynamics, cosmology and many other branches of physics, just as we will find attractors in any dampened system, that is, any system in which thermodynamics plays some role. A crucial question is, then: if patterns and attractors are necessary descriptive tools for a *level theory* of weak downward causation, what is the *sufficient* condition for the constitution of a level? Our guess is that the answer provided by consistent weak downward causation must be that within the theoretical framework of qualitative dynamics there is no sharp boundary distinguishing the large cases of emergence (physics/biology, etc.) from, for instance, micro/macrophysical emergencies, or from intra-biological emergencies (singe cell/multicellular). There is a continuum from simple patterns to complicated patterns involving a large range of different, specific interactions between parts. But this implies that levels are not necessarily sharply delimited; however, it does not imply that levels do not possess any ontological status. Even if levels have a gestalt quality, they are not mere epistemological constructs, since the gestalts governing them are objective. In the weak downward causation opinion, then,

---

21 It is interesting to note that weak DC may equally be regarded as an idealistic, religious aberrance in the perspective of stronger DC versions. Weak DC's insistence on potentiality can be considered an insistence that everything is determined beforehand, the landscape of attractors is always already there, as if arranged during Genesis by a deistic God. On the other hand, the theology of the stronger version is not deistic, but rather theistic or even mystical: in any case of emergence, a creative force is at work, as if God had not finished by the sixth day.

emergence and downward causation must be formal ontological concepts in a complex mereology.[22]

We should stress that claiming the existence of weak downward causation is different from claiming that emergent properties are just epiphenomenal. In contrast to Jaegwon Kim, who holds that 'if emergent properties have no downward causal powers, they can have no causal powers at all',[23] we have argued that the attractor description could count as a good case for the existence of an emergent property (i.e. belonging to an attractor in state space)[24] without the very notion of 'causal power' having to be relevant at all. To us it seems that the ontology of abstract objects — forms, shapes, mathematical and topological relations — indicates that entities do not have to have causal powers in order to exist.

To sum up the position of weak downward causation: downward causation cannot be interpreted as any kind of efficient causation. Downward causation must be interpreted as a case of formal causation, an organizing principle.[25]

Form, causality, supervenience

It may be difficult to decide whether the medium or the weak version of downward causation is the most promising, and even if the strong version can easily be discarded, we, the authors of this article, do not hide the fact that we disagree with the choice between the latter two. The point of departure in both cases is the assumption of formal causality. As higher level entities (e.g., a cell) supervene on lower order entities (molecules), formal causality on the higher level supervenes on the efficient causality of the lower level. This can be interpreted as the selection — from a very large set of possible (efficient) interactions — of a small set of realizable (efficient) interactions on the lower level, on which the higher level then

---

22 One could argue that emergence and DC must be formal ontological concepts. If, on the one hand, they are mere epistemological concepts in a subjectivist sense of the word, they would cease to possess scientific interest and just become consequences of our present lack of knowledge. On the other, if they are material ontological concepts, they would pertain to specific material cases and there would be no conceptual interest in comparing the emergence going on between physics and biology with the one taking place between brain and psyche. The very concept of emergence (and hence of DC) presupposes that these processes share some crucial formal properties–which then in the weak DC interpretation are the gestalt structural organization of entities from the lower level.

23 Kim, this volume.

24 It could be any kind of attractor: point, cyclic, quasi-cyclic or strange. This is a central point where our interpretation of emergence and weak downward causation differs from that of Newman (1996), who requires the attractor to be strange (chaotic) in order to meet the requirement of unpredictability for an emergent phenomenon. We would argue that even though complex systems like living organisms can be modelled by non-linear dynamics as being deterministic chaotic (and thus non-predictable) systems, they are non-predictable at a deeper level (than represented by non-predictable chaos) due to their historicity, i.e., their genesis is dependent on mutations (that ultimately may be quantum-indeterminate) and complex contingent environmental fluctuations.

25 A prominent forerunner of such a position is Ernst Cassirer, who attacked the latter-day vitalists of his age and instead invoked a 'nicht-stoffliche Ordnung' as crucial in biology.

(formally) supervenes. In any case, in our view this is the only non-contradictory version of downward causation possible.

As regards weak downward causation, we interpreted the formal cause in terms of the attractor concept. This description of phase space evidently gives downward causation a legitimate scientific status without involving any untenable metaphysical idea of a temporal causal process from a higher level to a lower one (or vice versa, for that matter). What medium DC will add to this conception is the claim that *the very process of emergence will necessarily change the local appearance of phase space*, so that the higher level attractors are only created in the process of emergence — leading to the distinction between boundary conditions and constraining conditions. This idea leads medium downward causation to pay special attention to 'first time emergencies' where the creation of these allegedly new attractors takes place;[26] while weak downward causation with its more structural approach does not consider these attractors any product of creation or contingent historical processes, and, consequently, only regards the question of the first-time generation of an emergent entity as a problem of how to maneuver a system into the right corner of a pre-existing phase space where the interesting attractors lie.[27]

A precondition for a strict mathematical application of the dynamical phase-space description of any material system is that the very phase space can be precisely defined and its dynamical equations known before the study of specific trajectories that gives the system (i.e. its description) the characteristic forms of movement. In other words: the phase space must, as it were, be an abstract preformed structure with fixed parameters and boundary conditions within which one may follow the dynamical development of the trajectories (as revealed in a computer simulation) of the individual states of the system (represented by points in the phase space), which may be attracted to, for instance, chaotic attractors. Thus, if we want to apply such a description to the emergence of life, we face the problem that this very emergence will change not only the states of 'the system' (which is the big 'primordial soup'), but the very parameters that are important for the description of the system. The emergence of life seems to change the very phase space, so that it can no longer be considered a fixed structure; rather, new higher order attractors will appear. To say so, however, is to apply dynamical de-

---

26 That is, the very space of possible states (as characterized by a given set of parameters) undergoes change, and often new parameters or observables become relevant to the system description. E.g., describing the 'state space' of living cells after the emergence of life, a description of the system as a $6N$-dimensional state space of particles with $3N$ position coordinates and $3N$ momentum coordinates, will not be feasible. Rather, a genetic sequence space of possible genetic states (characterized by DNA sequences) may in a lot of cases be a more interesting model, compare Küppers (1992) and Eigen (1992).

27 In this respect, the dissension between the medium and weak DC positions may be seen in the historical context of the preformation versus epigenesis debate, as discussed by Moreno & Umerez's paper in this volume.

scriptive language (qualitative dynamics, non-linear systems) in a somewhat metaphorical sense.

References

BAAS, N.A. 1994. Emergence, Hierarchies, and Hyperstructures. In C.G. Langton (ed.), *A life III, Santa Fe Studies in the Sciences of Complexity, Proc. Volume XVII*, Redwood City, Cal: Addison-Wesley, 515-37.

BAAS, N.A. & C. EMMECHE 1997. Emergence and explanation, *SFI Working Paper* 97-02-008. Santa Fe Institute, New Mexico (submitted to *Intellectica*).

BECKERMANN, A., H. FLOHR & J. KIM (eds.) 1992. *Emergence or Reduction? Essays on the Prospects of Nonreductive Physicalism*. Berlin & New York: Walter de Gruyter.

BLITZ, D. 1992. *Emergent Evolution. Qualitative Novelty and the Levels of Reality*. Dordrecht: Kluwer Academic Publishers.

CAMPBELL, D.T. 1974. 'Downward causation' in hierarchically organised biological systems. In F. Ayala & T. Dobzhansky (eds.), *Studies in the Philosophy of Biology*. Berkeley: University of California Press, 179-86.

CASSIRER, E. 1991. *Das Erkenntnisproblem in der Philosophie und Wissenschaft der neueren Zeit*. Vol. 4. Hildesheim/Zürich/New York: Georg Olms Verlag.

EIGEN, M. (with R. Winkler-Oswatitsch) 1992. *Steps towards Life. A perspective on Evolution*. Oxford: Oxford University Press.

EMMECHE, C., KØPPE, S. & STJERNFELT, F. 1997. Explaining emergence–towards an ontology of levels, *Journal for General Philosophy of Science,* 28, 83-119.

GELL-MAN, M. 1994. *The Quark and the Jaguar*. New York: W.H. Freeman.

GLEICK, J. 1987. *Chaos. Making a New Science*. New York: Viking Penguin.

GOODWIN, B. 1994. *How the Leopard changed its Spots. The Evolution of Complexity*. New York: Charles Scribner's Sons.

KAMPIS, G. 1991. *Self-modifying Systems in Biology and Cognitive Science*. New York: Pergamon Press.

KANT, I. 1790. *Kritik der Urteilskraft* (*Critique of Judgement*, trans. J.H. Bernard. New York: Hafner Publishing Company, 1951).

KAUFFMAN, S. 1993. *The Origins of Order. Self-organization and Selection in Evolution*. Oxford: Oxford University Press.

KIM, J. 1993. *Supervenience and Mind*. Cambridge: Cambridge University Press.

KIM, J. 1995. Emergent properties. In T. Honderich (ed.), *The Oxford Companion to Philosophy*. Oxford: Oxford University Press, 224.

KÜPPERS, B.-O. 1992. Understanding complexity. In Beckermann, Flohr & Kim (eds.) 1992, 241-56.

KØPPE, S. 1990. *Virkelighedens Niveauer*. Copenhagen: Gyldendal ['The Levels of Reality'].

MORGAN, C. LLOYD 1923. *Emergent Evolution*. London: Williams and Norgate.

NEWMAN, D.V. 1996. Emergence and strange attractors, *Philosophy of Science* 63: 245-61.

SALTHE, S.N. 1985. *Evolving Hierarchical Systems*. New York: Columbia University Press.

SALTHE, S.N. 1993. *Development and Evolution.* Cambridge, Massachusetts: The MIT Press.

SPERRY, R.W. 1969. A modified concept of consciousness. *Psychol. Rev.* 76: 532-36.

SPERRY, R.W. 1980. Mind-brain interaction: mentalism, yes; dualism, no. *Neuroscience* 5: 195-206.

SPERRY, R.W. 1986. Macro- versus micro-determination. *Philosophy of Science* 53: 265-275.

SPERRY, R.W. 1987. Consciousness and causality. In R.L. Gregory (ed.), *The Oxford Companion to the Mind.* Oxford: Oxford University Press, 164-66.

Part II
Physics

2

Wholeness and Part, Cosmos and Man in 16th and 17th Century Natural Philosophy and in Modern Holism

TOVE ELISABETH KRUSE

For almost three decades there has been a renewed interest — seen mostly in English and American scholarship — in refining the study of the scientists of the late Middle Ages and the Reformation. They are no longer merely regarded as pioneers of modern empirical science and their medieval and natural philosophical heritage is no longer suppressed. Increasingly the natural scientists of the period are regarded as transitional figures between the old and the new — between the Middle Ages and early modern times.

In common with their contemporaries the scientists were deeply rooted both in a fundamentally religious universe and in the traditional perception of man as an organic part of nature. At the same time nature developed into a phenomenon which it was possible to regard and study as an independent object. Therefore, all natural scientists of the 16th and 17th centuries had to find ways of relating wholeness and part to one another.

In this article I intend sketching two identifiable and decisively different ways of relating wholeness and part, cosmos and man in the natural philosophy of the 16th and 17th centuries, since these two different elaborations of the relationship are highly relevant as 'A Distant Mirror' reflecting and putting into perspective the actual problems of the relationship between wholeness and part — especially as these problems come to expression in modern holism based on the natural sciences.

Macrocosm and microcosm

In the natural philosophy of the 16th and 17th centuries wholeness and part, cosmos and man are always connected, most often in the form of the ideas of microcosm and macrocosm.

The macrocosm is always a manifestation of God. In the creation and in the created, God manifests himself as nature and as the elements and processes of nature. God is the primal elements of all things; God is earth, water, fire and air, He is salt, sulfur and mercury. God manifests Himself in the chemical separation process of creation and in natures eternal cycles of growth and decay. Or God manifests Himself in Pan, who represents the great universal nature: Pan's two horns represent the great worlds two poles, Pan's fiery expression stems from the influence of the seven wandering stars of the heavens, Pan's spotted hide are evidence of the stars of the firmament. Pan's long beard depicts the rays of the sun, the moon and the stars. Pan's flute shows the harmony, which is created by the seven planets etc.

Since God is the primal element and origin of all things, creation is not just a process of chemical separation and nature is not just matter. Any element, all of the building blocks of nature and all of the processes of nature at the same time refer to something material and to something immaterial. All the elements and processes of nature are spiritual entities with a body, corporal spirits. The first creation and the eternally repeated creations in nature are at one and the same time a physical-chemical process and a religious manifestation. In the macrocosm God is naturalized and nature is spiritualized. Thus, knowledge of nature becomes knowledge of God.

The microcosm is created from the macrocosm, from Pan and the elements of great nature man is created:

Microcosmus is the little world and he is taken for man so called, because he hath in his composition a portion of every member of the great world.   *Fludd 1979: 78*

Man imitates great nature in every way. The English natural scientist Robert Fludd imagines that in the same way as God lives on the highest peak in the purest heaven, the spark of God takes residence in the most distinguished and highest regions of the small world — in the head. In the middle of the little world sits the heart, which serves the same function in the microcosm as the Sun does in the macrocosm: sending its life giving rays to all the parts of the organism. And in the same way as in the great world, Chronos carefully controls the heavenly movements of the planets and, with that, time itself, Chronos also regulates the movements and beating of the heart, and takes care that the expansion and contraction of the heart 'live together in peace and harmony in the same way as husband and wife do'. So that strife and disharmony are not created in the microcosm, blood circulates in the body in intricate and complicated ways corresponding to the circulation of rainwater in great nature. After having reached all the corners of the little world the rivers of blood are collected at the great 'mountains' of the body — the stomach, the lever and the spleen. It passes from here through the stony caves of the kidneys, finally to run out in 'the salt sea of the bladder.' And in the same way as the winds blow in the great world, in the little world southerly winds also blow from the moist areas of the liver and northerly blustery winds blow from the windswept areas of the spleen. Pan regulates these winds and their collisions, so that strange meteors and troublesome illnesses are not created in the inner of microcosm. The guts, which job it is to collect the earthly excrement, represents the earth of the great world and Urine is the salt sea. Finally man is equipped with 'sensory channels': two windows to look out of, two doors to listen with, two channels to smell with, a passage to taste with and finally touch to feel with.

Man does not just imitate great nature as a whole. Man is also like and corresponds to the single parts of nature, e.g., a tree:

This...growth is like a man. It has skin, which is the bark. It has head and hair, which are the root. It has its figure, its signs, its mind, its sense in the stalk, the lesion whereof is followed by death. Its leaves and flowers and fruit are for ornament, as in man hearing, vision and the power of speech. Gums are its excrement, and the parasite is its disease.

Paracelsus 1976: 229

In the same way as everything in great nature, which man is created from, man is both material and immaterial. In the same way as the bark on trees and the skins of fruit are bodies that hide another body, man has two bodies — the external body, which is material and worthless, and the internal body which is spiritual and divine. The microcosm carries the whole macrocosm in it. The Universe is both spiritually and materially an organic whole.

Even though man is created by the macrocosm and enfolds nature in himself, both materially and immaterially, and even though the universe is saturated with correspondences and analogies between the macrocosm and the microcosm, the relationship between the macrocosm and the microcosm is not a relationship of mutual influence. The hierarchy of the creation from macrocosm to microcosm — downward causation in its ultimate form — makes great nature, not least the stars, decisive in relation to man:

The stars compel and coerce the animal man, so that where they lead he must follow, just as a thief does the gallows..., a fisher the fishes, a fowler the birds, and a hunter the wild beasts. *Paracelsus 1976: 174*

This is true generally for the life and fate of man, and it is tangibly true for the individual areas of existence. In this way most of the diseases of man are determined by the stars:

for it is most certain, that diseases come to men for the most part from the power and influences of the stars upon the bodies of men. *Paracelsus 1975: 100*

The person who remains at his animal level will always be a slave of the macrocosm. But it is not man's destiny to be bestial, unwise and a slave of material relations. Originally God created man last and gave man the privilege of ruling over all creation and all creatures. When man does not occupy this, his rightful position it is because man does not know himself and his intrinsic powers:

man does not know or estimate himself or his powers, or reflect that he is a lesser universe, and has the whole firmament with its powers hidden within himself   *Paracelsus 1976: 174*

Man's task is to carry his wisdom, because in that way 'anyone can free himself', If man becomes familiar with his own powers and if man learns to use his powers correctly, the roles between microcosm and macrocosm are switched. It is then man who rules the macrocosm and its influence, and not the other way round:

The wise man can dominate the stars, and is not subject to them. Nay, the stars are subject to the wise man, and are forced to obey him, not he the stars.   *Paracelsus 1976: 174*

The macrocosm is a manifestation of God and, therefore, the macrocosm contains all knowledge of itself in itself: nature contains knowledge of its own qualities, its processes, its functions and it contains knowledge of the intentions of the creator. At the same time man is a microcosm, which in itself enfolds all of nature. The natural scientist and the man, who realizes his microcosmic potentials, can in this way meet, recognize and understand all things in and through nature, and can with alchemy as a tool recreate the metals, extract the divine essence of the material and create a universal medicine which consumes all diseases. The person who realizes his microcosmic potential can imitate God and perfect creation.

Nature is not explored, however, as an independent physical phenomenon, but as a spiritual magical reality. To study nature is to practice alchemy. And the results of alchemy are in the end the external manifestation of the unity and connection between phenomena and forces in nature, which are predestined through man's inner spontaneous knowledge of these. The unity between the world and man, between wholeness and part, makes it possible for man to recognize all things and to imitate both God and nature. The universe is magical because none of the levels of reality are independent of each other. Everything is leveled — the synthesis between wholeness and part is created by making everything equal.

The implicate order — man as a hologram

The majority of natural scientists in the 16th and 17th centuries were characterized by moving in the sphere between wholeness and science. Today moving in this field characterizes the few — the minority of natural scientists creating holistic theories. This minority, however, has to a high degree set the agenda for modern cultural debate. A debate that always touches on many fields of social and political life and reality since the perspective is that of 'The Whole', including the underlying question concerning the view of existence as meaningful.

Modern holism based on science is generally constructed as a vision of wholeness, allegedly founded on a piece of empirical natural science. This is the case e.g., with Professor David Bohm, who, with his theory of 'The Implicate Order', has been a leading figure in the discussion of a change in paradigm towards a holographic or holistic world view.

Thus, Bohm's starting point is quantum physics, more specifically the question of how to describe and understand the behavior of atomic particles.

The core of Bohm's theory is the perception that the particle — besides being influenced by the laws and forces of classical physics — is also connected to and influenced by a potential possessing qualities quite different from that which is normally accepted within classical physics. For Bohm this quantum potential is the carrier of all form and all information. It is non-local and is potentially active everywhere. It forms and directs matter in the sense that the quantum potential is activated when its energy enters the particle and hereby gives form and direction to the particle. Consequently the order the particle follows, influenced by the quantum potential, is seen as a manifestation of a hidden order lying behind it. An implicate order carried by the quantum potential, which is explicated when matter activates its enfolded information. To Bohm this rule applies to all created phenomena. Any outer manifestation has a hidden implicate order enfolded within itself. And behind all unique manifestations and their implicate orders is a common implicate order, the holomovement:

We have seen that in the quantum context, the order in every immediately perceptible aspect of the world is to be regarded as coming of a more comprehensive implicate order, in which all aspects ultimately merge in the undefinable and immeasurable holomovement.

Bohm 1980: 156

The holomovement is the foundation of all created, it gives form and direction to all that is created and is enfolded in every specific manifestation. Body and mind, spirit and nature, stars, animals, man, society, politics, and history — nothing and no one possesses more than relative independence from the common implicate order. Everything and everybody is a projection of one and only one universal unity:

...we will have to be careful not to slip back into regarding the various elements of any given total situation as having more than relative independence. In a deeper and generally more suitable way of thinking, each of these elements is a projection, in a sub totality of yet higher dimension'. So it will be ultimately misleading and indeed wrong to suppose, for example, that each human being is an independent actuality who interacts with other human beings and with nature. Rather, all these are projections of a single totality.

Bohm 1980: 210

For Bohm the concept of order, which he formulates in order to perceive the movement of particles in the quantum field, is thus shown to be a specific case of a general and hidden generative order. It applies to all things — not only spiritual but also material. Therefore, Bohm's concept of order has validity not only in the field of quantum physics, but in all areas of reality. In this way Bohm's analysis of the reality of quantum physics allows for unlimited generalization to all areas and levels of reality. Consequently the concepts and theories that Bohm constructs to describe reality on the level of quantum physics are distributed to all reality, and form the basis of Bohm's theory of cosmos and the origin of life, of man and consciousness, of upbringing and social interaction, of the development of society and the course of history.

Bohm's theory — based on quantum physics — thus, also offers a solution to the disastrous situation mankind, according to Bohm, faces today. Modern civilization threatens to destroy the earth and mankind, and for Bohm this threat is a result of an unfolded and stiff order and an uncreative consciousness. But man is a hologram. As a countermove man must come in contact with his inner enfolded order — his creative intelligence — which originates from the holomovement and therefore in its depths enfolds all knowledge and all that is good. Mans creative, enfolded intelligence is omnipotent — it can transform any unfolded structure and thus radically change man and his consciousness, society and history in new and positive ways.

It is most interesting to note that modern holism in its most elitist, intellectual and trend-setting form — holism based on natural science — significantly resembles the reductionist synthesis of wholeness and science of the 16th and 17th centuries.

As has been outlined above, the essence of this synthesis is the perception of the fundamental unity of all things. A unity that triumphs over all distances and differences and harmonizes all reality in a leveled and uniform universe. The unifying of faith, the vision of wholeness and science in the synthesis is achieved by God being naturalized and becoming apparent as e.g., the power to grow, the planets and metals. At the same time nature is made spiritual, making every physical phenomenon a spiritual phenomenon too. In this universe to know nature is to know God, and the vision of wholeness and science can replace, support and verify one another.

Of course language and form differ, but at crucial points one finds fundamental similarities between the synthesis of the 16th and 17th natural philosophers and David Bohm's theory:

- Body and soul, spirit and nature, mind and matter originate from one common source. In the natural philosophy of the 16th and 17th century God, for Bohm, is the holomovement. In this source everything is enfolded and from this source everything springs. And every manifestation enfolds the whole in itself.

- This is true of the smallest components of matter. Bohm's particle is both material and immaterial. It is a physical phenomenon, but its energy and movement is directed by the non-local and non-causal quantum potential. Corresponding to this the elements of 15th and 16th century natural philosophy are materialized spirit, spiritualist matter.
- This is also true of man. Man is a macrocosm or a hologram and enfolds all reality and all information, both about himself and about nature. By contacting his hidden forces man, therefore, can learn, experience and transform everything — spiritual as well as material.
- Reality is uniform. In both the natural philosophy of the 16th and 17th centuries and Bohm there is no fundamental distinction between God, particle, man and society. Deep down everything is identical and can be reduced to the same principle, the same order.
- Analogy, coherence and similarity degenerate to identity and the vision of wholeness that creates unity mutilates both God and science. God fades away as spiritual reality and ethical requirement and nature is not investigated as an independent phenomenon.

Bohm — like most other holistic scientists of today — aims to compensate one-sided rationalism, fragmentation and the general loss of meaning in a modern atomized world by reintroducing organic wholeness. But Bohm's theory does not expand our world view, on the contrary it makes it shrink. Bohm's theory makes our world far more anaemic and limited than before. The reason for this is unlimited generalization, that is to say reductionism. Bohm does not stick to the invariable distinction between specific concepts related to a defined part of reality and common concepts related to all of reality. Bohm thus starts off with concepts that might be of relevance to quantum physics, but ends up with a theory of everything without scientific validity. And furthermore with a theory that seems more than questionable in relation to morals and politics.

Synchronicity

In the natural philosophy of the 16th and 17th centuries, wholeness and part, cosmos and man are always connected. But the connection is not always organic and based on identity and it does not always lead to uniformity of the levels of reality and thus to reductionism.

In Kepler the relation between wholeness and part is figurative in a true sense of the word. Cosmos and man share primordial images.

In Kepler's understanding, as in all the understanding of all the natural philosophers of the 16th and 17th centuries, the universe and creation bear the fingerprint of God, it depicts his essence. But whereas the fingerprint in the idea of the relationship between the microcosm and the macrocosm is concrete and sensual, manifested in innumerable ways and bound together by the inscrutable network of analogies and correspondences, Kepler's God is present in the world in form and quantity — abstract and formal qualities. The basic form is the sphere, because it expresses and creates an adequate picture of the Holy Trinity itself. The center, periphery and radius of the sphere are, therefore, the perfect image of the Father, the Son and the Holy Ghost and saturate the world partly in the perfect form of the sphere, but more in all the geometric shapes that occur when the perfect circle is broken, is divided and is cut through by straight lines. The sphere and the innumerable geometric shapes that it gives life to are, thus, the basis for the other foundation of creation: quantity.

In this way the form of the Holy Trinity flows through the Universe from the sphere to the straight and to the curved and their internal relationships, onward through all quantity and into nature. The symbol of the Trinity is the archetype and model for all that is created — not least the cosmos. The sun, the fixed stars and the planetary system in the space between the sun and the fixed stars relate to the center, periphery and radius of the sphere, in the same way as the Father, the Son and the Holy Ghost.

The created world is thus in Kepler, on the one hand, intimately connected to God — in the sense that both the Trinity and nature relate to the symbolism of the sphere. At the same time the created world is saturated by quantity and as such a rational and formally logical phenomenon.

In the same way as the cosmos and nature man and his soul is also a work of God. And in the same way as cosmos and nature, man and his spiritual capacity in its basic substance are structured in form and quantity by God. When he enters the world man is not an unwritten page. The soul is not a clean slate. All forms, all geometry and all mathematics are already laid down in the soul. Quantity, numbers and the basic ideas of mathematics and the spatial and flat geometric shapes are, thus, not derived from outside through a conceptual structuring of the profusion of the world of the senses. Fundamental harmony exists a priori — as a human instinct.

Thus, for Kepler too, man contains all things within himself, but man is not a microcosm. Man does not contain macrocosm and man is not the point of departure and ultimate goal for all analogies and correspondences. The relation is figurative in the most fundamental meaning of the word — man and world share primordial images, ideas and concepts. The unity between man and the world is not organic and, for Kepler, never has the character of an actual identity.

At the same time the connection between wholeness and part in Kepler is neither hierarchical nor deterministic. Wholeness and part, world and man synchronously carry the same archetypal images within them. The synchronicity between outer and inner constellations activate an already extant potential. This idea saturates at all levels Kepler's experience of the relationship between wholeness and part, world and man.

The nature of love is one example:

The infatuated young man loves a girl and does not know why or what it is in her that he is so in love with. *Kepler 1982: 218*

The young man is not aware of the hidden but fundamental similarity between himself and the girl, which is the cause of this love. He is unaware of the inner primordial images which are the fuel of the infatuation: he is in love with her, because she is like him — or more correctly because something in her is like something within himself. But this similarity is not recognized in its pure form — the similarity has grown together with the girl who carries it — and therefore the object of the young man's love is the girl and not the similarity.[1]

Because of the idea of synchronicity Kepler's astrology is also based on a very different foundation than is the case with his contemporaries. Kepler disregards the zodiac and its partitioning of the firmament as the basis of astrology. The horoscope and its connection to 'houses', 'constellations' etc. are, in Kepler's view, created by man and random phenomena without an empirical basis in nature. Kepler finds the natural basis for astrology only in rays of light, the angles they form and the influence these angles have on nature and man. The planets affect nature and man, when the emanations of two planets form an activating configuration. The configuration touches the ability of the soul for insight and causes the soul's affect on itself. The affect of the configuration is thus based not on a force, which springs from the emanations of the stars and the angles of the emanations. The affect is dependent on the ability of the soul to activate itself.

Thus, nature and man are, in Kepler's opinion, not passive objects, which are affected by the planetary constellations — not victims of the power and influence of the stars. Kepler points out that 'the planets are not astronomers and know nothing of the angles their rays create on the earth'. Neither evil nor good, positive or negative, health or disease arise from the heavenly aspects. The emanations of the stars only have an activating influence on what terrestrial and not least human nature contain:

---

[1] Kepler's idea of the psychology of love — and in further understanding cognition — is, thus, in many ways parallel to modern psychology's ideas of the inner patterns, traces and images which are basic for the individuals meeting with the world. The similarity is striking, however, in relation to the Jungian psychology. Here it operates not just with individual patterns and images. Jungian psychology is fundamentally founded on the idea of archetypal, primordial images as the actual centres of energy in the soul — an energy which is for Kepler, amongst others, woken by and activated via specific constellations in the outer world. There are, therefore, fundamental similarities between parts of Kepler's ideas of the ways of knowledge and the foundation of Jungian psychology. W. Pauli has pointed this out in relation to the concept of the 'archetype' in Pauli 1955.

I am addressing astrologers ... I consider nothing in the heaven malevolent, for the ... reason ... that it is the nature of Man himself, exercised here on Earth, which by the emanations of the planets gains their influence for itself.   *Kepler 1981: 119*

Whether it is the case of the psychology of love or of the effect of the horoscope
the relationship between the external world and internal knowledge is, therefore,
the same. The primordial images, basic forms and constellations of the outer world
do not create anything new in the soul or in understanding. The soul is already
filled with primordial images, geometric patterns, psychological constellations etc.
Things that, because of the external stimulation, are woken to life for then to
recognize, rediscover or recreate themselves in action, activity and all the manifestations of the outer world.

This thought also saturates Kepler's lifework and possibly comes most clearly to
expression as the very backbone in what Kepler himself thought of as his masterpiece *Harmonice Mundi* from 1619. With this work Kepler wanted to — as the
title indicates — show how divine harmony flows through the world and where
divine harmony has its source.

Harmonice Mundi consists of five books. The first is about the origin or foundation of world harmony: the regular solids, which prior to all creation lay hidden in
the divine spirit and which in the creation are manifested as basic forms and
archetypes for all the created. From these solid geometrical figures the plane geometrical shapes also spring. The subject for the second book of *Harmonice Mundi*
is, thus, the congruity between the solid and the plane geometrical shapes. A congruity which consists of the angles which can be established when both the solid
and the plane geometrical shapes are intersected by straight lines. In the first and
the second book, Kepler works through the prerequisites for the proportions and
relations that occur in the division of the geometrical shapes which is the subject
of the third book of *Harmonice Mundi*.

The quantification of the geometrical shapes is the foundation of numbers and
mathematics, and numbers are the structuring principle of any harmony. A large
part of the third book is thus given over to the numbers, the principles of harmony.

Where the first to the third book are primarily about the archetypal figures,
images and proportions of geometry and mathematics, the fourth and fifth book
are about how archetypal primal shapes saturate the world. In the fourth book,
Kepler describes how the archetypal images are both laid down in the human soul
as well as in nature, and at the same time are constantly being activated by the
harmonious proportions of the emanations of the stars — so that divine harmony
exists both in the external and the internal, is both laid down in the soul a priori
and is continually being recreated. The fifth book is the culmination of Kepler's
work. The book is, in Kepler's own opinion, at the same time both a work on as-
tronomy and metaphysics. It shows the perfect harmony between the movements
of the planets on the one hand, and on the other, the intervals in song and music.

This shows how the human spirit, which forms hearing and musical expression, is the carrier of the same harmonic proportions that God has placed in the outer world in the form of the heavenly movements of the planets. Thus, Kepler has uncovered the harmony of the world.

In Kepler, as well as in the other natural scientists of the 16th and 17th centuries, cognition has the nature of recognition. For the alchemists recognition is instinctive or contemplative and in any case it is spontaneous and not open to discussion. The alchemist spontaneously 'tunes in' on the correspondences of nature and knows, because of inner experience, which plants, minerals, planets and metals correlate with which parts of the body and illnesses. The signatures of nature are read because of spontaneous inner information. The path of recognition is hidden and inaccessible for those who do not have access to the same mental and spiritual experience. At the same time the content of recognition needs no evidence in the outer world: the alchemist experiments and observations of nature only illustrate and show what the natural scientists already know because of their internal experience.

The case is different for Kepler. The problem of recognition is of central importance to him — a problem he consciously reflects upon and illuminates from many different angles in order to achieve clarity on the crucial question: how can internal and external experience meet? How can external experience based on the senses meet with internal spiritual experience based on the archetypal primal images? What is the criteria for, that recognition can take place? How can Kepler *know* that something in the external world really is harmonious, so that he can witness the true harmony of the world?

Kepler's lifework — to show the Holy Trinity in the created world in the shape of the planets and their movements and internal relationships — demands that God and nature are in relation to one another in such a way that the two things can be compared. It is, however, crystal clear for Kepler that no direct comparison is possible: God's inscrutable nature, God as love or mercifulness, God as an ethical demand can never be on the same level as the orbit of the planets or their mutual distances. The nature of God and the true profusion of nature do not allow comparison and scientific processing. What can be compared and processed scientifically are concepts — and in the final analysis images and symbols. The sphere is 'an image of...the Trinity', the form of the surface exists 'in imitation of the eternal manifestation of the Sun', which is 'symbolised and depicted' in this form. Radius is 'an...image of the creating spirit'. (Kepler 1982: 215)

'Image', 'imitation', 'symbol', 'depiction' — again and again Kepler stresses that the sphere with its center, radius and periphery is not the Trinity. What is talked about are images, symbolic expressions. Kepler knows he uses images, symbols and concepts, and that they are not identical with reality. In the same way Kepler knows when he is speaking allegorically. In Kepler's introduction to the

chapter in Mysterium Cosmographicum, where he describes the planetary system
as an image of the Holy Trinity the first lines are:

'Bear with me now, patient reader, if I trifle for a moment with a serious subject, and in-
dulge in allegories a little'. Thereafter follows the description of amongst other things 'the
Sun above being the image of God the Father'.   *Kepler 1981: 107*

In the same way as the sphere is a pictorial, symbolic expression for God, nature's
'true reality' is changed into an image; a concrete concept is created, a concrete,
materially based model, a concrete geometrical or mathematical expression, which
'illustrates' the empirical evidence.

   God and nature's actual and profuse nature denies intellectual and scientific understanding. They are qualitatively different and do not allow themselves to be
compared. Only indirectly can wholeness and part be brought into connection
with one another. They can relate in images, in symbols and in quantifiable things.
God and the individual parts of nature are not identical and the same. The connection can only exist by proxy: via the symbolic and conceptual expressions in
which God and Nature — each on their own — allow themselves to be expressed.
Only in this way is the comparison possible, which is not just central but crucial for
Kepler's theory of knowledge and all of his scientific work.

   The comparison between things in the external, sensory world, and at the next
step between the external sensory world and the internal primal images, is the final
test — if there is no concord then Kepler has found no true harmony.

   The basis for Kepler's vision of wholeness and scientific method is, thus, on the
one hand a special combination of the legacy of Pythagoras with medieval
Christian mysticism.[2] Kepler revises the Pythagorean idea of numbers as the foundation of the world and sees instead the geometric shapes as the archetypal point
of departure of the created. And these geometrical shapes are loaded with religious, symbolic meaning by Kepler: the sphere becomes the symbol of the Trinity.

   On the other hand, Kepler's scientific work is based on an unusual combination
of the Platonic theory of knowledge and the critical empirical method. Cognition
is recognition, but recognition is only valid if the external and the internal are exactly alike. This means that Kepler's scientific method of work resembles that of
Max Weber: on the basis of the empirical evidence an ideal type is formulated — a
concrete concept, a concrete theory which is compared with the internal primal
image — the general concept — which, thus, functions as a hypothesis. Or as the
method of work often is in Kepler's practice: the primal image forms the starting
point for a hypothesis, which has to be compared with empirical evidence in order
that it can be verified. Therefore Kepler, on the basis of the empirical evidence —
that is to say the astronomical observations — calculates a mathematical or geo-

---

2   Kepler gives Nicolas Cusanus as a crucial source of inspiration in connection with the idea of the geo-
    metric shapes as religious symbols. (Kepler 1981: 93ff.)

metrical model, which is then compared with the original hypothesis of the primordial image. If there is not concord then Kepler has not rediscovered or recognized the harmony in the external world. For Kepler observations and calculations serve not as illustrations of an already given a priori, internal knowledge. The empirical proof shows whether the internal primordial image only has the character of a subjective idea, or whether it is of objective validity. The exploration of the external nature has, thus, independent validity in the face of the internal, archetypal image of the hypothesis.

Kepler's approach to the relationship between world and man, wholeness and part allows for a connection that is not reductionistic. In Kepler's vision of wholeness, wholeness and part, world and man are synchronous. Different levels of reality manifest simultaneous phenomena and expressions, which have a joint core. But the synchronous relation is based not on organic identity, but on formal and pictorial likeness. And it is asserted that likeness means that x and y have something in common, whilst other things are different. Similarity between wholeness and part, world and man occurs, thus, as a phenomenon which demands that both that which is the same, and that which is different have equal weight. The levels of reality carry certain similarities, but similarity does not triumph over difference. Kepler maintains the completely decisive distinction between similarity and identity. Thus wholeness and part, world and man can be connected without being uniformed and leveled.

Thus there are important differences in the ways of relating wholeness and part in the natural philosophy of the 16th and 17th centuries. In a modern perspective, however, it is obvious, that the natural scientists of this period also share ideas that differentiate clearly from modern scientists. First of all none of them ever question the relationship between wholeness and part, cosmos and man. They just disagree — as sketched above — on the very nature of this relationship. Secondly they share essential ideas, that are crucial especially to their concept of order. In the scientific reformers of the 16th and 17th centuries, as in the middle ages order is based on and created by analogy and correspondence, similarity or even identity. But order is never based on difference and diversity as in most modern approaches. Order based on similarity belongs to a world-view, that values stability and community; to a society where change is not seen as progress but as disorder, an interruption leading astray from the original and eternal harmony.

Order based on similarity and order based on difference express and originate from completely different world-views, based on completely different values. In this interpretation the scientific concept of order does not stem from science but from history.

References

BOHM, D. 1980. *Holeness and the implicate order.* London: Routledge & Kegan Paul.

FLUDD, R. 1979. A Philosophicall Key. In A.G. Debus, *Robert Fludd and His Pholosophicall Key, being a Transcription of the Manuscript at Trinity College, Cambridge.* New York: Science History Publications.

KEPLER, J. 1981. *The Secret of the Universe.* New York: Abaris Books.

KEPLER, J. 1982. *Weltharmonik.* Munich.

PARACELSUS 1975. *The Archidoxes of Magic.* London: Askin Publishers.

PARACELSUS 1976. *The Hermetical and Alchemical Writings.* Ed. A.E.Waite. California: Shambala Publications.

PAULI, W. 1955. The influence of archetypal ideas on the scientific theories of Kepler. In *The interpretation of nature and the Psyke.* New York: Pantheon Books.

3

Macro and Micro-levels in Physics

PEDER VOETMANN CHRISTIANSEN

Abstract

Downward Causation in a physics-context is viewed as the influence of macro-scopic boundary conditions on the microscopic dynamics of a thermodynamic system. Three cases are considered, corresponding to the three phenomenological categories of C.S. Peirce: (1) The irreversible approach to the maximum entropy equilibrium state of a homogeneous phase. (2) A symmetry-breaking phase transition (emergence) forming a separating boundary between two phases, like the surface of a liquid. (3) adaptive behavior associated with the surface-modes such as self-organized criticality.

1. Wholes and parts

The metaphorical use of the words 'upward' and 'downward' in connection with 'causation' is generally understood as involving wholes and parts of a system. Thus, the system is a whole that is distinguished from its surroundings by certain boundary conditions, and inside the system we may find interacting parts. In general systems theory, words like 'inside' and 'boundary' also have a meta–phorical character: the system is not necessarily like a container in ordinary space; for example we may speak of the system of electrons in a metal as something separated from the system of elastic vibrations in the same metal, although the 'boundary' separating these two systems does not have the character of the wall of a container but is a sort of energetical constraint that connect the two systems weakly throughout the three-dimensional space of the metal.

We shall, however, in this chapter mostly be concerned with systems that really are containers, e.g., a gas that is separated from its surroundings by a solid wall. The gas as a whole has certain properties, like volume, pressure, and temperature that are conditioned partly by the wall and partly by properties of its constituent molecules. Thus, if the wall is heat conducting (diathermic) we may assume that the temperature has a fixed value, determined by the temperature of the surroundings, and the pressure and volume have a reciprocal relation to each other, whereas, if the wall is heat-insulating (adiabatic) both pressure and temperature will change, when the volume of the container is changed. The boundary conditions in this way determine the laws on the macroscopic level of the whole, i.e. the thermodynamic relations that are appropriate to the system, and they restrict the motion of the microscopic parts. We can therefore say that the boundary conditions exert a 'horizontal' and a 'downward' causation. Also, it is clear that there is an 'upward' causation in the system, because macroscopic properties, like the heat capacity of the system depends on microscopic features, like the shape and rigidity of the molecules.

One may say that the restricting influence of the walls on the motion of the molecules is not genuine downward causality, because the *laws* of molecular motion, like Newton's law of action and reaction, are unchanged by the walls. This, however, is a limited truth, because the boundary conditions determine *how* these laws are to be applied. We may state the law of action and reaction by saying that the force molecule A exerts on molecule B is equal in magnitude (but with opposite direction) to the force molecule B exerts on molecule A, but this law then presupposes that molecule A and B have individual existence, so that they do not react chemically with each other and form a compound or split into other parts that are not identical with the original molecules, and whether such reactions take place or not is determined by the boundary conditions, e.g., whether the walls are rapidly changing their positions or whether they are able to conduct heat from surroundings with a sufficiently high temperature.

The temperature is the most important macroscopic property that determines what type of laws describes the dynamics on the microlevel. One may say that temperature determines what type of parts we may consider as having individual existence. An examination of the concept of an ideal gas will illustrate that.

At room temperature we may consider a quantity of atmospheric gas as consisting of rigid diatomic molecules that are able to move freely in the three dimensional space within the confinement of the walls and perform free rotations around their center of mass. Thus, each molecule has 5 degrees of freedom in their motion, namely three translatorial motions and two rotational, and each of these degrees of freedom contributes on the average with a fixed amount $1/2kT$ (where k is Boltzmann's constant and T the absolute temperature) to the total energy of the system (assuming that the interaction between molecules is weak). The heat capacity of the system is therefore $(5/2)k$ times the number of molecules.

When the temperature is raised the heat capacity begins to increase, because the molecules cease to be rigid. When the two atoms in a diatomic molecule are able to oscillate relative to each other there will be 6 degrees of freedom per molecule, and this is also the case when the temperature induced oscillations become so violent that the molecules split into two atoms each having three translatorial motions. A further increase in heat capacity due to additional degrees of freedom for the microscopic motion becomes evident when the atoms begin to lose their electrons and the gas becomes a plasma of charged ions and free electrons.

We may understand the increase of heat capacity as due to the occurrence of new degrees of freedom, but once we have understood that molecules consist of atoms that consist of electrons and nuclei that consist of protons and neutrons that consist of ..., we are faced with a big problem: These additional degrees of freedom exist all the time in the molecules. How come that we do not 'feel' them at ordinary temperatures? How is it possible at all to speak of a well defined micro level of a macroscopic system when the parts themselves are wholes consisting of smaller parts that perhaps again may be subdivided in even smaller parts? It looks as if there is no 'bottom' for the physical description but rather an indefinitely descending hierarchy of microscopic levels. Where do we find the bedrock of microscopic dynamic from which the upward reaching causality extends to the macro-surface of thermodynamic systems?

This is one of the paradoxes that haunted classical physics around the turn of the century and led to the invention of quantum mechanics. The answer to the problem is that sub-microscopic degrees of freedom are 'locked' by quantization of energy, and the smaller parts we consider the larger is the separation between their energy levels. When the level differences are much larger than the average energy of thermic motion it is impossible to transfer heat to these parts and therefore they do not contribute to the heat capacity. Therefore we are allowed to consider the gas at room temperature as a collection of classically moving rigid bodies for the purpose of dynamics, although we know full well that they consist of atoms, electrons and nucleons. The laws of quantum mechanics come into play for higher temperatures to describe the gradual loosening of the motions of these smaller particles and also for lower temperatures to describe the locking in of motions that are free at room temperature.

We see, thus, that the downward causative influence of the macroscopic boundary conditions on the microscopic dynamics is far more profound than just to delimit a certain part of the state space as available (see the paper by Mark H. Bickhard, this volume). The very notion of a microscopic state depends crucially on our ability to heat and isolate systems, and this ability is not reducible to microscopic laws but depends on technology and intention. The physicists do not just isolate a natural system for closer study, but with their methods of preparation *create* the system, including the notion of microscopic parts and the laws that govern them.

The Nobel prize in physics for the year 1996 was given for the discovery of superfluidity of the Helium isotope He^3.[1] However, this property only exists below a millidegree above the absolute zero of temperature, and, as the background temperature of the universe is between 2 and 3 degrees, more than a thousand times higher, we can be pretty sure that superfluid He^3 only exists where there are physicists to study it.

2. Irreversibility and noise

All microscopic dynamical laws in physics are *reversible*, or *invariant under time reversal*. This means, that there is a certain mathematical operation that changes time t to -t in connection with changes of other variables such that the same law applies to these transformed quantities. In classical mechanics we have to reverse all velocities when we reverse time. If we look at a motion picture of a lot of billiard balls in motion and compare a certain situation with the same situation in the same motion picture run backwards, then we see the same positions of the balls but the opposite velocities, but we cannot by watching of the two versions of the film decide which is run the wrong way, unless there is a situation that points to the setup or preparation of the scene. If, for example, we see ten balls lying still in a cluster and one rapid ball moving into the cluster scattering the others in all directions, then we would guess that we see the events in the correct order of time. The time reversed show of a lot of balls coming together in a multiple collision and transferring all their motion to a single ball would seem too improbable to be natural. We would know that no billiard player, however skillful, would be able to create such a sequence of events, except by sheer luck.

There is nothing in the laws of motion that forbid improbable occurrences, for the very notion of probability is totally alien to the laws, like the notions of skill and intention. When we introduce such considerations we are jumping from the microscopic, reversible world to the macroscopic world, where the laws are irreversible. A film showing an egg being dropped to the floor and splashed all over it displays this macroscopic type of behavior, and nobody would be in doubt whether it is shown with the right or wrong direction of time.

Macroscopic irreversibility was first formulated in laws like Fourier's law of heat conduction and Ohm's law of electrical conduction. Later it was generalized by Clausius about 1860 in the law of the increasing *entropy*. This strange state function of thermodynamic systems has the peculiar property that it can only increase when it changes, and it does so whenever some *spontaneous* event takes place in an isolated system. We all know what such an event could be, e.g., self-ignition of

1   The Nobel laureates (Physics,1996) D. M. Lee, R.C. Richardson, and D.D. Osheroff discovered the superfluidity of He^3 in 1971.

burnable material, but the notion of *spontaneity* is just as alien to the microscopic dynamics as entropy and irreversibility.

In classical mechanics or quantum mechanics every change of the state of an isolated system is totally deterministic, being determined alone by the force-law and the present state. But in thermodynamics we cannot be sure that a quiet state of equilibrium will remain so. It may be a metastable state, and a transition to a more favorable equilibrium (with higher entropy) may be triggered by unforeseeable fluctuations in an explosive way. There is a profound connection between irreversible behavior and indeterminacy. If a system is able to reach a state of equilibrium in an irreversible way then there must be unpredictable fluctuations or *noise* in the system. Normally the noise will be sub-liminal, and it is neglected in laws like Fourier's and Ohm's. But there may occur situations where the future development may take several directions depending on marginal differences, and in such cases the presence of noise is crucial for the realization of macroscopic indeterminacy.

The intrinsic connection between irreversibility and noise is due to the statistical or probabilistic character of both.[2] This was illustrated with the example of the billiard balls, and in general we can use statistical models involving a moderately large number of particles to mediate between the seemingly irreconcilable paradigms of reversible micro-dynamics and irreversible thermodynamics.

The first attempt to reconcile these two physical disciplines was made by L. Boltzmann with the H-theorem from 1872. Boltzmann set up an equation to show how an arbitrary initial distribution of velocities of the molecules in a gas would be changed by collisions and finally stabilize itself in a statistical equilibrium. This was done by introduction of the H-functional that exhibited irreversible properties and could be used as a definition of entropy in statistical terms. Boltzmann was convinced of the correctness of thermodynamics, but his H-theorem was met with severe criticisms from mechanicists, Loschmidt, Zermelo, and Poincaré. The simplest objection was the *Umkehr-Einwand* by Loschmidt who simply pointed to the time-reversal symmetry of the mechanical laws and correctly concluded that no mechanical proof of the entropy law could be possible. The objection would not be so serious if it hadn't been put forward in a philosophical ground of mechanical reductionism. Everybody seemed to believe that Newton's laws of mechanics ought to explain everything, and the best arguments against this view and in support of Boltzmann were formulated by the physicist W. Gibbs and the philosopher C.S. Peirce, both in America and far outside the European mainstream of science at that time.[3]

---

2   The most general formulation of this connection is the *fluctuation-dissipation theorem* of Callen and Welton (1951).
3   J.W. Gibbs and C. S. Peirce were both born in 1839 and both graduated in chemistry and had some correspondence with each other. Gibbs developed his *Statistical Mechanics* about thev same time as Boltzmann. Peirce wrote about the philosophical aspects of chance and necessity (*The Doctrine of*

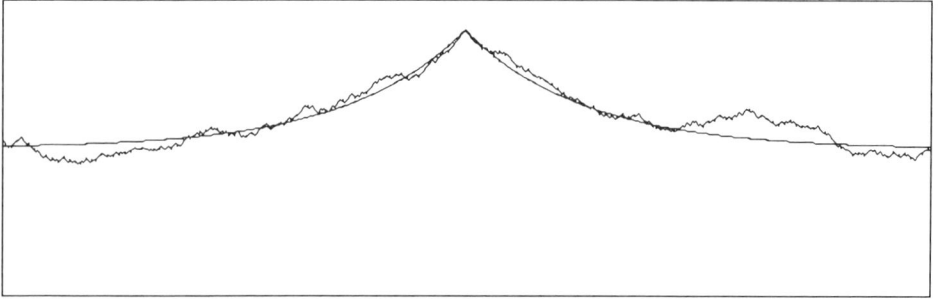

Fig. 1. The Ehrenfest diffusion model. Vertical axis (0-200) shows the number of particles in the right half container. Horizontal axis: time from -400 to 400. Ragged curve: simulation. Smooth curve: average relaxation.

In 1911, five years after the death of Boltzmann, Paul and Tatjana Ehrenfest published a thorough discussion of Boltzmann's theory and the objections against it.[4]
The *Umkehr-Einwand* was taken into consideration with a simple model of diffusion, that we shall briefly consider.

In the Ehrenfest diffusion model a collection of N numbered particles are distributed in two urns, or in the separate two halves of a container. Every second a
number is chosen randomly between 1 and N, and the corresponding particle is
transferred to opposite half-container. Figure 1 shows a simulation (or rather two
simulations) with 200 particles (ragged curve). At time zero in the middle there are
180 particles in the right half of the container. Time proceeds from zero to 400
from the middle to the right boundary of the figure and from zero to -400 going to
the left. See Fig. 1.

In this model, time is just a counting number of a random draw and it makes no
difference whether it is counted backwards or forwards. The leftward running
simulation (0 to -400) of course looks slightly different from the rightward running
(0 to 400) but that is just a statistical difference to be expected between two different simulations. The reversibility of the model is manifested by the approximate
left-right symmetry of the figure

In principle we could regard the whole run as one single simulation from -400 to
400. The resulting curve is a *fractal* with small fluctuations within larger ones and
one especially large fluctuation right in the middle. It is not *impossible* that such a
simulation result could occur but one gets suspicious that the large deviation in
the middle is *prepared*, because the most probable distribution of particles is 100
in each half of the container and large deviations from that number are extremely

---

Necessity Examined, 1892), defended Boltzmann's views against mechanicists and pointed to the need
for a new mechanical theory of atoms.

4   P. and T. Ehrenfest. *The Conceptual Foundations of the Statistical Approach in Mechanics*, New York,
     Dover Publications 1990. (Original article in german published in the *Encyclopädie der Mathematischen
     Wissenschaften, 1911*).

rare. If a single simulation produced such a result we would be tempted to discard it because it is 'untypical' just as if a shuffling of cards had produced a deck with all the diamonds in a single cluster with no other suits mixed in between. In fact, the probability of a random occurrence of 180 of the 200 particles in the right half-container is about 10^{-33}, so if we draw one number per second we would have to wait about $3*10^{25}$ years before such a combination could be expected to occur once if there was no 'cheating'. Considering that the universe is only about 10^{10} years old we are almost allowed to say that such a large fluctuation is impossible.

Knowing, however, that the situation at time zero is *prepared* by the experimenter and that in reality there are two simulations, one counting forwards and one counting backwards in 'time' there is nothing strange in the picture. If we make a lot of simulations from the same initial condition and calculate the average number of particles in the right container for each step of time, the result is the smooth curves in Figure 1 showing exponential relaxation of the initial large deviation in both directions of time. The reversibility of the model is *exact* for the two relaxation curves taken together, although the phenomenon of exponential relaxation in physics is always connected with irreversible phenomena. The *forward* relaxation curve looks exactly like the discharge of a capacitor through an Ohmic resistance. Ohm's law alone will give the smooth exponential, and the deviations from it shown by the simulation correspond to the Nyqvist-Johnson noise from the resistor as filtered by the capacitor.

How can the reversible Ehrenfest model then account for the irreversibility described by Boltzmann? By showing that irreversibility is a result of the experimenters ability to prepare an improbable initial state and letting the dynamical situation proceed *forward* in time. It is only the right half of Figure 1 that can be regarded as a physical model of diffusion. The experimenter can have the 180 particles put into the right half of the container at time zero and then let the system run its course by itself, but he cannot choose an initial state like the one at time -400 that will evolve by itself to the very improbable state at time zero. If the experimenter had a 'memory of the future' he could perhaps do the trick, but he only knows the past and he therefore cannot select one of the few initial states that will develop into a conspicuously deviating state from among all the many similarly looking states near equilibrium.

The question of how irreversibility arises is thus transferred from the domain of microscopic dynamics to the irreversible behavior of the experimenter. How can it be that we only have a memory of the past and that our sense of time always proceeds in the same direction? This question cannot be answered reductionistically by considering a human being like a collection of molecules that act together according to the laws of mechanics, for, as we have seen, these laws are all reversible and have no sense of 'time's arrow'. But the human body works as it should only if it is inserted in an ecological system with available food and clean air and water,

a thermodynamic system far from equilibrium. Such a system has a tendency to re-
lax towards equilibrium producing entropy and it is this tendency that nourishes
the organism and provides it with a sense of time. If the ecological system were
isolated in the universe it would run down to equilibrium and the organisms would
die. But it is maintained in the non-equilibrium state by a flow of low-entropic
energy from the sun that can be converted into high-entropy heat radiation and
scattered out into the background radiation of the universe. The question of the
origin of irreversibility is thus pushed upwards as far as 'up' goes in physics: to
the irreversible evolution of the whole universe.

The recognition of this multi-level downward causation from the ecosystem
through the experimenter's ability to select improbable initial states for a thermodynamic system changes the status of the phrase 'the entropy increases' from a
paradox to a tautology. This is because the prerequisite for being able to say
something is that the entropy of the universe is higher after the saying than it was
before. The same entropic condition applies to any significant event, to every difference that makes a difference, i.e. rises appreciably above the noise level of fluctuations.

3. The emergence of boundaries

In the early universe matter is uniformly distributed in a gaseous state of internal
thermodynamic equilibrium. In such a state there are no boundaries, it is impossible
to separate a system from its surroundings, and no signs or significant actual
events can exist. Nothing marks the space, and gravitation is cancelling itself out.
However, the increasing scale or expansion sets up an external control parameter
that gradually forces internal symmetry breaking choices that set up ordering
fields acting as internal control parameters for the creation of significant boundaries, limitations, and constraints.

A specific type of order, created by spontaneous symmetry-breaking may generalize itself by the action of the ordering field it makes. For example, a larger con-
centration of matter in a volume creates a gravitational attraction towards its center such that surrounding material gets sucked in making the gravitational pull
even stronger. The resulting local inhomogeneity of matter creates a spreading
tendency to form nucleation centers for matter in space. Gravitation, previously
lying dormant, in this way becomes generalized to a habit of the universe, and
becomes *significant*.

According to Peirce this is *semiosis* at work. A slumbering affinity or similarity is
an *icon*, an actual difference is an *index*, and a habit or general rule is a *symbol*.
Symbols are general ideas that spread and lose intensity but become associated
with other ideas whereby new symbols are created. This is Peirce's *law of mind*.

The phenomenology and metaphysics of C.S. Peirce distinguishes between three ontological modes or categories:

1.   **Firstness:** This is the mode of *potentiality* and *being*.
2.   **Secondness:** *Actuality* and *individual existence.*
3.   **Thirdness:** *Generality* and *reality.*

The categories follow each other such that Secondness presupposes and contains Firstness, and Thirdness presupposes and contains Firstness and Secondness.

The emergence of a boundary separating between spatially extended qualities is a Secondness arising as an actual distinction between Firstnesses. If we think of something like a water surface we can imagine how the constrained space of the surface evolves its own laws by downward causation, and indexical signs like drops of water become generalized and symbolized to rain and rivers and oceans (with birds, boats, and fishes).

Internally there is no qualitative difference between a gas and a liquid. There is no long range order and the molecules wander erratically around. So, if it is at all possible to distinguish between gas and liquid it must be due to the existence of a surface that separates the denser liquid from the rarefied gas. Secondness enters the picture through the surface that distinguishes between the internal Firstnesses of the two phases, but while the gaseous phase keeps its unconstrained Firstness, the liquid is contaminated with Secondness, for the surface belongs to the liquid it confines. The surface introduces a *tension* that keeps drops of liquid together.

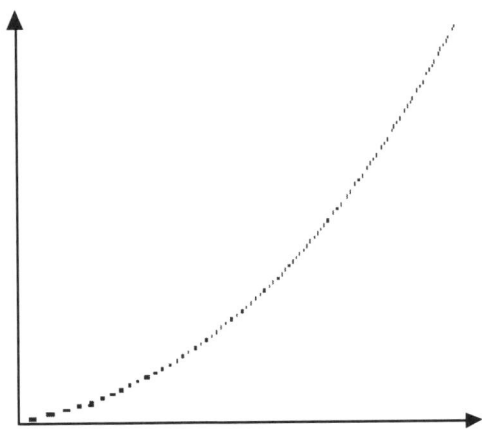

Fig. 2. Reduced pressure of saturated vapor as a function of reduced temperature according to van der Waals.

The qualitative features of the gas-liquid transition were first described mathematically with the Van der Waals equation of state (1872). This equation explains the existence of a *critical point* (P_c, T_c) in the pressure-temperature plane, such that the distinction between gas and liquid only exists for certain pressures when the

temperature is below the critical temperature T_c. Van der Waals' equation has become paradigmatic, not because of its quantitative agreement with measurements
for real gases (which is not impressive) but because it gives a simple conceptual
scheme for the discussion of *order-disorder transitions* (or second order phase
transitions). The hypostatic abstraction of this concept was perfected by L.D.
Landau in the *mean field theory of second order phase transitions* (1950)[5] and
by R. Thom in the so-called *catastrophe-theory* (1978).[6] The gas-liquid transition
exemplifies the *cusp-catastrophe* of Thom, and this is the simplest model for describing how a type of order nucleates spontaneously and is able to induce similar
ordering in its surroundings. By means of Van der Waals' equation one is able to
formulate a law of *corresponding states* for different gases. For example, the *reduced pressure* P/P_c of saturated vapor is a universal function of the *reduced temperature* T/T_c as shown in Figure 2

As shown in Figure 3 the cusp catastrophe requires two control parameters, *a*
and *b*, where *a* is the 'external' control (temperature) and *b* the 'internal' control
(ordering field). For the case of the gas-liquid transition *b* is roughly proportional
to the deviation of the pressure from the critical pressure. The *a*- and *b*-axes in
Figure 2 are made to cross in the critical point. Above this point (for higher values
of *a*) no ordering is possible (no surface), but below there is an interval of *b* values
where the two phases may coexist.

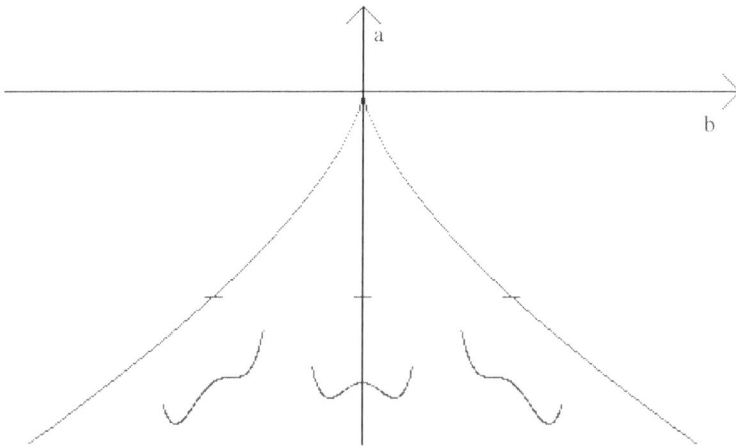

Fig. 3. The cusp catastrophe. Potential as function of order parameter shown for marked
points below the cusp.

5   L.D. Landau and E. M. Lifshitz, *Statistical Physics*, Pergamon Press, London, 1959.
6   T. Poston and I. Stewart, *Catastrophe Theory and its Applications*, Pitman, London 1978. The name
     Catastrophe Theory was invented by E.C. Zeeman (1972) to denote Thom's theory of differential
     topology, outlined in the book R. Thom, *Stabilité structurelle et morphogenese. Essai d'une theorie
     general des modeles*, Benjamin, Reading, 1972.

The ordered phase is described by an *order parameter* which for the gas-liquid transition is the difference in density between the two phases separated by the surface. The equilibrium value of the order parameter is one that minimizes the thermodynamic potential (Gibbs' free energy). The *catastrophe set* in the control plane is a curve that exhibits a cusp in the critical point. This curve separates a region where this potential has two minima below the cusp from another region where it has only one minimum.

The left minimum corresponds to the gaseous phase and the right to the liquid phase. Close to the critical point, where the saturated vapor pressure is equal to the critical pressure, the two phases may coexist in equilibrium only on the line $b=0$. Normally in thermodynamics one assumes that the lowest minimum is the stable one, such that the two phases may coexist only when the two minima have the same height, i.e. on the a-axis below the cusp. This assumption corresponds to the so called Maxwell convention. In reality, however, there may be a region with 'superheated liquid' to the left of the a-axis and a region with 'supercooled vapor' to the right and these regions of metastability may extend to the catastrophe curve, but not beyond, which is the convention of 'maximum delay'. Where the transition actually takes place is determined, among other things, by characteristics of the surface. Very small bubbles of liquid have a high surface tension which increases the internal pressure such that the bubble may be superheated.

The emergence of the phase separating boundary to a liquid phase in a gaseous region is a complicated cooperative phenomenon. A mist of small droplets appears, and gradually these droplets coalesce whereby the pressure is regulated through the action of surface tension (and perhaps gravitation). When the external control parameter is lowered (a, the temperature) large density fluctuations will begin to appear, and these will adjust the internal control (b, the pressure deviation) so as to pass through the critical point. Below criticality the fusion of droplets will tend to keep the system in the close neighborhood of the a-axis, $b = 0$, the line of saturated vapor pressure.

The emergence of boundaries like the liquid surface is the first step in the *semiosis* of natural pre-biological evolution. It is the transition from the slumbering Firstness of icons to the specificity and actuality of indices. But the law of mind comes to play by the downward causative influence of habit formation. A habit is an emerging generality, a Peircean Thirdness that presupposes the significant difference of Secondness. An occurrence governed by habit is facilitated by its own previous occurrence. In this way the habit implies a self-reference that makes it a suitable third factor or *interpretant* of a symbolic sign relation.

We have seen that the surface tension is a feature that arises by downward causality. But liquid surfaces and other types of emergent boundaries tend to develop specific habits that do not belong to the world of microscopic dynamics. The significance of singular shapes in the control space, like the cusp and the line of coexistence in Figure 2 is due to a tendency of boundaries to proliferate themselves, and this is done most efficiently in the neighborhood of critical regions. The phenomenon of *self organized criticality* that has been described by Per Bak *et al* [7] seems to be a most important fact for the understanding of semiosis in evolution. The simplest example is that of the sand dune that maintains a critical slope because just this slope has the maximal ability to respond to every disturbance by avalanches of all sizes.

Phase separating boundaries create a confined space for special types of disturbances, like ripples on the water.

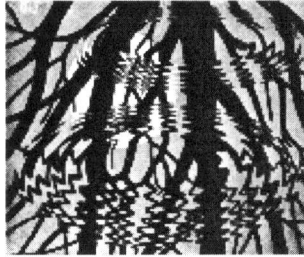

Fig. 4. Rippled surface by M. C. Escher. Lino-cut 1950.

These surface modes have dynamic properties determined by overall metrical properties of the surface, like its fractal dimension. On the other hand, these modes have the function of maintaining the overall characteristics of the surface that maximizes the diversity of internal motion which is close to the critical region of marginal instability. The working of the pre-biotic *law of mind* may thus be described as a complex interplay of upwards and downwards causality.

7   P. Bak, C. Tang, & K. Wiesenfeld, Self-organized Criticality, *Phys. Rev. A* 38, 364, (1988).

4

Causation, Control, and the Evolution of Complexity

H. H. PATTEE

Abstract

Causation is a gratuitous concept for events described by the laws of physics. The concept of causation is useful only in the context of events described as controllable. To understand the continuous evolution of stable complex forms, it is essential to distinguish two complementary types of control models, a semiotic model exerting upward control from a local isolated memory, and a dynamic model exerting downward control from a global network of coherent, interactive components. Semiotic control models are heritable and provide efficient search processes for discovering adaptive and emergent structures. Dynamic control models integrate networks of components constructed under semiotic control. Dynamical models do not explain the discrete, rate-independent, orderly, heritable sequences of languages, nor do semiotic models explain the coherence and integration of complex networks. Evolution and learning require both types of control.

Is causation a useful concept?

It is not obvious that the concept of causation, in any of its many forms, has ever played a necessary role in the discovery of the laws of nature. Causation has a tortuous philosophical literature with no consensus in sight (e.g., Hart & Honoré 1958; Bunge 1959; Taylor 1972), and modern physics has little interest in the concept. Nevertheless, causation is so ingrained in both the syntax and semantics of our natural language that we usually feel that events are somehow causally explained by almost any grammatically correct declarative statement that relates a noun and a verb phrase to the event: *Why did the ball roll? Because John kicked the ball. Why did the ball bounce? Because the ball hit the post.* In Aristotelian terms, the verb is a form of efficient cause, and either the subject or object can act as a material cause. If the subject happens to have a large brain we may also attribute a formal, teleological, or intentional cause to the event: *Why did John kick the ball? Because John wanted a goal.* As children we figure out that these linguistic forms are transitive and always lead to a vicious circle or an infinite regress, but we are usually told that it is rude to continue to ask *Why?* when presented with one proximal cause. The major weakness of the concept of causation is this Whorfian dependence on natural language. Thus, the richness and ambiguity of causal forms arise more from the richness and ambiguities of language than from any empirical necessity or from natural laws.

Naive causation requires a direction in time

This naive concept of causation is formed from our perception of certain sequences of events. One condition is temporal antisymmetry. That is, when we say an event B is caused by an event A, it must be the case that A occurred before B. If temporal order were reversed any cause and effect relation would also be reversed, although some philosophers have questioned this assertion (e.g., Dummett 1964). The concept of causation therefore presupposes a model of time, usually a tacit model. Our everyday concept of time is directed in one dimension, and so we ascribe causation to events that can be decomposed into simple strings of local ordered events or actions. High-dimensional and diffuse concurrent influences that cannot be localized are seldom viewed as causes. However, like the concept of time, the meaning of causation does not easily lend itself to deeper analysis. When we try to define more precisely the concepts of time and causation we find they are entirely context or model dependent. Furthermore, these concepts are often not consistent between contexts and levels, as in the case of reversible and irreversible dynamics. To make matters worse, they usually appear as irreducibly primitive concepts at all levels.

Causation is gratuitous in modern physics

The Newtonian paradigm of state-determined rate laws derived from a scalar time variable and explicit forces only strengthens the naive concept of one-dimensional, focal causation. Reductionists take the microscopic physical laws as the ultimate source of order. At this lowest level, causation was classically associated with the concept of *force*. According to one statement of Newton's 2nd law, a force is the cause of objects changing their motion. The concept of force can also be interpreted in many ways, but in practice most physical models are of systems with a very small number of forces, or more precisely, of systems where the equations of motion can be easily integrated or computationally iterated. However, in the case of the famous n-body problem (n > 2) that is generally nonintegrable, the forces are so interdependent that no focal causes exist. The motion of one body in an n-body model might be seen as a case of downward causation, but this does not add anything to our understanding of the fundamental problem.

The fundamental problem is that the microscopic equations of physics are time symmetric and therefore conceptually reversible. Consequently the irreversible concept of causation is not formally supportable by microphysical laws, and if it is used at all it is a purely subjective linguistic interpretation of the laws. Hertz (1894) argued that even the concept of force was unnecessary. This does not mean that the concepts of cause and force should be eliminated, because we cannot escape the use of natural language even in our formal models. We still interpret some variables in the rate-of-change laws as forces, but formally these dynamical equations define only an invertible mapping on a state space. Because of this time symmetry, systems described by such reversible dynamics cannot formally (syntactically) generate intrinsically irreversible properties such as measurements, records, memories, controls, or causes. Furthermore, as Bridgman (1964) pointed out, 'The mathematical concept of time appears to be particularly remote from the time of experience.' Consequently, no concept of causation, especially downward causation, can have much fundamental explanatory value at the level of microscopic physical laws.

Do statistical laws give a direction to time?

The answer to this question is still controversial. It is a near tautology to state that on the average the more likely events will occur sooner than the less likely events. In the more precise form of the second law of thermodynamics this is still a useful near tautology. Here the word 'sooner' appears to give time a direction, as does the second law's increasing entropy or disorder with time in an isolated system. But on careful thought we see that sooner and later are concepts that presuppose a direction of time. This statement, and the second law, would still be true if time were reversed since sooner and later would also be reversed. Assuming an isolated system with less than maximum entropy, the plot of entropy vs. time would show increasing entropy in both directions of time without favoring either direction (e.g., Tolman 1950). Nevertheless, it has been argued on many grounds that the observer's psychological time must be consistent with the second law, and furthermore, using the weak anthropic principle, both must correspond to the cosmological arrow of time (e.g., Hawking 1988).

What is important to recognize is that the concepts of causation have completely different meanings in statistical models and in deterministic models. A reductionist will assume that cause refers to events in a lower level model. That is, if we ask what is the cause of temperature, the reductionist will answer that it is caused by molecules exchanging their kinetic energy by collisions. But notice that the measurement of temperature is practical only because measuring devices effectively *average* this exchange without requiring measurement of detailed initial conditions of all the molecules. Averaging is not part of the microscopic model but is a statistical process of a higher level model. A deterministic microscopic model cannot cause an average to be an observable. There is also the model of flipping a coin. Here the reductionist will again say that it is the detailed initial conditions that determine the result, but in this case precise enough measurement of initial conditions is not practical, and therefore flipping a coin is modelled as a random event.

Measurement gives a direction to time

Many people are satisfied by the reductionist's detailed 'causes' and feel that these microscopic models have explained the macroscopic observations. However, a skeptic will observe that averages, coin equilibria, dissipation, measurement, and all other irreversible or stochastic events cannot be derived from reversible, deterministic models, and therefore cannot be adequately reduced to, or explained by, such models (e.g., Coveney & Highfield 1991). In the two examples above, what forces an asymmetric direction of time in our models is not the microscopic behavior of the system, but the *measurement process*. In the case of temperature, the irreversible process of averaging is done by the measuring device, the thermometer, not the reversible dynamics of the molecules of the system being measured. For the same reason, the macroscopic observables of heads or tails of a coin appear only after the reversible dynamics of the coin have been dissipated and the coin has come irreversibly to rest. Dissipation here simply means that the useful details of the motion have become unmeasurable.

Of course, simply stating that irreversibility results from measurement does not settle this classical issue since when a measurement actually occurs is still controversial. For example, the argument has been made that it is ultimately the erasure of the results of measurement, not the measurement itself, that is irreversible (Bennett 1982). While there is no doubt that erasure is irreversible (by definition), it is also the case that measurement used to control must be irreversible otherwise the 2nd law of thermodynamics could be violated.

From this line of argument we conclude that our concepts of the direction of time and hence our concepts of causation arise from our being observers or controllers of events, not from the events themselves. Consequently concepts of causation are subjective insofar as they cannot be separated from the observer's choice of observables and the function of measuring devices. According to this model one might be tempted to say that it is the observer who causes a direction to time, not physical laws, but this would overstate the causal powers of the observer. Physical explanations require an epistemic cut between the knower and the known, and a model of the observer on one side of the cut makes no sense without the complementary model of the laws of the observed system on the other side (e.g., von Neumann 1955).

Universal causes are not explanatory

The reductionist's answers above are examples of universal causes. It is a metaphysical precondition for physical laws that they must hold everywhere for all observers. Laws are inexorable. That is, we expect every event at any level of complexity to satisfy these laws no matter what higher level observables may also be needed for a useful model. Therefore, just as it is correct to say that the temperature in this room is caused by atoms following the laws of physics, it is equally correct to say that the cause of my writing this paper is the atoms of my brain following the laws of physics. But since such statements hold in all conceivable cases they give no clue to the level of observables necessary for a useful model in each case. It is only our familiarity with this linguistic form that often leads us to accept uncritically such universal causes as explanations.

Complementary models require complementary causes

We know from the two fundamental levels of physical models, the microscopic laws and the statistical laws, that it is a wasteful exercise to try to abstract away the differences between these models since they are complementary. I am using complementary here in Boltzmann's and Bohr's sense of logical irreducibility. That is, complementary models are formally incompatible but both necessary. One model cannot be derived from, or reduced to, the other. Chance cannot be derived from necessity, nor necessity from chance, but both concepts are necessary. In his essay on dynamical and statistical laws, Planck (1960) emphasizes this point: 'For it is clear to everybody that there must be an unfathomable gulf between a probability, however small, and an absolute impossibility ... Thus dynamics and statistics cannot be regarded as interrelated.' Weyl (1949) agrees: ' ... we cannot help recognizing the statistical concepts, besides those appertaining to strict laws, as truly original.' And similarly, von Neumann (1955) in his discussion of measurement says: 'In other words, we admit: Probability logics cannot be reduced to strict logics.' It is for this reason that our concept of a deterministic cause is completely different from our concept of a statistical cause. Determinism and chance arise from two formally complementary models of the world. We should also not waste time arguing whether the world itself is deterministic or stochastic since this is a metaphysical question that is not empirically decidable.

It is significant that both complete determinism and complete chance can be invoked as causal 'explanations' of events, showing the extreme forms and model-dependencies of our many uses of causation. These extreme forms of causation are often combined to describe what we see as emergent events that require new levels of description as in symmetry-breaking and dissipative structures in physical models (e.g., Anderson and Stein 1988), or what Crick called 'frozen accidents' in biological models.

Useful causation requires control

As I noted above, the use of causation at the level of physical laws is now considered as only a gratuitous manner of speech with no fundamental explanatory value. Naturally the question arises: At what level of organization does the concept of causation become useful? To explain my answer to this question let me first jump up several levels of complexity. Clearly it is valuable to know that malaria is not a disease produced by 'bad air' but results from Plasmodium parasites that are transmitted by Anopheles mosquitos. It is also valuable to know that the lack of vitamin C will result in scurvy. What more do we gain in these examples by saying that malaria is *caused* by a parasite and scurvy is *caused* by lack of vitamin C?

I believe the common, everyday meaning of the concept of causation is entirely pragmatic. In other words, we use the word cause for events that might be *controllable*. In the philosophical literature 'controllable' is the equivalent of the idea of *power*. Bishop Berkeley thought it obvious that cause cannot be thought of apart from the idea of power (e.g., Taylor 1972). In other words, the value of the concept of causation lies in its identification of where our power and control can be effective. For example, while it is true that bacteria and mosquitos follow the laws of physics, we do not usually say that malaria is caused by the laws of physics (the universal cause). That is because we can hope to control bacteria and mosquitos, but not the laws of physics. When we say that the lack of vitamin C is a cause of scurvy, all we mean is that vitamin C controls scurvy. A fundamental understanding or explanation of malaria or scurvy is an entirely different type of problem.

Similarly, when we seek the cause of an accident, we are looking for those particular focal events over which we might have had some control. We are not interested in all those parallel, subsidiary conditions that were also necessary for the accident to occur but that we could not control, or did not wish to control. For example, when an aircraft crashes there are innumerable subsidiary but necessary conditions for the accident to occur. When we look for 'the cause' of the accident we are not looking for these multitudes of necessary conditions, but for a focal event that, by itself, might have prevented the accident but maintained all other expected outcomes.

In our artificial technologies and in engineering practice we also think of causes in terms of control. For example, the electrical power that provides the light in my room is ultimately caused by nuclear fission in the sun that drives the water cycle and photosynthesis, or by nuclear fusion on earth. Many complex machines and complex power distribution systems are also necessary in the causal chain of events lighting my room. So why do I think that the cause of the light in my room is my turning the switch on the wall? Because that is where I have proximal, focal control, and also because switching is a simple act that is easy to model, as contrasted with the complexities of nuclear reactions and power distribution networks.

We view the causal aspects of all our machines in this way. We do not think of any very complex system or diffuse network of stochastic influences as a cause. This is one reason that downward causation is problematic. In other words, we think of causes in terms of the simplest proximal control structures in what would otherwise turn into an endless chain or network of concurrent, distributed causes. A computer is a useful modelling device because the simple, controllable steps of a program are the pragmatic cause of the computer's behavior. It is also significant that at the cultural level of jurisprudence it is *only* those causes that are focal, explicit, and believed to be controllable that are admissible in determining guilt or innocence. No jury will acquit by reason of downward causation.

The origin of control

The lack of any obvious explanatory power or utility of the concept of causation at the level of physical laws led to the question of what level of complexity causation does become useful. I support the classical philosophical view that causation is a useful concept only when associated with power and control. This leads to the next question: At what level of organization does the concept of control become useful? The concept of control does not enter physical theory because it is the fundamental condition for physical laws that they describe only those relations between events which are invariant with respect to different observers, and consequently those relations between events over which the observer has no control.

At the least, control requires, in addition to the laws, some form of local, structural constraint on the lawful dynamics. Pragmatic control also requires some measure of utility. To say the riverbed controls the flow of the river is a gratuitous use of control since there is no utility, and the simpler term 'constraint' serves just as well. Following the pragmatic requirement that concepts of causation and control must have some utility, I would say that utility makes sense only in terms of some form of fitness or function of a system that is separate from, but embedded in, an environment. Just as the concept of measurement requires an epistemic cut between the measuring device and the system being measured, so the concept of control requires an epistemic cut between the controller and the controlled.

Living organisms are the first natural level of organization where we know these concepts of functional control and fitness in an environment clearly make sense, and in fact are necessary for a useful model. Of course artifacts are also functional, but these are products of living organisms. While there must be intermediate levels of organization from which our present forms of life arose, the fact is that present life requires semiotic control by coded gene strings. There are many theories of self-organization that try to fill in these intermediate levels (e.g., Eigen & Schuster 1982; Nicholis & Prigogine 1989; Kauffman 1993; Langton 1989), but at present there exists an enormous gap between these statistical physics and artificial computer-life models and the complex, coded, semiotic control of life as we know it. It is arguable whether the concepts of causation and control are necessary or useful in these intermediate-level models. Often the use of such high-level concepts of natural language to describe simple models obscures the real problem.

Why do most of us first think of the gene as the primary causal structure of the organism even though we know that some form of downward causation from the organism level is essential to control which genes are expressed? Again, one answer is that the gene's control activities are local, sequential, and relatively easy to model, as contrasted with the organism's downward control which is diffuse, parallel, and complex. However, there is a more fundamental reason: Genetic control is *heritable* — it is stored in a relatively simple, localized, semiotic memory that is easy to transmit. The organism's downward controls are not stored in memory, but are part of the time-dependent dynamics of the phenotype. Phenotypic dynamics are not simple, localized, or heritable.

Levels of control match models of causation

The pragmatic view of causation implies that different levels of causation will be associated with different levels of control. Downward causation is a difficult concept to define precisely because it describes the collective, concurrent, distributed behavior at the system level where control is usually impractical, rather than at the parts level where focal control is possible. Downward causation is ubiquitous and occurs continuously at all levels, but it is usually ignored simply because it is not under our control. For example, even in relatively simple artificial neural nets we know that collectively the hidden nodes exert downward control on the output.

Yet while we have some control training at the level of the entire net we rarely know how to explicitly control at the level of individual hidden nodes.

In real life the problem is much worse. In the real brain we may exert some control by drugs at the coarse level of awareness and moods, or somewhat finer control by brain surgery, but the firing of individual neurons is not controllable in any useful way. The same situation occurs at all levels in, for example, ecosystems, social systems, economic systems, and even in systems that are designed to be controllable but that have grown excessively complex. Some catastrophic system failures, including cancer, aging, death, and species extinctions, that might be viewed as a form of downward causation could just as well be described as loss of detailed control.

Evolution requires semiotic control of construction

This fundamental problem of how the dynamics of life maintains, or increases, its control of complexity, while most nonliving dynamics tend to decay, was one of Boltzmann's deepest concerns, but he found no satisfactory answer. The first hint of the answer was suggested by von Neumann (1966) in his discussion of complication and his theory of self-reproducing automata. Von Neumann was also motivated by the apparent conflict between structures that decay and structures that evolve. He focused on automata models, but it is clear that he had the contrast between thermodynamics and biological evolution in mind. He saw in Turing's universal automaton an example of a simple, fixed symbol system that could generate open-ended complexity. In order to translate this open-endedness to a physical system, von Neumann first postulated a universal constructor that could *interpret* symbolic descriptions. The universal constructor, like Turing's universal machine, was relatively simple, but the descriptions could grow indefinitely and consequently the resulting constructions could grow in complexity. *The essential property of semiotic description is that it can be read in two ways: it can be read syntactically to be transmitted, and it can be read semantically to control construction.*

Today we know in great detail how cells reproduce and evolve using this fundamental description-construction strategy. Over evolutionary time-scales the cell's construction machinery (tRNA, aminoacyl synthetases, ribosomes) remains more or less constant, but the gene grows in length and the organism grows in complexity. This dependence of life on the separation of genotype and phenotype has been implicit in evolution theory since Darwin, but it is only recently that the adaptive power of genetic search in sequence space and its redundant mapping to structure has begun to be understood. This power has been discovered largely by empirical exploration of adaptive systems by computer models of maps from sequence space to structure space (e.g., Schuster, 1994), and sequence space search using genetic algorithms (e.g., Holland 1992; Goldberg 1989). The combination of crossover and mutation has been shown to be surprisingly powerful for finding solutions to certain classes of problem that are otherwise intractable. It is not yet clear why genetic algorithms work well in some cases and not in others. The building-block hypothesis and schema theorem are part of the answer.

What is clear is that successful evolution depends both on the structure of the sequence space of the gene for efficient search, and on how sequence space maps to function space by control of constructions (e.g., Conrad 1990). The working out of the details of this mapping from genetic description to physical rate dynamics is a difficult empirical problem, but the fundamental requirement for open-ended evolvability is *the interdependence of the semiotic domain of the heritable genetic memory and the dynamic domain of construction and function.*

Artificial dynamics and self-organization

It is now well known history how semiotic rule-based systems dominated artificial intelligence models until the rediscovery of the potential of concurrent, distributed network models. With the development of connectionist machines and artificial neural networks, the study of nonlinear dynamic behavior has now largely replaced the rule-based symbolic models of classical artificial intelligence. In evolution theory there has also been a shift in interest toward dynamical models of self-organization as a non-exclusive alternative to the traditional heritable genetic variation and selection theory of evolution. The current controversy is over how much of evolution and development results from genetic control and natural selection and how much from self-organizing nonlinear dynamics. At the cognitive level the corresponding controversy is over how much of our thinking is the result of sequential semiotic rules and how much is the result of distributed, coherent neural dynamics.

These questions will not be resolved by either/or answers because (1) semiotics and dynamics must be intricately related at all levels of organization, and (2) semiotic and dynamic models are complementary, both conceptually and formally. It is precisely this semiotic-dynamic interaction that is responsible for evolving levels. Conceptually dynamical models describe how events change in time. Since time is viewed as continuous and one-dimensional, non-relativistic dynamical processes are conceptually viewed as concurrent, coherent, or parallel in time, no matter how many variables or other dimensions exist. Dynamical laws are state determined; we need only know the initial conditions; there is no memory. By contrast, semiotic models are based on discrete symbols and syntactic rules that have no direct relation to the laws of physics. One-dimensional strings of symbols are manipulated without regard to time or rates of change, or energy. Memory is fundamental for the existence of semiotic systems.

There is nothing wrong with trying to get as much self-organization as possible out of dynamical models, especially in the context of the origin of life before the genetic code existed. However, once coded, semiotic, description-construction exists, it is not productive to minimize its significance as a heritable mechanism for harnessing dynamical laws. There is no competitive model for efficient open-ended evolution.

One current computational approach to the problem of how semiotic behavior might arise from dynamics is the study of cellular automata that can be interpreted as both a dynamical system and as a semiotic computational system (e.g., Mitchell, Crutchfield & Hraber 1994). A cellular automaton is interpreted dynamically as a discrete mapping of the states of cells in a metrical space into the next state by a fixed rule that is a function of the states of neighboring cells. There are many ways to interpret the cellular automaton as a computer, but they all involve the initial state of cells interpreted as symbolic input and some later configuration of cells as the computed symbolic output. The emphasis in these models is on formal equivalences, and consequently the weakness of this approach is that there is no attempt to address how descriptions control actual physical construction, and how constructions relate to function.

The complementary approach to artificial evolution is the study of sensorimotor control in situated robots by various learning networks (e.g., Brooks 1992; Maes 1992, Hasslacher & Tilden 1995). This strategy couples the dynamics of artificial networks with the functional dynamics of sensors and activators in contact with the real physical world. Although this strategy has no direct interest in semiotic control, it is possible that such experiments may give us some clues about the origin of symbolic memory. The weakness of this approach is that this dynamic form of learning is not heritable, and consequently there is no evolvable self-replication.

When is downward causation a useful concept?

I have argued that causation is a useful concept when it identifies controllable events or actions. Otherwise it is an empirically gratuitous linguistic form which is so universal that it results in nothing but endless philosophical controversy. The issue then is how useful the concept of downward causation is in the formation and evolution of complex systems. My conclusion would be that downward causation is useful insofar as it identifies the controllable observables of a system or suggests a new model of the system that is predictive. In what types of models are these condition met?

One extreme model is natural selection. It might be considered the most complex case of downward causation since it is unlimited in its potential temporal span and affects every structural level of the organism as well as social populations. Similarly, the concept of fitness is a holistic concept that is not generally decomposable into simpler components. Because of the open-ended complexity of natural selection we know very little about how to control evolution, and consequently in this case the concept of downward causation does not add much to the explanatory power of evolution theory.

At the other extreme are simple statistical physics models. The n-body problem and collective phenomena, such as phase transitions, are cases where the behavior of individual parts can be seen as resulting from the statistical behavior of the whole, but here again the concept of downward causation does not add to the model's ability to control or explain.

A better case might be made for downward causation at the level of organism development. Here, the semiotic genetic control can be viewed as upward causation, while the dynamics of organism growth controlling the expression of the genes can be viewed as downward causation. Present models of developmental control involve many variables, and there is clearly a disagreement among experts over how much control is semiotic or genetic and how much is intrinsic dynamics.

The best understood case of an essential relation of upward and downward causation is what I have called *semantic closure* (e.g., Pattee 1995). It is an extension of von Neumann's logic of description and construction for open-ended evolution. Semantic closure is both physical and logical, and it is an apparently irreducible closure, which is why the origin of life is such a difficult problem. It is exhibited by the well-known genotype-phenotype mapping of description to construction that we know empirically is the way evolution works. It requires the gene to describe the sequence of parts forming enzymes, and that description, in turn, requires the enzymes to read the description.

This is understood at the logical and functional level, but looked at in detail this is not a simple process. Both the folding dynamics of the polypeptide string and specific catalytic dynamics of the enzyme are computationally intractable at the microscopic level. The folding process is crucial. It transforms a semiotic string into a highly parallel dynamic control. In its simplest logical form, the parts represented by symbols (codons) are, in part, controlling the construction of the whole (enzymes), but the whole is, in part, controlling the identification of the parts (translation) and the construction itself (protein synthesis).

Again, one still finds controversies over whether upward semiotic or downward dynamic control is more important, and which came first at the origin of life. There are extreme positions. One extreme sees the universe as a dynamics and the other extreme sees the universe as a computer. This is not just a useless argument, it obscures the essential message. The message is that *life and the evolution of com-*

plex systems are based on the semantic closure of semiotic and dynamic controls. Semiotic controls are most often perceived as discrete, local, and rate-independent. Dynamic controls are most often perceived as continuous, distributed and rate-dependent. But because there exists a necessary mapping between these complementary models it is all too easy to focus on one side or the other of the map and miss the irreducible complementarity.

Semantic closure at the cognitive level

Many comparisons have been made between the language of the genes and natural language (e.g., Jakobson 1970; Pattee 1980). Typically in both genes and natural language the symbol vehicles are discrete, small in number, and fixed but for the most structurally arbitrary, yet they have the potential for an unlimited number of one-dimensional expressions. These expressions are held in a memory structure that has more or less random access, i.e., not significantly restricted by time, rate, energy, and position dependence. The basic elements of the language syntax are context free and unambiguous, but as the length of expressions increases, the syntax and semantics become inseparable. When taken as a whole the semantics of the text becomes context dependent and more ambiguous, with the organism exerting more downward controls. At the many pragmatic levels the entire organism and its environment exert strong stochastic influences on meaning, function and fitness.

We know the explicit steps required to map the semiotic gene strings into the dynamics of enzyme control of rates of reactions, but almost nothing is known about the details of how the brain generates or reads the semiotic strings of natural language to produce meaning or dynamic action. Consequently, while the essential complementarity and semantic closure of semiotics and dynamics are apparent in both cases, there are certainly major differences in the structure of the memory and the dynamics and how they are coupled. First, the discrete symbols of natural language appear to be surface structures in the sense that they appear only as output of dynamic speaking or writing acts. There is no evidence that symbols exist in the brain in any local, discrete form as in the case of the gene. On the other hand, if we look at the gene symbols as input constraints on the translation and at the parallel dynamic folding process as producing the output action, this is not unlike symbols acting as constraints on the input layer of a neural network and the dynamics of network relaxation as producing the output action (Pattee 1985).

Conclusion

To understand life as we know it, especially the continuous evolution of stable complex forms, it has proven essential to distinguish two complementary types of control models. One type, a semiotic model exerting upward control from a local isolated memory, and the other type, a dynamic model exerting downward control from a global network of coherent, interactive components. The semiotic model explains how control can be inherited and provides a remarkably efficient search process for discovering adaptive and emergent structures. The dynamic model suggests how the many components constructed under semiotic control can be integrated in the course of development and coordinated into emergent functions.

Neither model has much explanatory value without the other. Dynamical control models do not explain the discrete, rate-independent, orderly, heritable sequences that form the individual protein molecules, nor do semiotic control models explain how these sequences fold or self-assemble and how coordinated enzymes control the rates of specific reactions. It is true that each model alone can account for a limited level of self-organization. For example, copolymers can self-assemble more or less randomly, and by chance form autocatalytic cycles. Dynamics can also generate innumerable complex autonomous patterns. But dynamics without an open-ended heritable memory or memory without dynamic coordination have very limited emergent and survival potential. The origin of life probably required the coupling of both self-organizing processes, but in any case, present life certainly does.

References

ANDERSON, P.W., & STEIN, D.L. 1988. Broken symmetry, emergent properties, dissipative structures, life; Are they related?. In F.E. Yates (ed.), *Self-organizing Systems — The Emergence of Order.* New York: Pergamon, 445-57.

ARISTOTLE. 1924. *Metaphysics* I.3. W.D. Ross (ed.), Oxford: Oxford University Press.

BRIDGMAN, P. W. 1964. *The Nature of Physical Theory.* New York: Wiley, 58.

BROOKS, R. A. 1992. Artificial life and real robots. In F.J. Varela & P. Bourgine (eds.), *Toward a Practice of Autonomous Systems.* Cambridge, Mass: MIT Press, 3-10.

BUNGE, M. 1959. *Causality,* Cambridge: Cambridge University Press.

CONRAD, M. 1990. The geometry of evolution. *BioSystems* 24: 61-81.

COVENEY, P. & HIGHFIELD, R. 1991. *The Arrow of Time,* New York: Ballantine

DUMMETT, M. 1964. Bringing about the past, *Philosophical Review* 73: 338-59.

EIGEN, M. & SCHUSTER, P. 1982. Stages of emerging life — five principles of early organization, *J. Molecular Biology* 19, 47-61.

GOLDBERG, D.E. 1989. *Genetic Algorithms in Search, Optimization, and Machine Learning,* Reading, MA: Addison-Wesley.

HART, H.L.A. & HONORÉ, A.M. 1958. *Causation and the Law.* Oxford: Oxford University Press.

HASSLACHER, B. & TILDEN, M.W. 1995. Living machines. In L. Steels (ed.), *Robotic and Autonomous Systems: The Biology and Technology of Intelligent Autonomous Agents*. New York: Elsevier.

HAWKING, S. 1988. *A Brief History of Time*. New York: Bantam Books, 143-53.

HERTZ, H. 1894. *Die Principien Mechanik*. English translation by D. E. Jones and J. T. Walley, *The Principles of Mechanics*. New York: Dover, NY, 1956.

HOLLAND, J.H. 1992. *Adaptation in Natural and Artificial Systems*, 2nd ed. Cambridge, Mass: MIT Press.

HUME, D. *An Enquiry Concerning Human Understanding*, Section 4-7.

JAKOBSON, R. 1970. *Main Trends of Research in the Social and Human Sciences*. Paris: Mouton/UNESCO, 437-40.

KAUFFMAN, S. 1993. *Origins of Order. Oxford:* Oxford University Press.

LANGTON, C. 1989. Artificial life. In C. Langton (ed.), *Artificial Life*. Redwood City, Cal: Addison-Wesley, 1-47.

MAES, P. 1992. Learning behavior networks from experience. In F.J. Varela and P. Bourgine (eds.), *Toward a Practice of Autonomous Systems*. Cambridge, Mass: MIT Press, 48-57.

MITCHELL, M., CRUTCHFIELD, J. P., & HRABER, P. T. 1994. Evolving cellular automata to perform computations: mechanisms and impediments. *Physica D* 75, 361-91.

NICOLIS, G. & PRIGOGINE, I. 1989. Exploring Complexity. New York: Freeman.

PATTEE, H. H. 1979. Complementarity vs. reduction as explanation of biological complexity. *Am. J. Physiology,* 236(5): R241-R246.

PATTEE, H. H. 1980. Clues from molecular symbol systems. In U. Bellugi and M. Studdert-Kennedy (eds.), *Signed and Spoken Language: Biological Constraints on Linguistic Form*. Dahlem Konferenzen Report 19, Weinheim: Verlag Chemie, 261-74.

PATTEE, H.H. 1985. Universal principles of measurement and language function in evolving systems. In J. Casti and A. Karlqvist (eds.), *Language and Life: Mathematical Approaches*. Berlin: Springer-Verlag, 268-81.

PATTEE, H.H. 1995. Evolving self-reference: matter, symbols, and semantic closure. *Communication and Cognition — Artificial Intelligence* 12(1-2): 9-28.

PLANCK, M. 1960. *A Survey of Physical Theory*. New York: Dover.

SCHUSTER, P. 1994. Extended molecular evolutionary biology: Artificial life bridging the gap between chemistry and biology. *Artificial Life* 1: 39-60.

TAYLOR, R. 1972. Causation. In P. Edwards (ed.), *The Encyclopedia of Philosophy*, vols. 1 & 2. New York: Macmillan, 56-66.

TOLMAN, R. C. 1950. *The Principles of Statistical Mechanics*. Oxford: Oxford University Press.

VON NEUMANN, J. 1955. *The Mathematical Foundations of Quantum Mechanics*. Princeton, NJ: University Press.

VON NEUMANN, J. 1966. *Theory of Self-reproducing Automata*, A. Burks, ed. Urbana, IL: University of Illinois Press.

WEYL, H. 1949. *Philosophy of Mathematics and Natural Science*. Princeton, NJ: Princeton University Press.

Part III
Biology and Psychology

5

Psychosomatics and the Pineal Gland

SIMO KØPPE

Psychosomatics is one of the most obvious domains of psychology which give rise to assumptions regarding downward causation. The concept is that psychological phenomena, mechanisms, functions, etc. can evoke somatic symptoms. Many discussions of psychosomatic theories begin with a survey of the psychophysical problem as analyzed in philosophy. The classical monistic, dualistic and pluralistic variants are described and discussed. Such an overview is often seen as obligatory, and contributes little to the formulation of concrete theories.

Therefore, in this paper, my focus will be on a concrete discussion of the transition between the psychical and the somatic as discussed in theories related to psychosomatic illnesses. One of the most precise concepts of this transition is Descartes' pineal gland. The pineal gland can be seen as a material terminal for the alternation of the psychical and the somatic — the hypothetical point at which the transition takes place. The question to be analyzed in this chapter concerns the means by which, and the form in which, the pineal gland has survived in psychosomatic theories, and the way in which these theories conceptualize the question of downward causation.

1. The coining of the concept

Even if the coining of a concept is rarely the first and primary formulation of its content, or indeed the most important, it is relevant here to recapitulate the coining of the concept psychosomatic.

It was the German psychiatrist Johan C.A. Heinroth (1773-1843) who introduced the concept in a book published in 1818. In the history of psychiatry the university psychiatrist Heinroth is always put forth as the best-known representative of the *mentalists* who, in the first quarter of the nineteenth century, were in opposition to the *somaticists,* represented by the asylum psychiatrist Maximilian Jacobi (1775-1858). As these denotations apparently imply, the theory of the mentalists is interpreted as the point of view that psychical illness is determined by psychical factors and cured by different forms of psychical treatment (or moral treatment, as it was called), while the somaticists, in contrast, were of the opinion that psychical illnesses have a somatic origin and that they are to be described, explained and treated like other medical illnesses. (This viewpoint of the two theories is expressed in Beyerholm 1937, for example).

This interpretation of the differences between the mentalists and the somaticists is incorrect. The somatic theories indicate clearly that no one at this time regarded the nervous system as the unique foundation for the psyche. In particular, the somaticists' view of the source of feeling in different organs (a hypotheses that goes far back in the history of science) indicates that the nervous system does not occupy the primary role as background for a biological and medical reduction. However, in continuation of this, the pathologization of the soul is indirectly a discussion of the possibility of a scientific description of the soul. Discussions of the extent to which the soul, as such, can become ill are implicitly discussions of the material foundation of the soul. The opinions of the two schools — the mentalists and the somaticists — were really the opposite of the interpretation they were given in the history of psychiatry. According to the mentalists, the soul itself could grow ill, while the somaticists believed that if it was necessary to maintain a soul tied to the body, then it must in itself be untouchable. Mental illness was to be viewed as a pathologization of those channels which materialized the soul, but the soul itself was above the dichotomy of health and illness. These two points of view are explicitly formulated by Heinroth and Jacobi.

In at least two ways it is Heinroth's mentalist theory and not Jacobi's somaticist one that is the more progressive. It is a condition for the psychologization of psychiatry that one operates with a concept of the psyche. The condition for this is that it is possible to see the soul, not primarily as a religious concept, but as something subject to material conditions, such as the possibility of being ill. Heinroth's point of view is a condition for the next step in the development: the localization of the soul to the nervous system and thus a proper concept of the psyche. Furthermore, Heinroth's view of psychosomatic illness is quite modern. He sees psychosomatic illness as based on a holistic psyche-soma entity connected with a health-illness dichotomy. Heinroth describes himself in his book as an adherent of what we would call neutral monism, whereby the apparent differentiation between the material world and the immaterial soul is viewed as apparent: the actual existence, in an ontological meaning of the word, is a third substance which nobody is able to grasp, and of which the two 'conventional' substances are different expressions. The psychosomatic angle implies that all illnesses are psychosomatic, because the psychical and the somatic are simply two expressions of the same thing. Heinroth sketches a holistic conception, which consequently implies that every imaginable illness is both somatic and psychical, the most widely-held point of view today (compare the discussion of Lipowski below).

In the history of science, the next important step took place within the neurosciences, that is neuroanatomy — with its mapping of the nervous system and the incipient division of the brain into centers, zones and areas — and neurophysiology, with its mapping of the nervous energy and the nervous impulse and its relation to the chemistry of the cell, along with the constitution of modern neurology based on a differentiation between sensory and motor illnesses (cf. Romberg 1844). The great step forward in psychiatry took place around the mid-nineteenth century supported by these developments and supplemented by the assumption that the psyche is not totally reducible to the nervous system. This reduction was first introduced into psychiatry in the last quarter of the 19th century with the neuropsychiatry which had at that point left the irreducible psyche behind.

Psychiatry had in the 18th century isolated a group of symptoms which did not have an organic basis. Psychiatrists called them *functional illnesses* and the number of symptoms included in this category rose in the course of the 19th century. Functional illness has existed ever since, and is defined in the same manner: the absence of a neuroanatomical or neurophysiological basis. A description of functional illness is often reiterated with the same words, i.e., that it does not have any provable or demonstrable somatic foundation. This does not mean that symptoms are psychical or immaterial: they indeed have a material basis, but this basis has not yet been proven. It is just a matter of time before the material foundation is found: until then, the symptoms are defined as functional.

The symptoms in the functional illness were explained by means of another diffuse concept, *neuropathic constitution,* defined as a hereditary vulnerability in the nervous system. Concepts like this are common in 19th-century psychiatry, and, as the absence of the material basis behind functional illness is declared again and again, so is the neuropathic constitution as the cause of the functional illness. Functional illness includes both neuroses and psychosomatic illnesses.

The scientific investigation into the substantial basis for the functional illness contributed greatly to the neurologization of psychiatry. The vulnerability which explained the neuropathic constitution was conceived as a substantial vulnerability, an increased sensibility in the nervous system. The point is, that it was nervous energy which became this substance. When a person suffered from ' bad or poor nerves' the attribution was meant literally as nervous energy which was too sensitive or too irritable. Nervous energy was attributed a qualitative aspect beyond its capability of recording and the capability of recording could express itself in extraordinary ways. In the 18th century one of the most distinguished neurophysiologists — A. von Haller — had defined the fundamental capability of the nervous system as irritability. He saw it as a capability of the nervous tissue, especially the receptors. Moreover, the irritability can — it seems — switch to ' irritation', able to exaggerate its function and pathologize. There are three elements in this hypothesis which must be separated. According to this hypothesis a fundamental capability of the nervous system becomes isolated — irritability (and sensation). It is one of the most essential qualities of the nervous system. Secondly, it is maintained that this quality itself has the potential capability of an etiological factor in a process of pathologization. Thirdly, it is a capability (like sensation) which is one of the main factors in the higher psychical functions, and forms an intermediate link between the somatic and the psychical.

One of the reasons for vulnerability comprising an etiological factor was civilization. The 19th century saw Romantic criticism of civilization, most sharply formulated by Rousseau. The well-known French psychiatrist Pinel wrote:

> The tremendous rise of man's ambitions striving for honor, wealth, academic and literary distinctions, fame; a sedentary life, detrimental of the secretions and muscular strength, ... ; the numerous artificial stimulations of weakening functions, lack of sleep, overworking excessive study, intense worries, never-ending troubles, the turmoil of passions in families ...
> *Cited by Riese 1960: 121-22*

It is the civilized way of life which itself strains the nervous system and makes it irritable and vulnerable. It is the daily life which is filled with unhealthy conduct which forces the nerves to the utmost. It is like balancing on a razor's edge — the pressure can bring about a whole range of unspecific symptoms, the functional illness.

It is remarkable that the term functional illness is still used. In a book about somatization published in 1990 Bass writes:

> In recent years this phenomenon has come to be known as somatization, a term which essentially refers to the presentation of psychological disorders with somatic symptoms which are attributed by the patient to organic disease. It is a term that subsumes many psychiatric disorders, notably conversion hysteria, hypochondriasis and factitious illness, but also includes the more common somatic manifestations of anxiety and depression. These so-called 'functional illnesses' inhabit a borderland between psychiatry and medicine, and are often overlooked by both.
> *Bass 1990: xi*

The way that the term functional illness is used in this passage is significant, because it links the historical development of the psychosomatic illnesses to another concept, that of *neuroses*. Throughout most of the 19th century, functional illnesses were identical with neuroses. The development of the concept of neuroses before Freud is relatively unexplained, but it is possible to see a developmental connection between neuroses and psychosomatic illnesses by looking at the way in which the concept of neuroses developed in the last 50 years of the 19th century.

In this period the concept of neuroses was divided into two groups. It is possible to link the modern concept of psychosomatic illnesses with one of the groups. Before the neuroses could be divided, the concept of functional illness was used to dissociate neuroses from neurological illnesses with a somatic basis. In the 18th century and the beginning of the 19th century the term neurosis was identical with nervous illness — which we today call neurological illness. The concept of functional illness was used in the first place as a criterion for the separation of neuroses without an organic basis from neuroses with an organic basis (identical with neurological illness). The functional illnesses are thereafter divided into illnesses with a cause which relates to nervous energy and illnesses with a cause which primarily relates to ideas (representations), i.e., psychical elements.

NEUROSIS		
Anatomical based illnesses	Functional illness	
	Energetic - hypochondria - anxiety neurosis - neurasthenia - epilepsy	*Ideogene* - hysteria - traumatic neurosis - compulsive neurosis - phobia
	Freud's classification of neurosis	
	Actual neurosis - anxiety neurosis - neurasthenia	*Psychoneurosis* - compulsive neurosis - conversion hysteria - phobia

Table 1

As shown in Table 1 this differentiation is directly continued in Freud's constitution of the psychoanalytic classification of neurosis (cf. Andkjær Olsen and Køppe 1985). The crucial point is that the two groups of neuroses are differentiated by the presence of ideas in the etiology of the neurosis. The decisive factor in the differentiation of the two categories is the extent to which somatic energy is transformed to psychical energy and linked to psychical representations, or , alternatively, whether the somatic energy stays at a somatic level. While according to Freud the causes of neurasthenia and anxiety neurosis are in the present, and mainly linked to the management of genital sexuality, the causes of psychoneurosis are always psychical constellations of ideas, where psychical energy gives way to replacement ideas which in turn form part of the symptoms. Conversion hysteria is an intermediate type because the psychical energy in conversion hysteria is converted back to the somatic level. In the formation of the neurosis there is a symbolic choice of somatic expression: conversion takes place as a transformation backwards of the psychical energy to the somatic, but is linked with a symbolic content in the symptom. This symbolic function does not constitute part of the formation of the actual neurosis.

A major problem in relation to psychosomatic illnesses is whether the somatic energy expresses a symbolic content or not. If it does, the symptoms are to a greater degree unspecific in that they are not permanently linked to anatomically provable change in tissue, although this is possible in chronic types of conversion hysteria.

2. Psychosomatic degrees

Before exemplifying and discussing certain concrete psychosomatic theories, I would like to review briefly those symptoms included in the category of psychosomatic illnesses. It will become apparent that the types and numbers of illnesses designated psychosomatic are completely dependent on the way the concept is defined.

The most extensive definition, and probably the most widespread, is that all illnesses in whatever etiological form have a psychical element. The multifactorial way of defining etiology dominates medicine today, and the consequence is that every illness has a biological-psychological-social etiology. We could say cautiously that it is not possible to totally eliminate the likelihood of a psychical component among those factors which influence illness. The same can be said of social factors. In an article about the historical development of the concept psychosomatic, Lipowski chose this broad definition. His very thorough historical examination concludes with a sharp rejection of the point of view which he calls *psychogenetic,* i.e. that there are psychical causes to somatic symptoms:

Indeed, the entire notion of psychogenesis, one incompatible with the currently prevailing doctrine of multicausality of disease, is no longer tenable, hence the psychogenic connotation of the word ' psychosomatic' should be explicitly discarded. ... The word ' psychosomatic' should not be used to imply causality in any sense or context, but only to refer to the reciprocal relationships between psychosocial and biological factors.

Lipowski 1984: 167

The concept psychosomatic must not imply any distinct causality, only the diffuse multifactoriel. The question is whether this point of view really solves anything: it is certainly watertight, because nothing is said of the way in which the psychical and the social are defined. A reductionist could share the opinion that what we call psychical is just a temporary designation of something which in itself can be reduced to the nervous system and the body. If the meaning of the concepts 'psychical' and 'societal' is not explicitly described we are back at our starting point again.

A more narrow definition, according to which the number of illnesses is smaller, takes the premise that the psychical are irreducible to the somatic. The psychical are in one way or another relatively autonomous, and psychosomatic illnesses are those which are characterized by somatic symptoms, but where there is no somatic cause. There are two subgroups. In the first subgroup are those illnesses in which it is possible to prove actual damage to the tissue or other abnormalities which form the direct basis for the symptoms (but do not constitute the provoking factor). A classic example is the ulcer, where the symptoms emanate from damage to the tissue, but the cause of the damage is at a psychic level. The second subgroup of psychosomatic illnesses shows somatic symptoms as well, but has no provable anatomical or physiological basis. The classic example is hysterical paralysis or other so-called conversion symptoms, which for a routine procedure are identical to analogous illnesses with an organic basis. This group and the functional illnesses discussed above are identical.

The third definition is the most narrow, because it excludes the functional illnesses on the basis of an interpretation of the missing anatomical basis: because there is no basis at all — the symptoms are only psychical — the sufferings are not in any way psychosomatic.

It is then possible to differentiate between three conceptions:

(a)   The holistic definition, identical to that originally stated by Heinroth at the beginning of 19th century: every possible illness is in a certain way psychosomatic.

(b)   A second definition in which psychosomatic illness is defined by two subgroups: the functional illness with somatic symptoms and illnesses in which the somatic manifestation has become chronic, in the sense that the symptoms emanate from damaged tissue.

(c)   A third and narrow definition which includes only the anatomically based somatic manifestations with a psychological background.

In relation to the question of downward causation there appears to be no compelling reason to exclude the functional illnesses from discussion. If a person suffers from a hysterical paralysis, the symptoms of which are clinically and descriptively impossible to separate from symptoms which have an organic basis, this must be an argument for psychical causality.

3. Psychosomatic theories in the 20th century

Let us return to Descartes' pineal gland. The intriguing factor is that it points out the exact and precise transformation point between the psychical and the somatic. The question may be asked: what are the functions of the pineal gland in different psychosomatic theories? It is necessary to point out that the entity — if there is one — which can be reached from both sides must be something which has a somatic basis and simultaneously a direct connection to the psychical. It is further necessary that the connection with the psychical be of such a nature that 'psychi-

cal problems' have, in a very broad way, direct access to the point of transformation. Three 20th-century theories are discussed below.

One of the psychosomatic theories most frequently quoted and discussed is the
German psychoanalyst Franz Alexander's so-called specificity theory. From the
1940s to the 1960s the specificity theory was the most dominant within the field
(see Taylor 1987 regarding its further development, and Andkjær Olsen and
Køppe 1996). Lipowski regards Alexander as the most significant representative
of what he calls the psychogenetic point of view. The theory is in fact very old:
Hippocrates makes the point that emotions are able to influence the function of
the body and cause illness. Throughout medical history there are an infinite number of repetitions of this and, as we shall see, it is also the emotions which provide
the anchorage in Alexander's theory. The problem with the emotions, however, is
that they themselves contain the psychosomatic problem. Independent of the degree of emotional intensity — whether it arises from an ordinary everyday emotion
or a passionate affect — the emotions themselves invariably involve concomitant
bodily phenomena, like forms of excitation in muscles, feelings of cold and warmth,
buzzing, respiratory difficulties, raised pulse, increased heartbeat etc. In many theories the relation has been reversed and it is maintained that emotions are nothing
but the registration of bodily conditions. The classic James-Lange theory of emotion asserts, for instance, that fear arises as a perception of the body: fear manifests
itself when we discover that we are running like hell from something threatening.
This point of view is correct as far as it goes, in that it is very difficult to imagine an
emotion without a body, an un-bodily emotion. The whole scale of emotional in-
tensities is certainly accompanied by bodily feelings in a varying degree but the
question is whether it is possible to reduce emotions to a perception of this. One
could also maintain that emotions only exist if they are conscious perceptions. It is
very difficult to imagine an emotion which is not perceived consciously. If an
emotion is not perceived, is it then an emotion at all? Hardly. Both 'bodilyness'
and consciousness are necessary conditions for emotions. (For this reason, unconscious emotions do not exist — but unconscious precursors of conscious emotions
do).

Alexander developed his theories at the beginning of the 1930s, when he still
worked in Berlin. When he later emigrated to the USA his theories gained a
widespread acceptance. It is one of Alexander's basic suppositions that there
exists a physiological correlate to every emotion. Some of these are obvious —
weeping, laughter and blushing. They can be seen as physiological and bodily reactions to grief, amusement and shame, respectively. The connection between
emotions and their bodily manifestation is dense and incidental — when the emotion passes, so does the bodily manifestation. If emotions are involved in more
permanent emotional conflicts and in this way become chronic there will be at the
physiological level a corresponding chronic physiological concomitant. It is this

chronic condition that in the long run is able to cause anatomical damage to tissue. The difference between the ordinary emotional manifestation in weeping and the chronic emotional conflict is, according to the theory, a question of consciousness. When the emotion is felt, that is when the emotion gains a psychical manifestation in consciousness, it will also be discharged: the process by which the emotion becomes conscious *is* the discharge. In repression, the emotion will be prevented from reaching consciousness and will remain at a non-conscious level, where it can enter into a chronic emotional conflict. In classical conversion, hysteria, in which the emotional content is repressed to the unconscious and the energetic side of the emotion is manifested at the bodily level, Alexander noticed that the physio-logical concomitants frequently concern that part of the nervous system called the volitional nervous system. This involves the muscle and the senses, and exactly those physiological processes which are involved in ordinary non-pathological manifestations. The main difference between the ordinary emotional manifestation and that involved in conversion hysteria is that the underlying psychical phe-nomenon is unconscious. When the emotional basis is unconscious, the manifesta-tion will be symbolic and will not be directly readable, as it would be if the condi-tion were conscious. Alexander *rejects* this group of manifestations and symptoms as not psychosomatically relevant. The physiological feature defining those he considers relevant is that they belong to the autonomic nervous system, i.e. com-pressing all those physiological processes relevant for the life of the body.

The autonomic nervous system handles the vegetative processes and is divided into subsystems, the parasympathetic and the sympathetic nervous system which each has a general function. The general role of the two subsystems is to maintain and build up (parasympathetic functions) and to enable the organism to react ap-propriately in threatening situations (the sympathetic nervous system), enabling the organism to fight and fly. Alexander set out to prove that there are basically two types of emotional conflict, each having physiological manifestations, which belong to the parasympathetic and the sympathetic nervous systems. Through his work, Alexander isolated a number of illnesses he believed had an obvious psy-chogenetic etiology, that is, based on emotional conflicts, and which later became classics among the psychosomatic illnesses. They are often called the 'seven holy ones' and include peptic ulcer, bronchial asthma, essential hypertension, thyro-toxicosis, ulcerative colitis, rheumatoid arthritis and neurodermatitis. Alexander's theory can be summarized by means of Table 2.

Alexander's theory is called *the theory of specificity*. In his major work, pub-lished in 1950, Alexander retained the localization and description of the two spe-cific types of emotional reactions. It is possible to combat displeasure — for in-stance, in anxiety-provoking situations — in two ways, either actively, that is by trying to manage one's aggression, or passively, by withdrawing from the anxiety-provoking situation and returning to a state of more or less infantile security and dependence (Alexander 1950, p. 69).

The nervous system		
Volitional regulates relation to the outer world	*Autonomic* regulates the inner vegetative processes	
Conversion hysteria Other psychoneuroses with somatic manifestations	*Parasympathetic* conservation and building up	*Sympathetic* situations of threat, fight and flight
	peptic ulcer, ulcerative colitis, thyrotoxicosis bronchial asthma	rheumatoid arthritis, essential hypertension, neurodermatitis

Table 2

These two reactions are in themselves non-pathological. If they are blocked, if a person's aggression is not manifested or he does not reach his security base, the blocking will bring about the concomitant physiological processes in the sympathetic nervous system; alternatively the parasympathetic nervous system will in the long run be locked in a chronic condition causing tissue damage. Alexander and others have tried to bring the specificity further in a mapping of seven emotional conflicts as background for the seven illnesses, but the results are controversial and Alexander's theory is not dependent on these seven types, only on the two basic ones. It is worth observing that Alexander does not maintain that there exist only these two basic types of emotional conflict: there are many others, but the concomitant physiological phenomena do not exclusively relate to the vegetative functions.

What is the 'pineal gland' according to Alexander? Alexander's view of the pineal gland rests on two premises, one of which is rarely alluded to, even by Alexander himself. *The first assumption* concerns the relation between the emotional conflict and physiology. The general model for this is that a number of different emotional conditions automatically give rise to one of two sorts of appropriate reaction: competitive aggressiveness and infantile dependence, respectively. If these reactions *are not* blocked the emotions will give rise to an appropriate bodily reaction. If the emotions are blocked, and the appropriate physiological reactions are not usable, the organism responds with a chronic condition of excitation, resulting in tissue damage. The decisive point is that it is possible at a psychical level to block a reaction which can result in a chronic physiological condition. However, this statement only explains the passage from the psychical to the somatic by postulating that the two dimensions are unbreakably connected. The implicit assumption is that blocking specific emotional reactions will *always* cause physiological chronification, because they are two sides of the same thing. There is no explanation or description of the pineal gland in this.

The second assumption, which is crucial and the only way that Alexander's theory can elucidate the main question, is that the connection between emotions and physiology is based on the ontogenetic formation of the psychical. According to this view, there is an obvious temporal connection between the physiological maturing of the vital organs and the development of the corresponding emotional registrations, which themselves take part in the formation of the psychical. From a genetic point of view, the psychical are developed by emotional registrations of physiological processes. If we go further back, to the differentiation of the psychical, we see that it is clearly linked to the constitution of the emotional representations of the physiological processes. There is an overt connection between the maturing of the digestive system and early relations of dependence and likewise an overt connection between managing aggression and the hormonal processes involved in this. This assumption is in fact necessary to understand the difference between animals and humans and the cultural variations in psychosomatic illnesses. If there is a downward causation from the psychical to the somatic it is only because there was once an upward one, and they are each other's reflection.

In the 1960s and 1970s another theory took over the status which Alexander's psychogenetic theory had enjoyed until then, namely *the theory of stress*. Both theories were inspired by Cannon's concept of homeostasis, and the stress theory was formulated by Hans Selye as early as Alexander's theory of specificity, that is at the beginning of the 1930s. Both theories agree about the frustration or blocking of the bodily reaction to a threat, relating this to the autonomic nervous system and those hormones which are involved. The main difference is that the theories of stress are mainly non-specific, describing stress as a general physiological reaction form which causes the organism to be more vulnerable to the development of a number of illnesses. Selye formulated the so-called general adaptation syndrome (GAS) the course of which follows three phases. (1) In the first alarm phase the body prepares itself for fight or flight. The autonomic nervous system brings about a change in the secretion of adrenaline and noradrenaline from the adrenal medulla. (2) The second resistance or adaptation phase involves the hypophysis and the two hormones, cortisone and cortisol, secreted from the adrenal cortex. (3) Finally, the process concludes with the exhaustion phase when resistance and adaptability are reconstituted. Today it is assumed that the three phases can exist separately and result in different types of illness.

The immense quantity of stress research carried out in the past 30 years can be divided into three areas of investigation. The first has examined the factors that can act as stressors and the conditions, situations etc., that can function as stress-inducing. The second has examined more carefully the physiological basis for stress and the physiological concomitants. The third has investigated the specific illnesses that arise from stress related physiological processes. According to Elsass (1992, p. 126) there exists no unambiguous and coherent theory of stress which the researchers concerned can agree upon. Different theories give high priority to different aspects of the three fields of research. The investigation of stressors culminated at the end of 1960s with the so-called Social Readjustment Rating Scale, which presented different sorts of scales to show the degree of stress a given life situation can provoke. Numerous extensive studies were summarized in huge inventories, in which the stress weighting of different situations, such as the death of a spouse (100%), the raising of a bank loan (17%) etc., could be read. In time there appeared so many individual differences that the idea of a general weighting was abandoned, and today it is necessary to evaluate the life history and constitution of the individual person (see Mirdal 1990, pp. 63-91). It is assumed today that stress is a general cause of illness which manifests itself in many different ways and can be relevant to any illness. Stress theories are often used in holistic models which show all illnesses to have bio-psycho-social causes.

In this context it is important to emphasize that far from difference of opinion there is general agreement about the assumption that stress acts as an unspecific reaction in the organism, as a result of which the organism becomes vulnerable to different illnesses. Even though modern stress research differentiates between varying types of personality as vulnerable/resistant to stressors, the stress condition itself is the same, being evoked by something different in different persons.

Within psychosomatics, one of the newest theories is the theory of psychoneuroimmunology. Its point of departure is the same as that adopted by stress research. Before the explosive development of immunology in the 1970s the nervous system and the hormone system were considered the two main regulation systems in the organism, and biology and medicine had a fair description of the coordination between the two systems in neuroendocrinology. With the growing insight into the immune system it is today regarded as a third main regulation system, which has a value parallel to the two other systems. The complexity in the coordination of these three systems becomes huge with the addition of a fourth factor in psychoneuroimmunology: the psychical. While stress theories have demonstrated a connection between the psychical, the nervous system and the hormones, PNI theories have attempted to survey possible connections between the immune system, the nervous system, the hormone system and the psychical. A recent Danish thesis focusing on PNI theories has examined and discussed known empirical studies and concluded:

Although still a relatively new field of scientific endeavor, psychoneuroimmunology is slowly increasing our understanding of some of the mechanisms linking the brain with immunity and inflammatory processes. Our knowledge of these links also provides information about psychoneurophysiological mechanisms that may mediate the known effects of certain stressors and negative affective states (e.g., bereavement and depression) on immunity. Albeit limited, there is also evidence to suggest that such influences may have an negative effect on an individual's physical well being. *Zachariae 1996: 200*

PNI theories can be seen as a continuation of stress theories. They extend the number of variables by adding the immune system, and they have apparently established a connection between negative emotions, such as grief and depression, and the immune system. It is obviously interesting to note that the immune system can be placed under the same bio-psycho-social umbrella, but in reality PNI theories do not contribute decisively to the question relating psychosomatic illnesses to the elucidation of the causal relation between the psychical and the somatic.

If we look back at the functional illnesses of the 19th century, we see an astonishing resemblance between those theories and the theories of current interest. An imprecise and unspecific concept of functional illness is based in both cases on a postulated general neurophysiological function which relates the physiological to the psychical without attempting to explain how that happens. The pineal gland simply disappears or seems to be so unspecific that the arguments come close to tautology. In reality it is precisely the same concept of a vulnerable nervous system filled with a substance which is itself both somatic and psychical, and which itself can be overworked and in that way generate pathological conditions. What is the connection between emotions and their neurophysiological foundation based on? The connection is based only on the *conscious* sensation of emotions with somatic concomitants. It is in the last resort the conscious testimony of the somatic basis for emotions that provides the foundation for the dissolving of the problem according to psychosomatic theories. We have not moved on and are only able to repeat that psychosomatic illnesses are connected with a vulnerable nervous system.

4. The importance of ontogenesis and the representational pineal gland

To reach a step further we can try to transform the problem by asking another question, the question of the precise way in which the body is represented in the psychical. If psychology could offer a reasonable theory for this the solution to the psychosomatic question could be derived from it. A number of difficulties in this area are related to the assumption that emotions form the psychosomatic hinge. Emotions themselves constitute a representation of the body in the psychical, but are not the only relevant representations.

One of the most advanced models of the representation of the body in the psychical has been put forward on the basis of modern developmental psychology by Daniel Stern (Stern 1985, 1995). Stern criticizes earlier conceptions of the infant as a passive being, who, for a relatively long period, simply receives impulses from the outer world and from a psychical point of view merges with the caring subjects. According to Stern, the infant is active from the beginning of its life and has at its disposal a number of representational functions, including amodal perception, spatial-temporal vitality affects and an ability to organize relations to other subjects by generalization to interactional schemas. The psychical are built up by a number of representational or schema modalities. Stern uses the concept of emergence to emphasize the organizing activity which integrates a swarm of sensations and existing schemas into coherent experiences. According to Stern's theory the following can be stated:

(a)   From the time of birth the infant is actively related to the environment in a constant and prolonged process of construction. In this process there are constituted an indefinite number of representations. These representations enter into a complex hierarchy which in the long run is the basis for the highest and most complex organizations: the personality, identity, etc.

(b)   The constitution of the psychical can be viewed as an sliding emergent process, but the infant is equipped from the beginning with a core self, which can be understood as a center of attention and is active in the constituting process. Even if Stern's theory can be used as a description of the complex process of representation, it cannot support a genetic view of the psychosomatic relation: the core of the psychical is inborn and as such a priori.

(c)   The concepts of representation and schema in psychology are used in both a neuropsychological and psychological sense. The concepts are as ambiguous regarding the psychosomatic relation as the concept of emotions and cannot in themselves be used as the basis for a criterion. They can, however, be used as building blocks and as a common concept in the sense that the lowest level of the representational hierarchy is local and neurobiological, while the superior constructions are psychical.

(d)   It is possible to add a neurophysiological representational model, put forward by Hughlings Jackson (1835-1911), which is consistent in a certain way with Stern's. According to Hughlings Jackson the nervous system is built up by a hierarchy of centers, where each center represents a certain (both sensory and motor) physiological unit. This reflects a hierarchy of domination in which the highest centers are the most complex and the most dominant. Should a center in the hierarchy be damaged, underlying centers take over the function handled by the former center. The important point in the theory is, that the same neurophysiological unit is represented in a great number of centers. The representation of a finger has its own center, but also forms part of many other centers: the center for the hand, the center for part of the arm, the center for the whole arm. In this way a function is not localized to one particular place, but is represented in relation to other functions. This multilocalization is important for Hughlings Jackson as a neurologist because he would not otherwise be able to explain why damage to the brain need not necessarily destroy certain functions. Other centers are able to take over the functions, though often in a more primitive and less complex way.

A newer theory (than Hughlings Jackson's) which uses a parallel concept of representation (module, schema, concept) has been put forward by Gerald M. Edelmann. The relevant assumption in this connection is that the nervous system is constituted by modules of neuron circuits of varying degrees. Further, it is assumed that every element of memory enters into a great number of relations and combinations in the cortex. The primary unit in Edelmann's theory is not representation, but patterns of excitation (produced by the single module). The point is, that the patterns (which carry information) are reproduced all the time and that they relate to each other hierarchically, in such a way that the building of patterns of patterns occur.

If we interpret the theories proposed by Stern, Hughlings Jackson and Edelmann from a psychological point of view, and assume that the psychical core is not inborn (as Stern maintains) but is something which every infant constitutes individually, then it is possible to conclude that the problem is a question of complexity. The organization of the totality creating representations *is* simply the psychical and constitutes the psychical as such. It is not possible to specify exactly *where* the representational hierarchy changes into the psychical, but it may happen in connection with the integration of the componental representations of the body to a whole. The implicit assumption in this is, of course, that the psychical is not able to exist without a body, but the reverse is also true: the body is not able to exist without the psychical. The pineal gland is not a demarcated localized entity, as Descartes maintains, but neither is it reduced away, thereby avoiding a definition of the psychical. The pineal gland is not manifested in each 'psychical cell', as holism maintains, but is a non-localizable field of structured representations.

Before this view can be discussed in relation to causality is must be elaborated. One of the conceptual obstacles for the enlightenment of psychosomatics is the degree of permanence ascribed to the psychical. The pineal gland is interpreted as the mediating link between a permanent physiological soma and an equally permanent psyche, seen either as parallel universes or as sharply demarcated zones able to interact. If we insist on the non-permanent (but dynamical) hierarchy of representations we reach the conclusion that the representation of the body in the psychical is something which is produced incessantly (except during periods of sleep), a form-constructive activity which is stable but not permanent, in the sense that it is constituted once and for all.

This view of the dynamic between the somatic and the psychical is consistent with the assumption of a simultaneous and not a temporally displaced process. As we have argued in the chapter 'Levels, Emergence and Three Versions of Downward Causation', both upward and downward causality concepts are not consistent with the idea of serially connected and temporally displaced entities, between which causality relations exists. It is not appropriate to look for autonomic and localizable causal connections. Downward causation must be conceptualized as a constantly producing dynamic representational process which looks like a hierarchy from one angle (below), being neurophysiological and therefore somatic, and from another angle (above) appears psychical. The view can be sharpened if related to the two notions of causality discussed in the above-mentioned chapter and here called medium DC and weak DC respectively.

(a) Medium downward causation

In medium DC the basic assumption is that higher order entities, in this instance psychical ones, can act as constraining conditions for the potential emergent activities of entities at a lower level. It is necessary to distinguish between two different problems: the psychosomatic relation in general (which is a variant of the psychophysical problem) and the psychosomatic relation involved in the creation of psychosomatic illnesses.

The psychosomatic relation may, in general, be understood in such a way that the bodily somatic condition at a given time *invariably* has the possibility of realizing a number of emergent complexities, which are psychical. The bodily somatic condition manifests a number of initial conditions which are always greater than the ones realized at a psychic level. (This is analogous to the relation between the constituent chemical parts of a biological cell and the manifested cell: the chemical parts can be combined in a number of ways, but the concrete cell is just one of several possible ways). At a given time or moment the organism is able to realize a great number of different psychical phenomena, that is it has a great number of psychic phenomena as a potentiality. The psychical does not float free in space in its own universe, and, at a given moment, there exist at the somatic level a great number of potential psychical phenomena and a number of manifested psychical phenomena at the psychical level. The potential somatic elements can be seen as the initiating condition for the selection, emergent creation, etc. of the concrete psychical phenomena. Those psychical phenomena which will be manifested are selected by the existing psychical elements: not chosen freely, but selected in accordance with the relation between initializing and constraining conditions. The psychical elements function as constraining conditions of the initiating possibilities, they constrain the possible developments to exactly those conditions to be realized. The psychical constraining conditions are in the last resort dependent on the subject's life history — both as a biological and a psychological organism — that is, the whole individual history from birth on, and will therefore always be specific to the individual. Note that this view is in accordance with the assumption of the existence of representational centers. When the center is multilocalized and hierarchical, the concrete process of selection, which is inherent in the constraining conditions, will in itself be represented in higher centers and as such support the individuality of the life history.

In the creation of psychosomatic illnesses it is possible to use a model originally proposed in a working paper by Freud (Freud 1895). Freud's name for the model was 'the theory of translation' and the theory claims that repression is to be understood as a *lacking translation* of recollections (object-representations/*Sachvorstellungen*). The lacking translation is to be understood as a lacking naming of the existing objectrepresentations. It is a condition for verbalization of memories and recollection that they are related to a word representation, and, if they are not verbalizable, they are repressed. The only way an object representation can be verbalized, and therefore conscious, is if it is associated with a word representation. If we ignore the question of what object and word representations are, it is reasonable to view the lacking translation as a lack of representation. In particular those psychosomatic illnesses that imply a symbolic relation between etiology, conflict and symptom can be interpreted as a representation which is excluded. Certain specific representations are excluded from the hierarchy and only exist as elements at a somatic level, as potentialities, which are not selectable in the emergent development. They are not then integrated into the subject's life history.

The autonomic nervous system also has representations at the psychic level. There are no isolated bodily functions or organs which are not represented at the psychical level. We have to conclude that somatic dysfunction resulting in damaged tissue is also to be understood in this representational way. The somatic dysfunction can be triggered by missing, lacking, twisted functional representation, representation which at a certain level of complexity is psychical.

(b) Weak downward causation

In the theory of weak downward causation, higher order entities act as attractors for the dynamic processes of the lower entities. It may be possible to view what are here called representational centers as micro-local attractors, which in themselves are organized hierarchically, and the development of dysfunctions as a consequence of the relations between attractors, a development which in itself would be an attractor.

References

ALEXANDER, F. 1950. *Psychosomatic Medicine*. New York: W.W.Norton (1987).

ANDKJÆR OLSEN, O. & KØPPE, S. 1985. *Freud's Psychoanalysis*. New York: New York University Press.

ANDKJÆR OLSEN, O. & KØPPE, S. 1996. *Psykoanalysen efter Freud*. Copenhagen: Gyldendal.

BASS, C. 1990. *Somatization*. London: Blackwell.

BEYERHOLM, O. 1937. *Psykiatriens historie*. Copenhagen: Munksgaard.

EDELMANN, G. M. 1989. *The Remembered Present*. New York: Basic Books.

ELSASS, P. 1992. *Sundhedspsykologi*. Copenhagen: Gyldendal.

FREUD, S. 1895. *Aus den Anfängen der Psychoanalyse*. London 1950.

HEINROTH, J. C.A. 1818. *Lehrbuch der Störungen der Seelenlebens*. Leipzig: F.Vogel.

HUGHLINGS JACKSON, J. 1874. *Selected Writings*. New York: Basic Books, 1931.

LIPOWSKI, Z. J. 1984. What does the word psychosomatic really mean? *Psychosomatic Medicine* 46: 153-71.

MIRDAL, G. 1990. *Psykosomatik*. Copenhagen: Munksgaard.

RIESE, W. 1960. *The Legacy of Philip Pinel*. New York: Springer.

ROMBERG, M. H. 1844. *Lehrbuch der Nervenkrankheiten des Menschen* I-II. Berlin: A. Duncker.

SHORTER, E. 1992. *From Paralysis to Fatigue. A History of Psychosomatic Illness in the Modern Era*. New York: The Free Press.

STERN, D. 1995. *The Motherhood Constellation*. New York: Basic Books.

ZACHARIAE, B. 1996. *Mind and Immunity*. Copenhagen: Munksgaard.

6

Downward Causation at the Core of Living Organization

ALVARO MORENO & JON UMEREZ

Abstract

In this paper we argue that biological systems cannot be explained only in terms of physical laws, but that their organization also depends on the action of informational records which control the construction of the organism's phenotypes. This information is shaped by natural selection through a collective and historical process. By controlling the lower level of molecular interactions, information acts as a kind of explicit formal cause which restructures matter according to a given pattern. As the construction of informational patterns is an open process, essentially independent of the dynamics of their material support, information exhibits compositional capacity which, besides allowing open-ended evolution, constitutes the main difference between formal and physical causation.

1. Introduction. The idea of downward causation

'Downward causation' has experienced the common fate of any suggestive idea and has been widely used in many different contexts, both to support or to attack it, and frequently it has been given much broader meanings than the originally intended one. It would, therefore, be helpful to start with the recollection of the formulation of the principle within its own context. In a recent paper Campbell (1990) restates, with very slight rewording, the 'four principles for the relationship between organic and inorganic laws' which he first introduced in Campbell (1974). In his new presentation he explicitly combines, as he already did in the original one, a 'physicalist world-view' with the 'hypothesis of several ontologically 'real' levels of organization (and the endorsement of teleonomy):

1. All processes at the higher levels are restrained by and act in conformity to the laws of lower levels, including the levels of subatomic physics (a 'reductionist' constraint).

2. The teleonomic achievements at higher levels require for their implementation specific lower level mechanisms and processes. Explanation is not complete until these micromechanisms have been specified (a 'reductionist' constraint).

3. (The emergent principle) Biological evolution, in its meandering exploration of segments of the universe, encounters laws, operating as selective systems, which are not described by the present laws of physics and inorganic chemistry, and which will not be described by the future substitutes for the present approximations.

4. (Downward causation) Where natural selection operates through life and death at a higher level of organization, the laws of the higher level selective system determine in part the distribution of lower level events and substances. Description of an intermediate-level phenomenon is not completed by describing its possibility and implementation in lower level terms. Its presence, prevalence, or distribution (all needed for the complete explanation of biological phenomena) will often require reference to laws at a higher level of organization as well. Paraphrasing Point 1, for biology, all processes at the lower levels of a hierarchy are restrained by, and act in conformity to, the laws of the higher levels. *Campbell 1990: 4*

There are several issues which deserve attention in this arrangement.

One is that the physicalism behind the explicit combination of what are considered reductionist and emergentist principles is not at all of the 'nothing-but' kind. This is precisely what allows for an attempt of association without the risk of self-contradiction from the very beginning. This point may appear obvious and even shallow but is worth stressing because it is going to help us draw the difference between a narrow physicalism and a more general one, a generic materialism.

Another one is the exact formulation of the principle of downward causation which is specifically construed in terms of natural selection; as well as the specification of the 'effects' of this higher level cause — natural selection — as presence, prevalence, or distribution' of biological phenomena. Stressing what might appear to be merely a detail, is due to the importance of being fully aware of any kind of extrapolation we may wish to carry out with the idea of downward causation in order to be able to clearly separate those vices (or virtues) which might stem from the very idea and those which stem from the obscurities of the particular domain to which it is being extrapolated. As we will see, this is going to become a major problem for the assessment of the explanatory legitimacy of downward causation.

A final one, for the moment, is the use of a very broad concept of 'law' as can be deduced from its undifferentiated appearance in points 1, 3 and 4. This may, again, raise some reproach from the less sympathetic angles, but, in this case, our task will be mostly defensive in two consequent ways. On the one hand, showing that this terminological scarcity cannot hinder the richness behind the intuition so expressed and, on the other, providing an alternative way of putting it by distinguishing between laws and constraints (following the path indicated by Polanyi, 1969 and Pattee, 1972).

2. Who is afraid of downward causation?

Before going ahead we should mention, at least, some of the most common or representative criticisms raised against the idea of downward causation. Along with this we should try to explore (and evaluate) the assumptions (explicit and implicit) which underlie and empower most of these criticisms. It is true that there are not many explicit considerations of downward causation on those terms, but what is more frequent is finding related issues in discussions around reduction, emergence or the status of the special sciences. Therefore, we will have to address at least some of those issues, but let us begin with a couple of representative and direct criticisms.

A) Kim is perhaps the author who has addressed the issue of downward causation more consistently in his writings. In a recent paper, Kim (1992), referring to an excerpt from Sperry and connecting Campbell's downward causation to psychophysical action, comments the following:

This is an instance of what has been called 'downward causation' [here the footnote refers to Campbell (1974)]. The idea is that when certain wants and needs, aided by perceptions, propel a bird through the air, the cells and molecules making up the bird's body, too, are propelled, willy-nilly, through the air by the same wants, needs, and perceptions. If you add to this the further thesis, as Sperry [1984] would, to the effect that these psychological states and processes, though they 'emerge' out of biological and physicochemical processes, are distinct from them, you are apparently committed to the consequence that *these 'higher-level' mental events and processes cause lower-level physical laws to be violated,* that the molecules that are part of your body behave, at least sometimes, in ways different from the way they would if they weren't part of a living body animated by mental processes.   *Kim 1992: 120, italics in the original*

Besides the question of whether to consider this example (or any case related to mental or conscious events) an instance of downward causation (at least in Campbell's spirit) we would like to expose now an inferential mistake in the argumentation. Notice that there is no logical implication from the example to the consequence, but, more significantly, *not even* from the italicized consequence to its explanatory rewording. First of all there is no violation of physical laws which might be hinted by the example; as far as flying is a physical and mechanical action accessible both to living organisms and mechanical devices, regardless of the intentional or unintentional nature of the trigger. In other words, what we think is the right way to describe the propelling factor of the action, does not at all change the circumstance that the cell and molecules are also propelled 'willy-nilly' through the air by the same factor, whichever might this be, but which will never belong to the same level of the cells and molecules themselves. Second, and more importantly, the rephrasing takes for granted that if 'the molecules that are part of your body behave, at least sometimes, in ways different from the way they would if they weren't part of a living body animated by mental processes' implies the presumed violation of lower-level physical laws. This is totally unwarranted because for a molecule to behave differently within a living organism does not, by itself and without further argumentation, imply that a violation of physical laws is being committed.

What appears behind this argument is a confusion between laws and constraints as explanatory and/or causal principles. What is different in the behavior of the molecules of a living organism, with respect to a non-living system, is not their obedience to physical laws (which we take for granted), but also to biological constraints. We will come back to this question in next section.

B) In a paper on 'micro-determinism and concepts of emergence', Klee (1984) tries to show that all kinds of emergence — he distinguishes four — either are compatible with micro-determinism or are illegitimate. Campbell's downward causation is listed among the fourth conception of emergence which is characterized by the feature that the emergent property 'has direct determinative influence and effects on at least some of the properties' in the micro-structure (p. 48). In case of surviving the analysis, Klee asserts that this kind of emergence is the most threatening to micro-determinism. But, then he tries to distinguish Campbell's position from Sperry's and he states that 'Campbell's type of biological emergence can be seen to involve intersystem determinative connections' (p. 59). Klee thinks that this shifting from intrasystemic to intersystemic considerations leaves the way open to all kind of reformulations in micro-determinative terms. Let's just recall the main features of this intended translation in order to point out its biological mistakes:

As a result of this, Campbell's kind of macro-determination does not seem to me to be, after analysis, inconsistent with a thorough-going micro-determinism. The particular sort of case Campbell has in mind, the interaction of a biological population and its environment, is the interaction of two distinct systems of properties. (...) Interestingly enough, most systems affect each other by the interaction of certain of their respective micro-properties. To take Campbell's natural selection case: it is true that overall environmental properties have a determinative effect on biological populations contained within the environment. But the effect is not one involving a direct macro-determinative influence of the population by the environment. (...) Natural selection 'works' through differential rates of reproductive success for different phenotypes in the population in question. (...) Thus the property (...) is still ultimately micro-explainable, within any given individual, in terms of the micro-determination of phenotypes by genotypes.   *Klee 1984: 62*

First of all, Klee leads us from an indirect relation regarding populations, to a direct one involving first organisms and then phenotypes, without any indication of how these different levels relate to each other or even without properly acknowledging he is dealing with levels. The inferential gap between natural selection working through the selection of phenotypes to the micro-determination of phenotypes by genotypes is too wide to let it go unmentioned.

Second, the organism-environment separation is not as clear-cut as it appears here but of a much more complex interrelation (see, for instance, Lewontin, 1983) making the 'two distinct systems of properties' approach certainly inadequate.

Third, even at the organismic level there is no micro-determination from genotypes to phenotypes but, again, a much more complex relation where a many-to-many relationship is established between them. Not only the same phenotype might be 'caused' by different genotypes (a case perhaps of multiple-realizability) but also the same genotype might give rise to different phenotypes (Lewontin, 1992).

In summary, in both cases we have the presupposition of microdeterminism being both the presumed consequence of an argument and the undisputed basis of this very argumentation. And in the case of Kim, in most of his papers regarding interlevel relations (i.e., Kim 1978, 1992, and other in Kim 1993), we have several metaphysical and epistemological presuppositions, such as the causal physical closure or the causal explanatory exclusion, playing an essential role in a very frustrating axiomatic way. We shall discuss briefly these presumptions.

There are several important issues lurking beneath the uneasiness produced by the idea of downward causation. Causality, by itself, is probably one of the most difficult and endlessly discussed concepts in our understanding of the world, both scientific and philosophical. Troubles range, to mention just global ones, from radical empiricist skepticism about causal claims to contemporary discussions over indeterminism. To make matters worst, the directionality implied by 'downward causation' does not only inherit those intricate questions related with causality, but specific ones concerning the spatial structure, functional relation and temporal development of the 'furniture of the world'. These have to do with questions of reduction or emergence, monist or pluralist ontologies and one-dimensional or multi-layered views of the world.

In the next sections we will discuss in more detail two of these questions. The first one concerns the opposition between hierarchical and reductionist views of the world, and the second one is related to the different conceptions of causality.

3. Opposition between hierarchical and reductionist approaches

The root of this issue is implied by the directionality of the term 'downward' and the set of questions underlying it in relation with the assumptions regarding the structure of the world. This directionality would probably cause less trouble if we

adopted a dualistic framework in which both directions would be totally dis-
jointed. Then, we would have the old Cartesian problem of relating the two domains, but for anyone who would accord some preeminence to a higher principle
or realm, the consequent acceptance of a top-down determination would not
require any assumption further to the original dualist one.

Conversely, in the case we are dealing here, we begin with a different starting
point, a materialist one, which carries with it additional difficulties regarding the
relationship of the levels of organization, insofar as we are presuming there is a
'down' and an 'up'. That is, a materialist stance which rejects dualism needs to
give account of the upward dimension as well as of the downward one, and, more
imperiously, of the interrelation between both of them. But, moreover, this account
requires further hypotheses which need to be argued for, apart from the original
materialist presupposition. In summary, the questions of reduction or emergence,
monist or pluralist ontologies and one-dimensional or multilayered views of the
world that we mentioned above.

First of all, there is a subjacent assumption of some kind of priority of order
among levels, both in temporal terms and in degree of 'complexity', which need
not be challenged (it seems reasonable to ignore for the moment the case of a strict
holism which would assign a complete priority to the whole). But, perhaps, the
identification (as a metaphysical assumption) of that bottom level *qua* physical
with the domain of the material, which represents the domain of the 'acceptable'
and 'real', should not be kept undisputed. Campbell is, of course, aware of this
issue and, before stating the principle of downward causation, he formulates, in his
third item, the principle of emergence which is intended to give account of the
implicitly prior upward direction. Adopting a hierarchical approach for the understanding of the world implies qualifying carefully many of the allegedly self-evi-
dent claims of a materialist position. This perspective would immediately render
compatible some degree of upward determination (the emergent direction) with
some degree of higher level autonomy, and allow us to undermine somehow the
canon of the 'physical closure of the world'.

A second point should be to realize that physical laws are just able to determine
very basic and general features within the realm of the possible. But they still
leave plenty of room for equally possible instantiations which might be actualized
further due to factors ranging from mere chance to any kind of selective process,
passing through weaker types of constraining influence. Actually, physicists take
this into account all the time when they introduce constraint equations (to express, for instance, boundary conditions, besides the very initial ones) to simplify
their calculations, i.e., they explicitly *reduce the degrees of freedom* of the system
(Pattee, 1969, 1972). Therefore, depending on the system under analysis, it may
well happen that we are able to give a physical causal explanation which deter-

mines only a range of possibilities which need to be supplemented with an additional causal explanation at a different level.

The idea of constraint is therefore different from that of physical law. In physics, constraints are embedded boundary conditions which human observers selectively impose in order to simplify the description of the action of laws. In this sense, constraints are not reducible to laws. However, the question of how constraints can arise (here in the form of physicists' minds) remains unanswered. For, if we do not postulate the possibility of naturalizing the origin of constraints (i.e., the origin of natural systems endowed with autonomous constraints), we face either an infinite regress or a radical dualism. The problem of the role that constraints could eventually play in the explanation of those systems that autonomously produce themselves (which we claim is the case of all biological systems) leads us to the question of whether explanations of complex systems — and of biological systems in particular — in modern science require a basic and unique type of causal principle or, by contrast, they use and need other types of causes. Hence, the role played by internal autonomous constraints in biological systems (along with its irreductibility to physical laws) is what is going to allow us to overcome the problem of the 'causal explanatory exclusion' which, in conjunction with the physical closure, alleges to make downward causation spurious.

Consequently, a hierarchical approach would readily accept Kim's suggestion to adopt as pertinent a criterion which he designates as *Alexander's dictum*: 'to be real is to have causal powers' (derived from Alexander, 1920). This is so because we think there are good reasons to adopt an open conception of causality where causes at different levels may contribute to the effect (of certain degrees of complexity) without any of them pretending to exhaust in isolation the relation of determination. A hierarchical approach sets the ground to develop a complex causal structure where circular, relational, multifactorial, interlevel and even semantic forms of causality happen at different domains of phenomena, without precluding each other and, this is crucial, depending on the aspect of the world they are called upon to explain.

The opposite approach to the one we have just described here is tied to reductionism, which implies the rejection of downward causation. One important requirement of reductionism is that all systems are made up of separate parts. Accordingly, through isolating and understanding these parts, we could understand the whole. Thus, the reductionist research program in biology proceeds by identifying separate mechanistic models and then concatenating them into larger models. Though it may take millions of steps to describe completely a biological system, the reductionist research program claims that it is at least theoretically possible to form a complete description of the whole system with a finite number of isolated mechanistic models. In this way, we can associate some types of processes to complex aggregates of parts, and then call similar aggregates in a system

a level of organization. If we find a complex system where its internal levels of organization seem to play some causal action, reductionism will deny downward
causation, because such new levels will be explained in terms of their constituent
parts. For reductionism the global level, the 'whole', is deprived of any causal
power, which lies ultimately in the parts.

However, in a biological system some components will not be able to be parti-
tioned into disjoint sets. We do not find most of the complex biological molecules
outside living organisms, and it is easy to test how quickly proteins decay outside
the cell. When we try to understand why such components exist within cells, we
find that a complex web of chemical interactions continuously generates, maintains and replaces them. Accordingly, biological components appear integrated in
a complex organization. On the other hand, all these molecular components do not
belong to the same (unique) level, but they are organized hierarchically. Hence,
the very logic of the biological organization is at odds with the reductionist approach. We will come back to this question in sections 5 and 7.

4. Beyond a monist vision of causality

The mechanistic legacy of what is normally considered *the* Scientific Revolution
of the XVIIth century,[1] supported by a mixture of atomistic and reductionistic features, reinforced an equally mechanistic conception of causality.

This narrow but powerful conception paved the way for an undeniable scientific advancement which implied neglecting other more encompassing views, but
less able to yield applied results. This process might be described as a gradual replacement of a previous Aristotelian and, hence, plural approach by a monist one.
There was therefore an impulse to build an unified view of causality, aimed at ful-
filling the whole range of possible relations meant by the cause-effect link, following the successful model of physical causality. The question now is whether the
current state of scientific knowledge may still develop further keeping that model.

In this context we should consider a complaint that a steadily growing number
of scientists (not only philosophers) have about our scientific outlook. Namely, a
protest against what they see as the impoverishing restriction of a more encompassing and plural Aristotelian conception of causality to but one of the four ways
of answering the question 'why' studied by the Greek philosopher.

Anyway, the predominant view on causality until the present day is dominated
by a reductionist concern. Even though every author does not share the same idea
about the way to understand the nature of this physical causality, there is indeed
more agreement in considering this kind of causality as the only compatible one

---

1   See Cohen, 1985; Cohen, 1994; Shapin, 1996 for a review of different opinions regarding the nature
     (such as its uniqueness or even its existence) and characteristics of this historical episode.

with a scientific explanation of any material phenomenon, either biological, mental or social.

If we frame the question in Aristotelian terms, many authors tend to understand this physical or 'basic' causality as efficient. But it may also be stated that physical causality refers somehow to the material one, due to the fact that the root of such efficient causality lies in the laws intrinsically embodied by matter. Or even if the specificity and intrinsically active condition of matter are considered as causal principles, physical causality allows also for a kind of platonic interpretation in terms of inherent formal cause.

Notwithstanding, all these different views regarding the nature of physical causality share the basic idea of its universality and *exclusivity* as causal principle. In our opinion this is the main idea behind the expression 'causal physical closure'. Most contemporary criticisms to downward causation have deep roots (consciously or not) in this sort of assumption about causality in terms of causal explanatory exclusion. It is therefore natural to hear expressions as 'inheritance of causal powers' or 'derivation of causal potential from physical properties' (i.e., in Kim, 1993). However, it is possible to admit the principle of the universality of physical causality (which we may call 'materialist principle') and, simultaneously, reject its *exclusivity* as explanatory principle for every kind of systems. We are in fact pleading for a plural vision of causality. Fortunately, we are beginning to see defenses of more open approaches to causality as Brandon (1996), Dupre (1993) and others, some of which might be traced back to Harre & Madden (1975).

Our argument in favor of a plural vision of causality lies in the necessity to postulate the existence of another type of causal link in biological systems (and in other kind of complex systems as well). This is not in contradiction with the principle of universality of physical causation, because anyway such new type of causal link requires complex underlying levels of physical organization.

Indeed, biological systems cannot be explained unless we take into account, in addition to physical causality, internally generated constraints. Biological organisms generate and result from a certain kind of boundary conditions which selectively constrain those dynamical processes which constitute their identity. This type of causal action is 'formal'[2] in the sense that it infuses forms, i.e., it *materially restructures matter according to a form*. It acts materially, in the sense that formal causality implies the requirement of complex and specific aggregates of matter and specific and controlled flows of energy. And this restructuration of matter is not an

---

2   We should make clear that we are using formal cause in a significantly different sense from the Aristotelian one. In Aristotle, both formal and material causes are intrinsic, whereas efficient and final ones are extrinsic. In our view of formal cause being efficient and being intrinsic do not exclude each other. In a sense, formal cause is intrinsic inasmuch as it is inherently generated in the very system which becomes an autonomous complex system. Anyway, formal cause can also be extrinsic with respect to some levels or subsystems (or even systems) which allow for relatively autonomous kinds of description.

implicit process, but the consequence of a given pattern (whose domain of possible structures is autonomous from dynamical considerations) which brings forth and stabilizes possible — but improbable — complex organizations of matter (i.e. proteins, cells, pluricellular organizations, etc.).

The basic type of formal causation in biological systems is genetic information, which consists in a complementary and recursive interaction between certain records (which are the result of previous processes of organization that shape some conservative molecular components) and a set of components in the individual systems that are restructured depending on the causal activity of such records. We will explain this question in more detail in section 7.

Accordingly, formal causation is a quite different kind of causality than physical causality. Physical (or 'material') causality lies on the intrinsic activity of matter, whose processes occur in intrinsic time and energy, and do not require underlying levels of organization. On the contrary, formal causality needs underlying levels of material organization (enormous amount of systems and time) and consists in explicit re-arrangements of matter (in fact, it is an autonomous over-determination of matter in formal terms) and, at the causal level, processes occur at arbitrary times and costs of energy. Hence, the idea of formal causality advocated here differs from physical causality in its matter re-arranging and non-intrinsic character.

It is therefore important to emphasize that causal explanations of a kind beyond the mechanical efficient are as legitimate as this one, insofar as materially and scientifically sound connections are provided. In this sense there seems to be no reason to accept an a priori contradiction between emergence and causality, unless we had good reasons to prefer a narrower conception of causality which we certainly find difficult to come with when dealing with the complex objects of study on which science is focusing nowadays (not only in biology but in general in non-linear physics, not to mention psychological or sociological domains)

5. The cell organization as a web of causal relations

In order to analyze the questions addressed in sections 3 and 4, we propose to take as a case of study the problem of the relation between the level of molecular interactions in a cell and the global level of the cell as a whole. In a second step, we will try to show why this organization cannot be fully understood unless we consider it embedded in a collective and historical dimension.

The organization of the cell is a highly complex web of chemical reactions. In this organization many classes of components take part, but the extreme precision of this organization relies in the fact that practically all the biological reactions are controlled by a kind of molecules: enzymatic proteins. Hence, we will focus first of all in the case of proteins.

If we inquire after the 'agent' that produces a given protein (in Aristotelian terms, the efficient cause of this particular protein), the answer would involve several molecules. Concretely, the synthesis of any protein is a direct consequence of the action of tRNAs and peptidyltransferases protein molecules, both involved in the formation of the string of aminoacids. Therefore (in Aristotelian terms) aminoacids would be considered to be the material cause of the proteins. As Aristotle himself admitted, these different causes may act together.

But proteins are highly specific and complex. This complexity is manifest in their three-dimensional structure, which results from the folding of a specific one-dimensional string of about one hundred small molecules (aminoacids). As the proteins are constituted by 20 different aminoacids, and the average length of a protein is of about one hundred, there is an incredible high number of possible proteins (about 20^{100}). Given that in the cellular organization enzymatic functions are highly specific, one fundamental problem is to determine which are the causal mechanisms for explaining the synthesis of every specific protein in a given cell.

As it is well known, the answer to this question at the level of an individual cell is that the specific sequences of aminoacids, that constitute the proteins of this particular organism, are related ultimately to the specific sequences of the nucleotides of DNA molecules. DNA (and RNA) acts, then, as an 'in-formational' template for the synthesis of proteins, because such template contains the necessary instructions for guiding or regulating the production of proteins. Hence, we can say, in Aristotelian terms, that DNA molecules are the formal cause[3] of proteins in biological cells, because their specific sequence of nucleotides convey the 'idea' or 'form' of the latter. In fact, the causal role that DNA plays in the synthesis of proteins is, in addition, in-formative in an explicit sense because it is possible to establish explicit mappings between the sequence of the DNA and the primary structure of those proteins whose construction is driven by it. In the context of the cell, the DNA as the carrier of an explicit form causes the synthesis of the proteins, inasmuch as it selects certain specific forms of polymerization for the different aminoacids building up highly improbable sequences. However, this formal causation also implies the participation of more components. Since a code mechanism is necessary to link the sequence of nucleotides (of the DNA/RNA molecules) to the sequence of aminoacids, the translating process requires a complex number of steps in which (some of) the proteins themselves are involved (specifically, the DNA 'in-formative' causation of proteins involves also other enzymes, like tRNAaminoacil shyntethases). As Pattee (1982, 1995) has pointed out, the expression of this in-formation is only possible as an organizationally closed process of self-interpretation, which he calls 'semantic closure'. Last, but not least, all these

---

3   Except that, in this case, such *formal* cause would be extrinsic to its effect.

reactions imply many energetical exchanges, involving other components like ATP.

This is an important fact because it implies that formal causal action cannot be understood, as it seems it is in Emmeche, Køppe and Stjernfelt (this volume), independently of energy and time. Informational causal relation should therefore be considered as the transfer of a given pattern in material terms, i.e., implies the dissipation of a certain amount of energy.

To sum up, when we try to give account of a given protein, it turns out that it is caused by a large set of other molecules within the cell (DNA, other proteins, ATP ...). And the same happens with other cellular components. For instance, if we consider which are the cause of nucleic acids we will find several proteins, particularly the DNA polymerase. Even if we look at their intrinsic functionality, like the (self)replication based in its template capacity, it cannot, in practice, be performed without the participation of several specialized proteins.

Thus, we can say that all cells share the property that the functional molecules of their material make-up (DNA, proteins, fatty acids, etc.) are fabricated within internal processes of the cell itself. One could say that the functional hardware of the cell is continuously changing as new proteins are translated and other molecules synthesized. The first conclusion, then, is that those components that make up the system as a whole are at their turn, generated through the web of interactions of the whole system.

As biologists like N. Rashevsky (1954) and R. Rosen (1958, 1959) have pointed out, living organization can only be explained in relational terms, i.e. every component in a biological organism will have an explanation in which the other components of the system are involved, and conversely. In other words, the cause of a given component is the cell as a whole (i.e., the explanation of the parts of the organism are given within that organism). In general, what we see when we try to give account of the functional biological molecules is that they are caused by other functional molecules within the system. Hence, the proper answer to the former question is that the cause of a given functional component in a cell is the whole network of (recursive) reactions that constitute the cell itself.

Accordingly, we are talking about an operationally closed system where the components modify and generate each other through a network of interactions (Moreno, Umerez & Fernandez, 1994). To consider, in such a frame, the whole network as a result of a former (and lower) level made up of simpler components whose properties determine their interactions, would be partial. The reason is that many of these components can only exist as such as a consequence of the recursive maintenance of the whole network. In other words, complex components depend on the whole system. But stated this way, the origin of such systems seems trapped in a vicious circle (the so-called 'chicken-egg' problem). It is therefore necessary to find a bridge between models of chemical systems whose behavior can be explained in classical terms, and the simplest case of organizations in which a form of downward causation appears. In the next point we will examine two different models. Both have the advantage of an enormous simplicity with respect to the most primitive living cells known nowadays on this Earth. However, at the same time, as it will be argued, they constitute an important step in the origin of the simplest systems which exhibit forms of downward causation.

6. Looking for the origins

Our first example is taken from a plausible prebiotic scenario, where relatively simple organic molecules give rise to autocatalytic sets. From the chemical point of view, a process in which, starting from sets of less complex components, certain boundary conditions trigger the appearance of autocatalytic networks is completely understandable. Once these are formed, they will create the conditions for the production of new components. Such new components might lead to new forms of global organizations, and so on. Many models of prebiotic autocatalytic networks have been studied, and computer simulations show their robustness (along with other interesting properties). A well known example are Kauffman's autocatalytic sets, based on peptide-like polymers with non-specific enzymatic capacities (Kauffman, 1986; Farmer, Kauffman and Packard, 1986). This model shows that for a given set of boundary conditions, a small number of relatively simple components can generate a growing autocatalytic network, in which new molecules can be formed. The key of these capabilities lies in the fact that some 'passive' components (substrates) can become 'active' ones (i.e., convey catalytic functions). For example, certain polymers behaving as substrates, along with others acting as catalysts may produce new polymers by a bonding reaction. This way, every new component has a given probability to catalyze a new reaction and, under certain conditions, the whole network can reach a robust self maintenance capacity, or even (if a critical level of interactions is attained) can grow indefinitely. Another more abstract model of this kind of systems can be found in Fontana's work on 'Algorithmic Chemistry' (Fontana, 1992). Interestingly, the process of continuous unfolding of new components depends precisely on the upper levels of organization created by the process itself.

Although slightly different, the theory of autopoiesis of living organization could be also considered to be an interesting example of a primitive system where certain components exist as a consequence of the whole system. The autopoietic organization has been defined by Varela (1979) as

... a network of processes of production (transformation and destruction) of components that produces the components that: (1) through their interactions and transformations continuously regenerate and realize the network of processes (relations) that produced them; and

(2) constitute it (the machine) as a concrete unity in the space in which they exist by specifying the topological domain of its realization as such a network.   *Varela 1979: 13*

In this model a recursive network of component production generates the set of components forming a physical border or membrane. This border will topologically enclose the network of production of components, avoiding its diffusion. And, by constraining topologically the molecular interactions of the system's components, they realize such network. Thus, recursivity can be partly achieved because of the membrane. The autopoietic organization as a whole is thermodynamically open (it implies interchanges of energy and matter with the surrounding), but is closed from the logical point of view (operational closure).

Though neither Maturana or Varela would recognize different levels of organization in the autopoietic organization, one of us has argued elsewhere (Moreno, Fernandez and Etxeberria, 1990) that, when considering the type of causal actions of the different parts in an autopoietic system, two levels appear. First, a 'microscopic' level, constituted by the molecular components and its chemical relations, and second, another 'macroscopic' one, constituted by the whole membrane, acting as a boundary condition for the chemical network it encloses. As soon as the membrane has been created, it acts as a macroscopic constraint, harnessing the motion of the microscopic components within it, in a very simple but important way: avoiding diffusion, and hence, increasing reaction rates (and even, allowing them). In other words, the membrane should be considered as a functional structure.

Certainly, these two models do not display informational components in order to secure a robust and reliable mechanism of reproduction, needed to allow an open-ended evolution. But they are interesting because they are operationally closed component production systems. As such, certain emergent structures (resulting from non-linear processes occurring at the microscopic interactions in the system) are functionally causal, in the sense that they contribute to the reproduction of the conditions of their genesis. Therefore, the appearance of this kind of operationally closed or 'functional' systems is a necessary, but not sufficient, condition to understand the origin of biological systems.[4] The other condition, genetic information, makes it possible to talk properly about the appearance of new kinds of causal relationships: formal causation through records. Thus, what enables us to speak in terms of a double causal action — upward and downward — is precisely the conjunction of a circular causality with two different levels of organization, one of which is constituted by informational components.

---

4   Such systems devoid of informational components — which Rocha would consider 'distributed memory selected self-organizing systems' (1996: 377) — are bounded to restricted forms of evolution. Following the ideas of von Neumann and Pattee, this author holds that, without a form of localized memory for achieving reliable reproduction, open-ended evolution is not possible.

7. The historical and collective dimension of living organization

So far we have discussed the complex causal relations of the basic living organization and some (possible) models of more simple organizations which may help us understand how this organization could appear. But, as we have said, biological organization is more than mere *individual* recursive reaction networks. One of the main features of life is its capacity for evolving by natural selection. This capacity represents a crucial difference between full-fledged living organizations and other prebiotic forms of organization, like the aforementioned individual autocatalytic or autopoietic networks. This crucial difference lies in the fact that evolving organizations possess some components able to act as records which transfer to the individual cells a set of patterns, generated in a collective frame. This patterns are, in their turn, autonomously interpreted as specifications or instructions by every individual cell. Once expressed, selective pressures discard many of such embodied patterns.

The transmission of these patterns generated historically requires a kind of molecule suitable for (self)replication, storage and transmission of patterns, along with the capability to admit — and transmit — some local changes without alteration in its remaining functions. In other words, it requires a kind of polymer which, on the one hand, possesses a high template capacity and, on the other, does not make easy that sequential changes could affect this capacity. These properties make DNA the most suitable kind of biomolecule to establish a causal link between historical-collective processes and individual organizations. Even the increase in length of DNA molecules is generated through a collective process of natural selection. At its turn, the link with such long term, collective processes (which involve millions of individuals along thousands of generations) permits the open-ended increase in complexity of the individual organizations. This capacity depends on the encoding in specific non-dissipative structures like DNA/RNA molecules of the necessary specifications for the construction of functional proteins. This is the role played by DNA as a template or blueprint for the synthesis of proteins in the cell, what we have called its 'in-formative' or formal cause. In other words, the autonomy of the cellular organization cannot fully explain its own high complexity, because the functional organization of living systems is bounded to the recording of a (progressively) complex set of boundary conditions in informational components.

Now we come back to the causal explanation of nucleic acids. In section 5 we have explained DNA molecules by specifying the molecules which necessarily take part in the operations of DNA. As we said there, this process cannot be understood without the participation of the other components of the whole cellular network. But we did not answer the most important question, namely, where does (a given, specific) DNA come from? And the reason why we did not is that the answer to this question would send us to a more encompassing frame than the individual cell. In terms of the causal origins of living components, there is a fundamental difference between DNA and all the rest. DNA represents the material connection between the collective/historical dimension and the individual organization. The specific pattern that a given DNA molecule possesses (whichever its causal effects might be in the cell that expresses it) has been shaped through selective mechanisms that require a spatial and temporal collective dimension. This is why the informational role of DNA in the cellular organization is qualitatively different from the functional activity of all the other components of the cell.

In other words, a living organization requires a meta-network where the individual networks constitute a structure of synchronic (competition) and diachronic (transmission of characters via reproduction) relations. Hence, neither self-organization, nor information generated through natural selection, suffice alone to explain living organization; their mutual action is necessary. There is a 'bootstrapping' type of process between the setting-up of the individuals and the collective network where ultimately the information is generated, because the interpretation of this information occurs in each individual organism and constitutes it. This long-term collectively generated sequence of specifications is what at the level of individuals acts as in-formation, constraining the underlying dynamics of the chemical processes in every organism in a top-down way.

As information lies in non-dynamical and relatively stable material structures, whose changes are independent of rate and of energy (at the level of the individual organization), the informational domain is only contingently related to the domain of the dynamic organization where it is expressed. Then, information shows compositional capacity because the construction of informational patterns is an open process, essentially independent of the dynamics of their material support. This compositional capacity, in addition to allow open-ended evolution, constitutes the main difference between formal (informational) and physical causation. In functional terms, the causal action of information allows, on the one hand, the robustness of the processes of self maintenance in the early living systems and, on the other, the increase of their complexity. The informational components (records), shaped through a collective and historical process, materially rearrange material subsets of structures so that highly organized systems, with levels of complexity higher than previous systems, are generated.

Accordingly, this idea of formal causation is functionally similar to the one expressed by Campbell in the first section, when he defended the idea of Downward Causation as (the action of) the laws of the higher level selectively determining in part the 'presence, prevalence, or distribution' of lower level events and substances. However, this top-down action (downward causation) has at least two complementary meanings in the living organization:

(1)   at the level of each particular organism, the informational components (DNA molecules) constrain the lower level chemical reactions that constitute the cell.

(2)   considering life as a collective and historical phenomenon, the individuals are the result of this collectively generated historical information.

At its turn, the shaping of this information is only possible as a consequence of a selective process, consisting in a functional evaluation of the new forms at the level of the phenotypes. Ultimately, the selection process that shapes the information results from the viability or reproductive capacities of the phenotypes.

8. Conclusion

Biological systems cannot be explained unless we take into account that their organization generates and results from their internal boundary conditions (Polanyi, 1968, 1969; Pattee, 1972). Such boundary conditions, autonomously generated through natural selection, selectively constrain the dynamical processes of organisms, thus harnessing the physical and chemical laws. This process is usually described in biology in a language in which DNA molecules play causal roles. However, since biology can identify the material structures involved in these processes and understand every step of them, many biologists tend to consider that such description is an example of a successful explanation of living organization in physical terms.

Others, instead, more aware of the fact that explanations in informational terms do not belong to the physical language, propose simply to get ride of this vocabulary (autopoiesis school, Oyama, 1985). None of these attitudes seems to be useful for improving our scientific understanding of life.

As the daily practice of research shows, biologists do make use of (and need) functional and informational explanations (the grounds of which, in turn,, lie in the principles of natural selection). So far, we have tried to show how this special, downward kind of causation appears just when very complex (interwoven) meta-networks of recursive reaction networks arise in Nature. Not surprisingly, understanding such strange sets of self-describing molecular systems requires something more than standard physical explanations.

Acknowledgments

The authors acknowledge funding from the Research Project Number PB95-0502 from the DGICYT-MEC, and from the Research Project Number UPV 141.226-EA 114/96. Jon Umerez was supported by a postdoctoral grant from the Basque Government.

References

ALEXANDER, S. 1920. *Space, Time, and Deity*. London: Macmillan.

AYALA, F.J. & DOBZHANSKY, TH. (eds.) 1974. *Studies in the Philosophy of Biology*. Berkeley & Los Angeles: University of California Press.

BECKERMANN, A.; FLOHR, H. & KIM, J. (eds.) 1992. *Emergence or Reduction?* Berlin: De Gruyter.

BRANDON, R. N. 1996. Reductionism versus Holism versus Mechanism. In R.N. Brandon (ed.). *Concepts and Methods in Evolutionary Biology*. Cambridge: Cambridge University Press, 179-204.

CAMPBELL, D.T. 1974. 'Downward Causation' in Hierarchically Organised Biological Systems. In Ayala & Dobzhansky (eds.), 179-86.

CAMPBELL, D.T. 1990. Levels of Organization, Downward Causation, and the Selection-Theory Approach to Evolutionary Epistemology. In G. Greenberg & E. Tobach (eds.), *Theories of the Evolution of Knowing*. Hillsdale, N.J.: Lawrence Erlbaum, 1-17.

COHEN, I.B. 1985. *Revolution in Science*. Cambridge, Mass.: Harvard University Press.

COHEN, H.F. 1994. *The Scientific Revolution*. Chicago: University of Chicago Press.

DUPRE, J. 1993. *The Disorder of Things*. Cambridge, Mass.: Harvard University Press.

FARMER, J., KAUFFMAN, S. & PACKARD, N. 1986. *Autocatalytic replication of polymers*. *Physica* 22 D: 50-67.

FONTANA, W. 1992. *Algorithmic Chemistry*. In C.G. Langton, C. Taylor, D. Farmer & S. Rasmussen (eds.), *Artificial Life II*. Redwood City, Cal: Addison-Wesley.

HARRÉ, R. & MADDEN, E.H. 1975. *Causal Powers. A Theory of Natural Necessity*. Oxford: Basil Blackwell.

KAUFFMAN, S. 1986. Autocatalytic Sets of Proteins. *Journal of Theoretical Biology* 119: 1-24.

KIM, J. 1978. Supervenience and Nomological Inconmensurables. *American Philosophical Quaterly* 15(2): 149-56.

KIM, J. 1992. 'Downward causation' in Emergentism and Nonreductive Physicalism. In Beckermann, Flohr & Kim (eds.), 119-38.

KIM, J. 1993. *Supervenience and Mind. Selected Philosophical Essays*. Cambridge: Cambridge University Press.

KLEE, R.L. 1984. Micro-determinism and Concepts of Emergence. *Philosophy of Science* 51: 44-63.

LEWONTIN, R.C. 1983. The Organism as the Subject and the Object of Evolution. *Scientia* 118: 65-82.

LEWONTIN, R.C. 1992. Genotype & Phenotype. In E.F. Keller & E.A. Lloyd (eds.), *Keywords in Evolutionary Biology*. Cambridge, Mass.: Harvard University Press, 137-44.

MORENO, A., FERNANDEZ, J., & ETXEBERRIA, A. 1990. Cybernetics, Autopoiesis and Definition of Life. In R.Trappl (ed.), *Cybernetics and Systems'90*. Singapore: World Scientific.

MORENO, A., UMEREZ, J. Y FERNANDEZ, J. 1994. Definition of Life and Research Program in Artificial Life. *Ludus Vitalis* II (3): 15-33.

OYAMA, S. 1985. *The Ontogeny of Information*. Cambridge: Cambridge University Press.

PATTEE, H. 1969. Physical Conditions for Primitive Functional Hierarchies. In L.L. Whyte, A.G. Wilson & D. Wilson (eds.), *Hierarchical Structures*, New York: American Elsevier, 161-77.

PATTEE, H. 1972. Laws and Constraints, Symbols and Languages. In C.H. Waddington (ed.), *Towards a Theoretical Biology 4, Essays*. Edinburgh: Edinburgh University Press, 248-58.

PATTEE, H. 1982. Cell Psychology: An Evolutionary Approach to the Symbol-Matter Problem. *Cognition and Brain Theory* 5 (4): 325-41.

PATTEE, H. 1995. Evolving self-reference: matter, synbols and semantic closure. *Communication and Cognition—Artificial Intelligence* 12(1-2), 9-27.

POLANYI, M. 1968. Life's Irreducible Structure. *Science* 160: 1308-12.

POLANYI, M. 1969. *Knowing and Being*. Chicago: University of Chicago Press.

RASHEVSKY, N. 1954. *Topology and Life. Bulletin of Mathematical Biophysics* 16: 317-48.

ROCHA, L. 1996. Eigenbehavior and Symbols. *Systems Research* 13(3): 371-84.

ROSEN, R. 1958. A relational theory of biological systems. *Bulletin of Mathematical Biophysics* 20: 245-60.

ROSEN, R. 1959. A relational theory of biological systems II. *Bulletin of Mathematical Biophysics* 21: 109-28.

SHAPIN, S. 1996. *The Scientific Revolution*. Chicago: University of Chicago Press.

VARELA, F. 1979. *Principles of Biological Autonomy*. Dordrecht: Elsevier North-Holland.

7

Higher-level Descriptions:
Why Should we Preserve them?

CHARBEL NIÑO EL-HANI & ANTONIO MARCOS PEREIRA

Abstract

Non-reductive physicalism is committed to a description of the world where several levels of reality coexist. Such a multilayered model of the world renders necessary the preservation of higher-level descriptions. We claim that an apt formulation of non-reductive physicalism requires a combination of the notions of supervenience and emergence. We cannot give the notion of property emergence a reasonable account without examining the underlying assumptions concerning downward causation (DC). We make use of Emmeche, Køppe and Stjernfelt's three versions of DC, claiming that the medium version, understood as a kind of formal/functional causation, provides us with a sound understanding of DC. The notion of *biological meaningfulness* is here put forward as a justification for the convenience of higher-level biological descriptions, as medium DC prompts us to recognize that the relational properties of a complex system's components cannot be sufficiently described if we do not take due account of the formal/functional downward influence of the higher-level entity at stake.

The multilayered model of the world

For the last 300 years the reductionist program has been the paradigm in scientific explanation. Notwithstanding its pervasive influence, the reductionist model might lead us to situations such as the following, taken from a parable-like dialogue by Douglas Hofstadter:

Anteater: [...] imagine trying the following game: you must find a way of mapping letters onto ideas, so that the entire *Pickwick Papers* makes sense when you read it letter by letter.

Achilles: Hmm ... You mean that every time I hit a word such as 'the', I have to think of three definite concepts, one after another, with no room for variation?

Anteater: Exactly. They are the 't'-concept, the 'h'-concept, and the 'e'-concept – and every time, those concepts are as they were the preceding time.

Achilles: Well, it sounds like that would turn the experience of 'reading' *The Pickwick Papers* into an indescribably boring nightmare. It would be an exercise in meaninglessness, no matter what concept I associated with each letter.   *Hofstadter 1979: 326*

The rhetoric is somewhat exaggerated, but appropriately portrays the situation. Taken to its extremes – as, in fact, it has been taken, and the recent history of science provides us with several examples of such excesses[1] –, the reductionist program would force anyone, sooner or later, into a dead end, reflected in the exercise in meaninglessness of describing minute particulars of anything aiming at supposed worthy generalizations and the enhancement of our predictive power regarding the phenomena to be explained. As a reaction to this, several philosophers and scientists have been committed to a description of the evolution of matter that entails a non-reductive physicalism. One of the descriptions that cohere with such commitments may be named the *multilayered model of the world*, a label that intends to evoke the coexistence of several levels of reality.[2] Those philosophers and scientists hope to avoid both radical dualism, as it challenges ontological physicalism, one of the main tenets of the scientific thinking, and reductionism, since they believe that any description of the natural world should preserve the relative independence of those diverse levels of reality. While reductionist explanations are concerned with preserving the privileged status of low-level descriptions by claiming that such descriptions may limn the ultimate nature of reality, non-reductive physicalist explanations aim to preserve the diversity of vocabularies used to describe phenomena on the grounds that different descriptions fit different purposes, and are not necessarily mutually exclusive.

The evolution of matter, as described by a multilayered model of the world, gives rise to hierarchical orders of organizational complexity. Evolution can be thought of as a process that is at once continuous and discontinuous (Novikoff, 1945): on the one hand, evolutionary thinking entails that functional systems of 'higher' complexity are products of the evolution of simpler systems, and, hence, must be grounded in an underlying micro-structure; on the other hand, genuinely novel modes of organizing the relations among their components engender changes in

1   As to this issue, Midgley (1995) discusses some examples of such excesses, which she calls 'pieces of Reductive Megalomania'.
2   A theory of levels is consistent with both the idea that the levels are merely levels of description and the claim that they are levels of description as well as of ontology. Our attitude as to this issue can be stated as follows. Any time we set ourselves out to conceive some picture of the evolution of matter, we are bound to put forward a collection of sentences that can be interpreted as ontological claims. But if we believe, with Davidson, that there is no relation between non-sentences and sentences called 'making true', it will follow that such ontological claims cannot be seen as propositions about 'the way the world really is', but rather as 'convenient, but metaphorical, ways of talking about the world' (See Davidson, 1980, 1984; see also Rorty, 1991).

the behavior of the systems as they go beyond some threshold of complexity that seems to be properly understood as a discontinuity barrier between a 'lower' and a 'higher' level of organization. Consequently, the higher-level processes cannot be fully explained in the terms of the laws that govern its components in the absence of such organizational complexity (O'Connor, 1994: 92).

If the evolutionary process is, in a sense, continuous, then all the properties of a higher-level system will be supervenient on properties characterized in simpler systems. It follows from the notion of supervenience that substance dualism must be refused and ontological physicalism, accepted: there can be no complete disjunction of higher- and lower-level properties.

On the other hand, if the evolutionary process is, in a sense, discontinuous, the relation of supervenience between higher- and lower-level properties cannot be translated into reducibility. Hence, we must reject reductionist ontologies of properties and embrace non-reductive physicalism: there can be no complete conjunction of higher- and lower-level properties.

Non-reductive physicalism combines ontological physicalism with property dualism, claiming that higher-level properties constitute an autonomous domain that resists reduction to the physical domain (Kim, 1996: 212): the properties of the diverse levels of organization would be *identical in nature* (given that the evolution of matter is, in a sense, continuous) but *different in complexity* (given the discontinuity between the hierarchical levels of organization). That is, the properties of the relatively more complex levels of organization would be suitably seen as *emergent properties*, *higher level equivalents* of the properties of the relatively simpler levels (El-Hani & Pereira, in press [a]).

Once a material system attains a sufficient level of structural complexity, or, in other words, a higher level of organization arises in the evolutionary course, it acquires, as a matter of nomological but not metaphysical necessity, at least an emergent quality (O'Connor 1994: 92; Feibleman 1954). These emergent qualities are obviously supervenient on the properties of the composing elements, but if they are taken as the outcome of the coordinated assembling of these elements in a new system, they can be seen as the product of both an upward and a downward causation, and, hence, regarded as properties that are irreducible to, and unpredictable from, the lower-level material structure.

For instance, whenever a definition of life is put forward, it implies that a living system is emergent (Emmeche, in prep.).[3] Living beings are characterized by new 'rules' of dynamics that clearly set them apart from the chemical entities from which they have evolved. It is quite clear that the way living organisms evolve, reproduce, grow, learn, develop, organize knowledge, and use memory has no

---

3   Emmeche recognizes three definitions of life meeting his requirements, each related to a particular
     paradigm of theoretical biology, and, remarkably, the notion of property emergence is implicit in all of
     them.

analog among non-living systems (see Sacks, 1995: 102). This new behavior can be interpreted as the result of a change in the relational properties of the composing molecules due to the emergence of a different organizing principle in the newly evolving structure. Before the origin of living systems molecules had properties defined by the chemical systems they were part of, but as parts of a higher-order structure they are arranged into a biological form (or pattern) and acquire new properties on account of that form (El-Hani & Pereira, in press [a]). Biological systems act as constraining conditions for the relational properties of their components. They are now controlled, in the sense that they cannot enter in any kind of relation, but rather their relational properties are spatially and temporally restricted by the organization of the higher-level system. A cell, for instance, causes its components to have a much more ordered distribution and function in time and space than they would have in its absence (Emmeche, in prep.).

A middle road between radical dualism and reductionism stems from a picture of the material world combining the notions of supervenience and property emergence. In this picture, higher-level entities are *relatively independent* of lower-level entities, in the sense that they are at once grounded in and yet emergent from an underlying material structure (O'Connor, 1994: 91). While the concept of property emergence provides us with a way of reconciling ontological physicalism with non-reductive claims, the notion of supervenience seems to give us everything that a physicalist picture of the world requires, namely, the view that there are no concrete existents or substances in the world other than material particles and their aggregates. Thus, we may avoid a mistake that seems to be commonplace, that of defending 'a rather strong version of reductionism on the basis of the evidence for physicalism alone' (Trout, 1991: 390).

Supervenience and emergence

Many philosophers prefer supervenience to emergence when they engage in characterizing the dependence relation between entities or properties at different levels (Kim, 1996: 149; Emmeche, in prep.). Contrariwise, it is our contention here that supervenience physicalism alone does not suffice for a vigorous formulation of non-reductive physicalism. The idea of supervenience seems, at first, to fulfill the requirement of explaining in what sense higher-level properties are dependent on lower-level properties. Consider, for instance, the following formulation of supervenience physicalism:

(SP1) Higher-level properties supervene on physical properties in that for every higher-level property Q, if something has Q, it has a physical property P such that necessarily if anything has P it has Q.   *Adapted from Kim 1996: 223*

As Kim draws our attention to, physicalists widely share the assumption that 'higher-level properties are in some sense *dependent* on, or *determined* by, their lower-level properties' (Kim, 1996: 222). When claims like this are put forward, care has to be exercised. It is true that any non-reductive physicalist maintains that there is a dependence relation between higher- and lower-level entities and properties, since they are identical in their material nature. (SP1) must be observed, since in a physicalist picture of the world, nothing can produce a higher-level entity or property unless it produces its physical base. It follows from ontological physicalism that no complete disjunction of higher- and lower-level entities and properties can be supported. But neither a complete conjunction like that purported by reductionist ontologies of properties can be upheld. In a non-reductive physicalist stance, the interlevel relationship of properties is regarded as being that of relative dependence. If physicalists claim that higher-level properties are 'in some sense' dependent on, or determined by, lower-level properties, we have to ask to exactly what sort of dependence relation are they alluding. Kim, for instance, proceeds with his argument in the following way:

> More specifically, what higher-level properties a given entity has are totally fixed by the lower-level properties and relations characterizing its parts. Generally, then, a dependency relation characterizes both the entities and properties at adjacent levels. Higher-level entities are determined by the lower-level ones in that they are 'mereological' structures wholly decomposable into parts that belong to the lower level. It is this asymmetric and transitive part-whole relation that generates a hierarchy of level or tiers of entities.   *Kim 1996: 222*

In our reading of the multilayered model of the world, each and every quality an emergent system has is taken to be dependent on lower-level properties, but once such a higher-level system arises, it begins to manifest its causal powers, causally affecting lower-level phenomena. But these causal powers are of a rather special nature: they are to be understood not as a strict efficient causation, but as a kind of formal and functional causation, that is, as a new mode of coordinating and controlling the relational properties of the components that comes into being as a higher-level system appears in the evolutionary course.[4]

Suppose, then, that you were an eyewitness to the beginning of the evolution of matter. If you were a Laplacian calculator who had full knowledge of the laws of fundamental physics and the total distribution of matter at that point, would you possibly be able to predict all the subsequent evolution of matter (*cf.* O'Connor, 1994:92)? Can we interpret Kim's claim that higher-level properties are totally fixed by lower-level properties and relations in a sense that allows such a Laplacian prediction? If we take due account of downward causation (DC) as a kind of formal and functional causality, we may conclude that such a prediction

---

4   The four Aristotelian types of causality are here used as reinterpreted by Emmeche, Køppe & Stjernfelt, this volume.

could not be possible. No matter our complete knowledge of the laws of physics and the state of matter soon after its origin, we would not be able to anticipate and take due account of the emergence of new forms of behavior as the systems attain critical levels of structural complexity, giving rise to new modes of coordinating and controlling the relations among their parts. We would have but the slightest chance of predicting the fine structure of the configurations or patterns that would eventually arise in the evolution of matter, or, in other words, how the relational properties of the parts in increasingly complex aggregates of physical particles would come to be spatially and temporally constrained. The detailed structure of these aggregates of basic physical particles and the behavior of both the aggregates and their components would not be *a priori* predictable, since it follows not with logical but rather with nomological necessity from the subvening properties and entities. Form and function in these complex systems are contingent products of evolution, and, thus, cannot (even in principle) be predicted in advance, even though any material system, once it has evolved, is explicable in the terms of lower-level theories. As Küppers writes:

... a selective self-organisation of the microstates in sequence space seems only to be possible under the conditions of nonequilibrium processes, in the course of which an a priori indeterminable number of microstates is narrowed down to a few biologically relevant ones. The present results of the new paradigm of self-organisation show unambiguously that the process of molecular self-organisation is essentially subject to certain principles of selection and optimisation, and these can be reduced completely to the known laws of physics. However, the results also indicate an inherent limitation of the reductionistic research programme. Thus, although the existence of specific boundary conditions can be completely explained as a general phenomenon within the framework of physics, it is not possible to deduce physically their detailed structure. [...]. The fine structure of biological boundary conditions reflects the historical uniqueness of the underlying evolutionary processes [...].
Küppers 1992: 255

But the claim that higher-level properties are wholly fixed by lower-level properties and relations may be given other possible interpretations. It may allude to the idea that any macroproperties and regularities can be explained in the terms of micro-level theories. Be that as it may, it is essential to understand that this latter claim is not irreconcilable with non-reductive physicalism. The notion of supervenience implies that macroproperties and regularities must be explanatorily linked to micro-mechanisms. The multilayered model of the world entails that higher-level theories cannot be eliminated by means of a reductive maneuver, but reduction still plays an explanatory role in the model, as a tool for hooking the properties of the higher levels of organization on the underlying micro-structure. But as we require an explanatory maneuver through reduction without a concurrent ontological simplification, we have to distinguish between the ontological and explanatory roles of reduction. If we make such a distinction between, as we might call them, explanatory and ontological reduction, we will be profiting from the scientific payoff of providing explanations of the laws of the target theory in terms of the laws of a base theory, without engaging in the ontological simplification that is forbidden by a theory of levels (El-Hani & Pereira, in press [b]).

Supervenience physicalism seems, at first glance, to be a doctrine that can lay the foundations of a sound formulation of non-reductive physicalism:

Supervenience [...] opens up an interesting possibility: It may seem to provide us with a re-lationship that gives us *determination, or dependence, without reduction* [...]. For superve-nience seems, at least at first blush, consistent with irreducibility. [...]. Supervenience, therefore, looks like just what the nonreductive physicalist has ordered: It promises to be a nonreductive dependency relation that can do justice to both her physicalism and antireduc-tionism.   *Kim 1996: 223*

Nevertheless, it is an unsettled issue, as Kim recognizes, whether supervenience physicalism in the form of (SP1) is a viable form of non-reductive physicalism (Kim, 1996: 225), and since global supervenience also cannot avoid the likely reduction-ist commitments of (SP1) (For further details, see Kim, 1993: 79-91 and 161-171; 1996: 225-26), it remains an open question if supervenience physicalism in one of its various forms can provide a way of formulating a non-reductive physicalist stance (Kim, 1996: 226). It is not clear, in short, if the notion of supervenience brings the higher-level entities close enough to the physical so as to be consistent with ontological physicalism and yet manage to avoid reductionism. We may add that an argument developed by Kim himself shows how hard it is to maintain the autonomy of higher-level descriptions on the basis of the notion of supervenience alone (Kim, 1995; 1996: 230-32).[5]

Kim argues that the concept of supervenience leads to a dilemma. First, if the notion of supervenience fails, this means that we will have to invoke nonphysical causal agents when trying to explain higher-level phenomena. This would be no problem for a non-physicalist stance, since any theory aiming at a complete under-standing of physical phenomena would have, from this perspective, to invoke nonphysical causal powers. Nonetheless, this would never be acceptable to any physicalist, since it breaches one of the main tenets of physicalism, namely, the causal closure of the physical domain. For this reason, Kim claims that higher-level causation is, from a physicalist perspective, necessarily unintelligible if the super-venience of higher-level properties on physical properties fails.

But Kim goes further: he claims that even if the supervenience of higher-level properties on physical properties is held, higher-level causation is still unintelligi-ble. Briefly, his argument runs as follows (see Figure 1). Consider an event where a higher-level property Q causes another higher-level property Q*. If you apply the notion of supervenience, you conclude that both Q and Q* are supervenient on

5   Kim's dilemma is discussed in detail in El-Hani and Pereira (in press [a]).

basic physical properties P and P*. It follows, then, that higher-level causation collapses into physical causation: P causes P*, and Q supervenes on P, and Q* supervenes on P*. Kim's dilemma cannot be avoided:

(D) If the supervenience of higher-level properties on physical properties fails, higher-level causation is unintelligible; if it holds, higher-level causation is again unintelligible. Hence, higher-level causation is unintelligible.

We may claim that this dilemma indicates that supervenience physicalism alone does not warrant us to preserve higher-level entities as something valuable in our description of the material world, since it would not be of any service to postulate a domain of mere epiphenomenal properties, of entities whose causal powers cannot be understood.[6]

Further, if we conclude that higher-level causation is unintelligible even when the notion of supervenience holds, we are leaving the door open to nonphysical explanations. At last, higher-level causation is unintelligible in the event that the supervenience of higher-level properties on physical properties fails if we cling to physicalism and do not admit the refusal of the physical causal closure. Any physicalist, however, would reject such a surrender. Instead, he would pursue a way out of this dilemma. This is exactly what Kim did. He pursued an escape route through reduction to save mental causation: if mental causation collapsed into physical causation, the reduction of mental to physical processes would provide an explanation compatible with physicalism. But he also argued that mind-body reduction is hampered by qualia, the phenomenal, qualitative characters of our experiences, that as intrinsic properties cannot be reductively identified with anything else (Kim, 1995: 12; 1996: 236-37). Since he tried only this escape route through reduction, he could not help being entrapped in his dilemma.

Kim has to face yet another problem: while we have, in the philosophy of mind, eliminativists like Churchland arguing that all mental items must be banished along with the banshees (Dennett, 1991: 27), virtually nobody in the philosophy of biology, for instance, would feel comfortable with the claim that biological causation is unintelligible. Predicting such a counter-argument, Kim opens his section on reduction as a way out with the following question:

One good question to raise about the foregoing argument is this: Wouldn't the same argument show that all properties that supervene on basic physical properties are epiphenomenal, that their causal efficacy is unintelligible?   *Kim 1995: 8*

He maintains that there is no reason to worry about other supervenient properties, since

... with properties like biological and chemical properties, we are much more willing to accept a reductionist solution to the problem. That is, if the 'higher-order' properties can be

---

6   See, for instance, Alexander's remarks on epiphenomenalism (Alexander, 1920 vol. 2:8).

reduced to basic physical properties, [...] there is no <u>independent</u> problem of the causal efficacy of the reduced properties.   *Kim 1995: 9*

It is not so uncontroversial, however, that biological properties can be fully described in the terms of physical theories (El-Hani & Pereira, in press [a]). A growing
number of researchers believe that even though life is a physical phenomenon,
biological systems are so complex that we cannot in practice reduce biology to
physics. Genuine biological properties, such as self-reproduction, evolution,
metabolism, are inevitable in any list of the crucial properties of living beings
(Emmeche, in prep.). As Sober writes,

Adopting a physicalist view of the domain of biology simply means that one accepts the idea
that living things are physical objects. It is important to realize that this thesis does not say
what the relationship is between *biological explanations* and *explanations in physics*. Even if
living things are made of matter and nothing else, the fact remains that the vocabulary of
biology radically differs from that of physics.   *Sober 1993: 24*

In short, we cannot, as Kim assumes, simply eschew the problem of the collapse of
biological into physical causation by claiming that reductionism is more acceptable
in biology than in the philosophy of mind.

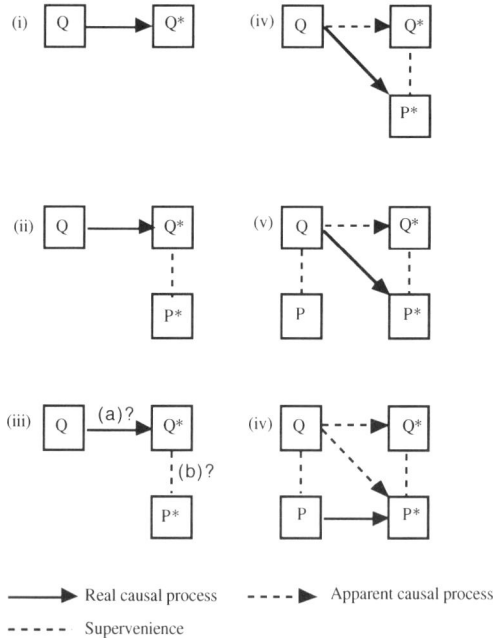

Fig. 1. The collapse of higher-level causation into physical causation. (i) A higher-level
property Q causes another higher-level property Q*; (ii) Q* is supervenient on a physical
base property P*; (iii) is Q* instantiated (a) because Q causes Q* to be instantiated, or (b)
because P* is instantiated?; (iv) an answer: Q causes Q* by causing P*; (v) Q itself is supervenient on a physical base property P; (vi) higher-level causation collapses into physical
causation: P causes P*, and Q supervenes on P, and Q* supervenes on P*.

We have claimed, in a previous paper, that Kim's dilemma can be solved if we follow an escape route through emergence (El-Hani & Pereira, in press [a]). This is a potential way out that Kim has not addressed, since he is not inclined to accept emergentist hypotheses (See, for instance, Kim, 1996). Nevertheless, as he neither admits, as a genuine physicalist, any sort of substance dualism, nor agrees with mind-body reduction, he cannot avoid the dilemma that apparently follows from the notion of supervenience. He closes his latest book, *Philosophy of Mind*, with the following assertion:

> It is not happy to end a book with a dilemma, but we should all take it as a challenge, a challenge to find an account of mentality that respects consciousness as a genuine phenomenon that gives us and other sentient beings a special place in the world and that also makes consciousness a causally efficacious factor in the workings of the natural world. The challenge, then, is to find out what kind of beings we are and what our place is in the world of nature.
>
> *Kim 1996: 237*

The crucial difference between Kim's line of argument and the escape route through emergence, as we conceive it, lies in the assumptions concerning the nature of downward causation (DC). At a certain step of his argument, Kim shows how the concept of supervenience poses a problem as to the claim that a higher-level property Q causes another higher-level property Q*. If Q* always occurs because its physical base property P* occurs, P* alone seems to be fully responsible for, and capable of explaining, Q*. We have to reconcile, then, this conclusion with the claim that Q causes Q* (Figure 1, iii). This can be done if we suppose that Q causes Q* by causing P* (Figure 1, iv). Notice, however, that DC is being depicted in Kim's argument as an effective top-down causation. Consequently, Kim's conclusion is inevitable: as Q itself has a physical base property P, higher-level causation seems to collapse into physical causation.

But suppose we understand DC in a rather different sense, not as a strict efficient causation but as a kind of formal and functional causation (Emmeche, Køppe & Stjernfelt, this volume; Emmeche, in prep.). We claim, then, that Kim's dilemma will be avoided if the notions of supervenience and property emergence are combined in an apt formulation of non-reductive physicalism:

(i)   The concept of supervenience holds. Every higher-level property Q is supervenient on a physical property P, but this relation only entails that, since Q and P are *identical in their material nature*, nothing can produce Q at *t* unless it produces P at *t*.

(ii)   The notion of property emergence also holds. Due to a *difference of complexity* between higher- and lower-level entities, or, in other words, an irreducibility of higher-order form and behavior, Q is an *emergent property* or *higher-level equivalent* of P.

Now, higher-level entities can retain their causal efficacy (Figure 2) (El-Hani &
Pereira, in press [a]). Suppose, again, that a higher-level property Q causes another
higher-level property Q*. In our example, the visual perception of a predator activates an escaping behavioral response in a prey. If you apply the notion of supervenience, you conclude that both Q and Q* are supervenient on the basic physical properties P (retinal photochemical events) and P* (muscle activity).
Nonetheless, it follows from our premises (i) and (ii) that Q and Q*, as properties of
a complex system characterized by irreducible form and behavior, are higher-level
equivalents of P and P*. In Kim's line of argument, as soon as we recognize both
supervenience relations, higher-level causation collapses into physical causation.
Here, we must inquire further: can the causal relationship between the visual perception of the predator (Q) and the escaping behavior of the prey (Q*) be sufficiently characterized in the terms of chemical and, ultimately, physical theories, as a
causal link between the retinal photochemical events (P) and the muscle activity
(P*)?

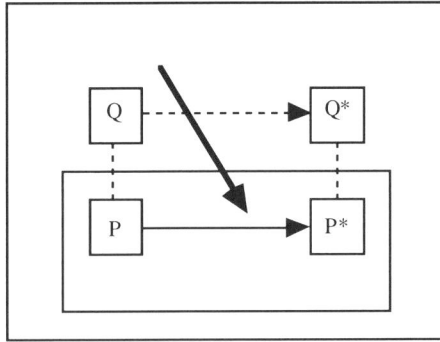

- - - - - - ▶ apparent causal relation arising out of subvenient molecular events

———————▶ causal relation between retinal photochemical events and adrenalin
synthesis in the context of a network of organic systems that ascribes
meaning to this very relation (see Fig. 3)

━━━━━━▶ coordination of sensory, cerebral and hormonal events that ascribes
meaning to the relation between retinal photochemical events and
adrenalin synthesis (biological top-down formal and functional
causation)

- - - - - - - supervenience relation

Fig. 2. The escape route through emergence. Q = visual perception of a predator by a
prey; Q* = escaping behavior elicited in the prey; P = photochemical events in the retina of
the prey; P* = adrenalin synthesis; PL = Physical/chemical level of organization; BL =
Biological level of organization.

The answer, arguably, is in the negative. If we do not take due account of biological top-down causation, understood as a kind of formal and functional causation,

we can hardly make any sense of the relation between the retinal photochemical events and the muscle activity: the relation between P and P* only makes sense if understood in the context of the coordination that acts over the relations among organic systems (see Figure 3) (El-Hani & Pereira, in press [a]).[7]

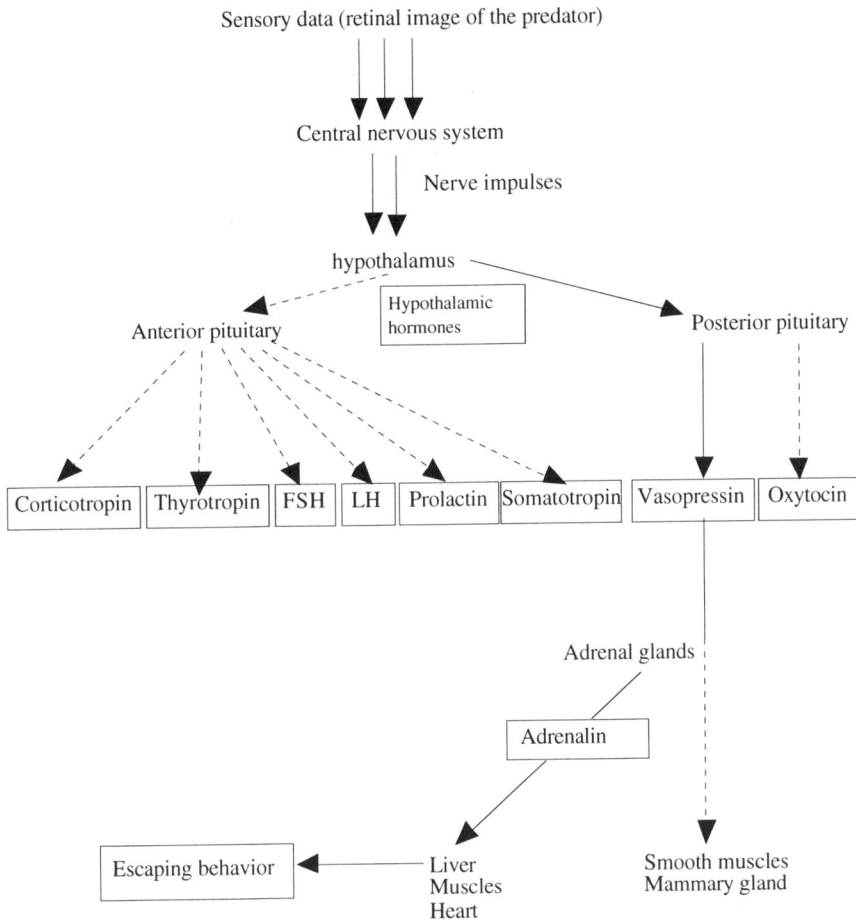

Fig. 3. Organic network coordinating sensory, cerebral and hormonal events involved in the relationship between the sensory perception of a predator and the escaping behavior of the prey (adapted from Lehninger, 1990:514).

We claim that this escape route through emergence solves Kim's dilemma: if the supervenience of biological properties on physical properties holds, biological causation is now intelligible, not as a kind of strict efficient causation, but rather as a formal and functional top-down causation. If, on the one hand, it is true that no new efficient causal powers can magically accrue to Q over and beyond the effi-

---

7   Notice that the arrow representing biological causation in figure 2 has its origin not in the higher-level property Q (as in Kim's argument, see fig. 1, iv), but in the biological level of organization itself.

cient causal powers of P, on the other hand, a non-reducible formal and functional
causal influence arguably emerges at the higher-level entity:[8]

(iii)   The retinal photochemical events (P), the physical supervenience base of the
         visual perception of the predator (Q), causes, *in the context of an organic
         network* coordinating sensory, cerebral and hormonal events, muscle activity
         (P*), and P*, in turn, instantiates its supervenient property, the escaping
         behavior observed in the prey (Q*).

Notice that the causal picture portrayed in proposition (iii) does not violate the
notion of causal/explanatory exclusion. Conversely, as it involves two distinct
causal modes, we may hold that it is entirely consistent with the claim that any
single event must have no more than a single sufficient cause, or causal explanation, or it will be causally overdetermined (Kim, 1996: 150). We are not claiming at
all that the escaping behavior (Q*) is causally determined by two different efficient causes. Rather, we only advocate that the causal powers of higher-level entities will be preserved, in the distinct sense of a formal and functional causation, if
it is recognized that the causal relation between P and P* itself cannot be properly
understood in the absence of the organizational complexity that characterizes the
network depicted in figure 3. To preserve higher-level events as causally robust
phenomena, we must change our view on causation so as to include other causal
modes in our picture of the world.

   As we claim that we need both the concepts of supervenience and property
emergence to lay the foundations of a vigorous formulation of non-reductive
physicalism, the next problem is to see how supervenience and property emergence can be interwoven in a single coherent picture. Van Cleve (1990: 220,
quoted by O'Connor, 1994: 95) suggests that the nature of the dependence of an
emergent property upon the lower-level properties of an object can be understood
if we think of emergence as a species of Kim's 'strong supervenience', which is
captured in the following:

(SS$_1$) A-properties supervene on B-properties = $_{df}$ Necessarily, for any object x and A-
property a, if x has a, then there is a B-property b such that (i) x has b, and (ii) necessarily,
if anything has b, it also has a.   *Kim 1984: 165*[9]

This definition, however, is intended to capture the supervenience of a property of
an object on some other property of that same object. We have, then, to modify
the definition to apply it to emergent properties, since they are rather characterized
in relation to the properties of the object's parts:

---

8   This stands in opposition to the following claim: 'There are no new causal powers that magically accrue
     to M [in our example, Q] over and beyond the causal powers of P. The approach to mental causation
     last pictured, therefore, is essentially reductionist: No new causal powers emerge at higher levels, and
     this goes against the claim of the emergentist and the nonreductive physicalist that higher-level proper-
     ties are novel causal powers irreducible to lower-level properties' (Kim, 1996: 232).
9   This definition is equivalent to (SP1).

(SS$_2$) A-properties of objects supervene on B-properties of their parts = $_{df}$ Necessarily, for any object x and A-property a, if x has a, then there are B-properties b, c, d ... (including relational properties) such that (i) some proper parts of x have (variously) b, c, d ... and (ii) necessarily, for any things collectively having b, c, d ... there is an object of which they are parts that has a.   *O'Connor 1994: 95-96*

The notion of supervenience entails two basic ideas concerning the relation between higher- and lower-level properties. Higher-level properties must be, first, *dependent on* lower-level properties: for each A-property there exists a B-property which is sufficient for that A-property, and, second, *determined by* lower-level properties: nothing can be just like a given thing as regards its own or its parts' B-properties without also being just like it concerning its A-properties. Nevertheless, these two features of dependence and determination apply both to qualities which can be suitably described as mere "results" of the properties of the object's parts[10] and to emergent qualities. We must distinguish between these two kinds of properties. One possibility is to claim, with Van Cleve, that we can tell emergent from resultant qualities as follows: ordinary supervenients, such as an object's shape or mass, would follow with *logical* necessity from the properties of the object's parts, while emergent properties would follow from the subvening properties only with *nomological* necessity, in the sense that they obtain under the associated base properties only in worlds with the same contingent causal structure as our own (See O'Connor, 1994: 96).

O'Connor does not regard this approach as a convenient characterization of emergence as a species of supervenience. He recognizes two basic problems in such an account of emergence. First, it counts a wide range of properties as emergents that clearly cannot be characterized as such. Second, as it requires a distinction between supervenients that follow logically or nomologically from their associated subvening properties, it implies the falsity of a stance on the relationship between an object's properties and its causal powers that takes it to be a logical necessary one. No matter if this stance is correct or not, it is not adequate to suppose that an explication of emergence could imply its falsity, and, hence, it is better to formulate this notion without relying on such a major assumption about the nature of causal necessity (For details, see O'Connor, 1994: 96).

O'Connor puts forward a different account of emergence that fits together the notions of *supervenience, non-structurality,* and *novel causal influence.* Based on these three features of property emergence, he defines it as follows (O'Connor, 1994: 98):

(PE) Property *P* is an emergent property of a (mereologically-complex) object *O*
        iff:

---

10 Alexander (1920, vol. I:11) calls them "resultant" qualities. Salt (1979), in his turn, refers to them as "collective" qualities. See O'Connor, 1994; Kim, 1996: 227; Odum 1988: 3-5.

(1)   *P* supervenes on properties of the parts of *O*;
(2)   *P* is not had by any of the object's parts;
(3)   *P* is distinct from any structural property of *O*; and
(4)   *P* has direct ('downward') determinative influence on the pattern of behavior involving *O*'s parts.

The second feature of emergence, that he calls non-structurality for lack of a better term, involves three components:

The property's being (a) potentially had only by objects of some complexity, (b) not had by any of the object's parts, (c) distinct from any structural property[11] of the object.

O'Connor 1994: 97

The third feature is the idea of novel causal influence, a term intended to capture, in O'Connor's view,

a very strong sense in which an emergent's causal influence is irreducible to that of the micro-properties on which it supervenes: it bears its influence in a direct, 'downward' fashion, in contrast to the operation of a simple structural macro-property, whose causal influence occurs *via* the activity of the micro-properties that constitute it   *O'Connor 1994: 97-98*

It is not clear what causal mode O'Connor has in mind when he characterizes DC as a direct determinative influence of *P* on the pattern of behavior of *O*'s parts, even though he claims that DC is to be understood as a sort of structural macro-determination, conceived as "a species of causation distinct from ordinary efficient causation through time" (O'Connor 1994: 103, note 18). Notice that, if DC is seen as a kind of formal/functional causation, it will be hard to see how it could be ascribed to the emergent qualities as such, while it seems proper and natural to attribute this kind of causation to the higher-level entity itself[12].

Emergentism and downward causation

Emergentism flourished during the first half of this century, as the first systematic formulation of both non-reductive physicalism and the multilayered model of the world (Kim, 1996:226). Nevertheless, this doctrine underwent a long period of oblivion and only recently has been revitalized by the sciences of complexity, that are concerned with the complex emerging properties of life and mind (Emmeche, in prep.; for historical accounts, see Beckermann, Flohr & Kim, 1992). Particularly, emergentist hypotheses have enjoyed a renewal of interest since the issue of con-

11   For details about the notion of structural property, see O'Connor (1994).
12   DC is, in O'Connor's definition, one of the criteria for the distinction between emergent and resultant qualities. Nonetheless, even if we ascribe DC to the higher-level object, it will still have bearing on the distinction between emergent and resultant qualities, not because that first kind of properties can be distinguished by their supposed causal powers, but due to the close relation between the emergence of genuinely novel properties in higher-level entities and DC.

sciousness has attracted once again the attention of philosophers and scientists, and now to talk about emergence is no longer perceived as something that stands in opposition to scientific thought or entails metaphysical dualism.

Emergentism can be thought of as consisting of the following four claims:[13]

1. [Ontological physicalism] All that exists in the space-time world are the basic particles recognized by physics and their aggregates.

2. [Property emergence] When aggregates of material particles attain an appropriate level of organizational complexity, genuinely novel properties emerge in these complex systems.

3. [The irreducibility of the emergents] Emergent properties are irreducible to, and unpredictable from, the lower-level phenomena from which they emerge.

4. [Downward causation] Higher-level entities causally affect their lower-level constituents.

In attempting to capture the sort of macro-micro relationship that appears between the several layers of organizational complexity one can perceive in the natural world, scientists and philosophers are often seduced by the intuitive appeal of the notion of property emergence. Nevertheless, the notion of property emergence is also regarded with suspicion, because (1) various formulations of this notion have been imprecise and not obviously reconcilable with one another; (2) it seems to violate the maxim that you can't get something from nothing (O'Connor, 1994: 91); (3) it entails DC, that presumably amounts to a violation of the physical causal closure (Kim, 1996: 232-33).

As to the first problem, it is quite clear that it does not require a rejection of the notion of property emergence, but rather a critical appraisal of its previous formulations. If we consider in some detail the idea that DC entails a breach of the causal closure of the physical domain, we will be able to answer the last two objections. Kim states this idea as follows:

... the nonreductive physicalist, like the emergentist, is committed to irreducible downward causation, causation of physical processes by nonphysical properties, and this of course means that the causal closure of the physical is breached. The emergentist perhaps will not be troubled by it, but the nonreductive physicalist, insofar as he is a physicalist, should be. [...] to abandon the physical causal closure is to retrogress to the Cartesian picture that does not allow, even in principle, a complete and comprehensive physical theory of the physical world. [...]. This is something that no serious physicalist will find palatable.

Kim 1996: 232-33[14]

---

13 We quote claims (1), (2) and (3) from Kim, 1996: 227-28. He also cites DC as a fundamental commitment of emergentism (see p. 229. Also Kim, 1993: 350).

14 We have argued, in a previous paper (El-Hani & Pereira, in press [a]), that Kim is not right when he claims that an emergentist would not be troubled by a breach of the causal closure of the physical and a presumable acceptance of a Cartesian picture of the world. How could any emergentist admit such a substance dualism, if she must be committed, as an emergentist, to ontological physicalism?

Emergentist hypotheses do not propose that living beings or minds bring with them nonphysical causal processes. Rather, they only stress a crucial difference between purely physical systems and highly organized aggregates of physical particles. At last, ontological physicalism does not claim that all concrete existents are the basic particles as described by physical theories, but basic physical particles *and their aggregates*. What an emergentist has in mind when she talks about DC and higher-level properties and entities is simply to highlight what happens in systems that are, indeed, identical to physical systems in nature but crucially different from them in complexity.

Kim uses in his reasoning a too narrow notion of 'physical'. It does not follow from the physical causal closure that any explanation which is not supposed to breach it must include only the basic physical particles as captured in physical theories. Instead, this principle can be broadly read as a claim against nonmaterial causation. If we maintain that DC lies in a change in the behavior of lower-level entities as they become parts of a highly complex aggregate of basic physical particles that acts as a constraining condition for their relational properties, it is clear that it cannot amount to a breach of the physical causal closure, for it has nothing to do with the causation of physical processes by nonphysical causal agents.

An emergentist conceives that all systems, no matter their complexity, are material, constituted by the very same basic physical particles, and the eye-catching difference between them lies not in any sort of substance diversity, but rather in their different levels of organizational complexity. The notion of property emergence does not violate the maxim that we cannot get something out of nothing, since emergentist hypotheses regard higher-level entities not as products of the advent of a new kind of substance, but rather of a new form of arrangement and behavior of a system's parts

Emmeche, Køppe and Stjernfelt describe three versions of DC:[15]

(1)   Strong DC: this version is related to the claim that higher- and lower-level entities are constituted by different substances, and there can be a strict efficient causality from entities or processes at a higher level to a lower one. This version of DC is invoked, for instance, by substance dualism in the philosophy of mind and vitalism in biology.

(2)   Medium DC: here, the higher-level entity, as a real substantial phenomenon in its own right, acts as constraining conditions (a kind of formal cause) for the activity of lower-level entities. In this version, DC does not amount to a direct efficient causation from an independent higher-level entity to a lower-level one, as in the strong account. Instead, the control of the part by the whole is seen as a sort of functional (teleological) causation, based for in-

---

15   See the original source in this volume for details.

stance in formal causation in a multinested system of constraints. Roger Sperry´s interactionism is an example of this kind of DC (Sperry, 1983).

(3)   Weak DC: in this version, the higher level is seen as an organizational level, characterized by the pattern or *form* into which its components are arranged. The higher-level entity consists of entities belonging to the lower level, but the forms of the higher level are believed to be irreducible.

If we take the crucial difference between medium and weak versions to lie in the claim, in the former, that the higher level constrains the development of lower-level processes according to its history, so that one set of entities at a lower level can be a starting point for different higher-level entities,[16] we may conclude that our remarks on this issue are more closely allied to a formulation of medium DC. We highlight that both the entanglement of matter and form and the role of higher-order structures as constraining and controlling conditions for the relational properties of a complex system's components must be seen as crucial features of higher-level entities.

   Anyway, our main concern here is to recognize that DC turns out to be a problem only for an ontology that allows only strict efficient causation (Emmeche, in prep.). Once we think of it not as 'effective' top-down causation, but rather as a kind of formal and functional causation, the notion of DC can be reconciled with the claim that all higher-level properties supervene on an underlying micro-structure.

   It is worth showing why this is a crucial point. Higher-level causation seems, at first, to be ruled out if the causal closure of the physical is held. Nevertheless, we can avoid such a conflict if we bring higher-level entities and properties into the physical domain. But, then, we face another problem: once higher-level entities and properties are taken to be part of the physical domain, doesn't that mean that they are nothing but physical properties and entities? How could we bring higher-level entities close enough to the physical so that the physical causal closure is not breached and yet not fully into it, admitting that complex physical systems lead a life of their own, as non-reducible aggregates of physical particles (Kim, 1996:148)? Our claim here is that such a middle road between reductionism and radical dualism should be grounded on the following two claims: first, that all kinds of entities that exist in the world are identical in their nature, and, hence, they are all into the physical (or material) domain; second, that higher- and lower-level entities show a difference of complexity, in the sense that genuinely new rules of 'dynamics' appear in higher levels of organization, that for this reason are not *fully* into the physical domain (Emmeche, in prep.).[17]

---

16   For a delightful presentation of this argument, see Hofstadter, 1979: 332-33.
17   Emmeche provides us with some apt examples: 'e.g., with the origin of human language, the linguistic rules of grammar were invented; with the origin of the first living organism, the 'rules' of the genetic

Paul Veyne offers us some thought-provoking metaphors when he engages in criticizing our usual understanding of causality. At first, causal events seem to be easily captured in some straightforward relations, such as 'fire causes the water to boil'. Fire is taken to be an agent that is obeyed by water, and water, a passive entity that makes what the fire wants it to make. Veyne claims that this ordinary view of causality emphasizes a misleading opposition between action and passivity: once we know its causes, any effect would be as predictable as the behavior of a billiard ball, as it is stated in the maxim 'same cause, same effect'.[18]

Nonetheless, we are all quite used to circumstances where the outcomes of complex processes are not so well-behaved. It is pleasing to read Veyne's provocative remarks: maybe we could talk about fire and boiling in quite different terms, recognizing only active elements. We would have to change our metaphors. Instead of talking about billiard balls following an entirely predictable path, we would talk about elastic gases with the potential to occupy all the space that is left to them. It would not be of any service, then, to put emphasis on 'the' causes to know what the gas will do. Veyne claims that we would be dealing with a polygon (or system) of small causes that would not allow us to predict its future configuration. Instead, the future configuration of the system would be revealed by its own development (Veyne, 1984: 47-48).

How should we interpret such a shift of metaphors with regards to our remarks on DC? Certainly, it can be read as a claim against the excessive emphasis put by our scientific tradition on efficient causation. It also tempts us into declaring that time is ripe now for investigating if other causal modes are not required for a proper description of the causal structure of the world. Since the gas metaphor coined by Veyne alludes to the expansion of a polygon of small causes, it is quite clear that it recognizes that the development of a complex system must be seen as an event that has, at its bottom, an effective causal process. But, on the other hand, it also sustains that the configuration, or form, of the system is unpredictable from this constitutive efficient causation. Rather, a higher-level system will have its form revealed by its own development. The top-down formal causation that will set the boundaries of the system and cause its components to have an ordered distribution and function in time and space is a contingent product of the evolution of the system, and while it is partly explicable in terms of (and for each particular system dependent on) lower-level effective causation, it must be seen as a causal phenomenon in its own right.

---

code were invented and the 'sequence space' of DNA-bases and aminoacid strings was invented on a much higher level than the 'physical state description of particles in dynamical systems theory''.

18 Levins & Lewontin (1985: 269) criticizes this same misleading opposition between active subjects and passive objects, regarding it as one of the ontological commitments of the reductionist program. A similar claim concerning an interchangeability of subject and object, of cause and effect, is found in Serpa (1991).

In higher-level systems, such as living beings and minds, formal, functional, material and efficient causation are fundamentally interdependent. Yet, while effective causal processes play a role in the underlying material structure that constitutes the system, the first two causal modes are better understood as top-down causation. Thus, while the components and low-level effective causal connections may be seen as material causes of any complex system, 'realizing' form and function within it, form and function constrain the possible effective causal connections involving the components. Formal causality supervenes on efficient causal connections that are selected by itself from a very large set of possible interactions at the lower level (see Emmeche, Køppe and Stjernfelt, this volume).

Biological meaningfulness

A higher level of complexity, e.g., living matter, differs from the preceding level, e.g., inanimate matter, due not only to the interactions among its elements, but rather to a new mode of coordinating their interactions. Compare, for instance, a mouse and a mass of mouse cells or molecules inside a test tube. Although a random collection of cells or molecules is certainly plenty of relational properties, no one in his right mind could deny the remarkable difference between that collection and the organism. We can reasonably claim that this difference lies in the event that although parts randomly gathered also display relational properties, there is no higher-level system coordinating these relations. The crucial difference lies in the coordination of the relations among the molecules, cells, or any other of its components by the biological system.

To 'make' a mouse with a collection of molecules, one would have to 'organize' the molecules in a 'form' corresponding to a mouse, that is, to restrain the possible spatial relationships among the constituting molecules so as to give the set of molecules the shape of a mouse. But this procedure would not be enough: one would also have to 'orchestrate' the 'behavior' of the molecules according to their mode of action as parts of a mouse, that is, to constrain their possible relational properties so as to establish the distinctive metabolism of a mouse. These are the peculiar features of a higher-level system: form and function. If we take due account of form and function, we will readily see how the emergence of genuinely novel qualities in higher-level systems, as a contingent product of the emergence of form and function in the evolutionary course, does not violate the maxim that one cannot get something from nothing. There we have the same basic particles, and the difference between the complex system and the lower level from which it has emerged lies in the peculiar mode of arranging the components, of constraining their relations. A higher-level entity would come into being, according to the medium version of DC, by the realization of one amongst several possible states on the lower level, with the previous states of the higher level acting as factors of selection (Emmeche, Køppe and Stjernfelt, this volume).

But then one may pose the following question: if the whole is *nothing but* an aggregate of interrelated parts, why should it be proper to maintain a higher-level description? You may be just alluding to the total set of interactions among the parts when you make use of the notion of higher-order coordination — or formal and functional DC — and, then, why should it not be enough to refer only to the relational properties of the basic physical particles and, hence, consider all higher-level properties as ultimately reducible to the predicates of the fundamental physical theories?

To go ahead with the argument, we must *make explicit* some of our commitments concerning the nature of knowledge. As long as we give up an essentialist point of view, the notion that our discursive practices may somehow be vehicles by which we grasp the 'real nature of nature', we are in a position to claim that it is better to ask how can we combine descriptions of the world in the terms of higher- and lower-level theories in a single coherent explanatory picture, than to engage in comparing and checking out the way our descriptions relate to the smallest chunks of the world. This metaphilosophical stance allows us to drop the notion that the vocabulary of physics is the most accurate vocabulary to describe any phenomena, and to drift towards the perspective that different ways of talking about the phenomena at stake are philosophically more interesting than just a unidimensional reductionist description. To suppose that the physics-oriented vocabulary of the die-hard reductionist may be able to overcome all other vocabularies is to forget that any description is not only a description *of,* but first and foremost a description *for.* So, once we deprive ourselves of reductionist dreams of finding the ultimate nature of reality, we may become more interested in exploring the consequences of the descriptions we advance for our understanding of the phenomena. Instead of deflating any claim from a special science like biology and offering it dried up as physics in disguise, we may try to develop descriptions that maintain the difference between the physical and the biological domains – a difference which is, at the very least, one of meaning.

Once we accept this metaphilosophical stance, the preceding question can be framed as follows: when we relate property emergence to a higher-order coordination, are we relying upon a sustainable, or, in other words, convenient, meaningful level of description, or can this coordination be sufficiently described in the terms of the relational properties of chemical/physical particles?

Even if we recognize that the coordinating influence that constrains the relational properties of, say, a biological system's parts to relatively stable patterns can be described in the terms of micro-level theories, this will not suffice for a commitment to reductive physicalism. Most causal links or relational properties in general, connecting cells, molecules, or other components of living systems, can hardly make any sense without the complex network that makes an organism an organism. In a previous paper, we have argued that the notion of 'biological meaningfulness' provides us with a sound basis to establish the convenience of a higher-level biological description (El-Hani & Pereira, in press [a]). This notion can be captured in the following conditional:

If P-P* is a relational property of physical/chemical particles that occurs on account of the organic network that coordinates events inside an organism B, P-P* does not make any sense and cannot be sufficiently described in the absence of a description of the organizational complexity that characterizes B.

The notion of biological meaningfulness entails the irreducibility of biological theories to chemical and physical theories, no matter if one believes or not that the biological macro-properties can be given a reasonable account in the terms of the relational properties of chemical/physical particles. In our view, we neither can dispense with the higher- nor the lower-level descriptions. Rather, multilevel descriptions will be required to capture the workings of the interlevel relationship between complex systems and their components, simultaneously hooking higher-level properties on the underlying material structure by means of reductive *explanations* and preserving higher-level entities as the coordinated networks that give meaning to the very relations among the lower-level entities involved in those explanations.

Our alternative escape route from Kim's dilemma is grounded in the notion of biological meaningfulness. We claim that the causal relationship between the visual perception of the predator (Q) and the escaping behavior of the prey (Q*) cannot be sufficiently characterized by means of a purely chemical description, as a causal link between the retinal photochemical events (P) and the muscle activity (P*), because the relation between P and P* does not make any sense outside the organic network that coordinates these events inside the organism.

One thing is to claim that any biological event must be *explained* in terms of micromechanisms. This sort of *explanatory reduction* is indeed required by any physicalist stance, since we should, as physicalists, hold that every *event* that falls under a law of a special science is, fundamentally, a physical event and, thus, also falls under a physical description.[19] Another quite different thing is to claim that any *property* mentioned in a biological law is nothing over and above a physical property and, thus, has to be exhaustively described in terms of the predicates of a physical theory. Such an *ontological reduction* overlooks the meaning of form

---

19 One can maintain that there are generalizations formulated by special sciences that refer to events whose physical descriptions have nothing in common, and, hence, there is no physical description which covers all such events. The multiple realization argument is put forward by Putnam (1975) and Fodor (1991). This shows how the identity between a higher- and a lower-level event does not entail the identity of the properties whose instantiation constitutes the events (Fodor, 1991: 431).

and function in higher-level entities and results in nothing but an exercise in meaninglessness (See Hofstadter, 1979: 311-36; Dennett, 1991).

Davidson claims that 'reduction' is a relation between linguistic items, and not among ontological categories (See Davidson, 1980, 1984).[20] He says that

> causality and identity are relations between individual events no matter how described. But laws are linguistic; and so events can instantiate laws, and hence be explained or predicted in the light of laws, only as those events are described in one or other way.
>
> *Davidson 1980: 215*

Following his line of argument, we can maintain that even if one accepts — as we do — that a biological event can and should be described in the terms of chemical/physical theories, this will not entail the conclusion that such a biological event is *nothing but* a chemical or physical event. Relational properties of physical/chemical entities cannot be substituted for biological entities in all true sentences about organisms, while preserving the truth and, consequently, the meaning of these sentences. Consider, for instance, the following sentence, framed in the distinctive vocabulary of biology:

(S₁)   The visual perception of the predator activated an escaping behavioral response in the prey.

Suppose, then, we translate it into the vocabulary of chemistry:

(S₂)   The retinal photochemical events caused a particular pattern of chemical activity in the muscles of the prey

(S₂) does not sufficiently characterize the biological event depicted in (S₁), since a sufficient description must take due account of the very organizational complexity that makes the relation between those chemical events possible. This means that if we translate a biologically meaningful sentence into a chemically/physically meaningful sentence, this will not capture all that is meaningful in a biologically meaningful sentence. The notion of biological meaningfulness entails that the concept of the organism must be preserved if we want to formulate true sentences about most relations that take place among its components, and this means, of course, that biological descriptions must be retained. This does not mean, however, that lower-level theories are not relevant to explain higher-level phenomena (Kincaid, 1988). Rather, a non-reductive physicalist stance requires micro-level accounts for the understanding of higher-order properties and entities.

O'Connor gives a comparable answer when he considers an objection to his account of property emergence (O'Connor, 1994:98): as the idea of supervenience implies that an emergent property is a consequence of certain base-level properties, its instantiation must be one of the potentialities of that subvenient set of

---

20   See also Rorty's interpretation of these Davidsonian thesis (Rorty, 1991).

properties. Hence, one can claim that there is no need to postulate an emergent property at all, since it provides no explanatory gain over an account that takes the further potentialities entailed by the notion of emergence as directly tied to the base properties. He pursues the following line of argument to answer this objection. Suppose that physicists have failed to provide an adequate understanding of systems of a rather high level of complexity (*n*) using a set of laws that accurately describes the processes of matter in all systems whose levels of complexity are lower than *n*. The presence of an emergent quality would be a reasonable assumption in this scenario. Nevertheless, it is clearly possible for the physicists to rework their formulation of the fundamental laws in order to provide an acceptable description of the phenomena related to that high-level system, owing to the necessary connection between the base properties and any emergent quality. But this does not provide us with a good reason to reject the presence of emergent properties, since the physicists' revised laws would themselves have a very odd complexity, involving tacked-on disjuncts covering the special cases. It seems that a higher-level description would still be required to make sense of those objects exhibiting that strange behavior and, thus, we would be in a position to maintain the diverse levels of complexity depicted in the multilayered model of the world.

Answering the question which is the title for this paper, we advance that we should preserve higher-level descriptions because where the reductionist explanations have become obstacles, blocking the way for new possibilities of approaching and understanding certain classes of phenomena, higher-level descriptions may work as the nourishment we need in order to keep up the good fight of trying not to sacrifice our search for a meaningful exploration of the world on the altar of low-level descriptions. After all, there is more to life than physics, just as there is more than reduction in the quest for thoughtful scientific understanding.

Acknowledgments

We are indebted to Claus Emmeche, Kelly Smith and Alvaro Moreno for their comments and helpful suggestions. We are also grateful to Jaegwon Kim for kindly sending to us several of his papers. Research partially supported by grants from PICDT-CAPES (C.N.E.) and PIBIC-UFBA/CNPq (A.M.P.)

References

ALEXANDER, S. 1920. *Space, Time, and Deity*. 2 vols. London: Macmillan.
BECKERMANN, A., H. FLOHR & J. KIM (eds.) 1992. *Emergence or Reduction? Essays on the Prospects of Nonreductive Physicalism*. Berlin: de Gruyter.
DAVIDSON, D. 1980. *Essays on Actions and Events*. Oxford: Clarendon Press.
DAVIDSON, D. 1984. *Inquiries Into Truth and Interpretation*. Oxford: Clarendon Press.

DENNETT, D.C. 1991. Real patterns. *The Journal of Philosophy* 88(1): 27-51.

EL-HANI, C.N. & A.M. PEREIRA. In press [a]. Understanding biological causation, in *Biology Meets Psychology: Constraints, Connections, Conjectures*, ed V. Hardcastle. Cambridge: MIT Press.

EL-HANI, C.N. & A.M. PEREIRA. In press [b]. PONDO. A casa em ordem: o debate reducionismo/antireducionismo. *Sitientibus*.

EMMECHE, C. In prep. Defining life, explaining emergence.

FEIBLEMAN, J.K. 1954. Theory of integrative levels. *British Journal for the Philosophy of Science* 5: 59-66.

FODOR, J. 1991. Special sciences, or the disunity of science as a working hypothesis. In R. Boyd; P. Gasper & J.D. Trout (eds.), *The Philosophy of Science*. Cambridge, Mass.: MIT Press, 429-41.

HOFSTADTER, D. 1979. *Gödel, Escher, Bach*. New York: Basic Books.

KIM, J. 1984. Concepts of supervenience. *Philosophy and Phenomenological Research* 45: 153-76.

KIM, J. 1993. *Supervenience and Mind*. Cambridge: Cambridge University Press.

KIM, J. 1995. What is the problem of mental causation? *10th International Congress of Logic, Methodology and Philosophy of Science*. Florence.

KIM, J. 1996. *Philosophy of Mind*. Boulder: Westview Press.

KINCAID, H. 1988. Supervenience and explanation. *Synthese* 77: 251-81.

KÜPPERS, B.-O. 1992. Understanding complexity. In A. Beckermann; H. Flohr & J. Kim (eds.), *Emergence or Reduction: Essays on the Prospects of Nonreductive Physicalism*. Berlin: de Gruyter, 241-56.

LEHNINGER, A.L. 1990. *Princípios de Bioquímica*. São Paulo: Sarvier.

LEVINS, R. & R. LEWONTIN. 1985. *The Dialectical Biologist*. Cambridge, Mass.: Harvard University Press.

MIDGLEY, M. 1995. Reductive megalomania. In J. Cornwell (ed.), *Nature's Imagination: the Frontiers of Scientific Vision*. Oxford: Oxford University Press, 133-147.

NOVIKOFF, A.B. 1945. The concept of integrative levels and biology. *Science* 101(2618): 209-15.

O'CONNOR, T. 1994. Emergent properties. *American Philosophical Quarterly*. 31(2): 91-104.

ODUM, E.P. 1988. *Ecologia*. Rio de Janeiro: Guanabara.

PUTNAM, H. 1975. *Philosophical Papers*. Cambridge: Cambridge University Press.

RORTY, R. 1991. *Objectivity, Relativism, and Truth, Philosophical Papers, Vol. 1*. Cambridge: Cambridge University Press.

SACKS, O. 1995. A new vision of the mind. In J. Cornwell (ed.), *Nature's Imagination: the Frontiers of Scientific Vision*. Oxford: Oxford University Press, 101-21.

SERPA, L.F.P. 1991. *Ciência e Historicidade*. Salvador, Brazil.

SOBER, E. 1993. *Philosophy of Biology*. Boulder: Westview Press.

SPERRY, R. 1983. *Science and Moral Priority: Merging Mind, Brain, and Human Values*. New York: Columbia University Press.

TROUT, J.D. 1991. Reductionism and the unity of science: introductory essay. In R. Boyd, P. Gasper & J.D. Trout, *The Philosophy of Science*. Cambridge, Mass.: MIT Press, 387-92.

VEYNE, P. 1984. *Acreditavam os Gregos em seus Mitos?* São Paulo: Brasiliense.

8

The Change is Afoot: Emergentist Thinking in Language Acquisition

GEORGE HOLLICH, KATHY HIRSH-PASEK,

MICHAEL L. TUCKER & ROBERTA M. GOLINKOFF

There is no plan. We posit that development, change, is caused by the interacting influences of heterogeneous components, each with its own take on the world. These are not encapsulated modules; indeed, development happens, behavior is fluid and adaptively intelligent because everything affects everything else. *Thelen & Smith 1994: 338*

... most everyday situations cannot be rigidly assigned to just a single script. They generally involve an interplay between a number of sources of information ... each aspect of the information in the situation can act on other aspects, simultaneously influencing other aspects and being influenced by them. *McClelland, Rumelhart & Hinton 1986: 10*

1. Introduction

A change is afoot in cognitive psychology. The great pendulum of theory in cognitive development has cycled from Skinnerian environmentalism to Piagetian constructivism to Fodorian and Chomskian innatism. As a result, over the last three decades, much of the field has been paralyzed by debates about whether cognitive structure and process are innately constrained or are shaped by input; whether processing is domain-specific or domain-general, whether learning is inherently constrained or associationistic in flavor (see Gleitman & Wanner, 1982; Elman, Bates, Johnson, Karmiloff-Smith, Parisi & Plunkett, 1996; Thelen & Smith, 1994). The field, however, appears amidst a kind of paradigm shift, poised to leap into an entirely new age in which many of these old debates are rendered obsolete and in which many of the old answers to our questions are being reformulated. What is this change? It is emergentist thinking: a process-oriented trend towards more fluid analyses and towards integrative approaches that do not parcel out innate from environmental influences, but rather seem to borrow the best from each of the prior theories. This view has been expressed in many areas of perception, action, and cognition (Elman et al., 1996; Karmiloff-Smith, 1992; Thelen & Smith, 1994). Some feel, however, that the final test of an emergentist theory (Elman et al., 1996) will be played out in the paradigmatic case of human intelligence: language acquisition. For as Pinker and Prince (1988) point out: 'language has been the domain most demanding of articulated symbol structures governed by rules and principles and it is also the domain where such structures have been explored in the greatest depth and sophistication, within a range of theoretical frameworks and architectures' (p. 78). Thus, these theories can only be said to truly explain the range of human cognition if and only if these symbol structures can be accounted for within them.

In this chapter, we will consider how this new metatheoretical perspective impacts on language: how the introduction of concepts like downward/upward causation, emergence, and boundary conditions (Bickhard, this volume; Campbell, 1990; Kim, this volume; Emmeche, Køppe & Stjernfelt, this volume) can fundamentally redescribe the problem space in a way that provides new solutions to long debated problems and suggests a concrete plan for the direction of future research.

With this goal in mind, this paper is broken into four sections. In the first section, we will define the problem space: briefly examining the phenomenon of language acquisition, the questions to be answered, and the classic theories that have evolved to explain them. In the second section, we discuss the new emergentist and interactive view and how it relates to the study of language acquisition. In so doing, we briefly review three recent (and somewhat different) incarnations of this interactive/emergentist perspective. In the third section, we demonstrate how our own work on language comprehension has benefited from the advancement in theoretical perspective, and how this perspective can speak to some of the questions raised in section one. Finally, in the fourth section, we argue that this new vantage point is more than just a redescription of old ideas: it requires a fundamental shift in the ways and means of empirical research itself.

2. A brief review of language acquisition

By most accounts, learning a language ought to be impossible. With enormous acoustic variation between human voices and words, the complexity of our grammar, and the sheer size of our vocabularies, developing children would seem doomed to failure in their attempts to make sense of it all. Indeed, Gold (1967) argued that to induce the rules of grammar from the input would take longer than a human lifetime.

Yet, like the bumblebee who goes on flying in spite of the mathematical impossibility of such a feat, children do learn their language — and quickly. Children utter their first words at around 12 months of age. By eighteen months of age, children's productive vocabularies increase rapidly to approximately 50 words and their development surges as they characteristically acquire, on average, 6 new words a day (Carey, 1978). Shortly thereafter, from ages two to three, grammatical growth becomes evident, going from two-word utterances to complete multi-word sentences in less than a year! By the time they are three-and-a-half years old, they are full communicative partners who have mastered the intricacies of their native tongue.

Given the ease with which children solve this learning problem and the inherent complexity of the task, it should come as no surprise that questions about language learning have been central to theories of cognitive development. That is, researchers continue to debate about how children learn to attach words to their meanings and how they learn to combine words into the regular patterns that comprise the grammar of their native tongue. Reviews of the empirical evidence on this topic have filled volumes (see Bloom, 1994). For the purpose of this exposition, however, we restrict our discussion to the arguments surrounding the learning of grammar, for it is grammar that is considered the *sine qua non* of the language field. It is through the learning of grammar that children come to manipulate symbols in regular ways and to create the propositions that allow them to represent and communicate relations between objects, actions and events in their environment.

2.1. Learning grammar and the nature-nurture debate

Grammar is composed of a set of linguistic units and of the relations that adhere among these units. Grammatical units come in a number of forms from nouns (e.g., cats and dogs), noun phrases (e.g., 'The cats' or 'the beautiful dogs'), clauses (e.g., 'The cats were found with the beautiful dogs') and even combinations of clauses (e.g., 'The cats were found with the beautiful dogs and the frogs were found with the ducks.'), to units like subjects and direct objects, among others. To learn the grammar of a language, children must discover both these units (e.g., Find the unit within the acoustic flux) and identify them (e.g., This is a noun). Unfortunately, linguistic units are not well-marked in the input stream. They are not punctuated for the learner with spaces, periods and commas. As anyone visiting a foreign country can attest, it is quite difficult to find the beginnings and ends of words if one does not already know the language. Thus, even the discovery of the language units is a most challenging task for the learner!

This discovery and identification of the units is even more difficult when we realize that units like nouns and noun phrases, verbs and verb phrases, (among others) bear a hierarchical relationship to one another such that nouns can and do occur in noun phrases which themselves occur in clauses (hierarchical embedding). Therefore, no simple *Markovian* (word by word) analysis will allow the children to discover or identify the many different units of language. The unit problem, therefore, exposes some of the complexity of what must be learned in language development and speaks to the kinds of processes that must be explained by any adequate theory.

Not only does the learner face the problem of finding and identifying the units of language, but also of noting the relationships that hold among units like noun phrases and verb phrases. Unit relations refer to the ways in which the units pattern to allow for some understanding of 'who is doing what to whom.' One relation that is often discussed is that of word order. For example, Steven Pinker (1994) eloquently points out that in the sentence, 'man bites dog,' it's not enough to know that men, dogs, and biting are involved. One must pay attention to word order in order to determine whether the sentence is big news or nothing special. English is a language heavily reliant on word order relations. Other languages like Imbabura Quechuan use inflectional marking to indicate the role of a unit within the language and hence dispense with word order cues almost entirely. By way of example, The English sentence, 'You saw me' would be rendered as riku-wa rka-nki (literally as, 'see, first person object past second person subject'). Speakers in non-word-order languages learn to paste together affixes, to specify the grammatical roles that the words play.

The use of different rules raises the stakes considerably. Not only must the naive learner discover what those rules are, but the learning system must be flexible enough to learn any of the grammatical relations that might be encountered in the environment. Babies cannot know, a priori, what language they will have to learn. Another, perhaps more problematic fact for the learner is that these rules — like the units over which they are realized — are not transparently represented in the input. Language relations are structurally or context dependent (e.g., structure dependency). This requires any reasonable theory of language learning to specify both the units and the ways children might attend to those units and their relations in ongoing speech. An example of structural dependency can be found in the formation of the question rule or relation from the simple declarative sentence. The question, 'Will John come?' might lead the child to suspect that question formation is achieved by inverting the first two words in a sentence. This simple rule quickly fails, however, when he sees the corollary question, 'Will John's sister come?' ('*John's will sister come.') and becomes even more apparent when the child is faced with questions derived from more than one clause: 'Will the man who will come be John?' (which 'will' do we use?). To solve the latter problem, children must know that the 'will' to be fronted is from the main clause.

The logical problem of language acquisition, therefore, is that children are virtual experts at using language by three-and-a-half years even though languages vary on certain critical grammatical parameters; even though the input seems to be impoverished (in that it offers no transparent solutions to finding unit hierarchies and structural dependent relations); and even though parents rarely if ever correct their children when they make incorrect grammatical utterances (as in 'I goes to the store,' see for example Bohannon & Stanowitz, 1988; Pinker, 1989). How can theorists explain children's remarkable success? They do so through appeal to either constraint theories (that are largely *nature*) or constructivist theories (that support a larger role for *nurture*).

2.2. Nature versus nurture/constructivist theories

Though we are about to embark on a quick review of these nature or nurture approaches, it is important to stress at the outset that there is no pure form of either position. Each class of theorists needs the other to explain language acquisition in total. Thus, the difference among the theories is more one of degree or emphasis than of kind. For those heavily weighted towards a nature account, nurture serves the role of triggering the internal grammatical system in highly constrained ways. Those who favor nurture explanations must come to explain how children direct attention to some aspects of the environment over others, thereby relying on some types of information as relevant to the task at hand while ignoring other types of information as irrelevant to the task. To say, for example, that children attend to certain rhythms in the speech stream or to certain types of acoustic information over others is to say that at least some predispositions exist for language learning, while recognizing that these are not, strictly speaking, linguistic abilities.

Despite the lack of pure cases, nature and nurture explanations have defined the theoretical playing field for explanations of grammatical development. These positions are reflected in various guises. Those endorsing the nature position tend to support domain-specific hypotheses in which the structures and processes that read 'input' are specific to the processing of language stimuli. The nature theorists generally endorse a constraints view of learning in which boundary conditions or biological predispositions are set that delimit the kinds of input that are relevant and the ways in which the units can be arranged into various relations. Nature theories often, though not always, support a modular interpretation in which language is served by specialized, encapsulated neurological architecture that is unable to draw inferences from non-language inputs (Fodor, 1983; Chomsky 1986). This view is characterized by Hirsh-Pasek and Golinkoff (1996) as the 'inside out' view of language development, in which pre-formed representations and structures must be linked to the outside input and are then fully realized as language units and relations within the native tongue.

In stark contrast to this view is the 'outside-in' camp of theorists. Again, this camp represents an eclectic group (Schlesinger, 1982, Bates, 1979; Bates, Bretherton & Snyder, 1988; MacNamara, 1982). Generally, however, this group endorses domain general learning and writes of non-modular learning mechanisms that are served by multiple sources of input. In many cases, the 'outside-in' group also supports a constructivist approach to the language learning problem. Heralded by researchers like Bates & MacWhinney (1989), Braine (1976), Piaget, (1952), Schlesinger, (1988) and Greenfield (1991) among others, this approach suggests that language is like other cognitive skills, and should be readily mapped onto existing cognitive structures and processes. Language structure, then, is constructed by the child, either in the context of pragmatically elaborate communicative contexts (e.g., Snow, 1986; Nelson, 1974, 1985) or as an extension of conceptual understanding, which is the logical precursor to language (e.g., Bates & MacWhinney, 1989). These researchers tend to designate primary explanatory prominence to the highly structured linguistic environment, rich in complex systems of grammatical, semantic and phonological patterns that bombard the young learner from the outset of life (Snow, 1986; Bates & MacWhinney, 1987). Thus, parents tend to highlight language units like noun phrases by using them at the ends of sentences, by giving them extra stress, and by repeating them more often. Parents also draw infants' attention to language by using a specialized speech register, termed child- or infant-directed speech (Fernald, 1991). The savvy infant who can read social cues and who is in a conversationally eliciting environment, can learn language units and rules by attending to social and functional cues as well as by computing statistical regularities in the use of these units (Nelson, 1985; Schlesinger, 1988; Snow, 1986) Rather than defaulting to an innately-specified language acquisition device (Chomsky, 1965; Lightfoot, 1989), the outside-in theories offer a position in which social partners compensate for the poverty of the input.

To date, each camp has its supporters. Yet, evidence in favor of nativistic explanations for language development has tended to rule the day (Bickerton, 1984; Chomsky, 1986; Lightfoot, 1989; Pinker, 1994; Gleitman, 1981). Much research suggests that language development does not tend to follow the path of general cognitive development — and hence is not governed by domain general rules. By way of example, it has been demonstrated that children with severe cognitive impairments nonetheless develop normal grammatical performance (e.g., Curtiss, 1977). If general cognitive devices were responsible for language (e.g., language was not unique) there should be a tight isomorphy between language and other cognitions and language development should not diverge from general cognitive development.

Evidence also suggests that children in all cultures learn language at about the same rate, and reach more or less similar levels of competence, regardless of the richness in their learning environments (see also Bickerton, 1984). Even deaf children of hearing parents who have little linguistic input tend to create a language (home sign) that has many of the grammatical properties evident in the language of children who receive a much richer language input (Goldin-Meadows & Mylander, 1984). That is, these children seem to derive hierarchical relations and structural dependency despite their limited input.

Finally, the fact that there are critical periods for language learning before which children can master new grammars and after which it is exceedingly difficult to learn these grammars is also used to buttress nativist claims (Johnson & Newport, 1991; Lenneberg, 1967). These are just of few of the many arguments that nativists raise in support of the 'language instinct' (Pinker, 1994), in support for the nature view of language development over the nurture view.

In short, while there is ample evidence that the environment does affect language development, especially vocabulary development (Tomasello, 1986), and to some extent grammar (Nelson, 1988), the social constructivist theories have yet to offer compelling explanations of how the child becomes a sophisticated speaker of her native language by age three or four. These theories still cannot offer a full or sufficient explanation of how it is that children can, say, multiply embedded sentences like, 'The man the girl kissed fled.' These theories still have problems in articulating how children come to discover and identify the units of language and the relations among them. Thus, after almost 30 years of debate, the nativistic position continues to dominate the field, mostly by way of default (it is argued that if it cannot be explained any other way, it must be a product of nature).[1] The burden of proof is on the social constructivists to address the logical problem of language acquisition and to show that domain general architectures can account for the timing and agility of the language learning process. It is at this point in history — with two seemingly incompatible theories in hand, that the new wave of thinking will make its mark by demonstrating that these two diametrically opposed ways of addressing the puzzles of language acquisition are not incompatible. What the new wave of theorizing in the field of cognitive development helps illuminate is that grammatical acquisition is the product both of innate constraints and socio-environmental inputs. In the newer theories, we begin to see that the nature-nur-

---

1   Bickhard (1995) argues convincingly that the traditional innatist account of language acquisition, and the field's tendency to 'default' to reliance on innate *grammatical* constraints is based on a false assumption about the arbitrary nature of these structures, and the underspecification of these structures from the linguistic environment (the 'poverty of the stimulus' argument). By contrast, Bickhard shows that key principles of linguistic structure, the UG, can be theoretically derived as *logical* constraints on any representational system that functions in the way language does: 'This (innatist) argument presupposes that experience and genes exhaust the possible sources of constraint on language and language learning ' (1995: 548). By adopting a functional account to explain linguistic constraints, showing how relationally structured representations can give rise to propositionally structured utterances, Bickhard's formulation permits the possibility that the so-called innate component in language development is actually *emergent* over developmental time through the refinement of a sophisticated relational-representational system.

ture debate has played a polarizing role in our conception of how cognitive processes develop. This debate crystallized some of the differences (rather than the similarities) between the major theories and created a situation in which scientists felt bound to one camp or the other with apparently no hope of reconciliation.

3. The 'New Wave'

Given the twin facts that the field of language development has been polarized by a potentially false dichotomy and that parts of each of the theories mentioned can account for a substantial amount of the variance in language acquisition, it is time for a reconciliation. We agree with those who suggest it is time to 'rethink innateness' (Elman et al., 1996), to break the conceptual paralysis that has gripped the field, to pose a reformulation of the entire nature-nurture question, and indeed, to reformulate cognitive developmental theory in general. In this new formulation, the question of 'where' language structure 'exists' before it is realized in development has given way to a set of entirely different questions, questions like: Under what conditions and under what constraints (either domain-specific or domain-general) does the child construct language? Are there multiple inputs to emergent word and grammatical systems? Most importantly, what is the process by which these inputs interact to create complex systems?

  As we will demonstrate, the different instantiations of this new wave of thinking represent divergent points of view within cognitive developmental psychology. Despite their differences, however, all of these newer theories share the dominant theme that it is no longer profitable to be caught on the horns of the nature/nurture debate. In the next section, we will consider this 'new wave' of thinking and the ways in which it is changing research in language development.

3.1. Emergence of the 'New Wave'

This new thinking within the field of cognitive psychology starts as all good ideas do, not by reinventing the wheel, but by at least recognizing its elegance and its place in the history of the domain. In this case, the old wheel is 'interactionism'. It has been suggested recently that the term, because of its heavy baggage and history, has been voided of any universal meaning (Oyama, 1985). In one way or another, everyone is to some extent an interactionist. Chomsky and his nativist followers are interactionists in the sense that all children must interact with the input to discover the grammar of their native tongue. The social pragmatists are interactionists in that it is through interaction with a socially sophisticated linguistic partner that we are guided in the construction of language. Indeed, interactionism is not only a loaded term, but is a term that is not operationally well-defined within the field.

Of interest for us here, however, is the current speculative notion that true inter-actionism is 'emergentism.' That is, if we wish to discuss a domain like language, questions that start 'Where does structure X come from' should be given only passing attention. Several theorists have recognized that a developmental expla-nation of such a complex system cannot rely on the 'smoking guns' of genes or environment for much longer. We must instead consider a more flexible and tem-porally variable array of input sources, some of which are more heavily available early in the process, like acoustics, and some which come into play much later in the language game, like semantics or syntax. (Nelson, 1996)

Thus, at a time when the field of cognitive psychology is coming to stress the importance of interactionism and studying systems as dynamic entities, psycholo-gists are becoming aware that mathematical theories to describe these phenomena already exist. These theories have many faces, and have been alternately called dynamic systems theory, developmental systems theory, success-driven learning theory, distributional learning theory, nonlinear dynamic theory, or chaos theory: to name a few. Whatever the name, they share three common themes: 1) Simple regularities when iterated can produce extraordinarily varied and complex behav-ior that is emergent from the interaction at the lower levels (upward causation). 2) Each problem space has its own set of constraints or boundary conditions which serve to limit the behavior of the system and which can produce discontinuous patterns of behavior, or phase shifts, from a single nonlinear process. 3) Finally, there is a beginning realization that, often the emergent whole may affect the lower levels as well: downward causation.

3.2. Three recent instantiations of the 'New Wave'

In the past five years, there has been a proliferation of these dynamically-flavored theories within cognitive development. In this section, we present a cursory re-view of three such instantiations. We will then use these three as a base from which to further elaborate on the central themes of the new wave outlined above. As with any cursory review, we will of necessity simplify and gloss over what are major differences in an effort to highlight what has changed. Let us apologize at the outset for any injustice that will be done here. After reviewing and extracting these common themes, we illustrate one use of the new trend in Hirsh-Pasek and Golinkoff's (1996) coalition models of grammatical and word learning.

3.2.1. Thelen and Smith: The dynamic systems perspective

Thelen and Smith (1994; Smith & Thelen, 1993) were among the first to import chaos theory and systems theory into the field of cognitive psychology (see also Thelen 1989, Oyama, 1985). In contrast to many of the theories we have already examined, the hallmarks of dynamic thinking are attention to process rather than to structure. The dynamic theorist is less concerned with looking for sources of static, unchanging structure, either in the environment or in the 'head' of the individual. Instead, this view proposes that structure is dependent on process. Through a highly contingent, multiply-caused and multiply informed constructive interplay of organism and context, systems emerge in developmental time.

Thelen and Smith demonstrate this theory by considering the problem of learning to walk: 'locomotor development in cats, as well as in frogs, chicks, and humans, is [made up of many components] and context sensitive. Cats can generate patterned limb activity very early in life, but walking alone requires more — postural stability, strong muscles and bones, motivation to move forward, a facilitative state of arousal, and an appropriate substrate. Only when these components act together does the cat truly walk' (p. 20).

One attractive feature of this perspective is that it defuses some of the conflict between the either-or views of environmental and innatist theories. Language is not 'learned' in any traditional sense, where learning means a transparent mapping of environmentally-given information. Likewise, language does not simply evolve out of biological, programmatic instructions. Instead, this view allows that multiple sources of information (both in the input and in the biological prerequisites) compel the process in a nonlinear, non-additive fashion. This thereby combines aspects of both nativist and constructivist theories.

In the same sense, language development can be seen as being composed of many different components. It is only when words, grammar, social-interaction, environmental cues and a biologically appropriate substrate 'act together' that the child can be said to 'truly' construct grammar, in the fullest sense. Thus, the study of language, and indeed, any developmental phenomenon, for Thelen and Smith, involves a consideration of the dynamic interaction of multiple factors: both biological and socio-environmental. (See Tucker & Hirsh-Pasek, 1993, for a fuller treatment of the way in which these ideas can account for phonological and grammatical development as well as Hirsh-Pasek, Tucker & Golinkoff, 1995; Hirsh-Pasek & Golinkoff, 1996.)

A theoretical perspective with attention to the dynamic interaction of multiple factors has led to some interesting caveats. First, although the precise evolution of any system may be unpredictable, the interaction will almost always conform to some kind of pattern, or attractor, for behavior. For example, although one might have trouble predicting the exact path a boulder might take when rolling down a mountain, one could quite accurately predict the stable end state (the bottom). Moreover, one could mathematically induce the kinds of forces necessary to produce a general path and end state: even to the point of modelling the system on a computer. Indeed, one of the great advantages of such an approach is to be able to predict qualitative behaviors of dynamic systems. That is, we can predict the kinds of things such a system can and can not do, the paths of language development that a child can and cannot take.

Second, many systems even have more than one possible attractor, or stable solution. Thus, a fertilized egg could become either a boy or a girl depending on the interaction between the genetic sequence and its intercellular environment. Likewise, French, German, and Italian all represent stable solutions to the language problem, with each seeming to work equally well for their practitioners.[2]

Finally, some solutions are better than others depending on the functional context. This can lead sometimes to sudden phase shifts in behavior. So children who initially use their fingers to count might suddenly shift to rote remembering, and a person who wants to get somewhere quickly might suddenly shift from fast walking into running. In the language domain, children who might differentially rely on semantic cues at one age may come to rely on syntactic or grammatical cues at a more advanced level. By way of example, the child who hears the sentence, 'Baby feeds mommy' might assume that mommy is feeding the baby because semantic and pragmatic cues dictate that interpretation despite the grammatical cues. The sophisticated toddler of three or four, however, lets the grammatical information dictate the interpretation.

According to Thelen and Smith, development — language or otherwise — is the evolution of a system, from an initially unstable starting point to higher and higher levels of organization, successive stable attractors. The study of development, then, is the induction of the processes and boundary conditions which serve to produce the patterns of behavior (attractors) seen.

---

2 Campbell (1990) provides a similar example in recognizing the contributions of upward and downward causation, of macro- and microdeterminants of form, in the formation of the jaws of the soldier ant. These creatures serve a single purpose in the social order of the ant: their jaws are specially designed to pierce other organisms. So, in one sense the genetics of the ant (and Archimedes' laws of levers) selects functional pincer forms over others. This would be an incomplete picture, however, since we must also appeal to the sociological laws of 'division-of-labor social organization' to explain why some ants are only food-gatherers, while others like the soldier ant, are utilized only for defense. Retreating to either the sociological or the biological (or, indeed, the mechanical) in explaining a) the role of the soldier ant in a colony's sociology and b) the shape of its unique mandles greatly oversimplifies the issue.

3.2.2. Karmiloff-Smith: Representational redescription

Thelen and Smith (1994) speak of interactionism in terms of dynamic systems theory. For Karmiloff-Smith (1992), the neuvo interactionism is codified through representational redescription. Her theory was motivated by the need to shift one of the staples in interactionism, a focus on failure-driven learning (Piaget, 1955). A most outspoken interactionist in the truest sense, Piaget argued that qualitative shifts in forms of thought arose through discrepancies between an existing structural organization and some environmental condition. Children may have mental structures that do not allow them to see that two beakers of water of different shape contained the same amount of liquid. In order for the child to reconcile this apparent contradiction in between their mental structure and the world, something had to change. In most cases, the change that occurred was within the child; more formally, the mental structures contributing to notions of conservation were modified to accommodate this new understanding. In this way, old forms of thinking gave way to new in a continuous process of equilibration, or movement from lower to higher forms of mental coordination. Qualitative, adaptive changes in thought take place when discrepancies between the expected and the manifest engender a cascading structural reorganization, a change in the child's representations of the problem and its solutions.

Karmiloff-Smith suggests that failure-driven models of learning ignore important developmental changes that occur when a given cognitive system is procedurally successful. Karmiloff-Smith's alternative is the model of representational redescription (the RR model hereafter; Karmiloff-Smith 1992). This model consists of four levels of representation, each of which arises through the redescription, or re-encoding, of the prior level. At each successive level, these representations become more explicit and hence more available to linguistic expression. Thus, development proceeds from implicit representations of basic behavioral procedures to successively more abstract, explicit, and flexible structures. Through this developmental process, representations become successively more adaptive, enabling the organism to enhance interaction with the environment, without appealing to failure of previous engagements.

Karmiloff-Smith's model provides a mechanism, albeit a speculative one, by which representational change occurs developmentally without appeals to failure, and remains faithful to an emergentist approach emphasizing domain- specific constraints (or boundary conditions) on development that are decidedly non-modular. Children need not come to the task with a finely tuned storehouse of language-relevant representations to explain what they eventually acquire. Finally, the RR model attempts to explain the emergence of domain-specific representations that are explicit and amenable to linguistic description through the representational redescription of implicit perceptual or motor procedures.

It may be useful to consider the RR model a sort of 'constrained constructivism'. Karmiloff-Smith remains essentially true to a constructive epistemology, arguing that we need not attribute sophistication to our naive learners in order to explain how they know what they know. Language, like other domains of knowledge, may capitalize on innate perceptual biases (e.g., constraints on attention) that lead the child to focus strongly on some input classes while virtually ignoring others. So, we might speculate that the child will find human speech, and child-directed speech in particular, more interesting than the sounds of cars moving outside the home, or the random noises made by household appliances. This places the RR model, and the specific formulations of micro-domains within language, at a place midway between and slightly above the old nature-nurture dichotomy. However, it is important to recognize (as others have, Bickhard, 1995) that while Karmiloff-Smith apparently rejects the old nature-nurture dichotomy in toto, the fact remains that her model does not completely eradicate the old idea. For example, it is still, in this developmental approach, we find that the tired question of *where* information comes from is still answered by the age-old answer, one still clinging to a limited, albeit more interactionist, set of developmental propositions. In her formulations, Karmiloff-Smith fails to embrace an emergentist approach of the sort advocated elsewhere in this volume. That is, in asking the question of *where* the information derives, Karmiloff-Smith closes off the alternative possibility that the question is based on a false premise and a fruitless reliance on a strict deterministic (or temporally and logically 'upward causation') answer (see Bickhard, 1995).

One particularly attractive feature of the RR view is that it allows for domain-specific learning that is not initially modular. Modularity may be the product of development, not its cause. In particular, Karmiloff-Smith argues that building in such fine-tuned and highly specified representations prior to language learning makes the system too rigid to account for variability in language use among children: *'The more complex the picture we ultimately build of the innate capacities of the infant mind, the more important it becomes for us to explain the flexibility of subsequent cognitive development'* (1992, p. 9, emphasis in original).

What does the RR model offer? First, it makes a useful distinction between procedural knowledge at the behavioral level and representational knowledge that later becomes amenable to linguistic expression. Karmiloff-Smith argues that behavioral mastery of a domain (say, mastering the articulatory gestures involved in producing understandable speech sounds) is the first step in internalizing knowledge about such behavior. Second, this theory provides a putative mechanism (the 'system-internal dynamics') by which initially implicit procedural representations become available outside of the initial domain through redescription into more abstract symbolic forms.

Additionally, Karmiloff-Smith herself has recently 'redescribed' certain aspects of this approach, and it is to this more current instantiation of these ideas we turn in the next section (Elman et al., 1996). However, we should emphasize again the relevance of this view for our central argument here. In this RR model, appeals to domain-specific structures or representations are rejected in favor of biases or perceptual constraints. Incidentally, this idea has become popular in other conceptualizations of language acquisition as well (Jusczyk & Bertoncini, 1988; Hirsh-Pasek & Golinkoff, 1996; Tucker & Hirsh-Pasek, 1993). Over time, these initial predispositions may indeed become more insulated and modular in character (a process referred to as emergent modularity, Greenfield, 1991, Karmiloff-Smith, 1992, Tucker & Hirsh-Pasek, 1993). Importantly, they did not start out that way, and it is this critical factor that makes emergentist views so distinct from traditional nativist accounts.

3.2.3. Elman et al.: Rethinking innateness

... we argue that some innate predispositions — architectural, chronotropic and, rarely, representational — channel the infant's attention to certain aspects of the environment over others. Our view is that these predispositions play different roles at different levels, and that as far as representation-specific predispositions are concerned, they may only be specified at the subcortical level as little more than attention grabbers so that the organism ensures itself of massive experience of certain inputs prior to subsequent learning. *Elman et al. 1996: 108*

In this last and current instantiation of interactionism, we see the most recent of Karmiloff-Smith's perspective as it melds with what has been called 'new age' connectionism. Connectionism is a way of modelling computer learning in ways thought to be compatible with the activity and structure of the human brain. A connectionist (or parallel distributed processing) network generally contains three layers of units called nodes. The inputs consist of one layer, outputs another, and in between these is a layer of so-called hidden units in which processing takes place. Processing in a network like this takes the form of activation of nodes from input, through the hidden units, to output. Changes in the activity of the net are achieved by altering the weights among connections, and these modifications are achieved either directly by the modeller, or through experience, via the inputs the network receives. 'Learning' in a network, then, is operationalized as modifications of the node connections in response to cascading waves of input sequences (epochs) that impinge the input layer.

Connectionist nets show themselves very flexible learning engines. Indeed, networks have attempted to learn everything from English phonology to the differences between regular and irregular verbs. Through tutoring and error-correct-ing (binary right-wrong distinctions) complex behavior 'emerges' from the network.

The network differs from traditional algorithmic programming in several respects. First, nowhere in the network are propositional representations of the things it 'knows': in the most sophisticated networks, say, for learning English verb morphology, there are no verb nodes, or regular and irregular nodes. These features emerge out of the activity of the whole network, based on the network's training history and present sources of input. The 'solutions [are] contained in the structure of the problem space' (Elman et al., 1996). This problem space includes the network itself, its architecture, its history, and the context of inputs and outputs it is receiving and producing, respectively.

Finally, and perhaps most important considering our early discussions of constraints, the net has no innate preprogrammed structure beyond the architecture described above. The weights merely represent 'attentional constraints' in the broadest sense of the term. The system simply begins with a bias to attend to certain aspects of the input over others, as we saw in Karmiloff-Smith's earlier model. By limiting the source of information in these initial ways (a 'sensitive dependence on initial conditions,' Gleick, 1987), the complexity of subsequent behavior falls out of the activity of the network.

There are other facets of this modelling technique that we will ignore for the present. Instead, let us consider what Elman et al. (1996) have asserted, based on these facts about connectionist architecture, and what implications these ideas might have for an emergentist program.

First, as their title suggests, ideas about innateness fundamentally change. Indeed, Elman et al. (1996) suggest that innateness takes place on several levels, including the architecture of cells in the brain, the arrangement of neurons in cortical and subcortical patterns, and so forth. Other aspects of innate constraints can include: innate representations,[3] innate mechanism or procedures, and constraints in developmental timing.

Second, we are no longer theorizing with one hand tied behind our backs. That is, the old formulations about nativism and constructivism allowed only either-or dichotomies, nature or nurture. Here we see how one can incorporate biases (or principles, or constraints) into one's model of development without adopting strong preformationist-style innatism. The biases begin the process. Attention to some kinds of information is stronger at the outset. These biases, however, do not constitute knowledge in an abstract or explicit sense, and simply start the ball rolling.

---

3   The possibility of innate representation is a proposition that Elman et al. (1996) argue is least likely, but which has been advocated extensively by structural-innatists like Chomsky (1965) or Fodor (1983).

Third, it is certainly the case that many different patterns of development may lead to similar outcomes, but these outcomes (solutions to the problem) are not uniform in any strict sense. Here we see again the attractiveness of ideas about individual differences and complexity. Uniformity on one level gives way, with more refined focus, to dynamic differences in performance, competence, and representations.

Fourth and finally, modelling of a connectionist sort leads to the supposition that qualitative changes at the behavioral level need not be governed by qualitative changes at the representational level. This final point is perhaps most controversial to those coming from a more traditional constructivist background, since many theorists, including ourselves, suggest that fundamental changes in representational capacity are necessary to explain cognitive advances.[4]

Applying these ideas to the language arena, we see that the position of Elman et al (1996) mirrors much of what we saw in both Thelen and Smith's and Karmiloff-Smith's accounts of learning. Cognitive behaviors are emergent from rather scant beginnings that help the system focus on domain relevant stimuli in the environment. In each account, the system is sensitive to multiple inputs from numerous sources (e.g., from social inputs and biological inputs). In each account, the line between the contributions of nature and nurture is blurred if not obliterated. In each account, emergent behaviors are governed simultaneously by upward causation, downward causation and boundary conditions. Taken in combination, these three theories allow for a fresh look at specific behavior like language development and allow us to re-frame many of the old questions that had so dominated the field.

3.3. Riding the 'New Wave' in language

As we look at the three theories discussed above with a broad stroke, we see some commonalities that incorporate themes of upward causation, boundary conditions, and downward causation. Indeed, these new trends seem to forecast a number of central assumptions that could fundamentally change both the study of cognition and the field of language acquisition. It is thus worth exploring how each of the three themes of emergentist thinking impact upon the picture of language development that was sketched earlier.

---

4   Indeed, our extended discussion of the implications of a connectionist architecture solution to the nature-nurture dilemma should not be misunderstood as an endorsement of a connectionist model of human cognition. While neural nets provide an interesting approach to modelling cognition, it does not logically follow that they accurately reflect the processes and representations involved in real-time human cognition, and they fall well short of providing a detailed explanation of language use or acquisition.

3.3.1. Upward causation

The first change in thinking reflected in the above theories is the growing recognition that answers to questions about the sources of linguistic structure ('Where does grammar come from?') are not going to be found in transparent accounts of external sources ('From the grammar that you heard when your parents spoke to you') or from the promise of biologically-determined language organs in the brain ('From the maturation of innate linguistic stuff'). Instead, there has been a renewed interest in structure that emerges with time, and is not reducible to early structure or to static processes that can be observed environmentally. This more process-oriented theorizing has shifted the focus of attention from 'Where'-type questions to 'How'- type questions, and leads us to expect that emergence, truly considered, may provide many of those answers. Thus, upward causation becomes central to theories of development.

In the field of language development, this emergentism also seems to be couched in a distributional learning model. Children are seen as miniature statisticians noting distributional and statistical regularities among many input sources to determine the characteristics of words or of grammatical properties (e.g., Saffran, Aslin & Newport, 1996; Saffran, Newport, & Aslin, 1996). So, for example, Golinkoff and Hirsh-Pasek (1996) suggest that infants may use a form of guided distributional learning to find classes of words like 'nouns' in the input stream. Scanning for evidence of heavy prosodic stress and sentence position, children might be able to use minimal structural and acoustic cues to construct a grammatical category, from the bottom-up.

3.3.2. Boundary conditions and phase shifts

The new perspective also supports a view of constraints or boundary conditions. Innate predispositions must be in place for the child to even extract the relevant information from the input (e.g., Elman et al., 1996; Karmiloff-Smith, 1992; Jusczyk, 1997). The infant listener is constrained to focus on certain human speech patterns and to ignore others as irrelevant for meaning.

By way of example, it has been argued that we hear 17 different acoustic sounds in every syllable of speech. Luckily, we do not attend to all of these acoustic variations when we want to extract meaning from the speech stream. In fact, we ignore large differences between a male and female voice both uttering the word 'stop,' but closely attend to seemingly small differences in the words 'stop' and 'spot.' If we postulate an unconstrained learner, randomly analyzing the input, language would quickly become impossible. Yet, the theories proposed above all propose a learner who is predisposed to focus on certain properties of the input over others.

It is important to note that in the new wave of thinking, boundary conditions do not restrict the learner to one universal solution to a cognitive problem, but merely assist in defining a set of more or less probabilistic solutions to that problem. Hence, constraints need not be universals that permit no variability. This view allows researchers to see not only the universal properties of language development that all children share, but also the variability that characterizes both individual development and language change (see Bates, Bretherton & Snyder, 1988) all within a unified theoretical paradigm.

3.3.3. Downward causation

Explicit reference to downward causation in language development is uncommon, although the ideas represented elsewhere in this volume are suggestive of the kinds of dichotomies we elaborated in previous sections. The either-or approach, the false dichotomy of development, is central to any mechanistic enterprise, and this reliance on a mechanistic research program (an efficient Aristotelian causality) pervades much of developmental thought. Stripped to its essentials, the approach is an attempt to either avoid the recognition of emergence (formal and final causality) or to *reduce* it to the level of epiphenomenon, vacuous or, at best, uninteresting (see also Overton, 1991). In their criticism of Klee's microdeterminism, Moreno and Umerez (this volume) highlight exactly the points the emergentist theories we advocate as plausible for the domain of language. The preformationist view of development in language mirrors the discussion seen in other domains, especially in developmental biology. Indeed, one fundamental tenet of the strongest innatist approaches has been that at its core, language development is a *biological*, rather than a psychological phenomenon.

Although downward causation models have not been as well-represented in the language-learning literature as have constraint or emergence models, downward causation might indeed play a critical role in theories of language in at least two ways: what we will refer to as internal downward causation and external downward causation. By internal downward causation, we refer to the idea that emergent properties of the system become self-organized at higher levels which themselves come to redescribe or constrain further processing (a medium-causation view, see Emmeche, Køppe and Stjernfelt, this volume). So, for example, each of the three theories presented above suggests that emergent modularity is a likely property of developmental systems. Once a child's cognitive system becomes modularized, it is likely that they will begin to process relevant input in different ways. By way of example, there is evidence in the area of developing phonology (the sounds of language) that children begin to process speech with an ear to all languages — readily distinguishing phonemes in Hindi, Japanese and English. Over time, however, the system becomes more specialized and seems less able to note those same distinctions in other languages when they are presented (Best, McRoberts & Sithole, 1988; Werker & Tees, 1984). Thus, the Japanese eight-month-old might hear the distinction between /r/ and /l/ that an older child finds more difficult to detect.

By external downward causation, we refer to outside influences from an organized system that directs lower level processing. Thus, the social interactionists could be said to represent downward-causationists in that sophisticated social partners impose order on the incoming stimuli that helps the child narrow the field of candidates for particular linguistic units. In word learning, for example, caretaker eye-gaze can direct the learner to expect words to have some meanings over others. If Mom is looking at a picture of an unknown animal in a book, the child may expect that when she utters 'aardvark' she is not referring to other objects in the room like the telephone or the pencil sharpener (Tomasello & Kruger, 1992)

Social inputs can also assist children in learning the differences in literal and metaphorical language. Thus, while initial interpretation of the sentence: 'it's raining cats and dogs,' might be quite literal, subsequent experience with the language in a social scene might lead to a more metaphorical interpretation. As Asch and Nerlove (1960) show, children seem to progress through stages of metaphor interpretation: initially being quite literal and only later able to routinely assign abstract meanings to new metaphors. Thus, growing and emergent abstract knowledge about the workings of language serve to constrain subsequent interpretation.

3.3.4. Putting it all together

Thelen and Smith's dynamic systems theory, Karmiloff-Smith's representational redescription and Elman et al's connectionist approach are recent models that represent dramatic changes within cognitive developmental psychology over the last five years. While they are theoretically distinct, it is our opinion that they have the potential to change the landscape in cognitive development by stressing several characteristic themes. The first is that the nature/nurture debate tends to dissolve, giving way to discussions of emergent behavior built upon distributional evidence. The second theme is that boundary conditions can and probably do exist either in the global architecture of the system or in the structure of the representation within the system. The third theme is that more complex systems can serve to drive the developing system and can provide yet another signpost for development through downward causation. None of these positions is really new. It could be argued that each of the warring factions (Chomsky vs. Piagetian alternatives) that traditionally characterized theories of language development can comfortably sit within one of these camps. What makes the new perspective really new, however, is that researchers of tomorrow will not have to choose from among these alternatives, but can begin to see these as mutually compatible and necessary explanations for complex behaviors like language development. This brings us to the final and perhaps most central point about the new wave. The real change in cognition and language development comes in the form of increased attention to multiple and mutually reinforcing sources of linguistic information that act in concert to ensure development. Each of the three representative theories above speak to this issue. Cognition will not and cannot be explained through appeal to exclusive reliance on either upward or downward causation or through boundary conditions. Single cause theories are too restrictive, are unnecessarily confining and are incapable of explaining the complexity of the various cognitive systems in a unified way. It is when we look instead to multiple sources of information: to a coalition of cues (Hirsh-Pasek & Golinkoff, 1996) that work in concert across developmental time that we begin to allow for the emergence and construction of word learning and grammatical development.

3.4. The 'New Wave' in our research: Hirsh-Pasek and Golinkoff's coalition government model of language comprehension

Hirsh-Pasek and Golinkoff's (1996) 'coalition model' embodies many of the characteristics of the newer theories. Though it represents a work-in-progress, we use it here to illustrate how ideas like emergence, phase shifts and boundary conditions can be profitably incorporated into a model of language development and how the resulting theories can be used to address the logical problem of language acquisition.

The coalition model embraces several key assumptions. First, Golinkoff and Hirsh-Pasek suggest that language comprehension is an emergent property of a complex system. That is, children begin to comprehend language when they compute the earliest relationships between inputs like sights and sounds in a very general and shallow way. This initial analysis of the input allows children to internalize chunks of sound (or visual input in the case of sign language) that will be language relevant and that will eventually serve as cues to the more sophisticated and abstract grammatical units of language.

Second, the model holds that children are confronted with a 'coalition' of inputs that are always available and highly redundant with one another. To learn the grammar of their language — to comprehend the language around them, children must mine the coalition of input cues.

Third, children are predisposed (boundary conditions) to attend to certain cues over others in each of the input arenas. Through what Hirsh-Pasek and Golinkoff (1996) call 'guided distributional learning' children are thought to attend only to certain acoustic cues in the input like fundamental frequency and vowel lengthening rather than to other cues like pausing (Jusczyk, Hirsh-Pasek, Kemler Nelson, Woodward & Piwoz, 1992). Not only do children attend to certain cues over others within a particular input, but they also differentially attend to different inputs over others across developmental time. Thus, prosodic cues are more heavily weighted within the first year of life while semantic and social cues become more prominent during the second year and grammatical cues more weighted during the third year. Language comprehension is affected by the change in the weightings of the input cues. Figure 1 depicts these changes over time.

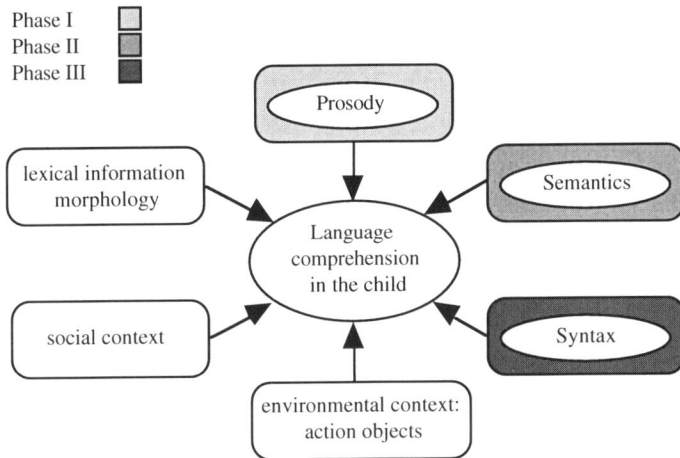

Fig. 1. A coalition model of language comprehension. Different cues are differentially weighted (as indicated by shading) during the course of development.

Fourth, changes in the weighting of cues from the input create phase shifts in the development of comprehension. These re-weightings of the input occur either when children require more elaborate language structures to achieve their communicative goals (Bloom, 1993) or when they fail in their communicative attempts — thus misinterpreting passive sentences, 'The man was bitten by the dog' as active sentences, 'The man bit the dog' because they attend to the order of the content words in the sentence.

Fifth and finally, one key assumption of the model is that the development of language comprehension through the phase shifts is empirically testable. Indeed, there is already a good deal of evidence to support the conceptualization of the phases suggested in the model. Current research is underway to assess the re-weighting hypotheses in both the comprehension of grammar and of words.

In what follows, we very briefly give the flavor of the model with some of the evidence that tends to be consistent with it. We then examine how such a model might explain the logical problems of language acquisition, finding the units and relations of language, and how it compares metatheoretically with the other models representing the new wave of research.

3.5. Three phases and some supporting evidence

3.5.1. Phase I

In this model, infants are said to already have some language comprehension from the second half of the first year of life as they attempt to make sense of the flux of acoustic and visual information surrounding them. Their job is seen as twofold: first to segment the fluid speech into some acoustically relevant chunks that will become language relevant units, and second, to use some of these acoustic units to assist them in discovering the objects, actions and events that surround them. Both of these initial processes are rather shallow and require only that the child attend to certain cues in the acoustic and visual environment and that they perform distributional and correlational analysis that will enable them to internalize frequently encountered units and events. Hirsh-Pasek and Golinkoff liken the first steps of the internalization process to 'cinema verite' in film. No interpretation occurs here. Indeed, in this first segmentation phase the child literally stores a number of meaningless but regular acoustic forms that can later become language relevant.

There is considerable support for the notion that speech is first segmented and extracted in language-relevant ways (see also Peters, 1983), and that these segments are further broken down and analyzed into their component parts. Hirsh-Pasek, Kemler-Nelson, Jusczyk, Wright, Druss, and Kennedy (1987, see also Jusczyk et al, 1992; among others) note that infants of just four and a half months of age are sensitive to the acoustic markings that correlate with clauses and that 9 month olds are sensitive to markings correlated with phrases like nouns and verbs.

There is also evidence that infants can do distributional analysis across phonological and rhythmic properties of the speech input even though they do not technically comprehend the meaning of these inputs. By way of example, Jusczyk and his colleagues (see Jusczyk, 1997) and Saffran, Aslin and Newport (1996) have demonstrated that very young infants of 6 to 8 months of age are sensitive to and perform distributional analysis across phonological patterns. Thus, infants appear to rely quite heavily on the acoustic system to get a leg up on early language units. This same literature suggests that these infants create a storehouse of acoustic information that can later be used for more sophisticated processing (see also Gerken, 1996 for a review).

While this segmentation and categorization is going on, Hirsh-Pasek and Golinkoff also speculate that children can use this 'acoustic packaging' to supplement their information about the linkage between sounds and events. They hypothesize that children make unbiased observations of the events that occur in the world, noting, perhaps, the temporal contiguities of sound, movement, cause and effect, as they take place in the environmental tableau. At this phase of input segregation, a young infant may observe, for example, that certain objects in the world (say, the family cat) tend to co-occur with certain sounds (say, the word 'CAT' and other references to cat attributes) more than other sounds. Further, the infant may notice that activity on the cat's part may be highly correlated with verbal comment about that activity and that these event segments may be similarly bracketed, such that the sound streams begin and end in concert with events that are observed in the world. It is important to note that while this phase is catalogued as the beginning of language comprehension, there is really nothing particularly linguistic about this phase. We do not place unusual constraints on the child's attention, save that they notice these things, and their likelihood of occurring together.

At the preliminary phase of perceptual segmentation and the extraction phase, the child begins to construct what Mandler (1988, 1992) calls 'image schemas'. These contain perceptual primitives such as AGENCY, CAUSALITY, PATH and CONTAINMENT. Further, this initial acoustic packaging may help the child to carve up events in the world, by providing a template or overlay onto ongoing scenes the child observes or the repeated and standard routines in which the child participates (Nelson, 1985). Although we don't expect that the child is making linguistic judgments about these packages, we argue that the structure of heard language may constrain possible event units in the perceptual arena. Evidence already exists showing that infants are more likely to attend to a visual event when it is highlighted by speech (Horowitz, 1974), and it seems reasonable that a first step towards building representations that may have linguistic correlates is to attend to those events that are being described or otherwise referred to linguistically. Further, it seems reasonable to assume that children will also use social cues, especially those present in discourse, to help tie the ribbon on their perceptual packages, further assisting their segmentation and storage of 'macroevents' and routines for later internal analysis. Much of this formulation is speculative but testable, and Hirsh-Pasek and Golinkoff offer some novel verification approaches for these predictions, some of which are currently being investigated in their laboratories. Indeed, it is difficult, to imagine a situation wherein something very much like this acoustic packaging did not occur as the first step in constructing linguistic representations in the first months of life as children try to integrate the multiple sources of the coalition in an attempt to make meaning in their world.

3.5.2. Phase II

Hirsh-Pasek and Golinkoff go on to describe the next step, a process of interpreting these perceptually stored acoustic packages. Beginning in the later months of the first year, infants are presumed to possess a small collection of these highly salient event packages that can be further analyzed into components that may have direct linguistic correlates like subject, verb and object. During this phase, infants move beyond prosodic mapping to what they call semantic mapping; in the coalition government, the voting power of the sound system gives way as the semantic system begins to assert itself. Children begin to use the correlates of prosody, semantics, and even syntactic cues (e.g., articles signifying nouns) to map individual words to their referents and thus to 'buy' a much more elaborate and rich system of communication and representation (Bloom, 1993).

One remarkable hallmark of Phase II interpretation is the growth of the lexicon. This remarkable feat, sometimes referred to as the vocabulary spurt, occurs after the child has already acquired roughly 50 words in production. The spurt seems to be a qualitative jump in learning — estimates are that between 7 and 9 new words are learned, albeit incompletely, daily (Carey 1982). To explain this rapid lexical growth, some researchers have suggested that the child must possess a set of constraints or principles to enable so-called 'fast-mapping' between the phonological and semantic representations of words (Slobin, 1982, 1985; Golinkoff, Mervis & Hirsh-Pasek, 1994).

Indeed, Golinkoff, Mervis & Hirsh-Pasek (1994) offer a two-tiered model of linguistic principles, developmentally realized, that may aid in such fast mapping of words with their referents: word-learning principles that are also considered to be developmentally emergent, in a coalition government fashion, out of the dynamic interrelation of multiple cues (Hollich, Hirsh-Pasek, & Golinkoff, in press). For example, initial word mapping may be governed by simple associative learning effects: words and objects are associated temporally and spatially (temporal contiguity). Later, children abandon this simple associative strategy and realize that words *refer* or somehow 'stand-for' objects, rather than simply being associated with them. This realization frees the child from the environmental requirement that all of the coalescing cues are there to support the word-referent connection.

The notion that word learning principles might themselves be developmental is consistent with work by Bloom (1993) and Jones and Smith (1993) and colleagues who have extended these findings to pre-vocabulary-spurt infants. Preliminary results suggest that these infants do, as predicted, use simple associative cues, like temporal contiguity and saliency to determine reference, while ignoring other cues like eye-gaze (Hollich, Hirsh-Pasek & Golinkoff, 1996).

Word learning is one of the defining characteristics of this period as are the rudiments of a grammatical system that is defined through the semantic functions and pragmatics. (e.g., Concepts like agents, actions and objects define grammatical categories, see for example, Bowerman, 1973; MacNamara, 1982; among others). What is striking at this age is the reliance on semantics or pragmatics as governing language comprehension. Semantically implausible sentences, for example, are simply misunderstood such that sentences like, 'Baby feeds mommy' will be understood as, 'Mommy feeds baby'. It is interesting that children at this age can attend to some grammatical cues like constituent structure and word order (see for example, Hirsh-Pasek & Golinkoff, 1996; Naigles, 1990; P. Bloom, 1990; among others), but that grammatical reliance gives way to semantic probability when the two systems are put into direct conflict. Note again that the child has many inputs at his disposal and differentially weights these inputs for the purpose of comprehension.

3.5.3. Phase III

By the time children are well into the vocabulary spurt, they are also recognizing certain regularities in the words they have learned, and the ways in which these words are arranged sententially to convey meanings. Words are categorized into form classes (open and closed class) as well as grammatical classes (noun and verb). Often these category assignments can be bolstered by prosodic variables; for example, in English, grammatical class can often be predicted by number of syllables and stress patterns. Nouns tend to have more syllables than verbs, and bi-syllabic words with syllable-initial stress tend to be nouns more often than verbs (cf. RECord vs. recORD) (Kelly, 1992). Also during this second phase, children are beginning to comprehend multi-word sentences and the complex grammatical relations indicated by word order. This ability is only readily apparent, however, when the complex social, semantic and syntactic cues are all 'in alignment'. This redundancy of cues is necessary here to bolster what Hirsh-Pasek and Golinkoff term the child's 'fragile comprehension'.

Beginning by about 24 months, however, this heavy reliance on a coalition of cues wanes as the child's syntactic system becomes more robust. It is one of the fundamental features of a linguistic system that the meanings conveyed by sentences are often (perhaps mostly) abstract and describe past or future events, feelings, and the like. So a child who expects language to only describe those events or objects immediately present would not get very far. Instead, as children grow more aware of the complex relationships among people and objects and events in

the world, and as their representations about these relations become more sophisticated, children will need to formulate (or discover) ways of communicating these
ideas (Phase III). This is essentially a paraphrase of L. Bloom's (1993) Principle of
Elaboration, but notice here how this idea is also fundamentally consistent with
representational redescription as Karmiloff-Smith conceived the term. Notice also
that this is not, strictly speaking, a failure-driven model, although we expect that
the child is highly motivated by certain inadequacies in their current repertoire of
linguistic forms. One strong impetus for further representational refinement is the
pressure to communicate abstract propositional ideas about feelings, past events,
and the like.

How can researchers distinguish between a Phase II and a Phase III child, a child
who is using syntactic cues and not simply semantic cues to meaning? Many argue that early semantic understanding is facilitated by what MacNamara (1982)
called basic sentences, characterized by a simple agent-action-patient format
(subject-verb-object). If children understand the individual meanings of the words
involved, and further, expect these sentences will have the semantic meaning of
'who did what to whom' they will be accurate a good deal of the time. Studies
using the intermodal preferential looking paradigm demonstrate that one-word
speakers can comprehend word-order in sentences like 'She is kissing the keys' or
'Big Bird tickled Cookie Monster', but the most conservative assumption is that
the child is engaging in a semantic, rather than syntactic interpretation (see Pinker,
1984; Bowerman, 1973). One way of showing movement to syntactic understanding would be to demonstrate comprehension of sentences that could only be understood by using syntactic interpretations. One such type of sentence is the
English passive, a construction that occurs rather later in children's productions,
and which violates word-order assumptions of basic sentences. (Other, more complex syntactic analyses are provided in Hirsh-Pasek & Golinkoff, 1996, and we
refer the interested reader to this source for discussion).

The English passive violates standard subject-verb-object form by introducing
the closed-class word 'by' and the closed-class morphology '-ed' on the verb:
'Big Bird is tickling Cookie Monster' becomes 'Cookie Monster is tickled by Big
Bird.' In order for a child to correctly identify the actor and patient in this sentence, the child must essentially ignore word-order and focus on closed-class morphology as a cue to meaning. This is especially interesting in that closed-class
items are routinely dropped from young children's productions, presumably because they tend to be unstressed in speech to children (Pinker, 1984). Recent evidence suggests however that even though children omit these items from their
speech, they are nonetheless sensitive to this higher level grammatical information
in comprehension (Golinkoff, Hirsh-Pasek & Swiesguth, in press; Shipley, Smith &
Gleitman, 1969; Taylor & Gelman, 1989; see also Gerken 1996 for a review). These
data along with others help to explain why children in Phase III are able to cor-

rectly interpret passive sentences, whereas children in Phase II misinterpret them in a prototypical (albeit incorrect) agent-action-patient format.

3.6. The coalition model: Similarities and differences with other models in the emergentist perspective

In this model language comprehension is described as a move from a non-linguistic, perceptual-acoustic system to one that is semantically-driven, to one that is finally rich with syntactic understanding (see Figure 1). This model provides a clear and rigorous application of the emergentist program, in that development truly rules the day. The model is also consistent with those theories that stress boundary conditions in that children begin the process of language comprehension constrained to notice certain cues over others; cues that will lead them towards the discovery of grammatical units and relations. Indeed, the discovery of language units is nicely accounted for in this model as progressing from attention to acoustic cues (nouns are marked by high stress at the ends of sentences), to semantic cues (these acoustic units generally correspond to persons, places and things — see also the semantic bootstrapping theories of Grimshaw, 1981, Pinker, 1984), to syntactic cues for form class assignment (nouns are followed by 'the' and 'a').

As is evident above, the coalition model borrows the emergentist approach to solve the unit extraction and identification problem. Yet, this model also differs from prior emergentist models by suggesting that a coalition of information is available to the child at all times and that children mine the correlations between these systems to solve the language learning problem. That is, in the other models reviewed, an input domain like syntax would itself be an emergent property of the theory rather than an available but less heavily relied upon system of information. Evidence from our laboratory, however, suggests that children are sensitive to grammatical cues in the input at a very early age and that they can use these cues even though they do not often use these cues (see Hirsh-Pasek & Golinkoff, 1996, for a review). By way of example, children who have yet to combine their first words are nonetheless sensitive to constituent structure and to word order cues in the input. It is hard at this point in the development of the emergentist program to imagine how a theory that does not provide some a priori syntactic cues to the child could ever derive them. Thus, Hirsh-Pasek & Golinkoff suggest that some rudimentary cues to grammar must be available to children at the time when they learn language so that they can use them to bootstrap their way in to more sophisticated systems. The jury is out as to whether a truly emergentist theory will someday supplant the need for this jump start: as to whether we will eventually be able to explain both how children identify the units of grammar and learn the relationships between these units that signify mastery of the human language.

In sum then, Hirsh-Pasek and Golinkoff's coalition model provides one example, indeed one of the first examples, of how the principles of the new metatheory can be applied in explaining early language development. Using this model, they provide an empirically testable theory of how innate beginnings (boundary conditions) and emergent development (upward causation) can work in tandem to account for one significant aspect of human development.

4. The future of emergentism

In the foregoing sections, we offered the likely proposition that something of a quiet mini-revolution has taken place in the world of cognition and, in particular, in the area of language development. This revolution of thought has largely abandoned old issues of nature-nurture and initial modularity. Instead, the change afoot in the language acquisition arena seems to be the enthusiastic rendering of these old ideas in a new emergentist uniform, complete with a qualitatively different role for the social environment, the sounds of language, and perceptual biases or constraints that even neonates may possess. This mini revolution is in its inception within the field of cognitive development and it is yet to be seen how the theory will stand the test of time.

Like any new theory, emergentism will have to prove that it is not just a redescription of old ideas. It must prove itself specific enough to accommodate the old facts, and powerful enough to predict new ones. To be truly useful, the theory will also have to answer some of the stubborn and persistent properties of language acquisition; properties which have plagued so many others (like an adequate explanation of how children acquire the hierarchical units and structurally dependent relations of grammar). It will also have to be the guiding light for newer methodologies that examine variability and the weighting of cues over time. Like any new theory, emergentism — though still in its infancy — does have its critics. In this final section, we briefly raise some of the critical rumblings that can be heard throughout the field, we offer some speculations about the types of methodologies that will be required in the new perspective and close by suggesting that emergentist thinking might provide just the right sort of theoretical medicine to allow psychologists to move beyond the feudal wars and into an exciting new era of research.

4.1. Evaluating the 'New View'

Two questions dominate the criticisms that can be heard throughout the land. The first questions whether there is anything new here. The second asks whether such complex, non-linear and interactive systems can ever be falsifiable. Let's address each in turn.

4.1.1. Is there anything new here?

Some critics of the new approach have posed the question of whether there is anything new here or whether the emergentist theory is simply old wine in new bottles? Are we substituting redescription for explanation? (Bloom, 1992). There are two forms that this argument has taken. In the first form of this argument, theorists ask whether the new innatism merely displaces structural innateness with process innateness. That is, for the earlier theories in language development, language structure was thought to be inborn and the job of the child was to discover these internal rules by attending to computing the relations in the input. Today's brand of nativism puts the innate material in the boundary conditions or constraints that guide learners toward relevant information in the input — processes that ultimately serve to constrain structure through the back door. Perhaps emergentism, then has simply displaced the problem of the homunculus without solving it!

While this challenge is a serious one, the emergentist position has taken great pains to suggest that the boundary conditions being proposed are really quite different than those endorsed earlier. First, in many theories the innate processes are thought to be the product of evolution and of biological predisposition. Second, the burden of the new theories is not to ask how input triggers a pre-formed choice of internal structures, but how these predispositions work in concert with the input and task demands to allow for the development of sophisticated and tightly organized structures like language. Thus, at minimum, the emergentist theory with its connectionist proofs that complex behaviors arise jointly from a set of predispositions and simple behaviors forces us to truly 'rethink innateness'. We cannot make hand-wringing appeals to pre-existing knowledge to explain the occurrence of complex behavior in the growing individual.

A second way in which the 'is there anything new' criticism manifests itself is in the direct attack on computer modelling as an implementation of human behavior. This echoes prior debates within psychology (see for example, Rumelhart & McClelland, 1986; Fodor & Pylyshyn, 1988; Pinker & Prince, 1988; Clark &

Karmiloff-Smith, in press). While we applaud the attention to architectural and timing constraints implicit in this modelling endeavor, are we just making implementable machines? Are we saying anything meaningful about human cognition? Is it possible to move in the direction of a machine-implemented connectionist model and still remain true to the original goal of explaining human cognition? And even if we construct machinery which behaves in every reasonable way the way humans do, if it passes a Turing test of the highest magnitude, have we come any closer to understanding human behavior? Or have we simply sidestepped the issue, fortifying ourselves with a complex and elegant system that only seems to provide some insights?

Obviously, we believe this approach has merit. Ignoring for the moment the enormous practical benefits of having a thinking computer which could respond as a human, there are at least four other reasons to be encouraged by connectionist modelling: 1) Simply thinking about building such machines focuses on the right questions: how do we think; what functionally do we really do when we think; what input is needed to the thinking process; what constraints need to be built in; how specifically can this be implemented? etc.; 2) Any detailed study of complex interacting networks is bound to help us when it comes to making sense of the neurophysiological data; 3) We can test, lesion and experiment with models in ways that would be completely unethical with humans or animals. Thus even if the network is completely wrong, such studies could still suggest relevant variables; 4) It gives us a sense of starting points. If a completely unbiased network could learn grammar from scratch, then constraints theories have some problems. If it can't, then we can explore what specifically needs to be built in before the network can learn a grammar. The networks themselves, could thus be used to constrain subsequent theorizing.

4.1.2. The falsifiable question

One further criticism of the emergentist approach is that it is hard to build an *a priori* theory about development. Because so much of development now is seen as flux and variability, the proximal causes for change are often difficult to detect and empirically verify. If observation always changes the thing observed, if all data are theory laden, then we may have compounded an already difficult problem by piling up data points.

The response to this is yes, this does indeed make things much more difficult. On the other hand, no one ever said finding the truth was easy. We argue that single cause explanations, while certainly simple, are by their nature deceiving. Moreover, even if observation affects the thing observed, it is still possible to infer the processes and forces involved: even if one of them happens to be the observer.

Rather than simply to give up, the field will have to adopt new methodologies and techniques that either model the ways in which multiple inputs interact or can assess the ways in which children calibrate their learning to these inputs over time.

4.2. Methodological implications

As noted above, if the new emergentism is to be taken seriously, we will need to refine our looking glass (see also Tucker & Hirsh-Pasek, 1993; Hirsh-Pasek, Tucker & Golinkoff, 1996, for additional methodological discussion). If we are mapping domain-specific (microdomain) changes in linguistic comprehension, syntactic understanding, prosodic intuitions, and the like over time, then we must of necessity adopt a long view of the problem. This requires longitudinal research, multiple measures of behavior, and time-slices of behavior more time-constrained and context-sensitive than those most developmentalists have yet attempted.

Likewise, variability among individuals must be taken seriously. We must stop squinting our eyes when we look at on-line behavior and developmental milestones. We must no longer obscure differences by averaging our observations together. Thus, the mean behavior is no longer appropriate, because such an averaging process, while perhaps methodologically and theoretically expedient, has left us with too many holes to fill: too many 'statistical outliers' whose behavior is interesting but doesn't fit in with our established theories of language development.

Moreover, (Thelen & Smith, 1994) patterns of variability could provide critical information regarding the underlying processes and constraints. Mathematically speaking, any pattern can be seen as the result of a limited number of underlying functions. Thus, accurate specification of the types and kinds of variability, helps one know better what kinds of causes to seek. Of course, pragmatic time and cost demands prohibit this kind of research to some degree, but the tendency of cross-sectional data to exaggerate the stage-like quality of development and obscure individual variation must be acknowledged as a real problem in the interpretation of traditional developmental data.

4.3. Conclusions

In sum, we have argued that there is a much needed change afoot in cognitive psychology that is being played out in the area of cognitive development that has enormous consequences for the theory of language development. It is a change that is being seen widely in other academic disciplines from physics to biology; from economics to political science. In part, this change is the focus on change itself and the dynamics of any highly complex system. This focus manifests itself as an increasing awareness of the ways in which higher order structures can emerge from lower order interactions (upward causation), the ways higher order interactions can affect lower levels (downward causation), and a renewed focus on the kinds of boundary conditions and phase shifts that characterize any dynamic system.

As we attempted to show in this paper, the area of language development will prove a major testing ground for this new theory. Like so many areas, the field has been plagued by a series of feudal wars in which the participants tended to endorse one extreme explanation to the exclusion of others. However, as three recent theories illustrate, the newer emergentist view provides an escape from this quandary, and re-maps the path for future experimentation in such a way as to combine the best of previous theories and move beyond them. Indeed, in our own work, the coalition model allows us to adopt some of the emergentist assumptions and to test them in the highly debated arena of language development.

We are just beginning to apply these new lessons and to find out whether this hybrid approach represents more than lipservice to old theoretical persuasions, or whether this may indeed signify the start of something akin to a scientific revolution. As these ideas are applied to language development, we are cautiously hopeful. Any perspective that advocates a more rigorous empirical proving ground for complex multivariate interactions among causal components is worth exhausting. Any theory or class of theories that attempts a dialogue among polar extremists is sorely needed. And any explanation that places fundamental power on the backs of formal and final Aristotelian causality, toting complex interactions in lieu of more facile efficient narratives, is ultimately a more fruitful way to think about the problem. What remains, of course, is the messy empirical work.

References

BATES, E. 1979. *Emergence of Symbols*. New York: Academic Press.

BATES, E., BRETHERTON, I. & SNYDER, L. 1988. *From First Words to Grammar: Individual Differences and Dissociable Mechanisms*. Cambridge: Cambridge University Press.

BATES, E. & MACWHINNEY, B. 1987. Competition, variation, and language learning. In B. MacWhinney (ed.), *Mechanisms of Language Acquisition*. Hillsdale, N.J.: Erlbaum.

BATES, E. & MACWHINNEY, B. 1989. Functionalism and the competition model. In B. MacWhinney & E. Bates (eds.), *The Crosslinguistic Study of Sentence Processing*. Cambridge: Cambridge University Press.

BEST, C.T, MCROBERTS, G.W & SITHOLE, N.M. 1988. Examination of perceptual reorganization for nonnative speech contrasts: Zulu click discrimination by English-speaking adults and infants. *Journal of Experimental Psychology: Human Perception & Performance* 14: 345-60.

BICKERTON, D. 1984. The language bioprogram hypothesis. *Behavioral and Brain Sciences* 7: 173-88.

BICKHARD, M.H. 1995. Transcending False Dichotomies in Developmental Psychology — Review of *Beyond Modularity*. by A. Karmiloff-Smith. *Theory and Psychology* 5(1): 161-65.

BLOOM, L. 1993. *The Transition from Infancy to Language: Acquiring the Power of Expression*. New York: Cambridge University Press.

BLOOM, L. 1992. Commentary on Fogel, A., et al. (1992): Patterns are not enough. *Social Development* 1: 143-46.

BLOOM, P. 1990. Syntactic distinctions in child language. *Journal of Child Language* 17: 343-55.

BLOOM, P. 1994. Possible names: The role of syntax-semantics mappings in the acquisition of nominals. *Lingua* 92: 297-329.

BOHANNON, J.N. & L. STANOWITZ. 1988. The issue of negative evidence: Adult responses to children's language errors. *Developmental Psychology* 24: 684-89.

BOWERMAN, M. 1973. Structural relationships in children's early utterances: Syntactic or semantic? In T.E. Moore (ed.), *Cognitive Development and the Acquisition of Language*. New York: Academic Press.

BRAINE, M.D.S. 1976. Children's first word combinations. *Monographs of the Society for Research in Child Development* 41.

CAMPBELL, D.T. 1990. Levels of organization, downward causation, and the selection-theory approach to evolutionary epistemology. In Greenberg, G. & E. Tobach (eds.), *Theories of the Evolution of Knowing*. Hillsdale, N.J.: Erlbaum.

CAREY, S. 1978. The child as word learner. In M. Halle, J. Bresnan & G. A. Miller (eds.), *Linguistic Theory and Psychological Reality*. Cambridge, Mass.: The MIT Press.

CAREY, S. 1982. Semantic development: The state of the art. In E. Wanner & L.R. Gleitman (eds.), *Language Acquisition: The State of the Art*. New York: Cambridge University Press.

CHOMSKY, N. 1965. *Aspects of a Theory of Syntax*. Cambridge, Mass.: MIT Press.

CHOMSKY, N. 1986. *Language and Problems of Knowledge*. Cambridge, Mass.: MIT Press.

CLARK, E.V. & KARMILOFF-SMITH, A. In press. The cognizer's innards: A psychological and philosophical perspective on the development of thought. *Mind and Language*.

CURTISS, S. 1977. *'Genie': A Psycholinguistic Study of a Modern Day 'Wild Child.'* New York: Academic Press.

ELMAN, J., BATES, E., JOHNSON, M., KARMILOFF-SMITH, A., PARISI, D. & PLUNKETT, K. 1996. *Rethinking Innateness: A connectionist perspective on development*. Cambridge, Mass.: MIT Press.

FERNALD, A. 1991. Prosody in speech to children: Prelinguistic and linguistic functions. In R. Vasta, (ed.), *Annals of Child Development, Vol. 8*. London: Jessica Kingsley Publishers.

FODOR, J. 1983. *The Modularity of Mind*. Cambridge, Mass.: MIT Press.

FODOR, J. & PYLYSHYN, Z. 1988. Connectionism and cognitive architecture: A critical analysis. In S. Pinker & J. Mehler (eds.), *Connections and symbols*. Cambridge, Mass.: MIT Press, 3-72.

GERKEN, L. 1996. Phonological and distributional information in syntax acquisition. In Morgan, J. L & Demuth, K. (eds.), *Signal to Syntax: Bootstrapping from Speech to Grammar in Early Acquisition*. Mahwah, N.J.: Erlbaum.

GLEICK, J. 1987. *Chaos: Making a new Science.* New York: Viking.

GLEITMAN, L.R. & WANNER, E. 1982. Language acquisition: the state of the state of the art. In E. Wanner & L. R. Gleitman (eds.), *Language acquisition: The State of the Art.* Cambridge, Mass.: Cambridge University Press.

GLEITMAN, L.R. 1981. Maturational determinants of language growth. *Cognition* 10: 103-14.

GOLD, E.M. 1967. Language identification in the limit. *Information and Control* 16, 447-74.

GOLDIN-MEADOWS, S. & MYLANDER, C. 1984. Gestural communication in deaf children: The effects and non-effects of parental input on early language development. *Monographs of the Society for Research in Child Development* 49: 1-121.

GOLINKOFF, R.M., HIRSH-PASEK, K. & SCHWEISGUTH, M.A. In press. A reappraisal of young children's knowledge of grammatical morphemes. In J. Weissenborn & B. Hoehle (eds.), *Approaches to Bootstrapping: Phonological Syntactic, and Neuropsychological Aspects of Early Language Acquisition.*

GOLINKOFF, R.M., MERVIS, C. & HIRSH-PASEK, K. 1994. Early object labels: The case for a developmental lexical principles framework. *Journal of Child Language* 21: 125-55.

GREENFIELD, P.M. 1991. Language, tools and brain: The ontogeny and phylogeny of hierarchically organized sequential behavior. *Behavioral & Brain Sciences* 14: 531-95.

GRIMSHAW, J. 1981. Form, function, and the language acquisition device. In Baker, C. L. & McCarthy, J. J (eds.), *The Logical Problem of Language Acquisition.* Cambridge, Mass.: Cambridge University Press.

HIRSH-PASEK, K. & GOLINKOFF, R.M. 1996. *The Origins of Grammar: Evidence from Early Language Comprehension.* Cambridge, Mass.: MIT Press.

HIRSH-PASEK, K., KEMLER NELSON, D.G., JUSCZYK, P. W., WRIGHT, K., DRUSS, B. & KENNEDY, L.J. 1987. Clauses are perceptual units for young infants. *Cognition* 26: 269-86.

HIRSH-PASEK, K., TUCKER, M.L. & GOLINKOFF, R.M. 1995. Dynamical systems: Reinterpreting prosodic bootstrapping. In J. L. Morgan & K. Demuth (eds.), *Signal to Syntax: Bootstrapping from Speech to Grammar in Early Acquisition.* Hillsdale, N.J.: Erlbaum.

HOLLICH, G., HIRSH-PASEK, K. & GOLINKOFF, R.M. In press. Introducing the 3-D Intermodal Preferential Looking Paradigm: A new method to answer an age-old question. In *Advances in Infancy Research* 13.

HOROWITZ, F.D. (ed.) 1974. Visual attention, auditory stimulation, and language discrimination in young infants. *Monographs of the Society for Research in Child Development* 158.

JOHNSON, J.S. & NEWPORT, E.L. 1991. Critical period effects on universal properties of language: The status of subjacency in the acquisition of a second language. *Cognition* 39: 215-58.

JONES, S. & SMITH, L.B. 1993. The place of perception in children's concepts. *Cognitive Development* 8: 113-40.

JUSCZYK, P.W., HIRSH-PASEK, K., KEMLER NELSON, D.G., KENNEDY, K., WOODWARD, A. & PIWOZ, J. 1992. Perception of acoustic correlates of major phrasal boundaries by young infants. *Cognitive Psychology* 24: 252-93.

JUSCZYK, P.W & BERTONCINI, J. 1988. Viewing the development of speech perception as an innately guided learning process. *Language & Speech* 31: 217-38.

JUSCZYK, P.W. 1997. *The Discovery of Spoken Language*. Cambridge: MIT Press.

KARMILOFF-SMITH, A. 1992. *Beyond Modularity*. Cambridge, Mass.: MIT Press.

Kelly, M. 1992. Using sound to solve syntactic problems. *Psychological Review* 99: 349-64.

LENNEBERG, E.H. 1967. *Biological Foundations of Language*. New York: John Wiley & Sons.

MACNAMARA, J. 1982. *Names for Things*. Cambridge, Mass.: MIT Press.

MANDLER, J.M. 1988. How to build a baby: On the development of an accessible representational system. *Cognitive Development* 3: 113-36.

MANDLER, J.M. 1992. How to build a baby: II. Conceptual primitives. *Psychological Review* 99: 587-604.

MANDLER, J.M. & BAUER, P.J. 1988. The cradle of categorization: Is the basic level basic? *Cognitive Development* 3: 339-54.

MCCLELLAND, J., RUMELHART, D.E. & HINTON, G.E. 1986. The appeal of parallel distributed processing. In D. E. Rumelhart, J. L. McClelland & T. P. R. Group (eds.), *Parallel Distributed Processing: Explorations in the Microstructure of Cognition. Vol. 1: Foundations*. Cambridge, Mass.: MIT Press.

NAIGLES, L. 1990. Children use syntax to learn verb meanings. *Journal of Child Language* 17: 357-74.

NELSON, K. 1974. Concept, word, and sentence: Interrelations in acquisition and development. *Psychological Review* 81: 267-85.

NELSON, K. 1985. *Making Sense: The Acquisition of Shared Meaning*. Orlando, FL: Academic Press.

NELSON, K. 1988. Constraints on word learning. *Cognitive Development* 3: 221-46.

NELSON, K. 1996. *Language in Cognitive Development: The Emergence of the Mediated Mind*. Cambridge, Mass.: 1996.

OVERTON, W.F. 1991. The structure of developmental theory. In H. W. Reese (ed.), *Advances in Child Development and Behavior*, San Diego, Cal.: Academic Press, 1-37.

OYAMA, N. 1985. *The Ontogeny of Information: Developmental Systems and Evolution*. Cambridge, Mass.: Cambridge University Press.

PETERS, A. 1983. *The Units of Language Acquisition*. Cambridge, Mass.: Cambridge University Press.

PIAGET, J. 1952. *The Origins of Intelligence in Children*. International University Press.

PIAGET, J. 1955. *The Child's Construction of Reality*. London: Routledge & Kegan Paul.

PINKER, S. 1989. *Learnability and Cognition: The Acquisition of Argument Structure*. Cambridge, Mass.: MIT Press.

PINKER, S. 1994. *The Language Instinct: How the Mind Creates Language*. New York: William Morrow & Co.

PINKER, S. & PRINCE, A. 1988. On language and connectionism: Analysis of a parallel distributed processing model of language acquisition. Special Issue: Connectionism and symbol systems. *Cognition* 28: 73-193.

PINKER, S. 1984. *Language Learnability and Language Development*. Cambridge, Mass.: Harvard University Press.

RUMELHART, D.E. & MCCLELLAND, J.L. 1986. *Parallel Distributed Processing: Explorations in the Microstructure of Cognition*, vol. 1. MIT Press.

SAFFRAN, J.R., ASLIN, R.N. & NEWPORT, E.L. 1996. Statistical learning by 8-Month-Old Infants. *Science* 274: 1926-28.

SAFFRAN, J.R; NEWPORT, E.L & ASLIN, R.N. 1996. Word segmentation: The role of distributional cues. *Journal of Memory & Language* 35: 606-21.

SCHLESINGER, I. 1982. *Steps to Language: Toward a Theory of Native Language Acquisition.* Hillsdale, N.J.: Erlbaum.

SHIPLEY, E.F., SMITH, C.S. & GLEITMAN, L.R. 1969. A study in the acquisition of language: Free responses to commands. *Language* 45: 322-42.

SLOBIN, D.I. 1982. Universals and particulars in the acquisition of language. In E. Wanner & L. R. Gleitman (ed.), *Language Acquisition: The State of the Art.* Cambridge, Mass.: Cambridge University Press, 128-170.

SLOBIN, D.I. (ed.) 1985. *The Cross-linguistic Study of Language acquisition.* Hillsdale, N.J.: Erlbaum.

SMITH, L.B. & THELEN, E. 1993. *A Dynamics Approach to Development: Applications.* Cambridge, Mass.: The MIT Press.

SNOW, C.E. 1986. Conversations with children. In P. Fletcher & M. Garman, (eds.), *Language Acquisition.* Cambridge: Cambridge University Press.

TAYLOR, M. & GELMAN, S.A. 1989. Incorporating new words into the lexicon: Preliminary evidence for language hierarchies in two-year-old children. *Child Development* 60: 625-36.

THELEN, E. 1989. Self organization in developmental processes: Can systems approaches work? In M. Gunnard & E. Thelen (eds.), *Systems and development.* The Minnesota Symposium in Child Psychology, vol. 22.

THELEN, E. & SMITH, L. 1994. *A Dynamic Systems Approach to the Development of Cognition and Action.* Cambridge, Mass.: MIT Press.

TOMASELLO, M. 1986. Joint attention and early language. *Child Development* 57: 1454-63.

TOMASELLO, M. & KRUGER, A. C. 1992. Joint attention on actions: Acquiring words in ostensive and non-ostensive contexts. *Journal of Child Language* 19: 313-33.

TUCKER, M. & HIRSH-PASEK, K. 1993. Systems and language: Implications for acquisition. In L. Smith & E. Thelen (eds.), *A Dynamic Systems Approach to Development: Applications.* Cambridge, Mass.: MIT Press, 359-84.

WERKER, J.F. & TEES, R.C. 1984. Cross-language speech perception: Evidence for perceptual reorganization during the first year of life. *Infant Behavior and Development* 7: 49-63.

Part IV

Social and Communicative Systems

9

Material Sign Processes and Emergent Ecosocial Organization

J.L. LEMKE

Downward causation and the levels paradigm

Complex, self-organizing systems have traditionally been analyzed in terms of a hierarchy of organizational scales or levels. The phenomenon of 'downward causation' can be interpreted as the quasi-effect of higher-level emergent patterning on the dynamics of the lower-level constituents of a self-organizing system. But the significance of such an analysis depends on the assumption that the dynamical processes which constitute the system each operate at a single characteristic scale of space and time. I will call this the assumption of *scale homogeneity*, and I want to question its application to social, and more generally to social-ecological systems. I will propose that when relations of meaning as well as of material interaction co-determine the dynamics of a system, we must take into account *scale heterogeneity* or scale-mixing as well. If system processes at very different scales are tightly coupled with one another, we may need new paradigms for system analysis and a somewhat different interpretation of the meaning and significance of 'downward causation'.

I want first to summarize the hierarchical or 'levels' description of complex self-organizing systems which emerged in slightly different forms over several years' discussion between Stan Salthe and myself (cf. Lemke, 1984; 1995a, esp. chap. 2, 6, and the Postscript which updates Lemke, 1984). I will then consider the role of semiosis and human-scale, human-interest viewpoints in our description of systems at all levels. To provide an example, I will focus on the process of composition of a written text, and try to explicate the multiple relevant dynamical scales and the problem of modelling them in an integrated and comprehensible account which includes various forms of 'downward causation'. Finally, I will propose some alternative models and metaphors for describing complex social-semiotic ecologies.

Many classes of self-organizing systems can be construed as hierarchical (in the sense of Salthe, 1985, 1989, 1993), where the properties of constituents provide the conditions of possibility for the emergence of higher-level organization, and higher-level patterns represent the net constraints on constituent dynamics from the interactions of all constituents in a highly-coupled system. A radical alternative to the 'levels' approach, recently proposed by Latour (1993, 1996a, 1996b), considerably opens up the discussion, and I would like to sketch out the terms for a helpful synthesis of the two positions.

To anticipate briefly, Latour proposes that traditional systems theory has too narrowly assumed that each descriptive level must maintain a homogeneous dynamical (especially temporal-spatial) scale: that all interactions constituting the same 'level' or 'subsystem' have the same characteristic scale. He notes that many empirical investigations of human social systems, on the contrary, seem to suggest that scale-*heterogeneity* is the norm, and that isolating each scale on its own level makes the problem of integrating levels across scales artificially difficult. I believe that his notion of scale-heterogeneity addresses exactly the same issue as 'downward causation' but in a very different conceptual framework. In brief, I believe that his approach is more natural (but not always necessary) for systems significantly structured by the role of human semiosis and its material artifacts, whereas the 'levels' approach is more natural to elementary physical and chemical systems where scale-homogeneity is a better approximation. Organismic and ecological bio-systems fall somewhere in between, but all complex self-organizing systems which show emergent forms of order are ones for which adequate accounts must involve processes on significantly different dynamical scales. I would like to sketch our available options for performing this feat of analysis.

There is one further important point we must bear in mind in this inquiry. Emergent patterns of organization are identifiable only by privileging certain global system variables over others which *a priori* might equally well be used to describe the system (cf. Hasegawa, 1985). We construct variables which are relevant for our human purposes according to the cultural meaning formations in relation to which certain forms of patterning or order are salient for us. An analysis of the emergence of order in a complex system must always include the observers and their cultural criteria of meaningful patternedness as part of the system to be accounted for (cf. Bohr, 1934/61, 1958; and chapters by Finnemann, Voetmann, and Pattee in this volume). We therefore need a theory of self-organization in 'ecosocial systems' (Lemke, 1994, 1995a), in which both material-interaction couplings and meaning-mediated interdependencies in the action of (human, and so also nonhuman) constituents are taken into account. The dynamics and development of ecosystems which contain humans who act according to cultural meaning criteria cannot be adequately described without a description of the meaning-systems in use and how they bias matter and energy flows in ways not predictable from regularities described solely in thermodynamic or biological terms.

These considerations will lead us specifically to the role of semiotic practices as material processes in a complex self-organizing social-ecological system, and, anticipating again, to an account of how typological-categorial distinctions, and the artifacts that mediate them, add new emergent properties to bio-thermodynamic systems which otherwise depend solely on quantitative or 'topologically' varying parameters. This account will be seen to fit very well with Latour's emphasis on the role of symbolic artifacts in the organization of human social interactions across dynamical scales. (For other examples of the complementarity of semiotic and material causation accounts, see Finnemann on artifacts and Pattee on DNA-mediated evolution in this volume.)

Hierarchical organization and emergent order

Let's begin with the 'hierarchical levels' account of self-organization, emergence, and downward causation. Very simply, every level of patterning or order in a complex system is seen as being characterized by units of analysis and their characteristic mutual interaction processes, each with characteristic spatial and temporal scales (within, say, the same order of magnitude) deriving from their dynamics. Taking one such level, L, as 'focal' or 'in focus' for analysis (the focus of our human concern, note for future reference), hierarchy theory proposes that two other levels are also relevant. One is the level immediately 'below' (smaller spatial, shorter dynamical time scales), L-1, where constituents of the units at level L interact with one another to produce these higher-level units. The properties of the L-1 units and their interactions provide the basis for the set of possibilities that may emerge at level L. Units at level L *are* self-organizing patterns of order on a larger spatial and longer time scale than what matters at level L-1. The classic examples are elementary particles interacting to form atoms, atoms to form molecules, molecules to form more complex structures ... on up through various higher levels of organization to cells, tissues, organs and organ systems, organisms, populations and ecosystems. This view presents the classic account of 'upward causation' and is the basis of the so-called 'reductionist program' in natural science: accounting for phenomena at any level by analyzing constituents and their interactions at lower levels.

Nonetheless, however neatly the 'upward causation' model fits with the general political and ideological program of modern Euro-cultural societies (i.e. individuals as more fundamental than communities), we all know that our individual behavior is still profoundly shaped, controlled, or limited in various ways by our interactions with other organisms on our own scale, and since each of these others is also similarly affected, we sum up our net mutual constraints by reference to larger-scale entities like the family, the community, the environment, society, culture, etc. In our scientific models of ecosystems we see again and again that the behavior of organisms and populations, however apparently free and independent when viewed at its own scale, nevertheless collectively repeats the same larger-scale ecological patterns and cycles.

Any entity's L-1 constituents allow it a certain range of possible behavior — but most often we do not exercise this potential in a vacuum. We adapt to those other L-scale entities which impinge upon us, and they to still others, in ramifying chains of reaction that bind us together as communities, ecosystems, societies, cultures. As we all strive to adapt to one another, only some self-consistent collective patterns are possible for the whole swarm. They are the patterns of emergent order and organization at level L+1, and their effects on us are just as real and material as those rising 'upwards' within us from level L-1. The constraints of mutual interaction at level L, which are summarizable as the emergent patterns of level L+1, produce, when spoken of in the pervasive linguistic metaphors of agency (cf. Pattee, this volume), 'downward causation' effects on us at level L.

While our intuitions of such matters may be sharper for our own human scale, our scientific accounts of even the most elementary dynamical systems with multiple scales (thermodynamic systems, with a micro-scale and a macro-scale) now recognize that the collective order of molar scales (entropy) emerges from *correlations* that accumulate over time from even the random collisional dynamics of the molecular scale (Prigogine, 1980; Prigogine & Stengers, 1984). If I am being jostled closely in a large dense crowd, I can, intrinsically, move in any direction I choose, but if others around me are tending to move in one direction, then I am more likely to be pushed from behind than from this emerging common direction, and I am more likely to encounter an open space to move into in that same relative direction — and so is everyone else. Locally we self-organize into a micro-convection current, or align ourselves in a local 'magnetic' domain. There may be, in randomly buffeted molecules, an equal probability for reversing any particular motion in isolation, but in the crowd we are not in isolation and the net emergent dynamics of the whole is irreversible and, locally at least, negentropic. Order forms because there are only relatively few solutions to the problem of correlated motions, and when contrasted with an ideal of randomness in which all possible states of motion are equally likely, those few solutions stand out as 'orderly'.

This 'levels' model is very elegant, and when combined with the mathematical formalisms of statistical mechanics, renormalization theory, or nonlinear dynamical analysis it enables us to account for the production of order from chaos, the amplification of signals over many dynamical scales, and the emergent attractors of the dynamics of complex systems as descriptions of pattern at higher levels. In most of the cases where such models are applied in physics, chemistry, and biology the assumptions of scale-homogeneity and clearly separable levels are well justified (see Voetmann, this volume). An excellent test of this is the observation by Salthe (1985: 136 seq.) that phenomena characteristic of level L are relatively independent of the detailed dynamics of levels L-2 and below. Phenomena at level L are constituted by interactions of units at level L-1, but the very existence of these units as emergent patternings at level L-1 means that they are already collective 'averages' over the individual behavior of their own constituent units at level L-2. The L-1 units 'filter' at the same time that they organize 'noise' from level L-2, and they thereby 'buffer' level L from noise at level L-2. This is, I believe the correct interpretation of claims such as those of Varela and Maturana that self-organizing systems are 'autonomous'. Systems at level L cannot be autonomous in the sense of insensitive to L-1 or L+1, for they are defined precisely by their *selective sensitivity* (filtering) to these levels. But they are relatively autonomous to noise or detailed phenomena at levels L-2 and L+2 — *unless* levels L-1 and L+1 for some reason do not perform the filtering of which they are capable (see examples in Salthe, 1984: 142-3).

All this neat layering depends on scale homogeneity and relative order-of-magnitude differences in scale from level to level. Obviously effects from L-2 are already second-order negligible on the scale of level L, as well as buffered by the selective sensitivity and collective homeostasis that are constitutive of the intermediate level L-1. But 'downward causation' effects are not limited to systems for which these assumptions hold strictly.

Beyond levels: Homogeneity vs heterogeneity of scale

Most of my human behavior, particularly what we might call my socially meaningful behavior, however much it may originate endogenously in any particular moment, and however much it may be directed to immediate interactions with present surroundings, nevertheless manages to also be quite typical and characteristic of members of my community and my period of history, and of my gender, my age-group, my social class and many subcultures to which I in some sense 'belong'. Even if we grant that dialects, social norms, epochal and community or class 'cultures' are to some extent artificial intellectual constructs produced by recording and comparing many particular momentary behaviors, nonetheless the kinds of abstract similarities and contrasts construed in these ways seem absolutely essential to any adequate account of social interaction or social organization (cf. Lemke, 1995a: chap. 2). When I speak or act in any way, not only my internal constituency and my present surroundings, but my biographical history as a member of many communities or social networks plays a part. More than this, the tools with which and through which I so often act, whether developed as part of my

own body (neural nets and maps, muscular habits and skills, immune responses —
none present at birth and all specific to my individual history) or as prostheses
produced by others and typical of my community (eyeglasses, hearing aids, cloth-
ing, pens and pads), or as something inextricably both (dialects, depictional styles)
ensure that the history of my community, and the history of the tools themselves,
are also essential for accounts of the full ecological and semiotic signficance of my
moment-to-moment actions.

I write a short note to someone in my household and attach it with a small magnet to the door of the refrigerator in our kitchen. In the analysis of the prove-
nience, consequences, and meanings of such a culturally typical activity it is not so
easy to cleanly separate different spatial-temporal dynamical scales. There is the
basic human reference scale for action, on the order of seconds to minutes of performance of what counts as more or less a single coherent action or activity. Such
performances typically span spatial scales of the order of the size of the human
body, from millimeters of movement in the writing of the letters to perhaps meters
of movement in attaching the paper to the fridge. Even in this there are perhaps
three or four orders of magnitude in spatial scale and perhaps three in time. But
that is nothing. The words I write may refer to recent past or future events on the
order of a day or more distant from the moment of writing. The meanings of those
words for me and the person I write for may well have critical dependencies on
events earlier by months or years in the history of our personal relationship (a pet-
name, for example). And of course the most common meanings of the words were
learned by us probably in childhood, and their grammatical and semantic patterns
and relationships will have histories of the order of centuries. Shifting to a spatial-
extensional view of scale, personal history and community history insofar as it is
relevant to the usage of words involves social networks of from several or a few
dozen to tens or hundreds of thousands of people.

But even this is only the tip of the iceberg of spatial-temporal complexity of in-
terpenetrating scales. What of the pencil and the paper without which I could not
perform this culturally typical action? They too have a history, and that history
implies several more scales of dynamical complexity in the social-ecological system
in which my action is performable and meaningful. Where did I get them? Who
made them? How and from what materials, obtained where and when? How did I
learn how to use them? where and when, as part of what eco-social subsystem of
cultural practices and material processes? And on what scales do they have their
origins and take their present forms in relation to the specific functions they play
in my present action? If we say that they are like my own muscular habits and
neural memory, substrates for action at the organism level, then we need the characteristic scales of their dynamical processes to be small and fast compared to my
human action scale. But they are not; some of the relevant scales exceed the human momentary-action scale. And so also for the magnet, and the refrigerator, and

the architectural conventions that define kitchens and their functions and contents, and the cultural habits that make it likely that a note placed there will be seen fairly soon by its intended reader. The scale of my partner's daily life routines is also somehow implied in my activity of putting a note on the fridge.

Why is this not also a problem for the hierarchical scaling of biological systems? Perhaps it is. Sometimes the long-term developmental history of particular cells may equal or exceed the typical organismic scale, but this is unusual. For tissue structures and organ systems perhaps it is not so unusual. But the functions of these constituents of the organism as a whole do not depend on their *meaning*. Their significance for the organism is exhausted by their organic functioning. Insofar as their history matters at all, that history is embodied in structural form and operational behavior at the present moment. This is quite unlike the significance that attaches to the history of a word or a visual image, or even a tool. In the days before our present culture of radical commodification, the history of ownership of a famous sword, say, had very definite implications for when and how it would be used as a tool or as a symbol — implications that could not be derived from properties found anywhere in the object itself, but which were emergent properties that existed for that sword only in the context of a much larger human community with a social history and a social memory.

Scale-heterogeneity based on embodied memory and interpretive history is definitely not a problem for elementary dynamical systems where interchangeability and the absence of non-dynamical properties or degrees of freedom ensure that there is no individuality to which a history can attach. All electrons are exactly the same; no particular one can be labelled or its history accumulated over time-scales large compared to the interactions in which it participates (cf. discussion in Lemke, 1994, 1995a: chap. 6). But as elementary units on any scale interact with many others so that collective properties emerge, we rapidly reach levels of complexity of compound units for which there can be individual identity, memory, and history — if not yet semiotic significance (see below, and Lemke, 1994, 1995a).

The segregation of distinct temporal and spatial scales of characteristic dynamical processes is a small problem until we reach the threshold of meaning. Once meaning plays a role in material processes, once what humans do in the ecosystem depends on stories and histories, once meaning-categories influence the design of material artifacts which in turn amplify meaning's human-mediated effects on matter, then maximally different scales intersect. If we follow the connections of social practices through links attaching to both the people and the artifacts involved in them, just far enough to account for what happened here and now in terms of both material consequence and semiotic significance, then we will find that social-cultural and material-ecological processes of the widest range of scales are encountered without any clear passage from one scale-homogeneous level to another.

This point has been forcefully made by Bruno Latour in his critiques of macro-social systems theories and his interpretations of empirical studies of the role of artifacts and technologies in human cultural activity (see especially Latour, 1987, 1993, 1996a, 1996b; and studies in Lynch & Woolgar, 1990; Law 1991; Hutchins 1995; and Goodwin 1995). Latour has long argued for a heterogeneity of 'actants' (a term originally from Greimas' semiotics, cf. Greimas & Courtes, 1982) in the analysis of social practices, by which he means a more symmetrical treatment of the roles of material artifacts and human actors, a redefinition of 'agency' away from a paradigm of independently acting agents and towards a model in which all action occurs within systems or networks of human actors and their tools, artifacts, and technologies. But recently he has emphasized that the application of his theory in empirical studies consistently argues for a 'flat' rather than a 'levels' model (Latour, 1996a, 1996b), and the core of his reasoning seems to be that the actant-networks in these studies typically have connections of and between social processes with very heterogeneous spatial and especially temporal scales.

In its current form Latour's argument is essentially that human cultural artifacts and technologies are a way of 'black-boxing' their own origins and histories, so that they can function as if they were units on a smaller scale of spatial extension and temporal process than they truly are. This is another way of saying what I have argued above: that larger-scale processes over more extensive communities and their longer-term histories are always directly implicated in semiotic artifacts, and that this fundamentally changes the scale relations for ecological-semiotic systems as opposed to more purely thermodynamic ones.

I want to argue here that both the 'levels' view and the 'scale heterogeneity' view are important tools for conceptualizing downward causation, i.e. for accounting for how larger-scale, longer-term dynamical processes become relevant for smaller-scale, shorter-term ones. Indeed I believe that a synthesis of 'levels' analysis and 'heterogeneous scale' analysis of complex systems is even more important than a reconciliation of the paradigms of 'upward' and 'downward' causation.

Salthe (1985, 1993) has made some interesting efforts to reformulate Aristotle's classic 'four causes' to fit the 'upward and downward' causation paradigm of his hierarchical levels model of complex biological systems, and he has commented there as well about the limitations of the reductionist paradigm. I would like to close this section by noting a different but related view of the reductionist program, from within a 'levels' perspective.

How is it possible in principle for a component at level L-1 of a system at level L (or spanning a number of levels) to model the levels above it? How can human organisms model the higher levels (ecosystems, cities, societies) whose downward causal influence we feel? How has it come about that we appear to be adapted by evolution to do just this?

That some modelling of higher levels is adaptive can be seen again by scale considerations. An organism has a limited capacity to sample its environment, limited in scale of spatial extension and limited in time-scales. In any given interaction on the normal human scale we sample the environment over a period of seconds or minutes (before moving on to another interaction, perhaps in a different locale) and in a volume of a few cubic meters, or perhaps on somewhat larger spatial scales if we count distance vision and auditory input as interaction. But the ecosystem to which we belong, and which matters to our survival and the survival of our progeny, extends over much larger spaces and may have on-going processes on much slower time scales which require sampling over much longer time periods to assess. Our first asset in the struggle to know the opportunities and dangers of our habitat is memory: our bodies dynamically recreate past sampling interactions and (at least with, and perhaps even without semiotic mediation) can overlay these on top of present interactional circumstances so that we can 'see with hindsight' and act with foresight or planning. We cumulate our sampling over space and time, we comparatively register invariances and divergences.

Our second asset is communication. With symbolic resources comes the possibility of collective memory and pooling our samplings of the environment over much wider times and spaces. When the troupe travels together this effect is somewhat minimized in space but augmented in time as informational patterns are passed across age-cohorts and generations. When some members typically wander far afield and return, or when troupes exchange information, spatial extension also grows.

The key lesson here is that our means of modelling higher levels are fundamentally social and collective, and our models are built with group means (languages, vocal or gestural) and by collective actions (comparing and accumulating records and accounts). The role of writing in this activity (cf. Olson, 1994, and see Lemke, 1995b) and in the construction of other sorts of stable visual artifacts (e.g., navigational charts, scientific data archives, cf. Latour, 1987, 1990) has often been noted. Individuals do not construct detailed maps of a continent, nor could we do so without artifacts-as-records (cf. Latour's 'immutable mobiles').

In all this, we have adopted the habit of constructing the properties of wholes from samplings of their parts. Confined to the human scale in our specific interactions with the here-and-now, but benefitting from overlaying these with models of the there-and-then, we have had to learn to make sense of higher levels by piecing them together 'from below'. When this same adaptive strategy was turned to the analysis of levels below us (anatomical studies, mechanical and chemical theories) we found first that we were well-served by our technologies (our machines, built by assembling pieces into wholes), and then that we had to sample still lower levels, where changes happened too quickly for our eyes and where units were many. But we still thought in terms of aggregation and piecing together, we sampled and constructed always 'as if from below', our ancient phylogenetic trick, for which our symbolic systems of communication and representation were themselves long adapted. We were, not very surprisingly, most successful as reductionists.

But in order to make the reductionist program work it was essential that we leave *ourselves* out of the picture. For once we see our representations of the levels below as actually models of our human-scale relationships *to* phenomena at those levels, then the neat homogeneity of scale that defines the separability of levels is broken. This paradox was of course at the heart of the great philosophical debates over quantum theory: if the data only existed because of the measuring apparatus, and so as part of the human-scale (and larger cultural-scale) experimental program, then events on our scale somehow were critical for events on the atomic scale, and vice versa (cf. the infamous lives and deaths of Schroedinger's cat). Niels Bohr's 'complementarity principle' was born from a rethinking of the reductionist program that admitted extreme heterogeneities of scale, mediated by human artifacts and technologies, in the measurement interaction itself (Bohr, 1934, 1958).

Bohr was the first to recognize that the new quantum theory presented us with a view of experience in which different interactional arrangements resulted in complementary perspectives that need not be logically consistent, compatible, or commensurable, and in many critical cases *could* not be so. The reductionist trick was predicated on the assumption that the different 'pieces' or views from different perspectives could always somehow be neatly fitted together. But we now know that material processes cannot be comprehended, cannot be exhaustively described within any one single self-consistent formal discourse. They always overflow the limited possibilities of our semiotic models of them. It is only by building more and more semiotic-discursive models, each internally self-consistent, but not limited by requirements of mutual consistency with each other, that we can, by adding together such 'complementary' views, attain to the most complete possible account of material phenomena, including semiosis itself. Thus we still come back to a version of 'assemblage' but hopefully a more sophisticated one, one that takes into account our own role and perspective as observers, as well as the material means by which we observe, compare, and assemble — the material mediation of our semiotic practices.

The inclusion of the observers and our technologies, and the viewpoints we embody, in the analysis of the dynamics of systems across many scales (from apparatus to electron) are also discussed in Voetmann (this volume) and in some ways extended by Bickhard (this volume) to the later field-theoretic models in physics, which are again inherently non-local — that is, they do not necessarily respect scale: events remote in space and time become interdependent, even without any energy passing between them to communicate information. Kruse (this volume) provides us with fascinating accounts of the historical and contemporary forms of material 'holism', an alternative to reductionism which assumes that the same sorts of patterns will be mirrored on all scales and that there is a material unity of the universe that transcends divisions into scale-homogeneous levels of analysis.

Materiality of sign processes and scale heterogeneity

So we are now building up a picture of material artifacts and the artifact-like (i.e. embodying culturally learned patterns) properties of our own bodies as accumulators of information sampled on larger-than-human, greater-than-here-and-now time scales, from those of the family and extended communities to those of personal biographical trajectories and wider social history. The importance of these artifacts lies foremost in their mediation of the role of meaning in human actions, actions which are always also material processes entrained in the larger dynamics of eco-logical-social systems. In ecosystems-with-humans, *meaning* matters to material dynamics because humans act in terms of semiotic categorizations and evaluations as well as in direct biological and thermodynamic response to their material environments.

Meanings are collective phenomena; their impact on the material ecosystem is large exactly to the extent that the same categorizations and evaluations are relevant to the behavior of many individual human agents. And meanings are shared to the extent of, and because of, common past history of interactions. At the level of the individual organism this is the phenomenon of social and cultural learning, but at the level of the community it is an emergent phenomenon, one of the small number of possible solutions to the self-consistency problem of myriad cross-coupled interactions among humans, mediated by signs and artifacts, and between humans and all material Nature. The common meanings of words, the common structures of language, the shared ideologies and genres of communication and social activity generally — all of these emerge as characteristics of communities or subcommunities, and all of them change on time-scales long compared to cogent human moments, or even lifetimes, and as part of larger-scale ecosocial processes.

Linked through the role of meaning in the material dynamics of ecosocial systems, human organisms and natural or artifactual objects are the irreducible participants in the local dynamics of interaction. But the characteristic scales of the dynamical processes which engender them, determine how they participate in various interactions, and control how they change, develop, or evolve, are often very different for organisms and for artifacts. If we construct our models of ecosocial systems by following the chain of linkages — which agents and objects are essential here and now, which processes put them here, now, and in a form suitable for the interaction, what other agents and objects were in turn involved as essential participants in those processes, ... and so on in indefinite regression — then our models will be 'flat' with no distinct levels, they will be like complex intersecting networks of interactional processes with all the auto-catalytic and cross-catalytic feedback which engenders non-linear self-organization, and they will be heterogeneous in dynamical scale in the specific sense that the processes so linked will be constitutive of and constituted by systems with widely different characteristic spatial extensions and time-scales.

This view foregrounds the new feature of complex systems with semiotic as well as biological and thermodynamic processes: tight linkage across scales. But it will not serve our human purposes if it is our only model. If there are no intermediate levels of organization and order between the total ecosocial network and the human scale of organisms, artifacts, and activities, we will be at a loss to usefully model the many kinds of order that we do indeed find in language, culture, social structure, ideology, historical change, etc., or to account for these larger-scale patternings in the mutual interactions of myriad constituents at the human scale. I believe that we are adapted for survival as a species-in-an-ecosystem partly by our ability to piece together collective pictures of systems larger than our own scale of moment-to-moment living. The 'flat' models of scale heterogeneity, however, do provide for one key notion of intermediate organization: artifacts themselves.

Latour conceives of artifacts in part as 'black boxes', as material condensations of the histories and processes that gave rise to them and determine their functional potential, but at the same time as units of interaction at the human scale for which it is normally possible to ignore what is boxed up 'inside' them. If we generalize, as Latour himself usually does, from artifacts to technologies, conceived as practices in which these artifacts play a part (as tool, as product, as raw material), then we can regard artifacts as points of possible connection, points of possible relevance of the there-and-then to the here-and-now. From the viewpoint of the global actor-object-network, the dependency is very real. From the viewpoint of the human actor, the key question is whether the meaning of the object does or does not go beyond its form and function in the present circumstances. If we use the object without regard for its history and origins, i.e. for the larger systems and time scales its existence implies, then it remains a black box, an unanalyzed instrumentality. But we *can* always open this black box, or try to, and we do so typically when it fails to function in the expected manner as an instrumentality for here and now, or when we wish to challenge its suitability or value, or when we wish to change it for new purposes, and so on. Then our interactions with it and through it will begin to depend quite critically on larger-scale processes in which it, and now we, participate.

In this sense artifacts are the very material reality of 'downward causation' in social processes: not only the means through which larger scales of dynamical organization impinge on each moment, but also the means by which, in the production of artifacts, we both produce and model these larger scales. Latour (1987, 1990) notes, for example, that we produce artifacts such as data archives and maps as the tools by which we sum up over many sampling interactions with the environment at the human scale, and so build up more global models. At the same time, in using them, we become able to carry out different kinds of material human practices (mid-ocean navigation, global trade) that in turn alter the world on larger-than-human (as well as human) scales.

But if we also maintain the 'levels' perspective we will suspect that artifacts can hardly be unique in this respect, though they may represent an especially salient case. It is not at all clear, for example, whether language as an abstract structure, or even the sets of systematic relations in how people use language, are artifacts in the same sense as material tools or objects, but certainly they have all the same functional properties which Latour requires. Nor is it likely that one needs technological artifacts as such, since natural environmental objects can also function semiotically in addition to their biological and thermodynamic functions. Indeed the human body itself can function in this way (perhaps even pre-semiotically) insofar as it carries within itself its own history of previous interactions (cf. Bourdieu's, 1990 notion of *habitus* as embodied dispositions for action).

The key linkage seems to be that between matter and meaning. An artifact, a twist in the gut, or a tree outside my window may be just a tool-of-habit, just an enteroceptive sensation, just a source of shade from the sun ... or these things may also be more: the tool a shame to its maker, the twist in the gut an associative focus for a germinating and still unarticulated idea, the tree a totem of my clan planted by a particular ancestor. Material interactions and the entities we construe from them are inexhaustible sources of meaning: they overflow the terms, categories, and sets of properties that any semiotic system can assign to them. We may collectively or individually assign them only their minimal common functional meanings, or we may open them up as black boxes, or begin to pack them with links to new interactions — including our semiotic tales about them — even if they had none before.

Meaning is the link between matter and history; making the material meaningful potentially links the scale of humans, artifacts, and other same-scale ecological partners to the larger scales of their diverging histories and the dynamical processes that determine those histories.

Topological vs typological semiosis: Emergence of ecosocial systems

In order to further develop the perspective outlined in the last section, we need to see how our descriptions of ecosystems must change qualitatively when semiotic processes are at work in them. Our goal will be an account of how categorizations and valuations of material processes, by producing artifacts and other meaning-implicated material forms, transform the dynamics of ecosystems and lead to the emergence of new system properties.

The essential point is that our meaningful material interactivity in the world arises from two kinds of interdependence among specific interactional processes: a 'topological' interdependence, based on continuously variable phenomena, which is primary and characteristic of thermodynamic and biological systems without human culture, and a 'typological' interdependence introduced by those forms of human semiosis that operate in terms of discrete contrastive categories. The former tend to preserve separations of scales and allow more faithful and complete descriptions in terms of 'levels', while the addition of the latter tends to favor scale-heterogeneity. In particular, by filling the ecosocial world with artifacts designed at least partly according to typological semiotic principles, subsequent use of these artifacts in activities that further shape the world materially leads to an avalanche or cascade, a sort of chain reaction by which typological meaning colonizes the topological world. (For a fuller discussion of the 'typological' vs. 'topological' distinction, see Lemke, in press-c.)

We need, most basically, an understanding of semiosis as a material process in an ecological system. Our own cultural traditions in the centuries since Descartes have too radically disjoined the material and (under the older name of the 'mental') the semiotic. We have one set of discourses for talking about matter in the languages of physics, chemistry, and biology, and a completely different set for talking about meaning in the languages of semiotics, linguistics, and cultural anthropology. Yet we know that every sign has a material phenomenon as its representamen (sign-vehicle, signifier, carrier), that every process of semiosis is not just a social and cultural practice, but also a material activity in which not just humans but also non-human elements of the ecosytem participate.

From the ecological standpoint, we know that when an ecosystem contains a human society, we cannot account for the dynamics of the total system unless we take into account the beliefs and values of a human culture. Which trees are cut, which crops are cultivated, what kinds of raw materials transported where, depends not simply on the physical, chemical, and biological properties of human organisms or other components of the ecosystem (biotic and abiotic), but also on the cultural values assigned to actions, constructions, and objects. These phenomena depend on the beliefs of a community, depend on purely cultural customs. These customs must be consistent, in some broad sense, with the other material aspects of the ecology, but there is still such a broad latitude for differences of culture, for differences of meanings made that affect matter moved, that we cannot hope to account for the changes, for the total dynamics and trajectory of such an *ecosocial* system unless we take culture and semiosis as well as physics and biology into account.

What kinds of material systems can support semiosis? This will depend on how broadly or narrowly we define the making of meaning. If we take the broadest possible definition, the most inclusive one, then we have the opportunity to examine how semiosis itself has evolved with the processes of self-organization and complexification of the cosmos (cf. the similar project of C.S. Peirce who saw the processes of human semiosis as continuous with, and a veritable extension of the general tendency to self-organization in the evolution of the cosmos, which he referred to as matter's propensity of 'habit-taking' ; Peirce, 1992: chaps 19, 24). We can also examine the degrees of complexity of various classes of material systems with an eye to imagining how close they might come to what we would be happy to call semiosis *sensu stricto*.

I have tried to do this following Salthe's notion of a specification hierarchy (Salthe, 1985, 1989, 1993; Lemke 1994, 1995a: chap. 6). This is a formal scheme of nested classification in which each class of system is a subclass of the previous one, from an outermost class of systems whose dynamics can be adequately accounted for with the fewest assumed properties or characteristics, in the simplest discourses with the fewest number of primitive terms, to those which successively require more complex descriptions, adding to the descriptive apparatus needed for the less specified or more generic systems further properties which are newly relevant. This model would map smoothly onto an evolutionary model in which systems of greater complexity arise from systems of lesser complexity by successive differentiation, and by the emergence of new properties by processes of self-organization and symmetry-breaking within a matrix system possessing only the more general properties. Whether cosmological evolution, seen from the human viewpoint, follows the sequence of a specification hierarchy or not, the latter is still a very useful way to formulate the degrees of complexity in observable types of systems, and this suits our present purpose very well. (Emmeche et al., this volume, seem to assume that historical emergence follows the specification hierarchy, but I believe this view needs to be somewhat modified from an 'ascent' to ever higher levels to a *progressive interpolation* of ever more specified kinds of systems *between* less specified ones above and below; see Afterword below.)

The simplest dynamical systems we know are the ones I will call elementary dynamical systems. They are typified by the elementary particles of physics and their interactions. For purposes of describing their possible dynamical participation in an interaction, quantum theory requires that only a small number of properties be specified. Moreover, it appears that these systems can have no other properties than these essential dynamical ones. The number of degrees of freedom, the number of ways in which such a system can be identified by its behavior, is completely exhausted by the properties necessary to account for its fundamental interactions. For this reason, modern physics says that electrons have no individuality, no history, no culture that matters to their potential behavior under any and all circumstances. Every electron in the same quantum state will behave the same way with the same probability as any other electron. When two electrons collide, one cannot trace their identities from before their interaction to after it. Each could as well have taken the role of the other, and the experimental results agree only with this otherwise strange assumption.

Electrons and other constituents of elementary dynamical systems are truly simple, truly minimal in their complexity. They are not really even individual entities in the sense we expect for macroscopic systems like ourselves. Electrons and atoms do not age. They have no history, no individuality, no youth, maturity, or old age. They are generic, and their science is a science of the generic.

How complex, and complex in what ways, must a system be to show the history, individuality, and diversity characteristic of cultures and meaning-making systems? We know from the work of Ilya Prigogine (1961, 1962, 1980; Prigogine & Stengers, 1984) on irreversible thermodynamics and complexity theory that statistical ensembles of elementary dynamical systems begin to have histories that matter. They are systems for which we need to define an entropy. They break the time-reversal symmetry of elementary dynamical systems. Macroscopically they are still not truly individual, though microscopically perhaps they are. They do not yet have individualized macro-developmental trajectories. They suffer the irreversible effects of history, they are 'in time', but they do not yet have unique individual biographies, trajectories which matter to their dynamics. This further step is taken with the next more highly specified class of systems in our hierarchy, the so-called 'dissipative systems' which export entropy to their environments and feed on the order in those environments (on the maintenance of a gradient between system and environment) in order to self-organize, to increase their internal dynamical and morphological structure, to develop along a trajectory typical of their system type, from one dynamical regime to another. Such systems as flames and tornadoes, hurricanes and Rayleigh-Benard convection cells (see Table 1).

These systems develop, but they do not conserve the information acquired through interactions with an environment which shapes their development, nor transmit it to future generations. There is as yet no epigenesis, no evolution. There is, however, already one feature which will later prove crucial to our analysis of semiosis in ecosocial systems: the dynamics of the system as we ordinarily define it cannot be defined in terms of processes strictly internal to the system: the dynamics is always transvective, it always crosses the boundary of what we call 'the system'. Indeed the maintenance of the structural or dynamical integrity in terms of which it is possible for us to define it as 'a system' depends directly and critically on processes of exchange of matter, energy, and information with an environment. In this sense while it may be defined as an individual, it is not in any sense autonomous. It is, in fact, merely an isolable component of a larger dynamical system. It is always a subsystem, and to understand its dynamics, we must always examine

the supersystem of which it is an integral part. It cannot exist apart from its participation in this supersystem.

System Types	Additional Properties
Elementary Dynamical Systems (electrons, atoms, small molecules)	*Energy, mass, identicality*
Complex Systems with Irreversibility (paper clips, balloons, water droplets)	*Entropy, memory, aging, identity*
Dissipative Structures = Dynamic Open Systems (flames, dust-devils, hurricanes)	*Emergent organization, individuality, developmental trajectory*
Autocatalytic Self-Organizing Systems (Cairns-Smith clays, Eigen-Schuster hypercycles)	*Autocatalytic-crosscatalytic interdependencies*
Epigenetic-Developmental Systems (Salthe dust-devils, ...)	*Recapitulation of evolvable type-specific trajectory*
Genetic Evolutionary Systems (Ecosystems > organisms; A-life configurations)	*Recombinant, transferable genotypes*
Ecosocial Systems (Ecosystems-with-cultures > semiotic practices-with-persons)	*Meaning-construal-dependent material activities*

Table 1. Specification hierarchy nesting ecosocial systems

The properties of each class of systems we are describing are inherited by all the
subsequent subclasses of the specification hierarchy (see Table 1). A dissipative
system is a thermodynamic system, a thermodynamic system is a physical system
with the same parameters and degrees of freedom of elementary dynamical systems. As we shall see directly, an organism is a dissipative system, and so is an
ecosystem. Indeed they are two levels of organization in the same system, and that
system belongs also to the class of dissipative systems, and to all the classes above
it in the specification hierarchy, *a fortiori*.

Where are we headed in this sequence of classes of systems? Obviously the
concentric circles of subclasses of more highly specified types of systems is con-
verging on the point from which it is being drawn: on the cultural systems in

which humans and their ecologies make meanings about classes of systems. Along the way, we hopefully will gain some further insights into what makes meaning-making possible in a material system.

An *epigenetic system* is a developing system that recapitulates the major stages along a developmental trajectory typical of its kind. It is a system that develops according to its kind, recapitulating a sequence of bifurcations in its dynamics that may have evolved over many generations of its predecessors. I hope it is clear that while we have for some time now been using the language of living systems, that at no point in the specification hierarchy that we have been defining (complex systems with irreversibility, dissipative structures, developing systems, epigenetic systems) is there a clear transition to Life, as such. Hurricanes are alive in many significant ways; so is the Planet as a whole. Organismic life as we know it is based on a very specific strategy (DNA-mediated epigenesis), but ecosystems are also alive and use a different strategy. What is special about the class of epigenetic systems is that the developmental trajectories of individuals recapitulate a prior evolution of the trajectory of their type.

How is recapitulation possible? Epigenesis further specifies the nature of development: epigenetic development is development guided by an environment which is approximately the same for different individual systems and which changes relatively slowly compared to the lifetime of these systems. The sequence of bifurcations, of development, cannot be left entirely to chance, to random fluctuations, if there is to be recapitulation. Random fluctuations must be harnessed and guided by an external source of information, regulation, and control, and that can only reside in the environment of the developing system. An adequate analysis of a developing system must not only be extended in time, it must also extend beyond the system itself to examine system-environment interactions: it must extend to the immediate *supersystem* that contains both the system under focus and its immediate environment (cf. Lemke, 1984, 1995a: 159-66).

In epigenetic systems, a new bifurcation in the developing dynamics of an individual leads to effects on the environment that favor similar bifurcations in other individuals. A series of 'accidental' dust-devils in a narrow defile might erode landscape surfaces in a way that produces contours which favor the formation of other very similar dust-devils in that same place (cf. Salthe, 1993: 42-43). Globules of organic polymers in a tidal pool, engaged in autocatalytic chemical reactions (i.e. proto-life), might modify the surrounding silicate clays (their external, proto-DNA) in ways which tend to favor recapitulation of their latest chemical innovations when future globules develop in the same pool. In each case, along with epigenesis comes a supersystem (dustdevils-plus-landscape, globules-plus-clays-in-tidal-pool) and a hierarchical relation of system and supersystem. That hierarchical relation is one of *scale* (cf. Salthe, 1985, 1989, 1993, who clearly distinguishes scale hierarchies from specification hierarchies), in which the supersystem is more stable, changes more slowly, and exerts a regulatory influence on the dynamics of the now 'sub'-system. In the case of organismic lifeforms, the relatively stable 'environmental' molecules (RNA, DNA) were eventually internalized, incorporated into the supersystem which became the modern *cell*.

But epigenesis depends only on a system's being integrated into a supersystem which can in turn regulate the subsystem's development. It depends only on the possibility that innovations by individual subsystems can be recapitulated because information about them (or leading to them) is stored in the long-term 'memory' of the supersystem environment. The DNA strategy of organismic life is only one specific way in which this can happen. Epigenesis is simply development under an environmental guidance that enables recapitulation of type-trajectories in individual development. (For a more complete picture of how development and evolution are linked by DNA, including the complementary roles of 'typological', semiotic constraints and 'topological' dynamical ones, see Pattee, this volume. For a complex account of subsystem-supersystem relations and the interplay of type-specific equifinality and individuation along particular developmental trajectories, see the account of language acquisition in Hirsh-Pasek, Hollich & Tucker, also in this volume.)

My simple account of things (like many accounts of the origin of organismic life) is a bit backwards: there have always been supersystems, there have always been ecosystems, there has always been a planetary dynamical system. Particular self-organizing units always came into being in the context of supersystem environments. Life did not begin with micro-organisms that eventually got together to form ecosystems that eventually united into the living planetary system ('Gaia' after Lovelock, 1989). There was always Gaia, even before organic life, and there were always the chemical, atmospheric, oceanographic, and geological precursors of biological ecosystems. What has happened in the history of the planet is that new *intermediate* levels of organization have emerged *between* the total Gaia-system and her molecular subsystems (cf. the discussion of this issue in Moreno & Umerez, this volume). Ecosocial systems and the human cultures they sustain form one of those intermediate levels. These levels of organization, each on a different scale of physical size and mass, rates of change, energy transfer, etc. are (partially) regulated by their integration into the larger ones that contain them, and in turn (partially) regulate the smaller-scale ones that they contain.

All epigenetic systems belong to regulatory subsystem-supersystem hierarchies of this kind across a range of scales from the molecular to the planetary. At or near the human scale, organismic lifeforms are not the only epigenetic systems, there are also ecosystems.

Ecosystems are individuals. Their biographies partly recapitulate during ecological succession (Odum, 1983; Schneider, 1988) the trajectory of ecosystems of their specific type. Unlike organisms, ecosystems do not seem to die, but to undergo continual processes of local decay, replacement, and variable succession, resulting in a whole, a supersystem which is a mixed-age aggregate, a mosaic of ecological patches, each of which is itself an individual on a smaller space-time scale. Human communities exist as patches, and networks (see below), within natural ecosystems. Our communities are parts of larger ecosystems, and even our most artifactual cities show all the properties of ecosystems as a class. Any architectural survey will show the mixed-age mosaic, the mixed-use patches, the local diversity of 'species' types (person-types, artifact-types, natural types), in intimate dynamical interdependence.

But the dynamics of such an *ecosocial system* (Lemke, 1994, 1995a) depends not just on the volume and biotoxicity of wastes, the nutrient needs of the population, the structural properties of building materials, the available arable land; it depends also on cultural food preferences, on building styles, on technological histories, on political structures and social values. It depends on the activities by which humans not only move and transform matter and energy but also assign value and meaning. It depends on the critical link between activity and language (cf. Vygotsky, 1963; Leontiev, 1978), action context and meaning.

How can we describe this ecologically? Human networks of activity, like many of the dynamical subsystems of an ecosystem, are not strictly space-time localized 'patches'. As Latour has emphasized and his co-workers shown in so many cases (Latour, 1987, 1993; Law, 1991), networks of activity have a different topology from localized subsystems. I discuss this in more detail below (see also Lemke, in press-a), but the critical point for our purposes is that humans and the non-human species and material forms that co-participate in ecosocial and cultural practices and processes within a network interact over long distances, and even at considerable removes in time, more intensely in many cases than they do with objects and persons close at hand but not in that network. Our transport networks, our information and communication networks, our economic trade routes of exchange, have always had a 1-dimensional reticular network topology spread through a three-dimensional ecosystem. This is true also of the food-webs and carbon-exchange cycles even of ecosystems that lack human participation.

One of the functions of our network subsystems, one of the kinds of activities that takes place in them, is semiosis. But we have in mind now not semiosis *per se* in some idealist sense, not some mental processes with no consequences outside an immaterial 'mind'. We are concerned rather with a view of 'cognition' more like that of Gregory Bateson (1972) or of the situated cognition models of the last decade (e.g., Lave, 1988; Kirshner & Whitson, 1997; Lemke, 1997), in which the material substrate of semiotic processes extends always beyond the organism, is always in fact a process characteristic of the supersystem, and not internal to an organism (cf. Smith & Thelen, 1993; Lemke, 1996). We are not concerned with 'thought' that does no work in the ecosystem, because there can be no semiotic process uncoupled to the material systems which are its dynamical basis. Every 'thought' is part of a material activity, and its form and its consequences depend on the material systems and processes through which it occurs. These are only partly neurological (and neurohumoral) processes: they are also active, efferent and motor processes. From perception to memory to reasoning, all human neural activity includes both afferent and efferent connectivities (even if pre-emptively inhibited and/or re-entrantly diverted, cf. Edelman, 1992), and most human meaning-making occurs in the context of immediate motor activity. Our perception is the product of our action: the Umwelt made by our specific way of participating in the ecosystem (cf. Gibson, 1979 on affordances; von Uexkull, 1926; Smith & Thelen, 1993).

We need to represent semiosis as an integral part of activity in an ecosystem. Integral in that it is engendered by such activity, evolved to function as part of such activity, is shaped moment-to-moment by the activity, and has its consequences in the activity. In Bateson's famous example (1972: 458), the chain of differences that make a difference, which constitutes cognition or semiosis, is one aspect of activity itself, and its moment-to-moment trajectory derives from the loop of action (hefting an axe), consequence (interaction of axe and tree), feedback (perception of recoil), and modification of action (the next swing). However ethically questionable this murder of trees may be, it readily situates itself within the larger activities and networks of activities of an ecosocial system. The axe is swung initially as part of a larger activity (tree-killing) which depends on an economy, on cultural values for certain kinds of wood, on a technology (for use of the wood as well as for cutting the tree), on the people who will buy the wood, those who will use it, those who forged the axe-blade, and so on. Semiosis is always *in medias res*, plunging into the midst of events, at once material and social-cultural. There is no 'mind' outside of an 'ecology' which makes it materially possible and culturally meaningful. (Bateson's title is *Towards an Ecology of Mind* in this sense.)

Meaning-making is a material process in a material ecosystem. Its forms have evolved and are dynamically shaped from moment-to-moment as aspects of human-mediated activities in network subsystems of ecosystems. Materiality is as fundamental to an understanding of semiosis as is social function. Indeed these two are inseparable in a model of ecosocial dynamics. Every social practice is also a material process. As social practice it has semiotic relations to other social practices, construed by the semiotic activities of human communities. As material process, it participates in material, eco-bio-physical interactions with other process of the ecosystem. It is this double-connectedness that gives to ecosocial systems their enormous increase in complexity over other ecosystems. There are so many more possible couplings of processes/practices through the mediation of semiotic relations as part of the activities of humans (and non-humans) in the system.

Finally, we can begin to characterize the materiality of semiosis in two complementary ways (see also Lemke, in press-c). In the first, more general perspective
(analogous to Peirce's, see above), which I will call the 'topological' one, semiosis
arises in any self-organizing system to the extent that there are differences that
make differences, and that what difference a given difference makes depends in
turn on some other feature of the system (for this 'meta-redundancy' view of
semiosis, deriving from Bateson, see Lemke, 1984, 1995a: 166-174). This kind of
semiosis is quantitative. It need not depend on categories or contrasts, it rules in
the domain of the analogue and the continuously varying — a domain in which all
material systems are situated, including our ecosocial ones. The mathematical descriptions of classical physical science developed precisely to describe this sort of
quantitative covariation.

But mathematics itself initially grew out of a very different sort of semiotic resource: language, for which meaning arises by discrete (not continuous) covariation of categories and types. Classical semiotics, deriving from Saussure
(1915/1959, but see Thibault, 1997 for a re-appraisal in relation to dynamical systems and topological semiosis), foregrounded the principle of *valeur*, according to
which the meaning of a sign is a function of its place in a system of contrasts with
other signs. *Which* other signs it is relevantly in contrast with depends on the
wider context of its occurence, a fact which leads again to Bateson's differences
that make a difference in a fully contextual and relational model of semiosis (see
Lemke, 1984, 1995a: Postscript).

This is perhaps not the place to attempt an analysis of how typological semiotic
practices can arise from a topological substrate; certainly it seems plausible that
this phenomenon is itself akin to self-organization in complex systems, to the
emergence of attractors of the dynamics of a 'topological' system which then bifurcate into two regimes, each of which stands in potential 'typological' contrast
with the other. Of more relevance to our immediate concerns here is what happens
when human collective interaction in the ecosystem becomes self-organized in
such a way that linguistic and other semiotic categories play a role in human material actions in the larger system.

There are two particularly important cases, I think. One is the role of human
semiotic valuations in determining what species we favor or disfavor, what materials we accumulate or disperse, and the differential ways we treat various categories of our fellow humans that are also grounded in such valuations. The other,
coming full circle to Latour's arguments and the foregoing extensions of them, is
the role of human semiotic categories and categorial-conceptual reasoning in the
design and engineering and modes of use of our 'artifacts'. Whether we merely re-
shape the 'natural' environment (foraging, primitive gardening) or construct more
completely artificial 'kinds' (mechanical and electronic devices) with no prior history in the ecosystem, we are providing the material means for still further human

activity predicated on the use of these artifacts, and in most cases predicated also on the adoption of the categorial-conceptual logic of their functioning and use (if not always also of their design and production). Each new artifact, from a myth or a speech genre (cf. Bakhtin, 1953/1986) to a container or a computer, enables patterns of human activity in the ecosocial system that tend to multiply and project typological meaning into other domains. Typological semiosis is contagious, and artifacts are among its primary vectors.

One very simple way to appreciate the pervasiveness of the consequences of this chain reaction, in which typological distinctions in one domain or material medium beget typological differentiations in others, is to consider how insulated from the systems of cultural categories a child growing up in our ecosocial system could remain? Even in the absence of formal education or explicit family or peer tuition in such matters, merely as a result of operating the pervasive gadgets and technologies of daily life, categorial culture comes with participation in material-artifactual culture. The typological, conceptual-categorial dimensions of our culture are built into our artifactual worlds, inescapably.

Textproduction: Linguistic technology and scale heterogeneity

Are *words* artifacts? Certainly *documents* are, because of their obvious materiality, artificiality, and the role they play in our technologies of communication and representation beyond the scale of the immediate here-and-now. Spoken language is rather more evanescent, especially inner speech, which verges on thought itself. But materially the spoken word is a cultural modification of a natural feature of the ecosystem: of breathing and grunting, of cries of pain and danger, of vocalizations more topologically determined. Presumably for long periods prior to the spread of literacy technologies, oral traditions played an equivalent role to documents; and spoken dialects are examples of emergent features of on-going collective interaction, relevantly describable only for scales of systems well beyond the individual organism or the momentary dyadic interaction. The dialect we speak very certainly shapes or constrains the kinds of things we are likely to say or think — one of the most powerful of all the examples of 'downward causation' (for this neo-Whorfian view see for example Hasan, 1986, 1990, 1992a, 1992b; Silverstein, 1979, Lucy, 1992) .

Language is a phenomenon of seemingly inexhaustible complexity, and every linguistics has had to pay attention to only some of its manifold aspects. For present purposes it is perhaps best to think of language as the sum total of all resources for verbal meaning. That includes not just the words themselves and the typical grammatical patterns that link them into phrases, clauses, and sentences, but their systematic semantic relationships (synonymy, contrast, hyponymy, etc.),

the typical ways-of-speaking about various topics in a community (thematic formations, speech genres, discourse voices — see discussions in Lemke, 1995a, in
press-a, and references therein), and even the typical stories told in those ways (cf.
Threadgold & Kress, 1988; Lemke, in press-b). It also includes the meaning shifts
associated with the intonations and pacings with which we speak the words ...
and much else.

Now here is our central mystery: How does it happen that a particular writer (or
speaker) produces, word by word, and sentence by sentence, a text that is not
predetermined in detail by any explicit plan (perhaps only by some general goals
or an on-going activity of which the writing forms a part) — and which indeed
quite often actually surprises us when we see what we've wound up having written — and yet, in almost every case the resulting text can be seen as quite typical
of a particular genre of a particular culture and subculture in a particular historical
period? For all the creativity and indeterminacy of the process of textproduction
itself, certain 'constraints' of genre and discourse conventions will nonetheless
supervene from larger scales of the ecosocial system. (For a discussion of the historical evolution of written genres through their dynamic integration into larger
social-political systems, see Andersen, this volume.)

If we open the black box that is the finished and completed document, we expose the processes of its production: the other times and places, the other participants in the larger-scale systems of text production as a process. This reminds us
that documents are not produced solely at the human here-and-now scale we
imagine, that the relevant system in which production as a total process takes
place is not limited to this scale. Somehow the larger-scale social systems are
speaking through us, as in Bakhtin's metaphor of 'ventriloquation'. Bakhtin
(1935/1981, 1953/1986) offers us a germinal insight into these processes in his
more general notion of the pervasive 'dialogicality' of language in use. Every
word, every expression form, is something that we appropriate from another, and
with it comes a history, a collective memory of its uses in others' mouths and texts,
which fills out its connotative meaning and cannot be ignored in any use we make
of it. No word is entirely our own, and the richness of meanings in the words we
appropriate depends precisely on their partial otherness.

From Bakhtin's basic insight Kristeva (1980) and others (see references in
Lemke, 1985, 1995a) developed the notion of 'intertextuality'. As a principle, intertextuality reminds us that the meaning of each use of language here and now
depends in part on how we connect it to other uses of language there-and-then.
The relevant 'intertexts' of any given text are those which echo in its meanings as
we read and interpret it, but they are also those whose resonances contributed to
the original selection of words and form in our production of the text. (Naturally
many texts only imply and do not explicitly state, in footnotes or by citations, the

intertexts of their production, so that interpretation may bring to bear still other intertexts, resulting in further meaning possibilities.)

As I write I consult my notes, another text. I switch windows on my screen to view other papers I have written, and bibliographies, and half-formed essays to be incorporated here. I have stacks of books and papers by my side to which I refer, and some I cite for you here and some I do not. I recreate in memory the outlines and key expressions of still other texts I have read, and I do so under the stimulus of some of the materially present intertexts I have before me, as well as of my re-readings of this very text as I have written it so far. Later this first draft of my text will become an intertext for future drafts.

In all these ways the extent, the spatial and temporal scale, of this present text-production exceeds the immediate processes of here and now. But there are also more intermediaries of an artifactual sort. In addition to fully formed texts here present and remembered highlights of texts past, there are also the accumulated dispositions of my body and its memory, my 'know-how' for writing this academic style, for shaping the conventions of this genre, and less consciously, for writing my dialect of English in this historical epoch. Do I write as a man? in a masculine manner? with the semantic orientation of the upper-middle class? with the interests and emphases of an academic trained as a physicist? widely read in linguistics, ethnography, semiotics, philosophy? And can we say simply that all these dispositions are solely to be regarded as operating on the scale of my organism in isolation, as Bourdieu (1990, 1991) sums them in his notion of *habitus*? Yes, my bodily processes play critical roles — but insofar as I-as-writer am concerned, the *agency* of this writing is distributed more widely across a larger material system and longer time-scales than any which are characteristic of me-as-organism.

I cannot write without keyboard, display screen, and all that mediates between them, or without motor-facility with pen, and paper of the right sort. My writing is as much in my fingers as in my brain, for the feedback loops between them and my eyes' sight make it no longer possible to ascribe exclusive originary agency solely to one part of this integrated system (cf. Bateson's tree-and-axe loops above). Here the differences that make a difference, however, are not simply perceptual forms and tactile feedback as simple stimuli, but rather, American radical behaviorism notwithstanding, in human action and all the systems in which humans participate, their *meaning* matters as well. I do not write from a preformed plan straight through to completed text. At each step I read what I am writing, read back what I have written, and new associations are made. Meanings reinterpret what the words say, differently or more richly perhaps than they meant as I first wrote them; these meanings evoke still other intertexts, still newer meaning possibilities for re-writing and editing what I just wrote, and for writing a new next phrase or sentence that I would not have planned to write before (see Lemke, 1991). My own text as a growing artifact before me also has co-agency with my body and brain in this activity, not simply material co-agency, as the black boxes hidden in the writing loop do, but semiotic co-agency as well: contributors to developing meaning. The system in which meaning is being made is the larger supersystem. (Togeby, this volume, seems to suggest that text is *analyzable* in terms of fixed sets of goals; this may indeed be possible and useful, but I do not believe text is in general *produced* in this way, even though many of us probably believe it should be.)

My partners in writing include all those material intertexts I have already mentioned, and through them their agents of production, all the remembered and imagined texts, and the very dispositions to write in particular ways and utilize particular themes and ideologies, that enter in through my body's "writerly" habitus. I am saying very literally that my internal organism cannot be the sole author of the texts that get written by my hand, that text production is a process across all these system scales. The text is not being produced solely as part of a process on the scale of a meter or so around about me, and over times of the order of each attack on the keyboard or the composition of each sentence or paragraph. The text is also being produced as part of processes on much larger scales that operate over much longer characteristic times — as part of the evolution of a discourse formation or a genre in a subcommunity (cf. Andersen, this volume), as part of the evolution of a dialect. Textproduction belongs also to community- and ecosocial system-scale processes, as well as to organism- and artifact- scale processes. (See also in this connection Togeby's insightful discussion in this volume of textual coherence as a phenomenon across time.)

This rather radical picture of a process like textproduction has an even more radical implication for human consciousness. Textproduction is a special case of meaning making, and so of what we loosely call 'thought'. Together with the more topological material ground of consciousness (our being-in-the-world interactively, much of which is also scale-heterogeneous), this analysis implies that meaning-making consciousness need not be considered as a process confined solely to the organismic scale. Our meaning-awareness, and perhaps a good bit of our primary awareness prior-to-meaning, are also aspects of larger-scale on-going processes. Consciousness is a cross-temporal phenomenon; it exists on multiple time-scales simultaneously, and some of those scales may be very long indeed.

New paradigms for the study of complex systems

What I have proposed here is an effort to extend our usual paradigms and metaphors for understanding complex self-organizing systems from those which assume strict scale-homogeneity of levels of organization to ones which also allow us to think, when needed, in terms of scale-heterogeneity.

A great deal of further discussion and elaboration of these issues will be needed. I believe that it will be very fruitful to examine, across the widest range of different kinds of empirically researched systems, the extent to which the assumption of scale-homogeneity is justified and the extent to which it is helpful to supplement it with views that emphasize multi-scale processes and strong cross-scale linkages. I would like to end here by mentioning a useful, if slightly simplified, set of metaphors for thinking about levels and scale-heterogeneity.

Our classic view of hierarchical levels in general systems theory models each level or dynamical domain on a sphere: a three-dimensional region with a definite spatial-extension scale, in which processes on this characteristic scale take place with some corresponding characteristic time. Our view of subsystems at lower levels models them as spheres or three-dimensional regions of smaller spatial-extension scale within the larger spheres, and so on up and down the hierarchy. There are two intimately related assumptions in such a prototypical view: (a) that there is a single definable spatial and temporal scale for the processes identifiable within the sphere, and (b) that points which are nearer in space, and events which are nearer in time, are more likely to be linked by interactions, more likely to be co-participants in larger events, more likely to be constitutive components of the next larger system level, than those which are remote (and so far outside the characteristic sphere).

But this view fails to some extent even in non-artifactual systems. Two ecological zones within the same watershed, or riparian zones along the same river, or regions within the influence of the same oceanic current, are more likely to interact with one another than they are with many points that are nearer in three-dimensional space but are not linked by these natural quasi- one-dimensional networks. Pollution dumped into a stream may have effects far down-river but none a few meters inland from the dumpsite. The relevant scale here is the long distance along the one-dimensional network link, and not any three-dimensional sphere with that (or any other) characteristic spatial-extension scale. Artifactual examples include railway and road transport networks, and telephonic and signal-cable system nets (including today the global Internet). I am far more intensively in interaction (for some purposes) with individuals in Italy, Denmark, and Australia than I am with most neighbors in my own town or street. From the viewpoint of a scale-and-levels model of the 'spherical' type, these network artifacts produce scale-inhomogeneities in processes which are both local and global.

More generally there are always a number of different co-dimensional manifolds that can be embedded in a space of N dimensions. In 3-dimensional space, in addition to three-dimensional regions, typified by the interior of spheres with a single spatial scale parameter, there are also what we will call 'networks', which are of co-dimension one. They are reticula in 3-space which are one-dimensional 'internally' even as they spread out through two- or three- dimensional regions in

space (i.e. one moves along *lines* that connect points, which may be quite different distances apart, inducing the external scale-heterogeneity).

Finally there are, not surprisingly, though much less often taken as prototypical,
also what we can call 'lamina', which are of co-dimension two in our three-
dimensional space. These are sheet-like regions, with one characteristic scale (the
thickness of the sheet), such that points within the same sheet are more likely to
interact with one another (either locally or across many scales of distance) than
with points which are off or outside the thin sheet. Ideally, of course, lamina are internally 2-dimensional (the limit of zero 'thickness' of the sheets), just as networks
or reticula are 1-dimensional. Real network connections (cables, rivers, roads) of
course are characterized merely by a very large ratio between their length scales
and any other spatial extension, and real lamina by the large area of the layer compared to its 'thickness'. There are again certainly natural laminar systems, such as
the layered zones of lakes and seas by depth (and so also by salinity, temperature,
pressure, and light levels), and perhaps also such phenomena as 'canopy ecologies' in rainforests, or layers of soils, etc. Artifactually, there is some isolation of
connected underground levels of cities vs the surface and perhaps in some cases
also of elevated levels.

In the case of lamina, there may be a single set of parallel laminar surfaces, in
each of which interactions across both short and long distances within the sheet
take precedence over interaction with nearby points outside the sheet. There may
also of course be more complex 2-dimensional manifolds, the analogue of reticular
grids, but I cannot off-hand think of ecological or artifactual examples, though
there may be such phenomena in the complexly folded tissues of organisms
(neural sheets?).

Extending the repertoire of our prototypical images and metaphors of organizational complexity to include networks and lamina as well as spheres can help us to
integrate both the 'levels' perspective and the 'scale heterogeneity' perspective
in our analyses of self-organizing systems. My examples here have been based on
the easily visualizable models of spatial scale relations, but of course dynamic temporal scales are equally if not more significant. One could generalize the embedded
manifolds view of connectivity here from 3-dimensional space to an Einsteinian
space of three spatial dimensions and a fourth one for time, but I will not explore
this interesting approach here. It is sufficient to see that multi-scale and cross-scale
temporal processes, as well as space-scale heterogeneity, are implied by the generalized models sketched in this section and elsewhere in the paper. We need
many more detailed empirical studies to help us build up a repertoire of means for
representing how processes on different characteristic temporal as well as spatial
scales (deriving from common dynamical scales) are intimately relevant to one another. Where we identify such cross-scale phenomena against the background of
relative separation of levels, we may speak of 'downward causation', but I think it

should be apparent from the arguments advanced here that this notion has an even wider generalization and signficance when we consider systems character-ized by scale-heterogeneity.

Afterword

Throughout this chapter I have made cross-reference to other contributors to this volume. Most of the contributors met near Aarhus in 1997 to discuss their draft chapters and the unifying themes of the volume. I want to add here a few notes to place the perspectives of this chapter in the context of some of the other issues raised by the volume as a whole.

In their Introduction, Emmeche et al. offer a useful categorization of views on downward causation. I believe that my own approach most closely corresponds to their 'medium-strong' position rather than to their 'weak' version. I do believe, in agreement with Finnemann, and Bickard, that in the processes of emergent self-or-ganization the very most fundamental laws of a system are produced and changed. The development of a system over time and through interaction within an environment can lead to dynamical possibilities in principle unpredictable from a knowledge of the system at any one time. (Self-organizing, open dynamical sys-tems cannot in general be analyzed at single moments of time. They exist in a sense only over-time, and across many temporal scales; they move or die.)

This is a much stronger view than the 'preformationist' perspective, according to which all the possible futures of a system are fixed by its composition, i.e. from below. If emergent organization in the dynamics of a system can be represented by attractors of the dynamics, as Emmeche et al., Finnemann, Andersen, and many others have proposed, then my position is that in at least some forms of emergent organization for sufficiently complex systems the attractors themselves change as the systems' processes become entrained in interaction with still larger-scale pro-cesses. Along the historical developmental trajectory of such systems the very ground of dynamical possibility moves. This can happen, as chaos theorists have observed, because non-linear systems amplify 'noise' from levels below, turning it into information. I would only add that what kind of information it gets turned into also depends on the larger-scale processes of the environment within which the system is itself a constituent.

I also agree with Bickard's response to arguments such as those summarized by Kim: a physics in which non-local fields or dynamic processes, rather than enti-ties, are primary does not require that the behavioral possibilities of (process) con-stituents be independent of the organizational patterns in which they may be in-cluded. This is more obvious perhaps at the social level. People have radically dif-ferent behavioral possibilities because they live in a complex technological culture: possibilities which *were* not available to our remote ancestors not simply for lack of the technologies and social institutions, but also because our species' bodies and brains have evolved, and our individual bodies and brains now develop, in the context of these larger ecosocial systems and they now have different potentialities as well. In both Bickard's argument and mine, non-locality, or violation of the assumption of separable scales for constituent processes vs. aggregate processes is fundamental. A focus on entities, be they particles or organisms, makes scale-homogeneity seem more realistic than it actually is. 'Things' always fit neatly inside some sphere at some definite scale; fields and processes do not. Many arguments against 'downward causation' depend on the assumption of definite, separable scales. (So, of course, do many formulations of what 'downward causation' is.)

Such arguments also seem to depend on a synoptic perspective, that is, one that stands outside of time and ignores both history and change-in-progress. This is the temporal-scale analogue of non-localizability. Over time, the distinction between different scales which seem obvious at a single moment can become quite blurred (as in the example above of ecosystem effects on the evolution and development of brains, not to mention the role of changing brain capacities in altering ecosystems). Not only don't systems of the kind we are interested in really exist in single instants of time, the processes which constitute them are not confinable to characteristic time-scales.

I do still want to qualify my support for the medium-strong version of downward causation in two respects. First, like Patee and Moreno & Umerez, I do not believe that the metaphor or paradigm of cause-effect itself can be applied in an unrestricted way to the analysis of all phenomena. I believe it reaches the limits of its usefulness precisely (a) for systems of sufficient complexity that they must be treated as individuals with irreversible histories (and so for which there can be no question of same antecedents, same consequents) and (b) for cases where phenomena result from self-organization among many components and it is pointless to single out some of these as causal agents. I would rather say that the dynamics of constituent processes become entrained in the dynamics of larger-scale processes than that a larger-scale system simply 'causes' its constitutents to behave in novel ways.

Secondly, many arguments about downward causation assume a two-level model, whereas I believe that useful accounts must always consider at least three levels simultaneously. Processes at level L+1 represent selectional constraints on the possible ways processes at level L (in focus) can deploy the affordances they have by virtue of their constituents at level L-1. Historically, developmentally, phylogenetically, and probably cosmologically, we do not climb up from isolated quarks (or whatever) to complex organisms and ecosystems as the two-level, rung-to-rung model suggests. Instead, there is always already a higher level of organization (or at least of interaction; a quark soup, not just single quarks; ripples in the hyperdimensional continuum on many scales, not just the particle scale) and emergent self-organization produces more organized, more specified *intermediate* levels of order. We do not go from A to B to C to D ..., but from A-Z to A-L-Z to A-G-L-Q-Z .... In this view what should be meant by 'causation', either upwards or downwards, may thus ultimately have more in common with notions such as material and formal cause than with the classical notion of efficient causation.

References

BAKHTIN, M. 1935. Discourse in the novel. In M. Holquist (ed.), *The Dialogic Imagination* (1981). Austin, Texas: University of Texas Press.

BAKHTIN, M. 1953. *Speech Genres and Other Late Essays.* 1986 edition. Austin, Texas: University of Texas Press.

BATESON, G. 1972. *Steps to an Ecology of Mind.* New York: Ballantine.

BOHR, N. 1934/1961. *Atomic Theory and the Description of Nature.* London: Cambridge University Press. [reprinted 1987, Woodbridge, Conn.: Ox Bow Press]

BOHR, N. 1958. *The Philosophical Writings of Niels Bohr: Essays 1932-1957 on Atomic Physics and Human Knowledge.* New York: Wiley, 23-31. [reprinted 1987, Woodbridge, Conn.: Ox Bow Press]

BOURDIEU, P. 1990. *The Logic of Practice.* Stanford, Cal.: Stanford University Press.

BOURDIEU, P. 1991. *Language and Symbolic Power.* Cambridge, Mass.: Harvard University Press.

EDELMAN, G. 1992. *Bright Air, Brilliant Fire.* New York: Basic Books.

GIBSON, J.J. 1979. *The Ecological Approach to Visual Perception.* Boston: Houghton-Mifflin.

GOODWIN, C. 1995. Seeing in depth. *Social Studies of Science* 25(2): 237-84.

GREIMAS, A. & COURTES, J. 1982. *Semiotics and Language: An Analytical Dictionary.* Bloomington, Ind.: Indiana University Press.

HASAN, R. 1992a. Meaning in sociolinguistic theory. In K. Bolton & H. Kwok (eds.), *Sociolinguistics Today.* London: Routledge.

HASAN, R. 1992b. Speech genre, semiotic mediation, and the development of higher mental functions. *Language Sciences* 14(4): 489-528.

HASEGAWA, A. 1985. Self-organization processes in continuous media. *Advances in Physics* 34(1): 1-42.

HUTCHINS, E. 1995. *Cognition in the Wild.* Cambridge, Mass.: MIT Press.

KIRSHNER, D. & WHITSON, A. (eds.) 1997. *Situated Cognition: Social, Semiotic, and Psychological Perspectives.* Hillsdale, N.J.: Erlbaum.

KRISTEVA, J. 1980. *Desire in Language.* New York: Columbia University Press.

LATOUR, B. 1987. *Science in Action.* Cambridge, Mass.: Harvard University Press.

LATOUR, B. 1990. Drawing Things Together. In Lynch & Woolgar 1990. [= 'Visualization and cognition: thinking with eyes and hands' *Knowledge and Society* 6: 1-40. 1986.]

LATOUR, B. 1993. *We Have Never Been Modern.* Cambridge, Mass.: Harvard University Press.

LATOUR, B. 1996a. On interobjectivity. *Mind, Culture, and Activity* 3(4): 228-45.

LATOUR, B. 1996b. Pursuing the discussion of interobjectivity. *Mind, Culture, and Activity* 3(4): 266-69.

LAVE, J. 1988. *Cognition in Practice*. Cambridge: Cambridge University Press.

LAW, J. (ed.) 1991. *A Sociology of Monsters*. London: Routledge.

LEMKE, J.L. 1984. *Semiotics and Education*. Monograph in Toronto Semiotic Circle Monographs Series, Victoria University, Toronto.

LEMKE, J.L. 1985. Ideology, intertextuality, and the notion of register. In J.D. Benson & W.S. Greaves (eds.), *Systemic Perspectives on Discourse*. Norwood, N.J.: Ablex Publishing, 275-94.

LEMKE, J.L. 1991. Text Production and Dynamic Text Semantics. In E. Ventola (ed.), *Functional and Systemic Linguistics: Approaches and Uses*. Berlin: Mouton/deGruyter (Trends in Linguistics: Studies and Monographs 55), 23-38.

LEMKE, J.L. 1994. Discourse, Dynamics, and Social Change. *Cultural Dynamics* 6(1): 243-75. [Special issue, Language as Cultural Dynamic, M.A.K. Halliday, Issue Editor].

LEMKE, J.L. 1995a. *Textual Politics: Discourse and Social Dynamics*. London: Taylor & Francis.

LEMKE, J.L. 1995b. Literacy, Culture, and History. Review of *The World on Paper* by D.R. Olson. *The Communication Review* 1(2): 241-59.

LEMKE, J.L. 1996. Self-Organization and Psychological Theory. Review of L.B. Smith & E. Thelen (eds.), A *Dynamic Systems Approach to Development*. *Theory & Psychology* 6(2): 352-56.

LEMKE, J.L. 1997. Cognition, Context, and Learning: A Social Semiotic Perspective. In D. Kirshner & A. Whitson (eds.), *Situated Cognition: Social, Semiotic, and Psychological Perspectives*. Hillsdale, N.J.: Erlbaum.

LEMKE, J.L. In press, a. Analysing Verbal Data: Principles, Methods, and Problems. In K. Tobin & B. Fraser (eds), *International Handbook of Science Education*. Dordrecht: Kluwer Academic.

LEMKE, J.L. In press, b. Semantic Topography and Textual Meaning. In R. Stainton & J. DeVilliers (eds.), *Communication and Linguistics*. Toronto: Glendon College.

LEMKE, J.L. In press, c. Typological and topological meaning in diagnostic discourse. To appear in *Discourse Processes*.

LEONTIEV, A.N. 1978. *Activity, consciousness, and personality*. Englewood Cliffs, N.J.: Prentice-Hall.

LOVELOCK, J. 1989. *The Ages of Gaia: A Biography of Our Living Earth*. Oxford: Oxford University Press.

LUCY, J. 1992. *Language Diversity and Thought*. New York: Cambridge University Press.

LYNCH, M. & WOOLGAR, S. (eds.) 1990. *Representation in Scientific Practice*. Cambridge, Mass.: MIT Press.

ODUM, HOWARD T. 1983. *Systems Ecology*. New York: John Wiley.

OLSON, D. R. 1994. *The World on Paper*. Cambridge & New York: Cambridge University Press.

PEIRCE, C.S. 1992. *The Essential Peirce: Selected Philosophical Writings, Vol.1*. Bloomington, Ind.: Indiana University Press.

PRIGOGINE, I. 1961. *Introduction to the Thermodynamics of Irreversible Processes*. New York: Interscience.

PRIGOGINE, I. 1962. *Non-equilibrium Statistical Mechanics*. New York: Wiley.

PRIGOGINE, I. 1980. *From Being to Becoming: Time and Complexity in the Physical Sciences*. New York: W.H. Freeman.

PRIGOGINE, I. & STENGERS, I. 1984. *Order out of Chaos*. New York: Bantam.

SALTHE, S. 1985. *Evolving Hierarchical Systems*. New York: Columbia University Press.

SALTHE, S. 1989. Self-organization in hierarchically structured systems. *Systems Research* 6(3): 199-208.

SALTHE, S. 1993. *Development and Evolution*. Cambridge, Mass.: MIT Press.

SAUSSURE, F. DE. 1915/1959. *Course in General Linguistics*. New York: McGraw-Hill.

SCHNEIDER, E. 1988. Thermodynamics, ecological succession, and natural selection. In B.H. Weber, D.J. Depew & J.D. Smith (eds.), *Entropy, Information, and Evolution*. Cambridge, Mass.: MIT Press.

SILVERSTEIN, M. 1979. Language structure and linguistic ideology. In P. Clyne, W. Hanks, & C. Hofbauer (eds.), *The Elements: A Parasession On Linguistic Units And Levels*, 193-247. Chicago: Chicago Linguistic Society.

SMITH, L.B. & THELEN, E. 1993. *A Dynamic Systems Approach to Development*. Cambridge, Mass.: MIT Press.

THIBAULT, P. 1997. *Re-Reading Saussure*. London: Routledge.

THREADGOLD, T. & KRESS, G. 1988. Towards a social theory of genre. *Southern Review* 21: 215-43.

VON UEXKULL, J. 1926. *Theoretical biology*. New York: Harcourt, Brace.

VYGOTSKY, L. 1963. *Thought and Language*. Cambridge, Mass.: MIT Press.

10

Genres as Self-organizing Systems

PETER BØGH ANDERSEN

Abstract

The notion of 'downwards causation' is an old acquaintance in the humanities, for example in the notion of the hermeneutic circle, where textual parts and wholes mutually influence each other's interpretation. The phenomenon of genres is chosen as a possible example of downwards causation (genre constraints). A computer model is constructed on the basis of genre theory and run under various conditions. The model accounts well for the formation and bifurcation of genres, but could not be made to generate the well-known oscillations from the history of literature. The original model is replaced by another one that contains two mutually perturbing systems which can be made to oscillate. This final model does not invite an interpretation in terms of downwards causation; instead an interpretation hinging on semiosis between two systems on different scales is suggested.

1. Introduction

The basic question I want to discuss in this paper is whether genres only exist in the eye of the literary beholder (the nominalist position) or whether they are real existing entities with causal powers (the realist position); and, if the latter position is adopted, what it means for genres to possess causal powers.

Genre theory[1] has always had difficulty choosing between these two positions:

1. *Nominalism:* genres are merely collections of texts with a certain likeness which we have chosen to give a name. Genres only exist in the mind of the beholders and can therefore have no causal effect on the texts. Genres are historical and change when literary conditions change.

---

1   I thank the students attending my genre course of Fall 1995 for the good discussions and references.

2. *Realism:* genres are real existing entities that embody eternal laws governing the production of texts. Texts cannot be constructed freely, and the genres define the permissible/possible ways of writing texts.

Support and criticism are not difficult to find for both cases. Against the nominalist view speaks the fact that at least mass communication falls in classes whose members share so many characteristics that it is sometimes difficult to tell one from the other: detective, spy and police novels; fantasy and science fiction books; cowboy films, war films, action films, adventure films; television series, such as melodramas and comedy. There exist written recipes for some genres, and any reader or viewer can tell the different species from each other and give them a name; and if they are a bit unsure, they are offered ample help from marketing

which potentially includes discursive though non-cinematic elements such as advertising strategies, posters, stills, trade review, trade synopses, reviewing and so on.
Neale 1983: 14

And in fact there are obvious causes for such consistency: genres help the consumer reduce complexity and make choices easier; we do not have to search all the thousands of books in a bookstore, but can go directly to the shelf labelled 'crime' and make our choice from, say, a hundred books there. Furthermore, since we know the contract underlying the individual genre, consuming is made easier. We know how to interpret the clues given in a detective novel, and are rightly disappointed if the author does not keep his part of the agreement and fails to collect all loose ends in the last pages.

Genres may be defined as patterns/forms/styles/structures which transcend individual films, and which supervise both their construction by the film maker, and their reading by an audience.
Tom Ryall, quoted in Neale 1983: 7

If genres supervise construction as well as reading, they must be said to possess causal powers. In addition, there are clearly constraints as to which components can actually be combined in a worthwhile book or film. Not all combinations are equally satisfying.

However, the realist view will not stand up to scrutiny either: genres change, disappear and are born, and combinations of old genres are quite possible. The repertoire of popular genres are to a certain degree historical, and relate to important social oppositions and problems. Science fiction is unthinkable without modern technology, and the *Bildungsroman* needs the capitalist background of individuality and dynamics to catch the readers' interest. These facts speak against the idea of genres as an embodiment of eternal aesthetic laws.

The problem of the causal powers of genres is the main topic of this paper. It is obvious that these powers cannot be attributed to a concrete agent. There has never been a managing director of literary styles that can set up the rules for genres and control that they are obeyed. How are causal powers of emergent patterns possible without concrete agents to wield the power?

The literary genres are just an example of a much more general phenomenon, namely how it is possible to create complex, stable, and self-perpetuating systems from small interactions between the parts of the system. Hurricanes and dust-devils are examples from the physical world (Salthe 93: 51), biological ontogenesis is a biological example, and social systems, such as conversations, exemplify the phenomenon in the social domain.

In this paper I have borrowed concepts from non-linear dynamic systems theory. Here I shall introduce some key concepts from this domain (see Bøgh Andersen 1994, 1996 for a fuller version). The basic descriptive concept is a *dynamic phase space*. A phase-space is a representation of selected properties of a system. It consists of one or more dimensions that represent the attributes of the system. The values of the attributes are represented by a point in the corresponding dimension, so the state of the system itself is represented by a point in the total phase-space. For example, we can characterize physical matter by means of two dimensions, temperature and pressure (Fig. 1.1). This defines a two-dimensional plane, and the state of the system is a point in this plane (the 'representative point').

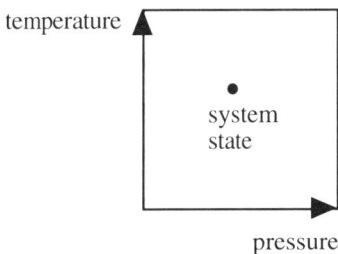

Fig. 1.1. Physical system.   Fig. 1.2. Fictional system.

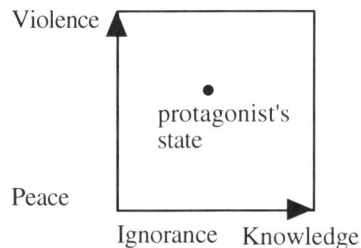

Another example is the plot of a fictional product, e.g., a detective movie (Fig. 1.2). Two important dimensions here are Peace/Violence versus Knowledge/Ignorance: there can be no detective movie without violence, e.g., a murder, and the plot of the movie is about the detective's state of knowledge. The actual state of the plot can thus be characterized by a point in the plane defined by the Violence/Peace and Knowledge/Ignorance axes.

A *dynamic* phase-space is a phase-space in which the representative point moves, i.e. a space that depicts a changing system. The movement of the point is called the *trajectory* of the system. Trajectories are assumed to follow rules; in the physical example, the rules are the laws of nature, in the fictional case the rules belong to the genre. A typical trajectory in a detective movie (Fig. 1.3) will start in the Peace-Ignorance part of the plane; a murder sends it vertically upwards to the violence part, and the actions of the detective are a trajectory leading from Ignorance to Knowledge.

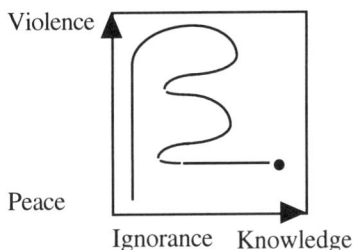

Fig. 1.3. Typical trajectory of detective movie.

Systems can undergo qualitative abrupt changes along the trajectory. In the physical example, the physical matter may change from a solid to a liquid state (ice melts) when the temperature is raised. In the movie example, we will very often have a climax where the detective reveals who dunnit; the revelation is often surprising and causes the viewer to revise his expectations in a fundamental way.

The system may gravitate towards a point or area of the phase-space and stay there on arrival. Such areas or points are called *attractors*. Attractors come in many types. In this paper I only distinguish between *fixed-point* attractors and *limit-cycle* attractors. The former consist of one point, the latter of a set of points. Most mainstream movies have a fixed-point attractor, i.e. there is one point that is felt as the natural ending of the movie. For example, detective movies must end in the knowledgeable state.

More sophisticated movies may have a limit-cycle attractor, i.e. they do not present a fixed solution to their problem, but oscillate between several possibilities. An example is a detective movie that ends without selecting one particular explanation of the crime.

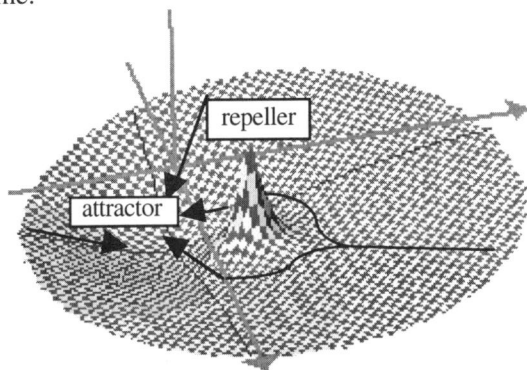

Fig. 1.4. An attractor and a repeller.

The trajectory can be specified in many ways. In this paper I use genetic algorithms, but often illustrate the dynamics by potential functions in the manner of
catastrophe theory. The potential functions can be understood as an energy landscape. The system is located in this landscape; it is influenced by the gradients of
the valleys and hills and will seek downwards towards the lowest position, i.e. towards the lowest level of energy. See Fig. 1.4.

If the equation defining Fig. 1.4 has a parameter in it, we can change the landscape by changing the parameter. If the change alters the number of attractors and
repellers, i.e. changes the equilibrium conditions of the system, we call it a *catastrophe*. A new landscape will cause the trajectory of the system to run in a different direction.

We shall restrict our attention to *recursive systems,* i.e. systems in which the
new state is calculated from the preceding state. In Fig. 1.4 the location of the system x_t is calculated from x_{t-1} by subtracting the gradient of x_{t-1} from x_{t-1}. If the rule
is parameterized we call the system a *perturbed recursive system*. The parameters
of the system describe its boundary conditions, i.e. the conditions that must be
fulfilled in order for the system to generate a certain set of trajectories. The reason
for concentrating on recursive systems is that examples of such systems are often
mentioned as generators of emergent complexity (for chemical examples, see
Prigogine & Stengers 1984: 134; mathematical examples are the Mandelbrot set
and other fractal shapes (Peitgen, Jürgens & Saupe 1992); biological examples are
given in Lindenmeyer 1968; cellular automata and genetic algorithms are also recursive systems, Davis 1996).

We can let two systems influence each other by letting the state of one system
act as the parameter of the other system, and vice versa. This means that we describe the systems as environments of each other. They *mutually perturb* each
other.

Ontologically the above ideas are heavily influenced by the theory of autopoiesis (Maturana & Varela 1980), especially in the sociological variant developed by Niklas Luhmann (Luhmann 1984, 1990). The main point is that autopoietic systems are operationally closed, that is, the maintenance and development of
autopoietic systems are their own doing and cannot be interfered with by their
environment. Autopoietic systems can be formalized as perturbed recursive systems. The interaction between autopoietic systems and their environment is a two-
step process: the environment first perturbs the system by changing the parameters of the recursive process which changes its internal dynamics; then the system
compensates for the perturbation by changing itself according to the new dynamics. This is for instance true of communication: the speaker cannot directly
change the beliefs of the listener, but only indicate that the speaker intends to
make the listener believe something. The actual adoption of the new belief is entirely up to the listener.

Now that these preliminaries are covered, let us return to the main problem of the paper, the nominalist/realist controversy.

2. Genres and self-organization

In this paper I shall explore a different conception that transcends the nominalist/realist dichotomy. I shall argue that genres are the result of self-organizing processes among texts, readers and writers, and as such are entities at a level above the individual text. However, even if genres emerge from interactions between texts, writers and readers at the level below, they are not merely sets of texts without causal effect. On the contrary, once stabilized in a loose form, they influence and constrain the possible new texts, and in this way may reinforce and maintain their own existence. Thus, genres are patterns of similarities of individual texts (the nominalist position), *but* they have causal powers controlling the same type of texts from which they were abstracted (the realist position).

In the following sections I shall argue that dynamic phase spaces can be used for defining genres, and I shall introduce and define the notion of levels and emergence.

2.1. Genres

When we use phase spaces to describe the driving force of whole texts or genres, the representative point can of course be a character, in which case the phase-space represents properties of that character, but it can also be the narrator or the reader.

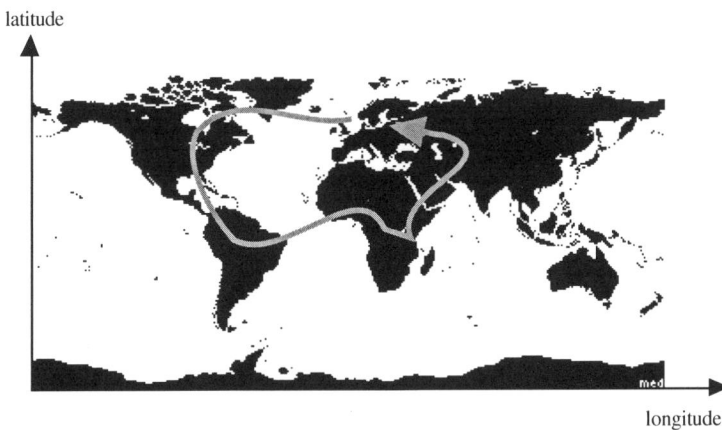

Fig. 2.1. Spatial phase-space of a travel novel.

In the first case, if the phase-space is the three Euclidean dimensions, the entity is a character, and the location of the character in the space represents his location in Euclidean space. A travel novel, for example, often follows the main character on a journey from home to foreign countries and back home (Handesten 1992). This composition can be represented by a trajectory of the character in the space (Fig. 2.1).

The second case, where the representative point represents attitudes of the reader, can be found in Todorov's analysis of the fantastic genres discussed below. Here the reader is continually oscillating between belief and disbelief in the supernatural.

Finally, we can define two main genres, *narrative* and *description*, by means of a four-dimensional phase-space, consisting of the three spatial dimensions plus time (Togeby 1982: 67 ff.), where the representative point is the author's or reader's consciousness. If it moves in time, the genre is narrative, whereas the genre is description if it moves in space but not in time.

Intuitively, narrative elements are those that contribute to the advancement of the plot, while nonnarrative elements flesh out the narrative universe and make it more vivid, without moving the plot forward.   *Ryan 1991: 125*

Text 1 contains examples of narrative and descriptive elements. It is a narrative about work incidents recorded by Klaus B. Bærentsen at a Danish power plant (Bærentsen 1996).[2] It starts as a narrative, then stops time and moves around in the plant, and finally goes on with the plot.

Narration: A couple of months ago we got a report from [tape change] insulation that had come off.

Description: It is a sort of a foam rubber, or something like that, sitting at the inside of the screw compressors we have. Sort of a silencer, on the casing, there is sort of a foam rubber that is rather heavy [...]

Narration: Then was, ... , then the plastic, the rubber came off. And then it had gone into something hot, then the card caught fire, and everything smelled awfully bad. And the compressor ran [...].

Text 1. Klaus B. Bærentsen: Interviews of machinists about incidents during work. Dept. of Psychology, 1988. Memory 4, Interview 20.

Fig. 2.2 shows a phase-space representation of the story.

The first paragraph tells about the initial incident, that some insulation fell off. The next one explains the location and function of the insulation, and the third one continues the narration.

---

2   *Narration:* For nogle måneder siden, da fik vi en melding fra [tape change] isolering, der er røget af. *Description:* Det er sådan noget skumgummi, eller sådan noget stads, der sidder på indersiden af de skruekompressorer vi har. Sådan for lyddæmpning så sidder der inde på casingen, der sidder sådan noget skumgummi, som er ret svær i det. [...] *Narration:* Så var ... gik der plastik, det der skumgummi af. Og så var det gået ind på en eller anden varm ting, så der var gået ild i kortet og det hele lugtede noget så forfærdeligt. Og kompressoren kørte [...]

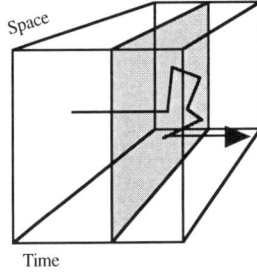

Fig. 2.2. Narration and description.

Dynamic phase-spaces seem suitable for representing the genre-concepts developed in Neale (1983), who bases his classification of film genres on the following basic understanding of narrative:

Narrative is always a process of transformation of the balance of elements that constitute its pretext: the interruption of an initial equilibrium and the tracing of the dispersal and refiguration of its components [in such a way that the] elements finally [are] replaced in a new equilibrium whose achievement is the condition of narrative closure.   *Neale 1983: 20.*

This analysis works with two types of dimensions, namely the dimensions of perturbation and the dimensions defining equilibrium conditions. Thus, the theory seems to be an instance of the perturbed recursive system from Section 1 (Fig. 2.3).

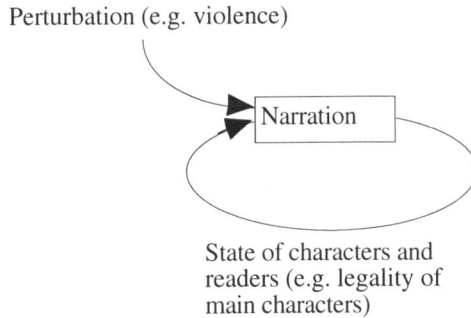

Perturbation (e.g. violence)

Narration

State of characters and
readers (e.g. legality of
main characters)

Fig. 2.3. Perturbed recursion as a narrative schema.

The genre itself is defined as a particular combination of the dimensions of perturbation and equilibrium (called 'discourse types' by Neale).

In each case, the marks of generic specificity as such are produced by an articulation that is always constructed in terms of particular combinations of particular types or categories of discourse.   *Neale 1983: 21*

For example, according to Neale, both gangster films and horror films use violence as the perturbator, but whereas the refiguration of equilibrium takes place in the discourse of Law (legal - illegal, presence - absence of legal institutions) in gangster movies, the trajectory of the horror movie lives in the dimension of the Monstrous with 'human' and 'natural' as opposites (Fig. 2.4 - 2.5).

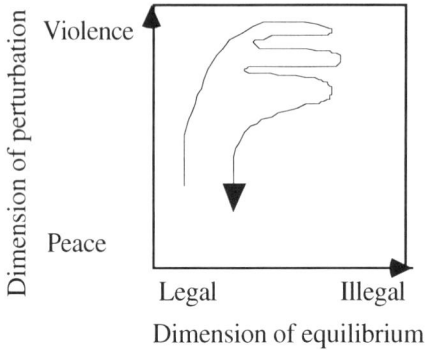

Fig. 2.4. The trajectory of gangster movies.

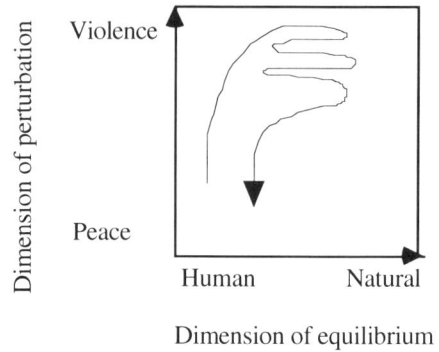

Fig. 2.5. The trajectory of horror movies.

On the other hand, whereas gangster and detective film both use violence as the perturbator, detective films are mostly concerned with the dimension of Meaning (Fig. 2.6):

In the detective film, the detective *and* the audience have to make sense of a set of disparate events, signs and clues. The 'risk' for the detective being represented in the narrative is a risk of violence and death. The risk for the audience is a loss of sense of meaning, the loss of a position of mastery.   *Neale 1983: 21*

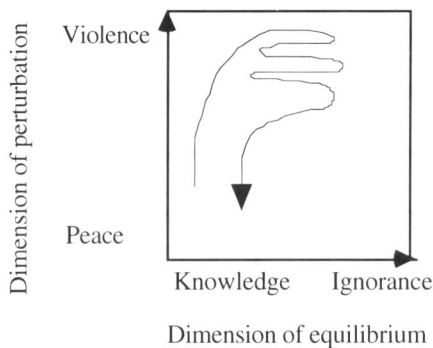

Fig. 2.6. The trajectory of detective movies.

But the space can also be a semiotic space, as in crazy comedies where the equilibrium dimension is the semiotic code articulated into *order* versus *disorder*, as in Marx Brothers films:

I know where the suspects are: they're in the house next door. — But there isn't any house next door. — Then we build a house next door. *Neale 1983: 24*

I need to say that Neale's theory is more subtle than is shown here. For example, the trajectory does not occur in two dimensions, but takes place in a multi-dimensional space, involving time, space, and other dimensions.

The idea of inequilibrium as genre-definition is of course not unique to Neale, but is used by many other authors, for example in terms of a contract that is violated.

Todorov (1970) has suggested that the Fantastic genre (exemplified by H.P. Lovecraft for instance) should be defined by means of a dimension of Belief with the endpoints 'natural' (the reader believes that the events have a natural explanation) versus 'supernatural' (the reader, and possibly the main character, believes that the events are supernatural). The defining characteristic of the Fantastic is that *the reader must keep hesitating, wavering between the two types of interpretation*. Thus, *X-Files* is Fantastic. If the narrative provides a natural explanation in the end, the novel is not *Fantastic* but *Shocking*, whereas it is *Wonderful* if the narrative is stabilized at the supernatural end of the scale.

In addition, Todorov requires the reader to accept that the text has a reference to actual persons and things: the reading may not be allegoric, where the literal sense of words are systematically replaced by a translation, nor poetic, which involves no reference whatsoever.

Thus, the Fantastic genre can be depicted as in Fig. 2.7. Novels that make a decision in the ending, such as *The Hound of the Baskervilles* by Conan Doyle, are depicted in Fig. 2.8.

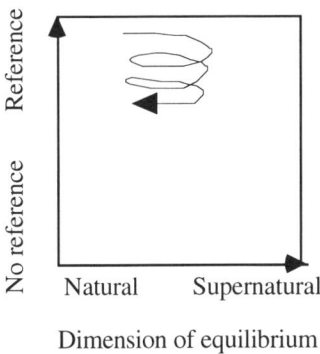

Fig. 2.7. The Fantastic Genre. E.g., H.P. Lovecraft.

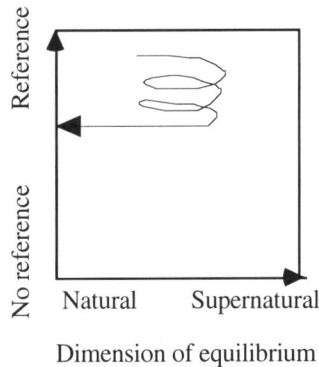

Fig. 2.8. The Shocker genre. E.g., *The Hound of the Baskervilles.*

If these examples can be generalized, *then genre can be defined by specifying the dimensions of the phase-space and the possible trajectories in it.*

In the latter task we can get help from the classification of possible trajectories from Section 1. For example, the mainstream film genres defined by Neale all have closure, i.e. they return to a state of equilibrium after having gone through

a series of oscillations that never exceed the limits of 'dramatic conflict' (that never, therefore, exceed the limits of the possibility of resolution).   *Neale 1983: 25*

We recall from Section 1 that a state or sequence of states which the system will enter after a certain amount of time, is called an attractor. If the attractor only comprises one state it is a fixed point attractor, whereas it is called a limit cycle if it contains more than one state. Fig. 2.9 shows the typical dynamics of Neale's mainstream movies: we start in a situation where the positive location begins to develop a repeller and thereby become an unstable equilibrium. If it is a gangster movie, the hero's legal status is jeopardized, and he starts sliding in the direction of crime and illegality. However, due to his actions, the situation changes, and the legal state once more acquires its status as a stable equilibrium.

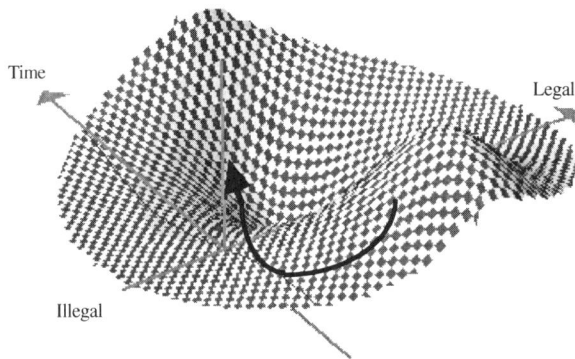

Fig. 2.9. The dynamics of gangster movies.

The initial inequilibrium of narratives must obviously be the result of a bifurcation causing the system to move towards the new point of equilibrium. In gangster and horror movies, the increase in violence is the boundary condition that makes the situation unstable and causes the story to begin. No liquidation, no retaliation, no gangster movie. No blood-sucking, no fear, no attempt to demolish monster, no Dracula movie.

It thus seems possible to define genres by means of the attractor type of the individual texts: the Fantastic genre must contain a limit cycle, whereas most of Neale's mainstream film genres must contain a fixed point attractor.

Let us now pass from the dynamics of the individual text to the dynamics of the genre, i.e. the collection of texts. According to Neale, genres ensure that the consumers of popular films or books can have both repetition and difference:

Genres, then, are not systems: they are processes of systematization. It is only as such that they can perform the role allotted them by the cinematic institution. It is only as such that they can function to provide, simultaneously, both regulation and variety.   *Neale 1983: 51*

The reason why this is desirable lies in the nature of — desire:

Desire is always a function of both repetition and difference ... Desire is [] founded on the urge to repeat and the impossibility of ever being able to do so. The reproduction of the signifier allows satisfaction, but it is a satisfaction marked by the gap between signifier and experience. The existence of the gap is the reason for the inexhaustibility of desire, but it also allows whatever satisfaction is attainable to be renewed. [...]

The mainstream narrative is nothing if not a 'text of pleasure': a text that regulates the subject's desire for pleasure, that functions, therefore, according to a precise economy of difference (the movement of desire, the subject ceaselessly in process) and of repetition (the containment of that movement, its repletion, the subject ceaselessly closed through the recuperation of difference in figures of tightly bound symmetry).   *Neale 1983: 48-9*

The key point here is that the media market is caught in a conflict if it is to satisfy the desire of the consumers: on the one hand it must provide stability and repetition because the radically new is discomforting and produces no immediate satisfaction; on the other hand, repetition produces boredom and a craving for the new.

In the preceding, the *contents* of novels and movies were described by means of the perturbed recursion schema. The relation between reader and text, i.e. the reading process, can be analyzed in a similar way. See Fig. 2.10.

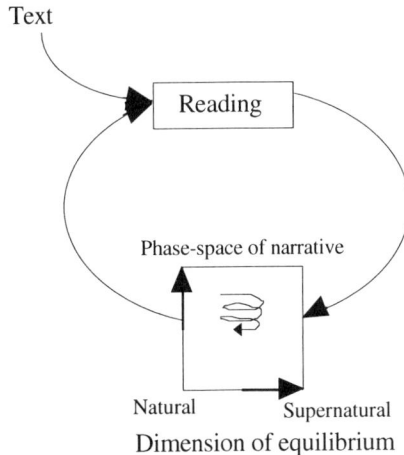

Fig. 2.10. The reading process.

The perturbator of the reading process is the text in its capacity as a series of visual and auditory elements. The iterator of the process is the phase-space, including its perturbator and iterator dimensions, its current trajectory, and its dynamics. Thus, reading a text or viewing a movie builds up the proper dimensions and their dynamics. In addition, the reading process includes the enacting of this dynamic space: the reading process is seen as a constructive process, where the text informs the building and enacting of dynamic spaces. This model explains why many narrative processes are not explicitly represented in the text, but interpolated by the reader: when the reader, guided by the text, has set up a dynamic space, this space takes over and executes trajectories that follow from the dynamics although they are not stated in the text. For example, it is enough that the film editor displays a shot showing the protagonist entering a plane followed by a shot showing the plane landing. We enact the middle part of the trajectory ourselves (cf. Bordwell 1985).

In this analysis, the perturbed recursion schema has a fractal self-similar geometry: the 'outer version' — the reading process — creates an inner version — the contents — with the same structure, namely a perturbator influencing a recursive process. And indeed, most symbolic processes do in fact exhibit a fractal self-similar structure: a text can embed other texts inside it (Ryan 1991), e.g., as a written dialogue, and a movie can itself refer to (fictive) movies. In Section 4.4 we shall elaborate further on the notion of self-similarity.

2.2. The dynamics of the art system

Whereas Neale offers a psychoanalytic explanation for the oscillation between repetition and difference, Yuri Lotman sees the pattern as a general mode of behavior for whole cultures (Lotman 1990).

His basic concept of a *semiosphere* seems close to the notion of a phase space. The semiosphere is 'the whole semiotic space of the culture' (Lotman 1990: 125), filled up with a diversity of languages and sublanguages. Lotman sees the semiosphere as a semiotic interpretation of the real physical space in which a culture lives;

The semiotics of space has an exceptionally important, perhaps even overriding significance in a culture's world-picture. And this world-picture is linked to the specifics of actual space.
Lotman 1990: 150

and describes the semiosphere as an abstract property-space, quoting the mathematician A.D. Aleksandrow:

When studying topological qualities we again are faced with the possibility of conceptualizing an abstract totality of objects having only those qualities. We term this totality abstract topological space.
Lotman 1990: 150

And further:

If by isolating a certain quality a set of continuously contiguous elements is formed, then we can speak of an abstract space of that quality. In this way we can talk of the space of ethics, of color, of myth. In this sense spatial modeling becomes a language in which non-spatial ideas can be expressed.

Lotman 1990: 150

The spatial notion enables Lotman to formulate many useful ideas for cultural analysis: a semiosphere is a real sphere with a center and a boundary. The center is the ruling culture defined by producing meta-descriptions intended to cover own practice as well as the practice of deviant cultures. Whereas the center strives towards consistency and harmony, inconsistency and conflict emerge as we travel towards the periphery. The boundary itself serves to give the culture its identity, dividing the world into a space of norms (us) surrounded by a space of normlessness (them):

Every culture begins by dividing the world into 'its own' internal space and 'their' external space ... The actual division is one of the human culture universals. The boundary may separate the living from the dead, settled peoples from nomadic ones, the town from the plains ...

Lotman 1990: 131

One can see the dynamics of a culture as a current running from the periphery to the center. Close to the boundary, the current is turbulent and disruptive, but as it draws closer to the center, its movements slow down and in the center of the culture, it reaches an equilibrium, stabilizes and freezes to ice.

A similar account is given by Nöth 1983. In opposition to language that strives towards states of equilibrium, Nöth considers the textual genres to be basically unstable. He quotes J. Tynjanov for the following account of literary code development:

1   In contrast to the automatic construction principle, a new opposed principle arises dialectically;
2   The new principle finds acceptance;
3   Its applicability expands, it becomes popular;
4   It becomes automatic and provokes opposed construction principles.

and continues

According to this model each new, opposed construction principle is a disturbance in the system of literature. The expansion of the principle is a process of negative [must be positive, PBA] feedback by which the disturbance is strengthened and the system finally changed, once it becomes automatic. Only during the process of automatization is the system in a state of equilibrium. But the new equilibrium is itself unstable, because a new phase of innovation must follow, and that means a new state of disequilibrium [...] literary codes have as their goal not equilibrium but the maintenance of the innovation process and thus of disequilibrium.

Nöth 1983: 119

We again see the same struggle between repetition/stability/automatization on the one hand, and difference/instability/creativity on the other.

The history of literature is a story of this battle: the age of Enlightenment in the 18th century rebelled against the orthodoxy of the baroque period, pitting reason and science against religion and superstition. New genres, like the encyclopedia, the essay, the satire (Swift), and the sentimental bourgeois novel (Fielding, Richardson) emerged from this battle. But to the romanticists of the 19th century, these genres appeared more and more soul-less and barren, keeping its public from emotional insights into the deep secrets of life. New genres appeared: the gothic tale (Hoffmann, Shelley), fairy tales (Grimm), folk poetry (Ossian), speculative philosophy (Schelling), the romantic poem (Blake, Burns, Coleridge, Byron).

But a new generation soon reacted to these genres under the banner of science and rationality, and we got the naturalistic novel, exemplified by Zola's novels, which was again opposed by the fin de siécle symbolism (Verlaine, Rimbaud, Mallarmé), and so on and so forth.

Oscillations like these have probably not always existed. In fact, Luhmann (1990) claims that they are caused by the differentiation of the art system as an autonomous social system in the 18th century. Only when art begins to free itself from direct influence from the church and patrons, and an educated public has been created, can an autopoietic art system organize itself.

Like the other writers, Luhmann emphasizes the craving for newness and the phenomenon of fluctuations — fashions, trends, schools — as characteristic of the art system:

The work of art is both the condition and obstacle for the autopoiesis of art. Without works of art there would be no art and without the prospect of new works of art no social system of art (but only museums and their visitors). 'New' means here, as it has since the seventeenth century, not only another example, but rather something that diverges from the foregoing and thus surprises. Genius lies in the accomplishment of discontinuity and it is clear that this temporal discontinuity presupposes a social discontinuity, i.e. the differentiation of art from the tutelage of other, above all religious and political interests.

Luhmann 1990: 195

But because of the inherent self-destruction of the concept of 'new-ness,' the art system is threatened by dissolution:

For whatever has to be new has for this reason no future. It cannot remain new. It can only be admired as that which was new. The social system of art is thus faced from this point on with the problem of the continual disappearance of newness.   *Luhmann 1990: 195*

Luhmann offers the concept of *style* as a remedy against this danger.

The particular qualities of the aesthetic form are functional for the organization of the experience of and communication about art. They are dysfunctional for the autopoiesis of the system of art itself. For how is it to continue? [..] Where does the 'organization' of autopoiesis lie if the work of art must put value on its own isolation? [...]. The question can be answered with the aid of the concept of style. [...] The function of style is to organize the contribution of the work of art to the autopoiesis of art, and in fact in a certain sense against the intention of the work of art, which aims for self-containment. *Luhmann 1990: 196-97*

Like genres, style is a means of ensuring the continuity of the autopoiesis of art, i.e. that one work of art can generate another work of art:

Style is thus, we may say, what joins work of art to work of art and thereby makes the autopoiesis of art possible. *Luhmann 1990: 203*

However, in order still to produce newness, the style/genres themselves must be subject to fluctuations:

The historicization of styles in the second half of the eighteenth century finally breaks with the traditional conceptions of time which had always allowed the unity of the beautiful, the true, and the good to be thought of as the acme of perfection. Only now can the work of art fully lay claim to its own singularity: for the individual uniqueness of the work of art is the surest guarantee that art always produces something new. *Luhmann 1990: 202*

And this finally produces the accelerating change of styles we witness in this century:

Certainly the tempo of change has increased — so much that change of style can no longer be explained by generational change. *Luhmann 1990: 209*

The argument is thus, as I understand it, that the characteristic of art lies in the production of newness and surprises. As emphasized by Neale, difference is a sine qua non of the work of art. But unlimited discontinuity will dissolve the art system as a social system, because there is no guarantee that the next work of art can be produced. Therefore styles/genres emerge that ensure a certain degree of continuity, but because of the demand for newness, style and genres cannot be eternal Platonic forms, as they were conceived in the Middle Ages. They must become historical and changeable.

   The existence of styles and genres presupposes that the demand of originality be relaxed, so that copying is allowed to a certain degree (Luhmann 1990: 198). In fact, in most genres a set of prototypical products can be identified. They are prototypical in several senses: on the one hand they embody the properties that are considered characteristic of the genre, and on the other, they have in fact been actual models for many members of the genre. For example, '2001' and 'Starwars' are typical science fiction films, 'The Stagecoach' a typical cowboy film, and 'Gone with the Wind' exemplifies the prototypical filmic melodrama.

   The next assumption I want to make is that the literary system is perturbed by social and cultural conflicts of both a historical and more general nature. The literary works of the Enlightenment, for example, responded to the social struggle between the feudal society and the rising bourgeois class, and the Romantic movement that followed reacted against the calculatory and materialistic world views of the rising capitalist society. Modernist schools in the middle of this century were concerned with the loss of values and meaning which followed in the wake of triumphant capitalism.

But since the art system is an autonomous system, it is not a mere reflection of the conflicts of society as some Marxist critics have suggested. The art system has its own inner logic that can be perturbed but not controlled by other systems. This enables the art system to pursue problems of a more general nature. Thus, although the travel novel can contain concrete political criticism of political systems, it can also discuss more existential problems. The theme of many of these novels, for example, is a basic feeling of non-belonging at home and a search for a new authentic identity abroad. In many cases, however, the problem cannot be solved, because, as tourists we do not belong to the places we visit, and, once there, the authentic life has moved on to another place.

The last assumption is that authors cannot pre-calculate the meaning assigned to a text by its audience. Although some authors guess better than others, the fact remains that textual interpretation emerges during the consumption process beyond the direct control of the producers. In this sense, the production process can be seen as a trial-and-error type of problem-solving process in a fuzzy and ill-defined problem area, where problems are defined by attempts to solve them. Furthermore, no person has direct access to new relevant themes (if such clairvoyants existed, they would be extremely rich). The social conflicts only reveal themselves through the trial-and-error process of writing texts about them.

This concludes the theory of genres and the literary market I would like to understand.

2.3. The dynamics of genre formation

The theory of genres following from these considerations can be summarized as follows:

1. The main process is a circular process whereby new texts are produced by recombinations of old ones. No writer or filmmaker starts from scratch but borrows some elements and varies others; any book or film enters a network of intertextuality with overt or hidden references to other texts.
2. However, this circle is perturbed by societal changes that outdate some problems and themes and actualize others. No person has direct access to the relevant problems and themes before they are written about.
3. Authors cannot pre-calculate the meaning assigned to a text by its audience.

4.   There exist more or less clear prototypes that are quite often used as models for new variations. A prototype is viewed as typical of the genre. Prototypes are in some sense 'central' with respect to their genre.

5.   There exist unsolvable contradictions generated by the general human condition and by specific historical circumstances (cf. 2) that authors still try to understand, come to grips with or even solve.

6.   Models for new texts are primarily selected from the set of prototypes in combination with their relevance for the unsolvable contradiction as perceived by the author.

7.   However, not all cultural production can be explained as recombinations of older texts. Evidently, revolutionary new ideas are created from time to time; in happy circumstances, these new ideas can themselves become the centers of new genres or replace old centers and thereby cause the genres to move.

Clearly, this theory needs further elaboration. For example, point 1 claims that 'new texts are produced by recombinations of old ones' but says nothing about the details of this process. For example, which elements are borrowed? Sentences? Themes? Characters? Endings?

I claim, however, that, elaborated appropriately, this model can explain important properties of genres, namely:

i   how they spontaneously emerge through the self-organizing processes of the individual texts, writers, and audiences;

ii   how they can stabilize themselves to such an extent that they prevent novelties from appearing;

iii how changes in the dilemmas create new genres, make old genres die out or bifurcate into subgenres that may become main genres as they drift apart;

iv   how a genre in the course of history may move to a new position and gradually change all of its former characteristics.

In short: how genres can be both dynamic and stable; how they can be both a result of an interaction between individual texts and able to constrain and change the texts that caused their existence.

How can I claim that points 1 - 7 explain phenomena i - iv? Well, I can't. One of the main reasons is that the theory only concerns local interactions among parts, whereas the claim concerns emergent properties of the whole. However, emergent properties are often difficult or impossible to predict from interactions of the parts; in addition, the domain of texts and genres is so large and complicated that it probably makes no sense to look for data that will prove our point. Instead of trying to prove that 1 - 7 in fact explains phenomena i - iv, I can set myself an easier task, namely to prove that 1 - 7 is a member of a larger class of theories — let us call them recursive theories (Fig. 2.11) — that has other members for which the claim can be proved. These members must be computational (Fig. 2.12), since I shall not be able to present analytical proofs, partly because I lack the skills, partly because techniques for such proofs may not exist (on use of computer models for understanding interacting distributed phenomena, see e.g., Casti 1997).

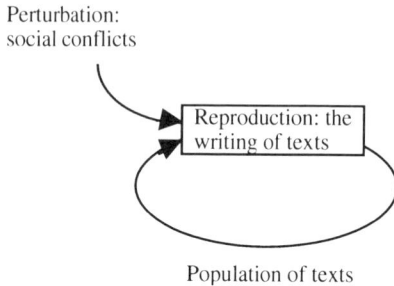

Perturbation:
social conflicts   Recursive theories

Fig. 2.11. The theory of genres as   Fig. 2.12. Model, Class of theories,
member of the general class of perturbed   and Theory of Genres.
reproduction theories.

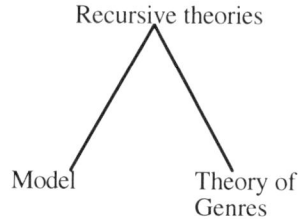

The goal of this paper is therefore very modest: to argue that the theory presented is a member of a more general class of theories that contains at least one member for which the claim can be proved. The goal is thus to prove that the theory is a possible theory.[3]

3. The model

In this section I describe the actual running model. Point (1) claimed that the main process was 'a circular process whereby new texts are produced by recombinations of old ones'. This indicates that the processes described by genetic algorithms (Davidor 1991, Davis 1996) could be relevant to the representation of the reproductive process in the computer program.

In the model the texts are represented by arbitrary sequences of 0's and 1's. Texts can be created in two ways, by *genetic recombination* and by *mutation*. Let us first illustrate *recombination*. Look at the two strings below:

(1)   001000000011
(2)   111000000001

Recombination means that we choose a section of the two strings and exchange them. Suppose we choose the section consisting of characters 2-3 in both strings. We then divide the two strings as shown in (3) and exchange the middle sections, which gives us (4).

---

3   Biologists have a similar problem, namely to explain the emergence of different species and their amaz-
     ing variety. See Todd & Miller (1997) and Werner (1997).

(3) 1-01-000000001   0-11-000000011
(4) 1-11-000000001   0-01-000000011

Finally, the two new strings are added to the population of strings.

Mutation merely means that we exchange an arbitrary 1 for 0 or vice versa.

Point (3) claimed that 'authors cannot pre-calculate the meaning assigned to a text by its audience'. This is concretized by defining the interpretation of the strings to be completely unrelated to their production process.

We divide each string into two halves and interpret each half as an integer. For example (2) is divided into 001000-000011, of which each half is interpreted as an integer. This gives us two numbers, 8 and 3. These numbers represent the *interpretation* or *value* of the string. Note that the construction of the string (recombination) analyses the string in a completely different way than the interpretation. In this way we represent the non-identity between construction and interpretation. The constructive process knows absolutely nothing about the ensuing interpretation.

The two numbers of the interpretation represent the location of the string in a two-dimensional phase space, cf. Section 2.1. The plane itself defines the set of possible themes, and the numbers locate the string in this continuum. However, the theory set forth in Section 2.1, namely that 'genre can be defined by specifying the dimensions of the phase-space and the possible trajectories in it', has been simplified somewhat. In the model the possible trajectories in phase spaces are reduced to a point in the phase-space representing the theme of the genre. Thus, the fantastic genre is defined by the location of its theme in the middle of the Natural/Supernatural dimension. This means that we can no longer distinguish between the Fantastic, the Shocking and the Wonderful. The reason for this simplification is not that the criterion cannot be implemented, but rather that it is more difficult and does not seem relevant to the main issues i-iv, which is the birth, differentiation and death of genres.

The theory of genres in i-iv now claims that texts are not distributed randomly in a thematic space but cluster together in certain areas. *Such clusters are the genres.*

Therefore, the first question is: can genres emerge if we start with a completely random distribution in the thematic space? The answer is: yes.

The secret lies in the requirement that central strings are more frequently used as parents to new strings than non-central ones. If this is the case, then it is an amazing fact that strings will cluster within specific areas even if the construction process knows nothing about the interpretation at all.

The program itself conforms to general schema for genetic algorithms and is an instance of the perturbed recursion schema:

```
Create initial population
repeat until some criterion is met
  choose two members of the population
        according to their value
  make two new recombined offsprings as
        indicated in 3-4.
  evaluate the offsprings
  choose two members of the population
        and kill them
  enter the offsprings into the population
end repeat
```

Code 3.1

The population of the algorithm is our texts. We are first required to find two good parents, and according to point (4) this search must be based on the prototypicality of the strings. In order to get a formal definition of this concept, we calculate the *isolation* of the strings. The isolation of a string x, I(x), is the mean distance between the string and its neighbors, e.g., the eight closest strings.

Since, according to (6), we want to reproduce central strings more often than non-central ones, we require that the probability of reproduction of string x and y, P(x) and P(y), must be inversely related to their isolation: the smaller the mean distance to its neighbors, the greater its chances for becoming a parent. Similarly, we calculate Q(x) and Q(y), which are their chances of getting killed, i.e. forgotten. These probabilities must be proportional to their isolation: the more isolated, the more likely it is to be forgotten.

The detailed construction of the formulas for P(x) and Q(x) is given in appendix A. The result is formulas (5-6), where K and L are constants depending upon the distribution of the total set of strings.

(5)
$$P(j) = \frac{K}{I(j)}$$

The probability of string j becoming a parent is inversely proportional to its isolation. The less isolated, the more chances of producing children.

(6)
$$Q(j) = L * I(j)$$

The probability of string j getting killed is proportional to its isolation. The more it is isolated, the greater chance it has of being the last of its kind.

3.1. Simulations

In the following I shall display some simulations that generate phenomena i-iv postulated in Section 2.4, but before presenting the results there are a couple of decisions made in the program that require comment.

The strings have the same length. This does not agree with our actual domain where texts have different lengths, and the decision is only motivated by ease of programming.

The number of strings is kept constant. Whenever a new central string is created, an old non-central string must die. To a certain degree this is motivated, since books do become obsolete and lose their significance for the literary process. However, the decision to use a constant population of strings is *not* motivated by the domain.

The system is based on concurrent processes. This is motivated since writers write in parallel, not sequentially, so that for example twenty new books may be written and published at the same time.

The isolation of a text is not necessarily calculated over the whole population but may *use a smaller subset of the closest neighbors.* For example, the isolation may be calculated as the mean distance to the five closest neighbors. This subset is called the *neighborhood*. This seems motivated by the domain. Neither writer nor reader can use the total set of books to interpret a book, since this presupposes a perfect knowledge of the market and unrealistic abilities to cope with the corresponding complexity.

Finally, the need for 'newness' (cf. Section 2.1) may prevent a certain central book which has been the parent of many books from being elected in the next period: as familiarity increases, boredom does too. To represent this we use a *familiarity* variable that is increased each time the strings are elected and decreased when they are not. Thus, instead of using (Appendix A)

(1)
$$Random\left(\frac{100}{P(j)}\right) = 1$$

to select new parents, we use

(2)
$$Random\left(\frac{100}{P(j)} + familiarity\right) = 1$$

For example, if P(j) — the chance of j becoming a parent — is 33%, then the program chooses it each time Random(3) = 1. However, if the familiarity value is 10, then it is chosen when Random(13) = 1. The corresponding probability has decreased to 7.7% chance of getting elected. Thus, increased familiarity counteracts the centrality of the string.

Run One. The first diagram in Fig. 3.1. very clearly shows that a random population of strings quickly clusters in one place, in fact after only 6 iterations.

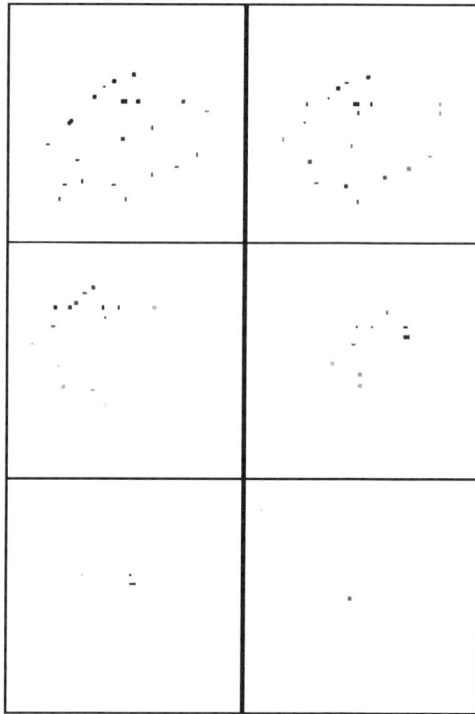

Fig. 3.1. Run 1. Dynamic diagram with a strong fixed point attractor.

We have a strong fixed-point attractor. The parameters of the diagram are shown in Table 3.1.

Length of strings	12
Number of strings	25
Number of iterations	10
Number of concurrent recombinations	5
Mutation rate	0.1%
Neighborhood	8
Increase in Familiarity	0
Decrease in Familiarity	0

Table 3.1. Parameters of Run 1.

The strings were 12 characters long, their number totaled 25, the number of iterations was 10 and in each iteration 5 concurrent recombinations were made. The mutation rate was very small (in fact no mutations took place), and the neighborhood used to calculate the isolation of the strings was 8. No increases in familiarity were used. If no new offsprings can be produced after a certain number of trials, the system begins to produce mutations.

The mean isolation of all strings decreased monotonely by a factor of 2.5.

Conclusion of first run: on the one hand, we have certainly proved point (i) in Section 2.4, but a little too much compared to reality: in the real literary market, we never end by reproducing copies of a single masterpiece! It seems as if the hardest problem is not — as we believed — to account for genre formation (regulation), but instead to account for the variety of genres!

In the next runs I experimented with various parameters. Here are the main results:

- In run two parenthood increased familiarity by 10, so that if a text had been the parent of another text it was less likely to beget children in the subsequent iterations. This medicine was not strong enough, since the strong attractor remained.

- In run three copying was prevented, so that children were always required to be different from their parents. This is well motivated, both for aesthetic and legal reasons. In this run, three clusters appeared and lived for a while, but eventually one of the groups won. The system ended in a state where no new texts could be produced; it went into an endless loop and had to be stopped by hand. The isolation measure no longer decreased monotonely. We seem to have proved claim ii: in the theoretical framework, genres can stabilize themselves to such an extent that they prevent any generation of new texts! Can the emergence of new genres be due to this type of literary indigestion?

- In run four the neighborhood was increased to 10, and the increase of familiarity remained at 10. Increasing the neighborhood is expected to slow down the growth of central strings. In this case we ended again in a situation with one cluster, but now the cluster stayed alive: there were no problems with generating new texts, and the cluster covered a regular space inside which it changed like an amoebae. By increasing the number of texts that are perceived as relating to each other and by maintaining the demand for novel texts, genres can be kept active while still constituting a coherent genre.

3.2. Social perturbations

In the previous runs we have only experimented with the *reproductive* function. Now we look at possible *perturbations*. We are interested in the stability of genres vis à vis social changes. For example, can well-established genres prevent new problems and dilemmas from being thematized in literature? And if they are thematized, can old genres move slowly to the new problem location or can new genres grow up around them?

By a dilemma I mean two antonyms (concepts that do not overlap) that both are attractive to authors and audience. The opposition between the natural and supernatural explanations of the Fantastic genre is a good example. As members of a secular society whose survival depends upon the natural sciences, we must endorse natural explanations in order to preserve our social reputation. On the other hand, natural explanations are boring and do not stimulate many people's imagination; faced with the dismal problems of the present society we all secretly hope that an unseen wonderful world may eventually reveal itself. Our brain and desire of social survival attracts us to natural explanations; but our heart and hopes for a better life move us in the opposite direction.

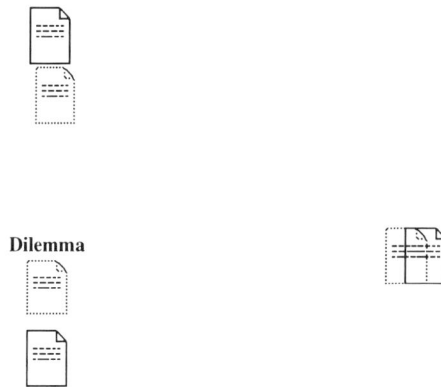

Fig. 3.2. Representation of dilemmas as distortions of a phase-space. Unbroken version: location in phase space without distortion. Dotted version: perceived location under the influence of the dilemma.

The hypothesis is that genres congeal around dilemmas generated by society, but that the actual position of the dilemmas is only revealed through discursive praxis. It cannot be observed directly through our senses but is gradually disclosed by trying to write about it.

In the model I have chosen to implement the force of dilemmas as a *distortion* in the phase-space: dilemmas are placed in the phase-space in the same way as texts are, but they only reveal their presence by shortening the distance to the surrounding texts (Fig. 3.2).

Dilemmas distort the interpretation of texts by attracting interpretations of neighboring texts to itself. This theory does not presuppose an objective interpretation of texts; it merely claims that dominant contemporary dilemmas bias the interpretation in a certain way. This explains why classics receive new — modern — interpretations in each historical era, and it explains why texts that have no relationship to each other in one period are viewed as having a common theme in another period: the semantic distances between texts are distorted by the dominant dilemmas of each era.

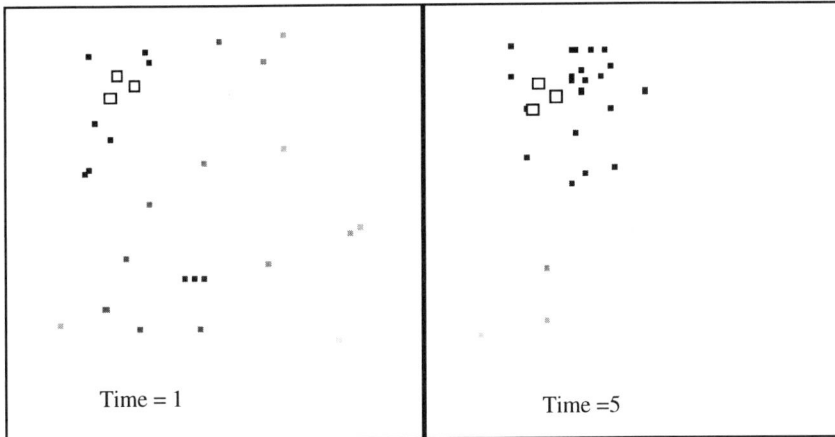

Fig. 3.3. Initial situation. The dilemma is   Fig. 3.4. Clustering around the dilemma.
represented by the three white boxes in the
upper left quadrant.

Run 5 showed a clear clustering around the dilemmas (Fig. 3.3 - 3.4). When I moved the dilemmas downwards, the original genre bifurcated into two: one stayed at the old location, another formed around the new dilemma (Fig. 3.5). However, after 29 iterations the new genres disappeared again and let the old genre reign supreme.

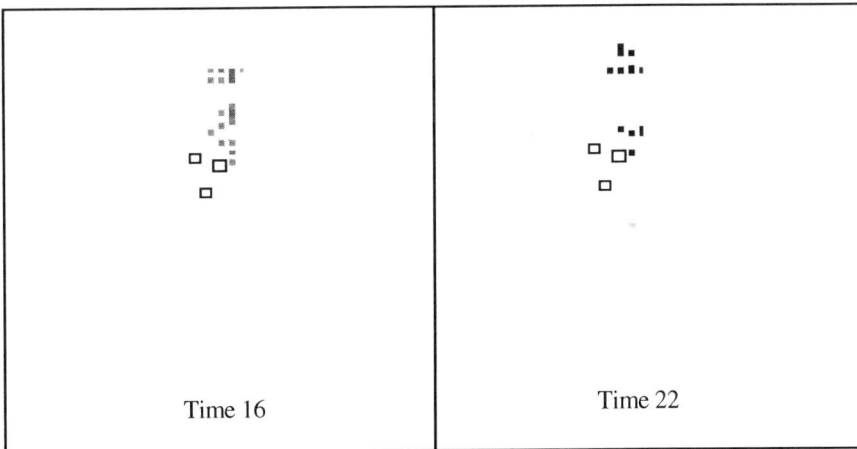

Fig. 3.5. Bifurcation of old genre as a result of a movement of the dominant dilemma.

A possible interpretation in terms of real texts is that after a change of social dilemmas, it is possible for a genre to bifurcate so that a new (sub) genre emerges around the new dilemma while the old genre still lives its normal life, although now devoid of social relevance. The immoral ending of this run is that obsolete tradition can have so much force that it kills its rival and re-establishes itself as the ruling genre.

We seem to have proved part of claim (iii), namely that in the chosen model genres can bifurcate into subgenres.

The model will also generate examples of perturbations that have no effect whatsoever on the existing genres. If we had moved the dilemmas to the bottom of the space, there would be no texts there to be influenced by the dilemma, the new distortion of the phase-space would have no effect on the isolation of the texts, and would therefore never be noticed by the literary market at all. In order for new dilemmas to be noticed, they must emerge in an area where they can cause re-interpretations of old texts.

3.3. Variety and repetition

In run 6 we add the constraint that no offspring may be equal to any of the old generation.

In a sense, this is not realistic, since an author does not have access to the whole population of texts. On the other hand, it stresses the demand for textual originality which grew in 19th century Romanticism. Each new text should be unique.

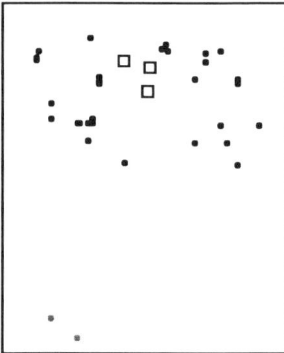

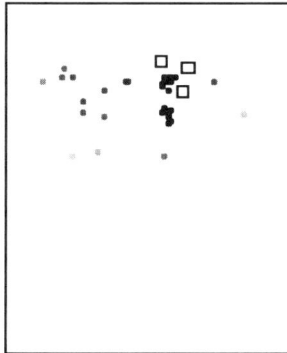

| Fig. 3.6. Weak clustering around dilemma. | Fig. 3.7. Clustering around dilemma. | Fig. 3.8. Genre is left behind. |

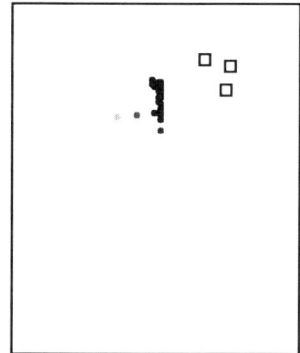

The constraint allows us to investigate the possible dynamics of authors caught in the dilemma of variety and repetition: on the one hand, the market demands repetition in the shape of genres; on the other hand, it expects every new text to be unique. Are the two opposing forces, regulation versus variety, irreconcilable, or is there a solution? A solution must consist in a collection of texts that are all distinct, but still cluster in the same area of the space. A set of texts that resemble each other but exhibit subtle shades of difference.

It turns out that there is a solution, but it certainly takes time to find it. Only in the 16th generation did texts begin to cluster, and it took 30 generations before two close-knit clusters formed.

In run 7 (Figs. 3.6-3.8) we move the attractors to the right and upwards for each iteration. In the beginning the texts clustered around the dilemmas, but the clustering seemed to be all too strong: although the dilemmas kept moving towards the right, the clusters stayed put. The genre was 'left behind' the social development! I could not simulate point (iv).

This example has made it abundantly clear that our theoretical framework has difficulty accounting for the ability of genres to adapt to new problem settings. When genre clusters have reached a certain critical size, they become insensitive to perturbations. The reason is threefold:

1.   They become self-sufficient. All strings lie in a confined cozy neighborhood so that their isolation is very low, and the distortion of the attractors plays a marginal role.
2.   Variety is insufficient. Close strings are similar; if all strings cluster in a small space, all strings are similar, and recombinations cannot produce offsprings that are markedly different from their parents.
3.   If mutations are isolated, they die too quickly to give rise to offsprings.

3.4. Chronic inequilibrium

In the preceding we have succeeded in describing patterns of genre formation based on local textual processes, but we overdid it: the genres turned out to be all too stable. I could not make the model sufficiently sensitive to changing social perturbations, nor create the internal chronic instability suggested by Nöth and Luhmann. Although this does not mean that no versions of the model can be made to accomplish this, it motivated the experiments with the following modification of the model.

The new idea is that literary codes keep oscillating between two phases, corresponding to two *cultural climates:* an innovative phase where old traditions are challenged and dissolved, and a stabilizing phase where the new ideas themselves become stabilized and standardized.

The preceding experiments provide a plausible reason for this oscillation: the important themes and contradictions of a cultural change as a result of changes in the rest of society — technology changes, commerce changes and the families' living conditions change — but although the themes are real, they are not floating around just waiting to be discovered. They need to be written about in order to become visible and socially accessible. Since they cannot be observed except at the moment of writing, the question is: how can we ensure that a social system discovers its own problems? Our experiments certainly showed that this cannot be taken for granted. On the contrary, it is easy to set up conditions that make genres so stable that they will not move when the problems move. Thus, situations where writers continue writing about problems that have become obsolete, and neglect problems that are pressing, can easily occur.

A built-in oscillation which forces the literary market into innovative, experimental climates could be one way to enhance self-reference.

The conjecture is that the class of theories we called theories of perturbed recursion does not seem to possess the desired properties. In the following we look at theories that involve two or more mutually perturbing systems.

The following model consists of two mutually perturbing systems, the literary market as we know it and the *Cultural Climate*. Both systems are controlled by processes with perturbators that can be influenced by the other system (Fig. 3.9).

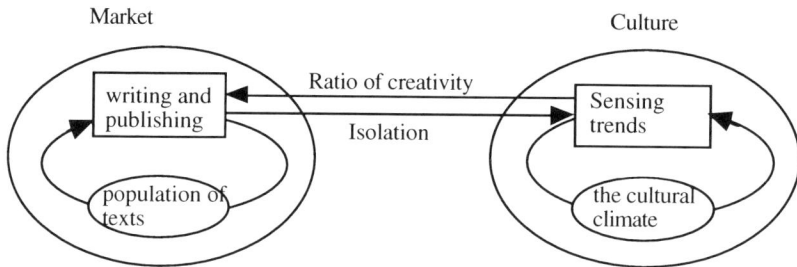

Fig. 3.9. The coupled systems model.

The two systems are autonomous in the sense that they do not directly interfere with each other: one produces texts, the other produces a general Cultural Climate (placing us an innovative phase (e.g., the early seventies) or in one where the most important task is stabilization of previously destroyed norms (e.g., the eighties). This means that writers do not take the temperature of the Cultural Climate and use that directly as a recipe for writing, nor can the public read books as explicit symptoms of cultural trends. The relationship between culture and the literary market is more indirect.

The writing process is basically concerned with creating new texts inspired by old texts, and is only perturbed by the Cultural Climate. In our model, the Cultural Climate determines the ratio of creativity, i.e. the ratio between recombinations and mutations, and not the concrete themes taken up by texts.

Similarly, the change of the Cultural Climate is mainly a function of the existing climate, but is perturbed by the actual main isolation (the variety) of the market.

Can this theoretical revision help us understand the real dynamics? In line with our methodology, we first check whether there are varieties of this theory that can describe the desired type of oscillations. And since the theory belongs to the non-linear type, we look again for a formal variation that can be experimented with on a computer.

Now let us return to developing the model.

In order to create a formal model, let N denote the number of new texts in each iteration. Then let R denote the number of texts produced by recombination, let M denote the number of texts produced by mutation, and let I denote the mean isolation of the texts, i.e. the mean distance of the texts to their neighborhoods.

We know that R + M must equal N

(1) $$N = R + M$$

and in addition we assume the R and M are related to I: the larger the isolation (variety) the larger the number of recombinations, and the smaller the number of mutations. See (2). In the following we use a function of I, C(I) the *Cultural Climate,* that is inversely related to I, so that larger I's give smaller functional values. This means that the larger I, the smaller C(I), and the larger the number of recombinations. Therefore, M is proportional to C(I) and R is inversely proportional. See (3).

(2) $$\frac{R}{M} \approx I$$

(3) $$\frac{M}{R} \approx C(I)$$

On the one hand, the more isolated and scattered the texts are, the more recombinations will take place, causing the literary texts to contract into fixed and localized genres. On the other hand, the less isolated the texts are, the more mutations will occur, causing the fixed genres to scatter into the whole problem space.

Solving (1) and (3) for R and M gives us

(4) $$M = N\frac{C(I)}{C(I)+1}$$

(5) $$R = N\frac{1}{C(I)+1}$$

Now we only need to determine how to calculate the Cultural Climate. The Climate must be a function that essentially yields values in intervals corresponding to the two phases: if Isolation is small (texts clot) then Recombination should be small, and if it is large (texts are scattered), Mutation should be small. Between the two intervals a small interval should exist where the Climate quickly moves from one value to another. One possibility would be to use catastrophe theory to do the job, cf. Section 1. In the following, we shall use the popular cusp:

(6) $\quad y = x^4 + ax^2 + bx$

The cusp family of equations has two parameters, a and b. By varying the b parameter, we can change the number and location of attractors, as shown in Figs.
3.10 to 3.12.

The idea is now to place an object inside the curve and let it be influenced by
the negative of the gradient of the curve. If placed on a slope it will roll down into
the nearest minimum, where it will stay. The location of this object is used to provide the values of the Climate controlling the ratio between Recombination and
Mutation. If the object is placed in the minimum of Fig. 3.10, it will stay there as
we increase b. It will rest in the right minimum during Fig. 3.11, and only begin to
change position in Fig. 3.12 for a sufficiently large b. The Isolation of the texts
perturbs the cultural system by being used as the b-parameter, so it is the Isolation
that causes the catastrophes in the cultural system.

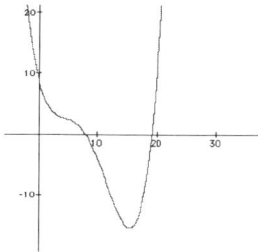

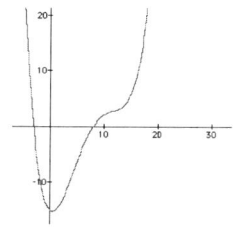

| Fig. 3.10 . b negative. | Fig. 3.11. b = 0. | Fig. 3.12. b positive. |

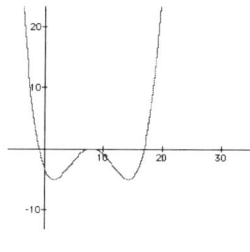

In this way we convert a continuous change — the change of the Isolation of the
texts — into a discrete change — a catastrophe — namely the change of Cultural
Climate that controls the proportion of expansion and contraction. In addition, the
location of the change when we go from expansion to contraction is different
from the location of the catastrophe when we travel in the opposite direction, from
contraction to expansion.

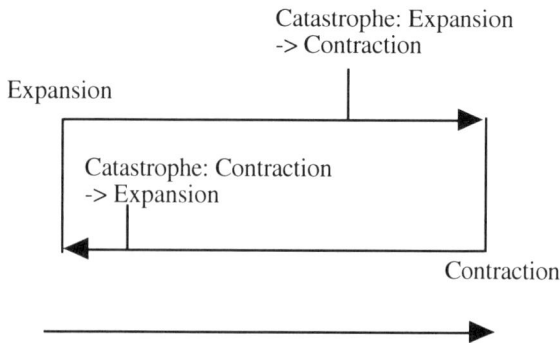

Catastrophe: Expansion
-> Contraction

Expansion

Catastrophe: Contraction
-> Expansion

Contraction

Fig. 3.13. The literary cycle.

When we move to the right in Fig. 3.13 (top trajectory), we are in a phase of renewal and dissolution. At the point to the right, the catastrophe occurs, and the ratio of mutation and recombinations is changed to the benefit of Recombination. The texts begin to clot and the isolation of texts decreases: we have entered the phase of stabilization (bottom trajectory).

This phase will continue beyond the point of the first catastrophe. When the next catastrophe eventually does occur to the left of the middle, the genres have had sufficient time to clot, and the cycle can now repeat itself. Thus, there is a built-in conservatism in the literary market, and it is in fact this conservatism that generates the oscillation.

After having chosen appropriate dimensions for the potential function and scaled the I in a suitable way, we let the new Cultural Climate C depend upon its own previous state and the isolation of the text of the market as shown in (7).

(7) $$c_t = c_{t-1} - f'(c_{t-1}, I_{t-1}).$$

(7) expresses the dynamics, i.e. the mode of development, of the Cultural Climate. It says that the climate moves towards the nearest attractor and that the nature of this attractor is determined by the isolation (density) of the products of the literary market.

The systems are of the kind Thom classifies as metabolic: the internal state of one system is used to perturb the other system, whose internal state again is used to control the first system.

A possible philosophical interpretation of this description is that the structure we experience in our world is the result of our own doing, that is: structures are the result of self-organizing processes. Even if a writer may complain of a hopeless Cultural Climate and feel it as heavy fetters around his neck, he has in fact himself participated in creating those fetters by his previous contributions to the market. But since the relation between his practical actions and their effects is non-linear, it is difficult for him to see that his chains are all of his own making: there are no eternal, mysterious laws of culture that govern the fate of civilizations and cultures.

The next examples verify that the formal system behaves as desired. Fig. 3.14 shows a typical run. The market starts in a scattered state, but it contracts quickly. The contraction reaches its maximum after 5 iterations, and then slowly begins to build up diversity again. The diversity reaches its maximum at iteration 25, and starts contracting again.

This proves that the type of theory we are working with has formal variants which do in fact produce the dynamics desired. But again: it does not prove that the theory is a correct theory of the actual domain of cultural innovation, only that it is a *possible* theory.

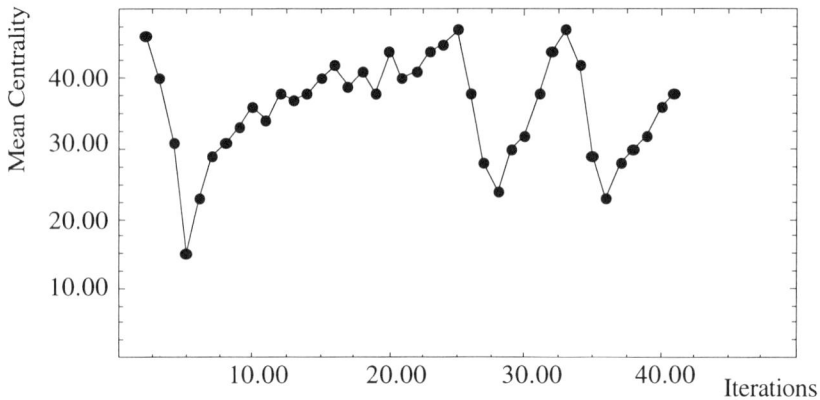

Fig. 3.14. Oscillation between contraction and expansion.

4. Types of causation

In this section we shall discuss two interpretations of the arguments in the preceding sections. The first interpretation uses the three types of downward causation described in Emmeche, Køppe & Stjernfelt (this volume). The second one exploits the notion of heterogeneous scales presented in Lemke (this volume).

4.1. Autonomous levels in texts

Let us first look at the notions of upwards and downwards causation as they occur in the human sciences. *Upwards causation* means that global patterns are created by the interaction of many parts, *downwards causation* means that these patterns can constrain and possibly change the self-same interactions that caused the patterns to emerge in the first place.

It is not unusual in the cultural sciences to assign some kind of autonomy to the superordinate levels. One reason is that if some kind of autonomy of levels did not exist, we would not be able to account for the actual literary battles and controversies of which text history is so full. If genres only existed in the eyes of the beholder, then it ought to be easy to break with the past literary styles and genres. One could just write a new text. But this is not how it works. On the contrary, new literary styles are nearly always accompanied by aggressive attempts from the new generation to free itself from the fetters of the old tradition. Therefore something must exist that needs to be fought. An account that only uses upwards causation ascribes too little stability and too much flexibility to genres.

We have the same problem in accounting for ideology. From a materialistic point of view, ideology can be considered an emergent property of the interactions of a group of human beings, of their material living conditions. If conditions are changed beyond a critical limit, the ideology changes too. Feudal society goes hand in hand with a hierarchical and static way of thinking, whereas capitalist society gives rise to ideas of dynamics and equality. Rich soil yields soft religion, poor soil engenders fundamentalism.

The problem is, however, that even if there is some truth in this idea, ideology seems to be all too stable for this explanation to hold. Romantic ideas that emerged in the 19th century still hold their grip on modern man. Obsolete ideology is the rule rather than the exception.

Furthermore, ideology exerts downward causation, i.e. it changes the material conditions from which it emerged. The clearest example is political ideology: the notion of equality, inherent in capitalism, may constrain the equal exchange of market economies in order to enhance equality in the consumer section of society (the welfare state).

This autonomy of levels is in fact an important ingredient in the *hermeneutic circle* which is assumed to occur during any kind of semiosis: reading the individual words helps create the global meaning of the sentences, and, conversely, the global meaning modifies the meaning of the individual words. This kind of mutual modification of parts and wholes does not stop at the sentence level but continues throughout the whole text (cf. the notion of *backward causation* in Togeby (this volume). In the beginning, the word 'rose' may mean a flower, but in the ending it may have acquired an elaborate non-standard metaphorical meaning.

In the hermeneutic circle one may say that the reader's interaction with the whole continuously modifies the rules by which he interacts with its parts. In addition, it is hard to point to external variables during the reading process that change boundary conditions. So during the individual reading of a novel or viewing of a film, we seem to have a closed loop where part and whole mutually reorganize each other.

That the level of texts and the level of sentences indeed form two autonomous levels can be seen from the practice of textual analysis. On the one hand, it is certainly possible to write a concise description of sentence patterns in a language, and on the other hand it is also possible to describe global patterns of textual organization (Propp 1975, van Dijk 1980, Johnson and Mandler 1980).

A simple sentence grammar could look like this:

SENTENCE	->	NP AUX PREDPH
NP	->	DET (ADJPH)* N (S)* I
		S
PREDPH	->	VP (PREPPH)*
VP	->	AUX V (NP) (NP)
V	->	givelseelrun

N   ->   boy|girl|ice| eat
DET   ->   the|a
....

which, with appropriate additions, would generate sentences such as 'The girl gave the boy the ice', 'The boy saw the ice', 'The girl runs', 'The boy saw the girl that ate the ice', etc.

An example of a text grammar is given in Johnson and Mandler 1980:

STORY   ->   Setting and EPISODE
EPISODE   ->   {Beginning event Cause DEVELOPMENT}*
                                   Cause ENDING
DEVELOPMENT   ->   COMPLEX REACTION Cause GOAL PATH |
                                   DEVELOPMENT Cause DEVELOPMENT
COMPLEX REACTION   ->   Simple Reaction Cause Goal
GOAL PATH   ->   Attempt Cause OUTCOME
OUTCOME   ->   Outcome Event | EPISODE
ENDING EVENT   ->   Ending Event | EPISODE

Note that these formally identical descriptions use completely different types of categories. Whereas the grammar categories are mainly defined by distribution criteria of morpheme classes, are eventually rewritten as actual morphemes, and involve only vague reference to meaning, the categories of story grammar denote global meanings that are assigned to larger stretches of sentences, they do not refer to specific grammatical structures, and they are not rewritten as actual morphemes. In fact, the terminal symbols of the text grammar (Setting, Beginning event, etc.) may cover whole pages in the text.

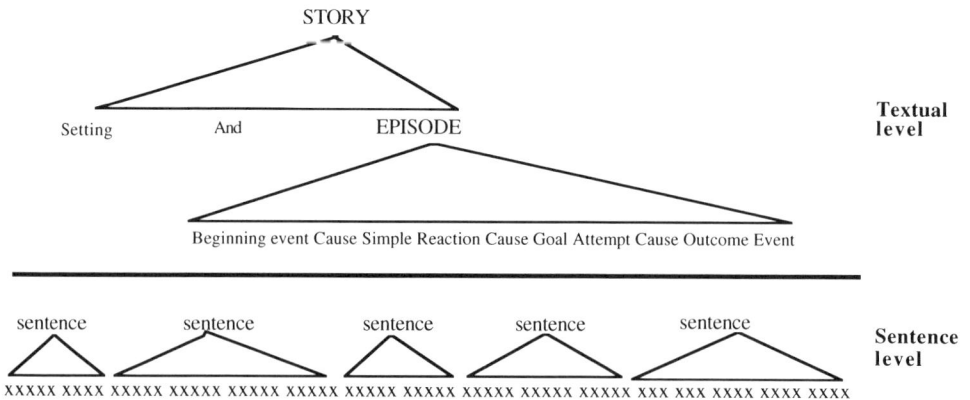

Fig. 4.1. The gap between text- and sentence grammars.

Thus, there are two levels, each with their own structure and categories, and separated by a deep chasm. As shown in Fig. 4.1, one can set up explicit descriptions of the textual level and of the sentence level, but not of the relationship between the textual and the sentential level.

We find the same difference when we compare the actants of Greimas (1979) to the cases of case-grammar. The subject of the *story* — i.e. the actant that desires to acquire an object and which may be hindered by an Antagonist and helped by a Helper — need not be the subject of its *sentences*. For example in *The Tinder Box* (Togeby, this volume) the soldier is the subject of the narrative but not necessarily the subject of the sentences. For example, the witch utters the sentence 'I'll give you my blue checked apron to spread out on the floor.' where the soldier is the recipient (dative). Still, the subject of the narrative in some genres may statistically tend to occur often as the subject of sentences, which in fact is the case in the quotation. The soldier *marches, meets a witch,* and *says things.*

What is certain, however, is that there is no simple logical relationship between the structure of the text and that of the sentence. One cannot derive one from the other in a simple fashion. Concepts like EPISODE, OUTCOME, Event are higher-level concepts that emerge from the reader's interaction with the lower-level words and sentences but seem to possess an objective existence, for example in the sense that people normally do not remember the actual wordings of the text, only the textual 'macrostructures' (Folke Larsen 1981).

If we compare these observations with the three kinds of downward causation in Emmeche, Køppe & Stjernfelt (this volume), it seems as if we have a type of *strong* downward causation: 'A given entity or process on a given level may causally inflict changes or effects on entities or processes on a lower level.' The authors associate this thesis with two assumptions:

Ontologically or materially, a higher level entity is constituted by the lower level, but even if lower level entities are a necessary condition for the higher level, this higher level cannot be reduced to the form or organization of the constituents. Thus, the higher level must be said to constitute its own substance and it does not merely consist of its lower level constituents.

A higher level entity is defined by a substantial difference from lower level entities. The morphological or organizational aspect is a necessary but not sufficient condition of a higher level entity. By emergence, an ontological change in substance takes place.

As well-known examples of new entities in the textual domain, we can mention *reference* associated with the level of noun phrases, *truth* (and other illocutionary effects) associated with the level of sentences, and *coherence* and *cohesion* associated with the level of text.

4.2. Signs as mediators between different scales

Although one can argue that semiosis involves strong downward causation, the coupled systems model in Section 3.4 does not fit well into this concept. In the model, the Cultural Climate must represent the upper level and the population of texts the lower level; each level is a closed system and upwards and downwards causation is represented by mutual perturbation between the systems.

However, the Cultural Climate does not have the texts as its parts, as should be the case if the two systems were to form a level structure. Rather than being part of a hierarchy, the two systems seem to be located at the same level but at two different scales. And even worse, the cultural institutions embodying the Cultural Climate, can be seen as a part of the literary market, since its products circulate in approximately the same channels as do the literary texts themselves and are read by overlapping groups of people. Thus, the level of the Cultural Climate is embodied as a part of the lower level from which it emerges! Something is clearly wrong here.

This motivates an alternative analysis that describes the relation between the two systems, not in terms of levels, but in terms of scales: the events of the market takes places on a lower scale than those of the Cultural Climate. To one change of climate corresponds many iterations on the literary market, and whereas the individual writer on the market can only observe a local and limited neighborhood of texts, the Cultural Climate observes average values of the whole population of texts. Thus, the Cultural Climate exists on a larger temporal and spatial scale than the literary market. Finally, we can point to social organizations that can be said to embody the Cultural Climate: the institution of literary criticism, publishers, schools and universities. The function of these institutions is to observe the development of texts over time-scales that may be rather large — hundreds or thousands of years, as in the case of the history of literature.

This makes Lemke's ideas of *scale heterogeneity* (this volume) attractive as an interpretation of the models. In this interpretation both the market and the Cultural Climate are social institutions that perturb one another, the difference between them being one of scale.

How is mutual perturbation possible between systems based on different scales? The question is relevant since there are many cases in which interaction between systems of different scales are impossible or difficult. For example, although I may observe and change properties of my arms or legs, it is very difficult for me to communicate with one of my cells; and although I know how to interact with a civil servant, I am not able to interact with his department as a whole.

The latter example shows one way of solving the problem of incommensurability of scales, namely by appointing representatives of scale i-1 for systems of scale i. The civil servant belongs to the same scale as me but represents a department of larger scale, in the same way as presidents and kings represent the state they govern. The technique is based on the rhetorical figure of *Synecdoche, pars pro toto*, and is thus a semiotic technique where something (civil servant, president) stands for something else (department, state).

The hypothesis is now that this observation can be generalized, so that interaction between heterogeneous scales is always mediated by sign-processes. In order to see this we have to take a closer look at signs.

An important property of signs is that they impose one set of distinctions on a substance that may itself contain no sharp distinctions (e.g., colors) or may contain many distinctions. Put differently, signs are used to classify, to recognize and to produce patterns. Signs do this in two ways simultaneously: they impose semantic form onto the signified, e.g., classify humans into man, women, adults, and children, and they impose phonological form onto the signifier, e.g., classify vowels into /i/, /e/, /a/, etc.

However, whereas the scale of the *signifier* remains constant, the scale of the *signified* may vary greatly. For example, whereas the signifier of the word 'now' is always realized as a sound that takes less than a second to pronounce or write, its meaning can denote very different time scales (this second ('Do it now'), this morning, this day, this year, this century ('The old enmity between Denmark and Sweden is now replaced by peaceful competition'). The word 'here' displays the same versatility with respect to location: it can mean 'here, close to me', 'here, in this city', 'here, in this country', and so on.

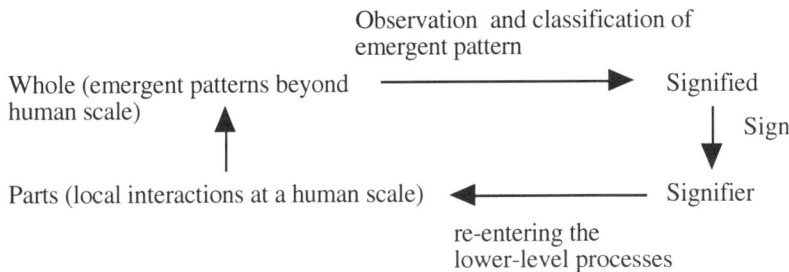

Fig. 4.2. The sign as realization of downwards causation.

Thus, although we cannot interact with the Tax Authority per se, we can certainly talk about it. Since, on the one hand, the scale of the signified can be of a size that precludes any human interaction and, on the other hand, the signifier is always on a scale which allows interaction with a human, *the locus of downward causation in scale-heterogeneous interaction is the sign,* i.e. in the relation between the signifier and the signified. The signified classifies emergent patterns of arbitrary size and its signifier guarantees that these types of patterns acquire a form that can enter into the lower level processes that generated the emergent patterns, and thus serve to stabilize the patterns (Fig. 4.2). For example, texts written by literary historians can span centuries and continents, but they all end up as a physical form that can re-enter the literary recursion, and thereby stabilize the patterns.

How do language users classify continuos perturbations? One way of describing this faculty (the 'categorial perception' described by Clark & Clark 1977: 200) is offered by catastrophe theory (cf. Section 3.4). Consider the strip in Fig. 4.3.

Fig. 4.3. Female body gradually changing to male head. From Saunders (1990: 94).

If one shows this strip to people by slowly disclosing each frame at a time, they will experience a sudden 'jump' of interpretation somewhere near the middle. There is no phase where we see something in between the woman and the man. In addition, people tend to be conservative in their interpretation, so if we start from the left, the male face is only seen to the right of the middle, whereas the woman appears to the left of the middle if we start from the right side.

In our example, two descriptions compete

1. The drawing is a female body
2. The drawing is a male face.

Under some perceptual conditions, the subject, 'the drawing', combines with the predicate, 'a female body', under other conditions it combines with 'a male face'. The experiment shows that as we continuously vary the perceptual features, the description changes abruptly, 'catastrophically'. Language imposes a discrete form onto a continuous visual stream. If we describe the forces of attraction between subject and predicate by means of the parameterized potentials of catastrophe theory (Section 3.4), and if we let the visual stream be identical to the parameters, then we can account for categorial perception, as shown in Fig. 4.4. The internal variable of the system (the horizontal dimension) represents the syntagmatic dimension of language, i.e. the before/after relation of morphemes.

In (1) the subject 'drawing' is attracted to an equilibrium position (a basin) to the left of the predicate 'female body' and we get 'The drawing is a female body'. In (2) the picture has become ambiguous, so two attractors exists, one with 'female body', another with 'male head', but since the location to the left of 'female body' is still an attractor, the subject stays there. In (3) the leftmost attractor has disappeared, the subject jumps to the 'male face' predicate, and we utter the sentence 'The drawing is a male face'.

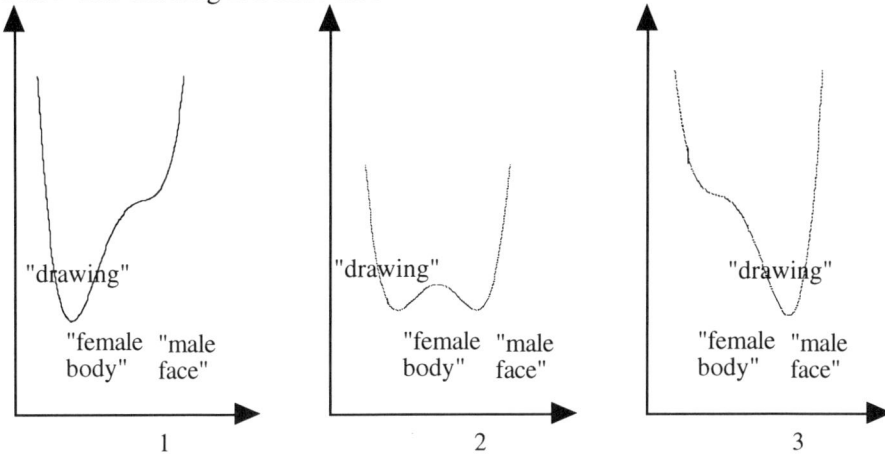

Fig. 4.4. Interpretation of visual stream.

In fact, the same technique was used in the coupled systems model of Section 3.4. Only here the input was not visual but cultural observations. Instead of observing a changing picture, the Cultural Climate system observed continuous variations of textual production, and, at a critical point, underwent a catastrophe where one set of attractors was exchanged for another. In the same way as in the face/body example, the attractors are assumed to regulate linguistic processes, which in this case is self-description, since the critics and philosophers describe a cultural situation of which they are part too ('The climate is conservative'). See Fig. 4.5.

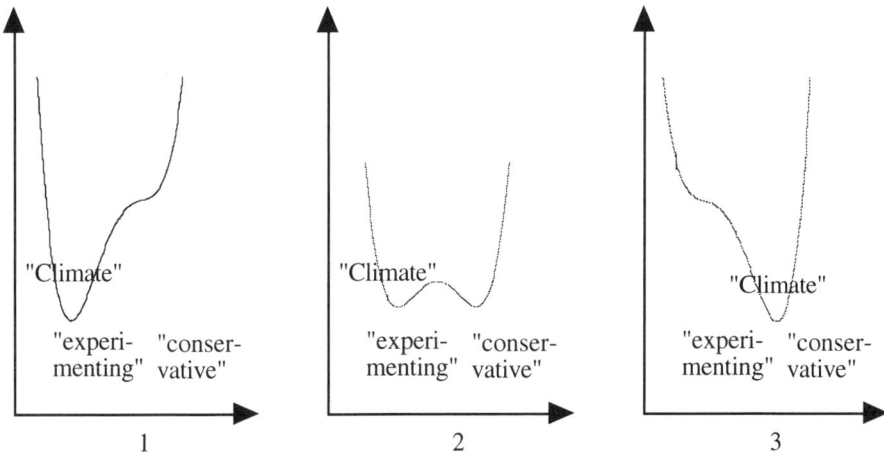

Fig. 4.5. Interpretation of a culture.

4.3. Observers and observees

In conclusion, we can generalize Fig. 3.9, which concerns the literary market, to Fig. 4.6 which encompasses all social processes.

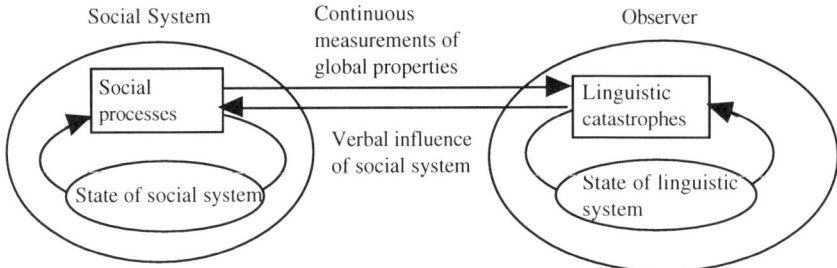

Fig. 4.6. General model of stabilization of levels.

The processes of a social system are iterative and strictly local. Normally we only perceive phenomena at our own scale, and we act according to this limited perspective. However, humans and their societies are capable of the paradoxical trick of observing themselves. The trick is paradoxical since in order to observe something one must (momentarily, at least) disentangle oneself from the object and keep a certain distance, but how does one disentangle oneself from oneself and keep a distance from oneself? In normal everyday work people simply stop working and begin discussing its problematic features (Andersen 1997: 406 ff). Or one can use a division of labor, so that one role observes another role, as when the coach observes the football players or management observes the economic development of the company. In these cases, emergent features are stabilized or changed by means of self-observation.

Lotman (1990) supports this argument. According to him, the stabilization of culture is due to self-description. The ruling culture in the center of the 'semiosphere' stabilizes itself by describing itself. Language is stabilized by grammars, and social norms by written laws and regulations.

The observer system, which is both part of the social system and (momentarily) distinct from it, is perturbed by continuous observations of higher-level emergent processes of the social system. Since the observer system is also a communicative system (which is also true of the social system itself), it converts the continuous inflow into discrete linguistic catastrophes, i.e. into general statements about emergent properties of the social system.

Since these statements are on a scale that can become a part of the state of the social system and thus can enter into its recursion, the observing system can re-influence the social system.

And since the observing system is assumed to be autonomous, the social system only perturbs it, that is, it only deflects the basic recursion of the observing system, but does not determine its precise course. Due to this autonomy of the observing system, we must assume that it performs many syntactical operations that cannot be seen as a direct result of the perturbation, and that properties of these sentences can be measured by the observed system. And indeed, the institution of literary criticism certainly does not stop at a cultural diagnostic, but normally also generates normative sentences that are intended to change the situation.

4.4. The fractal self-similar structure of meaning

If we collect the various examples of the perturbed recursion schema in this chapter, we discover that it can be embedded. For example, the signifieds of novels or films were analyzed as perturbator processes that set the narrative in motion by creating instabilities, and iterator processes that define equilibrium conditions. But this dynamic space is itself embedded into the reading process where the text works as a perturbator of the psychic system in which the narrative is enacted. These interpretative processes are themselves parts of the large-scale dynamics of the literary market where new texts are evaluated. The literary market, in its turn, functions as an environment of the literary institutions that are perturbed by market trends and generate new texts on the same scale as the market products.

Name	Perturbator	Iterator	Dynamics	State
Narrative (psychic system)	disturbance of equilibrium, e.g., violence vs. peace	equilibrium dimension, e.g., ignorance vs. knowledge	narrative process	state of presupposed reader or protagonist
Reading	text or movie	*Narrative*	creation and execution of Narrative	state of reader
Market(social system)	social dilemmas + cultural climate	population of texts	recombination and mutation (borrowing and invention)	state of market
Criticism	scattering of texts of *Market*	cultural climate	analysis and criticism	verbal description of climate

The perturbed recursion schema is thus self-similar in the sense that parts of the schema may itself be perturbed recursion schemas.

5. Summary

The main point of this paper is that signs work as stabilizers (and perturbators) of emergent patterns. The hypothesis predicts that the stabilization of emergent complex patterns has a qualitatively new nature in sign-using systems (cf. Pattee, this volume and Pattee 1987: 331). In these cases, continuous properties of large-scale systems (the observed systems) perturb small scale-systems (the observer system), which may even be a part of the observed system. The observer system generates signs with the large scale patterns as their signified and a normal human-scale signifier. The human-scale signifier can enter into the human-scale interactions of the observed system and thereby either disturb or stabilize it.

The line of arguments leading to this conclusion can be retraced as follows.

The empirical subject of the paper is genres because genres seem to be a good example of emergent and rather stable patterns which need the notion of downward causation for their explanation.

We started by reviewing the literature on genre formation and found that some theories of genres could be formalized in terms of attractors and trajectories in a phase-space which represents the thematic space of the texts. The dynamics of the phase-space was represented by perturbed recursive processes.

A description of the literary market was turned into an informal theory that was used to build a computer model driven by a genetic algorithm. Each text was assigned a point in thematic space (which is a simplification of the idea of trajectories) and new texts were generated by means of recombination (intertextuality) and mutation (invention). Parts of the algorithm could be interpreted in terms of real literary processes, whereas other parts could not.

As the computer model was run, it turned out that genre formation was a natural effect of the model. Thus, the problem of accounting for emerging genres turned out to have a natural solution in the model, whereas the real problem, surprisingly enough, was to provide sufficient variety. However, under certain boundary conditions, genres could retain sufficient variety, and it was shown how changing the boundary conditions could make genres bifurcate and move.

However, I could not make the model generate the oscillations of which literature history is so full. I conjectured therefore that an isolated recursive system was not a possible theory of genres, and added another component to the literary market, the *Cultural Climate* described by literary institutions. The two systems perturb each other mutually, one system acting as the environment for the other. This model did in fact generate oscillations in the representation of the literary market, shifting between periods of expansion and contraction.

The cultural climate was formalized by means of catastrophe theory. The internal variables of the theory represent the syntagmatic dimension of language, and the attractor change in the system (caused by perturbations from the literary market) therefore represents the formation of sentences. The role of the cultural institutions is thus to observe and describe emergent patterns of the literary market. The model showed that this can explain the unrest of literary genres. Note the word *can:* the argument only proves that the model belongs to a class of possible theories.

The initial hypothesis, that downward causation is needed for explaining the stability of genres, was thus replaced by another hypothesis that uses the arbitrariness of the sign as its pivot. The two sides of the sign differ in their scalar variability. The signified allows large variation as to the scale of the signified contents, whereas the signifier is always at the same (human) scale. In the alternative explanation, stability and change is explained by a semiotic interaction between two social systems of different scales, the observed and the observer system. In the case where the observer system is a part of the observed system the semiosis is self-description.

Appendix A. Calculation of selection probabilities

If P(x) denotes the probability of x becoming a parent, then we have that

(1) $$P(x) = \frac{I(y)P(y)}{I(x)}$$

since probability is inversely related to the isolation. From the fact that the total probability of all strings must equal 100, given that one string must be chosen from the set, it follows that

(2) $$100 = \frac{I(j)P(j)}{I(1)} + \ldots \frac{I(j)P(j)}{I(i)} + \ldots \frac{I(j)P(j)}{I(n)}$$

Putting I(j)P(j) outside the parenthesis we get

(3) $$100 = I(j)P(j)\left(\frac{1}{I(1)} + \ldots \frac{1}{I(i)} + \ldots \frac{1}{I(n)}\right)$$

from which we can calculate P(j), the probability of string j becoming a parent:

(4) $$P(j) = \frac{100}{I(j)\left(\dfrac{1}{I(1)} + \ldots \dfrac{1}{I(i)} + \ldots \dfrac{1}{I(n)}\right)}$$

If we set

$$K = \frac{100}{\displaystyle\sum_{i=1}^{n} \frac{1}{I(i)}}$$

(5)

then we can write (4) as the simpler

(6)
$$P(j) = \frac{K}{I(j)}$$

Since we will want to kill the non-central strings, the probability Q of their being forgotten must be proportional to their isolation; the larger the isolation, the more they risk getting killed.

(7)
$$Q(x) = \frac{I(x)Q(y)}{I(y)}$$

This leads us to calculate Q as

(8)
$$Q(j) = \frac{100 I(j)}{I(1)+...I(j)+...I(n)}$$

or putting $L = \dfrac{100}{I(1)+...I(j)+...I(n)}$

(9)
$$Q(j) = L * I(j)$$

again assuming that one string out of the total population must be killed. We now let the choice of parents be controlled by their P-probabilities, and their death by their Q-probabilities. In the model, we perform the tests

(10)
$$Random\left(\frac{100}{P(j)}\right) = 1$$

(11)
$$Random\left(\frac{100}{Q(j)}\right) = 1$$

to decide whether j should be a parent or die. For example, if P(j) = 3, it means that j has a 3% chance of being a parent. We implement these 3% by choosing random numbers in the range from 1..100 and answering 'yes' if the number is in the interval 1..3. The same effect can be achieved faster if we produce numbers in the interval $1 ... \dfrac{100}{3} = 33,3$, and answer yes each time the number is 1.

Appendix B. Calculation of distortion

This concept is implemented by scaling distances between texts and dilemma by formula (1):

(1)
$$scaling = \frac{\left(\dfrac{d}{w}\right)^2 + h + 1}{\left(\dfrac{d}{w}\right)^2 + 1}$$

As Fig. B1 shows, the scaling is strong in the vicinity of the dilemma, but decreases quickly and settles at the value of 1 which is 'no scaling.'

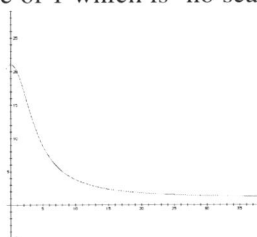

Fig. B1. Scaling with h = 20 and w = 4.

References

ANDERSEN, P. BØGH 1997. *A Theory of Computer Semiotics. Semiotic Approaches to Construction and Assessment of Computer Systems.* Cambridge: Cambridge University Press.

ANDERSEN, P. BØGH 1994. The semiotics of autopoiesis. A catastrophe-theoretic approach. *Cybernetics & Human Knowing* 2: 17-38.

ANDERSEN, P. BØGH 1996. Morphodynamic models of communication. In B. Holmqvist, P. Bøgh Andersen, H. Klein & R. Posner (eds.), *Signs of Work*, Berlin/New York: Walter de Gruyter, 151-217.

BEAUGRANDE R. DE 1981. *Introduction to Text Linguistics.* London: Longman.

BORDWELL, D. 1985. *Narration in the Fiction Film.* Madison, Wisconsin: University of Wisconsin Press.

BÆRENTSEN, K. B. 1996. Episodic knowledge in system control. In B. Holmqvist, P. Bøgh Andersen, H. Klein & R. Posner (eds.), *Signs of Work*, Berlin/New York: de Gruyter, 283-324

CASTI, J.L. 1997. *Would-be Worlds.* New York: John Wiley.

CLARK, H.H. & E.V. CLARK 1977. *Psychology of Language.* New York: Harcourt Brace Jovanovich.

DAVIDOR, Y. 1991. *Genetic Algorithms and Robotics.* Singapore, London: World Scientific.

DAVIS, L. 1996. *Handbook of Genetic Algorithms.* London: Int. Thomson Computer Press.

DIJK, T.A. VAN 1980. *Macrostructures : an Interdisciplinary Study of Global Structures in Discourse, Interaction, and Cognition.* Hillsdale, N.Y.: Lawrence Erlbaum.

GREIMAS, A.J. & J. COURTÉS 1979. *Semiotique: Dictionnaire Raisonné de la Théorie du Language.* Paris: Hachette.

JOHNSON, N.S. & J.M. MANDLER 1980. A tale of two stories: underlying and surface forms in stories. *Poetics* 9: 51-86.

LARSEN, S.F. 1981. Text processing and knowledge updating in memory for radio news. *Psychological Reports Aarhus 6: 4.* Aarhus: Dept. of Psychology, University of Aarhus.

LINDENMAYER, A. 1968. Mathematical models for cellular interaction in development, Parts I and II. *Journal of Theoretical Biology* 18: 280-315.

LOTMAN, Y.M. 1990. *Universe of the Mind.* Bloomington and Indianapolis: Indiana University Press.

LUHMANN, N. 1984. *Soziale Systeme.* Frankfurt: Suhrkamp.

LUHMANN, N. 1990. *Essays on Self-Reference.* New York: Columbia University Press.

MATURANA, H.R. & F.J. VARELA 1980. *Autopoiesis and Cognition. The Realization of the Living.* Dordrecht: D. Reidel.

NEALE, S. 1983. *Genre.* British Film Institute.

NÖTH, W. 1983. Systems theoretical principles of the evolution of the English language and literature. In M. Davenport, E. Hansen & H.F. Nielsen (eds.), *Proceedings of the Second International Conference on English Historical Linguistics.* Odense: Odense University Press, 103-22.

PATTEE H.H. 1987. Instabilities and information in biological self-organization. In F.E. Yates, A. Garfinkel, D.O. Walter & G.B. Yates (eds.), *Self-Organizing Systems. The Emergence of Order.* New York and London: Plenum Press, 325-38.

PEITGEN, H.O., H. JÜRGENS & D. SAUPE 1992. *Chaos and Fractals.* Berlin: Springer.

PRIGOGINE, I. & I. STENGERS 1984. *Order out of Chaos. Man's new Dialogue with Nature.* New York: Bantam Books.

PROPP, V. 1975. *Morphology of the Folktale.* Austin and London: Univ. of Texas Press. English translation 1958. Quoted from the paperback edition.

RYAN, M-L. 1991. *Possible Worlds, Artificial Intelligence and Narrative Theory.* Bloomington & Indianapolis: Indiana University Press.

SALTHE, S.N. 1993. *Development and Evolution.* Cambridge, Mass: MIT Press.

SAUNDERS, P.T. 1990. *An Introduction to Catstrophy Theory.* Cambridge: Cambridge University Press.

TODD, P.M. & G.F. MILLER 1997. Biodiversity through sexual selection. In C.G. Langton & K. Shimohara (eds.), *Artificial Life V.* Cambr. Mass.: MIT Press, 289-99.

TODOROV, T. 1970. *The Fantastic.* Cleveland: Case Western Univ. Press.

TOGEBY, O. 1981. *Brug Sproget [Use Language].* Copenhagen: Reitzel.

WERNER, G.M. 1997. Why the peacock's tail is so short. In C.G. Langton & K. Shimohara (eds.), *Artificial Life V.* Cambridge, Mass.: MIT Press, 85-98.

11

Anticipated Downward Causation
and the Arch Structure of Texts

OLE TOGEBY

In this article I will show that linguistic wholes such as an utterance, a speech or a text are determined not only by downward causation from the whole to its parts, as well as by upward causation from the parts to the whole, but also by anticipated downward causation from later events to earlier events. But first I will analyze the meaning of the words *whole* and *parts* in the domains of physical reality, visual perception of space, and linguistic interpretation of time.

Wholes in physical space-time are not the same as perceived mental wholes, so-called gestalts. And gestalts are not the same as temporal units or interpreted wholes in time. The criteria for wholeness are different for physical entities, mental gestalts and temporal wholes. What ties the parts of a temporal whole together are not the same forces as those that tie together the parts of a physical entity or a mental gestalt.

Physical entities

In the physical world we believe that there are things or entities, and that they are composed of parts, e.g., a cloud is composed of small drops of water floating in the air, a lake of molecules of water, a stone of molecules of some mineral. A chair is composed of the parts: legs, seat, and back, and a dog has head, body, legs, and tail as its parts. The properties of the whole are a function of the properties of the parts of which it is composed and the way they are configured or organized. H_2O is fluid water when the molecules move freely inside the boundaries of the surface, and ice when the molecules are fixed in a crystal grid. That is what is called upward causation or compositionality.

In physical space-time the criteria for calling a collection of parts one entity are the following (mentioned with the weakest first): contact in space, common permutability, unchangeableness, inseparability, stable spatial relations and configuration, and simultaneity. Elements not present at the same time will not be parts of one entity. The criterion of simultaneity is a necessary condition for wholeness.

In the physical world we also find emergent properties explained as downward causation on the organization of the parts from the boundary conditions. A cloud has form and color and can drift in the wind under the boundary conditions of temperature and pressure, a lake is liquid when temperatures are above zero, but can turn into a solid form when it is freezing. A chair can serve as a device for sitting upon, and a dog can run and wag its tail because it is a living creature born of another living creature.

The same collection of water molecules can emerge as different types of wholes (a lake or a huge piece of ice) controlled by the external variables (temperature and pressure). That is what is called bifurcation controlled by external variables in catastrophe theory. The molecules will not change, but the configuration of the molecules will change into a crystal grid when water suddenly stiffens into ice, and their organization in a crystal grid will break up when ice melts into water. The laws describing the relations between the boundary condition and internal organization of a physical system are reversible. Water can turn into ice, and ice into water.

Phenomenological gestalts

In the phenological world we don't talk of wholes as 'entities', but as 'phenomena' or 'gestalts'. When we perceive a phenomenon, we believe that the perceptual stimuli originate from an entity in the world. Most times we are right, otherwise we would not have survived as a species through the ages, but the thing and the phenomenon are not the same. In cases of sensory illusions we see something which is not there. We see a river as one phenomenon, but from a physical point of view a river is not one entity. 'You can walk into the same river and you cannot walk into the same river' (Heraclitus quoted from Næss 1996).

A perceived whole is often called a gestalt, i.e. a configuration or pattern of perceived elements so unified as a whole that its properties cannot be derived from a simple summation of its parts. The standard example is the drawing of two faces. Each of them consists of a circle, three straight lines and a curve. But as wholes they are seen as drawings of a smiling face and an angry face:

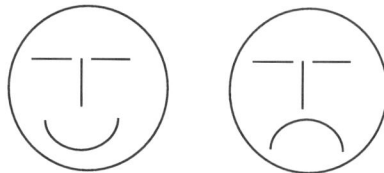

Fig. 1. The impression of the whole gestalt influences the way the parts are interpreted; the eyes look different in the two faces although they are identical.

We see the eyes of the smiling face as different from the eyes of the angry face, although they are physically identical. The impression of the whole gestalt influences the way you interpret the parts. In this case it can be explained by the principle of compositionality: the properties of the perceived whole are a function of the properties of the perceived parts and the way they are combined.

All phenomena are grasped as a figure on a background. The figure is perceived as one unit having a form that can be recognized and remembered, while the background is material and has texture but no form. From Gestalt psychology we know that the forces which tie many elements together to be perceived as an organized whole are the following (with the weakest first): similarity, proximity, the property of being a closed geometrical figure, continuity (the good curve) and simultaneity. Again, simultaneity is a necessary condition for wholeness. These gestalt laws can be seen from the following example:

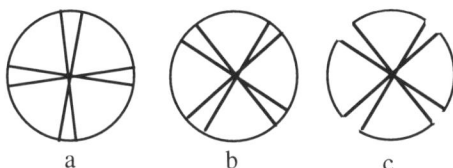

a   b   c

Fig. 2. Gestalt laws of a) similarity, b) proximity and c) closed figures.

Figure (a) is seen as a cruciform (+) in a circle because of the similarity; (b) is seen as an x in a circle because of the law of proximity, in spite of its similarity to a wide cruciform, and (c) is seen as a wide cruciform in accordance with the law of closed figures, in spite of the fact that the law of proximity would give an x in a circle.

A figure is always seen as having aspectual shape; we will always see a figure as something, as belonging to a category. One of the most famous examples is the Wittgensteinian duck-rabbit (Wittgenstein 1953):

Fig. 3. Seeming as. All figures are seen as having an aspectual shape. This figure is seen as either a duck or a rabbit.

We can see it as a duck or we can see it as a rabbit, but we cannot see it as both at the same time, and we cannot see it as neither of them. If we see the duck, we see it as composed of a head with one eye and two pieces of an open beak. If we see the rabbit, we see a head with one eye, a snout and two long ears.

All phenomena have aspectual forms, and if something has two or more aspectual forms, it is not the thing let alone its parts that determine the aspect under which the thing will be perceived. The decisive factors are the viewer's acquaintance with the category, and the relevance of the categorized thing in relation to the interests, wishes and desires of the viewer. And if the boundary conditions change, the gestalt will change too; we can change the interpretation at will, if we are able to see both of them.

The psychological gestalt examples are parallel to the examples of physical entities. The gestalt and the aspectual shape can be understood as emergent properties under the boundary conditions of the knowledge and interests of the person doing the viewing. The duck-rabbit is an example of reversible bifurcation controlled by external variables.

Sentences

The units to be investigated in this article are sentences and texts. Sentences are collections of morphemes and words which constitute a proposition, and texts are collections of sentences serving to communicate thoughts from a speaker to a listener in a real situation. (Sometimes a text consists of only one sentence which is uttered by the speaker to the listener in a given situation, but that is a marginal case, and I will make a distinction between the propositional content of a sentence and the social act of uttering a sentence. A one-sentence text could be called *an utterance* or *a speech act*.) In this section I will deal with the sentence, and in the next with the utterance.

In traditional linguistics the meaning of a whole is explained by the principle of compositionality (Partee 1984):

- According to the *principle of compositionality,* the meaning of a linguistic unit (e.g., a sentence) is a function of the meaning of its parts (e.g., the words and morphemes) and the meaning of the way they are combined.

In the Danish sentence *Eva elskede Adam* the word *Eva* has the meaning 'Eva', the word *elskede* has the meaning 'loved', and the word *Adam* has the meaning 'Adam'.

The rules for combining morphemes and words in Danish could be stated as follows: a sentence consists of a noun phrase (NP) as subject and a (finite) verb phrase (VP) which operates upon the NP to make a sentence. Another NP, the object NP, operates on the preceding transitive verb (Vtr) to make a VP. So the structure of the sentence is illustrated by a tree diagram:

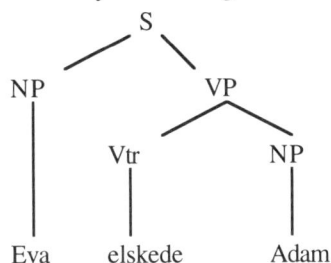

Fig. 4. Tree diagram showing the grammatical structure of the Danish sentence: *Eva elskede Adam.*

The meaning of the whole sentence *Eva elskede Adam* is a function of the meaning of the single words and the meaning of the way they are combined (*Eva* as subject, *elskede* as finite verb, and *Adam* as object), viz: 'Eve loved Adam'.

The meaning of the sentence *Can you pass the salt?* is, because of the word order finite verb + subject, analyzed as a question with *you* as the subject and *the salt* as the object; the verb phrase consists of a finite modal verb *can,* and an infinite main verb *pass*; and it has the meaning 'is the addressee able to hand over the saltshaker?'.

Most existing grammars are attempts to explain the meaning of sentences solely by upward causation according to the principle of compositionality; so are Chomsky's generative grammar, government and binding theory, categorial grammars, Montague grammar and so on.

Nevertheless, it can easily be seen that the explanation of upward causality is not sufficient to explain properties of a linguistic unit such as the sentence. Most morphemes and words, and most grammatical constructions are ambiguous, and this implies that most sentences have two or more readings according to the linguistic rules. The Danish sentence *Eva elskede Adam* can in fact, according to the Danish rules of word order, be analyzed in a different way than shown above, viz.

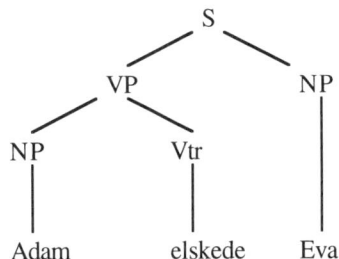

Fig. 5. Tree diagram showing another grammatical structure of the Danish sentence: *Eva elskede Adam.*

With this grammatical structure it means 'it was Eve Adam loved'. The two readings of the sentence can be found in different contexts. The first reading is found in the following context:

Eva vidste godt at Gud havde skabt både Adam og slangen. Men Eva elskede Adam, og hun frygtede slangen ... (Eve knew that God had created both Adam and the serpent. But Eve loved Adam and she feared the serpent)

And the second reading in the following context:

Før syndefaldet havde det første menneske kun rene stærke følelser i forhold til andre: Eva elskede Adam, Gud frygtede han og slangen foragtede han. (Before the Fall, the first Man had only pure and intense emotions towards others; it was Eve that Adam loved, God he feared, and the serpent he scorned).

The linguistic context is the determining factor, in one context the sentence will have one structure and one meaning, and in another context another structure and another meaning. The sentence has different functions in the first context (where it is first part of an opposition of two parallel feelings that Eve had in relation to Adam and the serpent) and in the second context (where it is the first part of a contraposition of parallel relations which Adam had to Eve, God and the serpent).

Consequently, the principle of compositionality cannot stand alone; we have to add the principle of functionality.

- According to *the principle of functionality,* the meaning of a linguistic unit depends on its function as a relevant part of the (linguistic) context in which it is uttered.

Utterances

Sentences can only have propositional meaning if they are uttered in some situation from a speaker to an listener. Referring devices such as noun phrases have no reference if they are not uttered in a sentence together with a predicate. And the reference does not depend on the noun phrase alone, but also on the situation in which is uttered. In isolation morphemes make no sense, they only have a number of potential senses.

In the sentence *Can you pass the salt?* (Searle 1979) the word *you* is highly ambiguous; it denotes the addressee in the speech situation and will change from one situation to another; this is a well-known fact about the so-called deictic words. But other words are ambiguous too. The words *the salt* can refer to 'the saltcellar, if the sentence is uttered at the dining table; if it is uttered in Isfahan by a man looking towards the great salt desert Dasht-E Kavir in Iran, *the salt* will probably refer to this desert. The word *pass* has many potential meanings: 'go through', 'deliver', 'go by', 'occur', 'spend', 'surpass', 'satisfy (finish)', and 'ratify'. At the dining table it probably has the meaning 'deliver', 'hand'; in Isfahan it will have the meaning 'go through'.

And if the sentence is uttered at the dining table, it is probably not understood as a question because the listeners know that the speaker knows that every one of them in fact are able to deliver the saltshaker. As a consequence, uttering this sentence with the word order of a question counts as a polite request: 'Please hand me the saltcellar!'. On the other hand, if the sentence is uttered in Isphahan, and the listener is the driver of an old jeep heading towards the great salt desert, the sentence will have the meaning: 'Are you able to go through the salt desert?'

The principle of functionality has to be reformulated. The meaning of a sentence not only depends on the linguistic context, but also on the whole situation in which it is uttered; who are the persons present, what are the immediate salient features of the situation, what do the participants know, and what do they know that the other part knows?

- According to *the principle of functionality,* the meaning of a linguistic unit depends on its function as a relevant part of the context and situation in which it is uttered.

This principle of functionality is a type of downward causality, we find emergent properties, the propositional content, emerging from the organization of the parts determined by the boundary conditions, i.e. the situation in which it is uttered. Two readings of the same sentence, *Can you pass the salt,* are what is called a bifurcation controlled by external variables. The laws describing the relations between boundary condition and the internal organization of a linguistic sentence are reversible. If we change the context or the situation, the meaning of the sentence will change.

In traditional grammar the criteria for the wholeness of a sentence are often described as similar to the criteria for the wholeness of physical entities and mental gestalts. The parts are contiguous or continuous (there are no pauses in a sentence), they are moved around in transformations, have common permutability, and are inseparable. But since the only relation between the parts of speech is succession (concatenation or chaining), the fact that one part follows the other, the description is not consistent. There is in fact no common permutability or inseparability because the parts are not simultaneous, and no transformations take place in real time.

But the grammatical rules can be formulated in a different way than in ordinary grammars; the grammar then describes the actions performed by the language users when they communicate. It is a joint rule for all people speaking the same language that something (A) counts as something (B) in a context (C). A standard example of this type of rule is the social construction of money: a piece of paper imprinted with some pictures, letters and numbers counts as the equivalent of one hundred kroner in the state of Denmark.

In the Danish and English languages, the most basic grammatical rule is that the utterance of a definite noun phrase counts as a subject-referring device in the context of a predicate, and a finite intransitive verb counts as a predicate in the context of a subject-referring device. The next rule could be: the utterance of a definite noun phrase counts as a predicate in the left hand side context of a transitive verb.

Along with traditional grammars, rules of this type will explain in detail how the utterance of morphemes of different types in special combinations functions as a tool for communicating meanings from one mind to the other. The vocabulary and the grammatical rules are conventionalized and are known and accepted by all users of the language.

The forces that tie together the parts of speech are in fact these grammatical rules and the principle of cooperation. The speaker would not utter the word *Adam* to the listener if it did not count as an object in the context of the transitive verb *elskede*, and *elskede* would not be pronounced if it did not count as a predicate in the context of the subject *Eva*.

The listeners are able to interpret *Adam* as an object because they keep a memory of the earlier pronunciation of the words *Eva elskede* as a context of the actual word *Adam*. The memory makes all three words present simultaneously in the mind of the listener although they are not pronounced simultaneously. By means of their memory of the immediate past, the so-called short-term memory, language users are able to grasp the meaning of a chain of words as if some of them were a figure on a ground consisting of the rest of the words simultaneously present. The short-term memory has only a limited capacity, namely the magical number seven plus or minus 2 (Miller 1956). It is not possible to remember the pronunciation of 50 words (with no sense). But most sentences have a length of not more than 7 constituents, so they can normally be kept in the short-term memory from the first pronounced word until the pronunciation of the last word.

The grammatical relations tying the parts together are not the same as the gestalt laws (similarity, proximity, closed figure, continuity and simultaneity). The grammatical relations are subordination (forward dependency of occurrence, backward dependency of occurrence), nexus (mutual dependency), and coordination (joint occurrence).

Temporal events and acts

The units dealt with in text theory are not at all like physical entities or phenomenological gestalts and not exactly like sentences, but rather they are units (wholes) of time. Examples of temporal units are the battle of Austerlitz, the American presidential election, a football match, the speech by the Danish Queen on New Years Eve, the fairy tale *The Tinder Box* by Hans Christian Andersen, and the sentence I uttered 20 years ago in Isfahan to a driver of an old jeep: *Can you pass the salt?* In general, temporal units are social events, actions or acts.

Every temporal unit consists of temporal parts (Clark 1996), i.e. shorter temporal units: the battle consists of preparations, attacks, movements, retirements and defeats, a football match of the kickoff, first half, second half, goals, free kicks, and the time-out whistle; a speech or a text of the introductory sentences, the middle sentences and the final sentences.

The criteria for wholeness in time are totally different from the criteria for wholeness in physical space-time and in phenomenological space. Especially the necessary condition of simultaneity of the parts forming the whole is untenable for wholes in time. The parts need not be contiguous or continuous (there is a pause in a football match or in a speech), they have no common permutability, and they are not inseparable. The question now arises: when none of the forces which tie the parts of physical entities and mental gestalts together are tenable for temporal wholes, what kind of forces tie the parts of temporal wholes together? In the case of the sentence we have seen that it is possible for the human mind to keep up to seven successive items in its short-term memory, and at the end of the sentence treat them as if they were simultaneous. But football matches, speeches, and texts (novels, reports) can last for hours, and that is too much for the capacity of the short-term memory.

Temporal units are events, and long or molecular events (episodes) are sequences of smaller, transitory or atomic events. An atomic event is a 'piece of time' which is interpreted in a similar way by two or more persons present. An atomic event is the difference that makes a difference. It is a figure on the background of time acknowledged as such by its salience compared to what precedes it and what succeeds it. This means that an atomic event involves a change from one state to another at the beginning of the event, and a change from the new state back to the previous state at the end of the event.

The referee's kickoff whistle is such an atomic event, the kick of the ball at a free kick is another, but the movement of the leg making the kick is not. A morpheme in a sentence is an atomic event, but a phoneme is not.

The difference between a kick and the movement of the leg, between a morpheme and a phoneme is as follows: the kick and the morpheme are differences that make a difference, they count as something in the social interaction with common interests and goals, a movement of the leg and a phoneme do not count as anything in the social interaction, they make no difference. Kicks and morphemes are atomic events that can proceed or follow other events, movements of the leg and phonemes are not. An event can only count as something if it is

known and recognized by the participants pursuing a common goal in the interaction.

It is my claim — and a rather strong one — that units in time, i.e. temporal
wholes that consist of successions of atomic events, are social phenomena with
joint goals and beginnings and ends salient to all participants. Physical entities are
not mental, they are wholes independent of any perception or knowledge of them.
Mental gestalt phenomena must be recognized as relevant categories, and consequently they presuppose memory, knowledge, wishes and desires, but they do not
presuppose ongoing social interaction. Events in time are successions of atomic
events, and they presuppose ongoing social recognition.

We can now address the crucial question again: assuming that none of the
forces which tie the parts of physical entities and mental gestalts together hold for
temporal wholes, then what kind of forces tie the parts of temporal wholes together?

Time is an endless flow, there are no breaks, no marks or milestones indicating
the different parts. The digitalization of time is made by the mutually recognized
atomic events indicating boundaries. The only force which ties a certain number of
atomic social acts together to form one molecular event is the joint recognition of a
common social goal for all the successive acts inside the boundaries of the whole
in one-dimensional time. The boundaries of a temporal whole are marked by one
salient atomic event signaling the beginning of the molecular event and one
salient atomic event signaling the end of the molecular event.

The temporal unit of the day has sunrise and sunset as its boundary events, and
is constituted by all the joint institutional acts and actions performed by the members of a society with the common goal of creating and maintaining the society.

In a football match the kickoff whistle and the time-out whistle are the acts indicating boundary. Only if all the players acknowledge them as indicating boundaries and behave accordingly, will the match exist as a game with the constitutive
goal of winning.

Texts

Texts are temporal wholes, consisting of smaller temporal units, namely sentences.
In describing the properties (interpretation) of texts we will face the problem of
the hermeneutic circle: We cannot interpret the meaning of the whole before having interpreted each of its parts, and we cannot interpret the parts before having
understood the meaning of the whole.

As the principle of linguistic meaning, the hermeneutic circle can be formulated
as a function of both the compositionality and the functionality of its parts: the
meaning of a linguistic unit depends both on the meaning of its parts and the mea-

ning of the way they are combined, and on its function as a relevant (obvious, fit and meaningful) part of the whole current situation in which it is uttered. This means that the same sentence has different meanings in different contexts. It also means that a sentence in the middle of a text has to be understood before the conclusion in the end of the text is pronounced, although the conclusion is the necessary context for understanding the function of the middle sentence.

As an example I will use the fairy tale by Hans Christian Andersen: *The Tinder Box*. Below is the first part of the story.

1. THE TINDER BOX
2. There came a soldier marching down the high road — one, two! one, two! He had his knapsack on his back and his sword at his side as he returned home from the wars. On the road he met a witch, an ugly old witch, a witch whose lower lip dangled right down to her chest.
1. 'Good evening, soldier,' she said. 'What a fine sword you've got there, and what a big knapsack. Aren't you every inch a soldier! And now you shall have money, as much as you please.'
2. 'That's very kind, you old witch,' said the soldier.
3. 'See that big tree.' The witch pointed to one near by them. 'It's hollow to the roots. Climb to the top of the trunk and you'll find a hole through which you can let yourself down deep under the tree. I'll tie a rope around your waist, so that when you call me I can pull you up again.'
4. 'What should I do deep down under that tree?' the soldier wanted to know.
5. 'Fetch money,' the witch said. 'Listen. When you touch bottom you'll find yourself in a great hall. It is very bright there, because more than a hundred lamps are burning. By their light you will see three doors. Each door has a key in it, so you can open them all.
6. 'If you walk into the first room, you'll see a large chest in the middle of the floor. **On it sits a dog,** and his eyes are as big as saucers. But don't worry about that. I'll give you my blue checked apron to spread out on the floor. Snatch up that dog and set him on my apron. Then you can open the chest and take out as many pieces of money as you please. They are all copper.
7. 'But if silver suits you better, then go into the next room. There sits a dog and his eyes are as big as mill wheels. But don't you worry about that. Set the dog on my apron while you line your pockets with silver.
8. 'Maybe you'd rather have gold. You can, you know. You can have all the gold you can carry if you go into the third room. The only hitch is that there on the money-chest sits a dog, and each of his eyes is as big as the Round Tower of Copenhagen. That's the sort of dog he is. But never you mind how fierce he looks. Just set him on my apron and he'll do you no harm as you help yourself from the chest to all the gold you want.'
9. 'That suits me,' said the soldier. 'But what do you get out of all this, you old witch? I suppose that you want your share.'

10.   'No indeed,' said the witch. 'I don't want a penny of it. All I ask is for you to fetch
        me an old tinder box that my grandmother forgot the last time she was down there.'

To illustrate my point about the relations between parts and wholes in texts, I will
now describe the function of the sentence in the text *On it sits a dog*, which is uttered by the witch to the soldier, starting with *See that big tree* (paragraph 3),
ending with *to all the gold you want* (paragraph 8).

In order to demonstrate that the internal pragmatic structure of a sentence is determined by the function of the sentence in relation to the text in which is a part, I
will introduce some new pragmatic concepts of informational elements in the utterance: basis, designators, predicators and message. a) The first constituent of the
sentence is called 'the basis' and is indicated by square brackets: [basis]. b) The
referring devices (noun phrases), are called designators, indicated by curled brackets: {designator}. c) Pieces of new information (verbs, adjectives, prepositions, indefinite noun phrases) in the proposition are called predicators, with no special notation: *predicators*. d) The predicate of the utterance that is most relevant to the
listener is called the message, indicated by bold type: **message**.

The pragmatic structure of the sentence *On it sits a dog* is the following:

   [**On** {it}] **sits** {a dog}

The rules regulating the pragmatic elements of the utterance are the following
(Grice 1975, Sperber and Wilson 1986, Togeby 1993):

1.   The speaker defines in the basis of the sentence the mental space of the pro-
        positional content in relation to the mental background of the listener: *[On
        it] sits a dog*.
2.   The speaker designates with the help of noun phrases and adverbials topics
        accessible to the listener in a formulation which is sufficient to distinguish
        the references and necessary to recognize them: *On {it} sits {a dog}*; the
        phrases are not: *the large chest* or *a bulldog* although the references are the
        same.
3.   The speaker informs the listeners about the true relations and properties of
        the topics in the mental space by the predicators of the sentence, using the
        strongest relevant formulation: *On, sits* and *a dog*; the wordings are not: *on
        the middle of it* or *sits and snarls*. Among the pieces of information in a sen-
        tence, the one most relevant to the listener counts as the message: *[On {it}]
        sits a {dog}*.
4.   A sentence uttered as part of a longer text is not necessarily relevant in itself
        to the listener but aims by its message at a later relevant message (the con-
        clusion) in the text; the aim is illustrated by the question answered by the

later relevant message: *[On {it}] sits a {dog}*_{AIM: and what is the consequence of that?} (...) *Snatch up that dog and set him on my apron.*[1]

5.   When the message has to be formulated as strongly as necessary to tell the whole truth, it is an implicature of the utterance that a stronger formulation would not be true: *[On {it}] sits {a dog}*_{IMPLICATURE: it just sits there, it does not snarl or bite.}

The function of a sentence in a text

The message of the sentence is taken to be *sits on* (which is one predicate) and not *a dog*, although both constituents are predicators in the utterance of the sentence. The reason for that is that *sits on* is more relevant to the listener than *a dog*. If *a dog* had been the message, the aim of the utterance would have been the answer to the question: AIM: and what about the dog?. This question is in fact answered in the subsequent sentence: *and his eyes are as big as saucers* with the message *are as big as saucers*_{AIM: and what is the consequence of their size?}. And that implicit question is not answered by the witch in her speech or in any other sentence of the fairy tale. To believe that *a dog* should be the message of the utterance would lead to a dead end.

If we take *sits on* to be the message with the aim: AIM: and what are the consequences of the fact that a dog sits on it?, the implicit question is answered by the sentence: *Snatch up that dog and set him on my apron,* with the message *Snatch up and set*_{AIM: and what then?}. And that implicit question is answered in the subsequent sentence: *Then you can open the chest and take out as many pieces of money as you please.*

This last sentence is the conclusion of the whole speech by the witch. The piece of information *take out as many pieces of money as you please* is the common goal for the communicative collaboration of the witch and the soldier. It is relevant in relation to the interests of the soldier to know how to get money.

In other words, if we take *a dog* to be the message, it leads to a dead end, if we take *sits on* to be the message of the utterance, it is a proper part of a temporal whole; it serves as a means to reach the goal of the whole collaboration, that is to inform the soldier how to get money, which is the meaning of the sentence that concludes the speech. And this is the reason for choosing *sits on* and not *a dog* as the message of the sentence.

This choice is an example parallel to the interpretation of the straight lines as being smiling or angry eyes in the smiling and angry faces respectively. The inter-

---

1   For every type of predicator there will be one type of question to be answered: state predicators elicit the question: AIM: *What's the consequence of that?* accomplishment predicators elicit the question: AIM: *and what then?*, and new topic predicators elicit the question: AIM: *and what about that topic?* There are more types of predicators and more types of implicit questions, but I will not go into details about that here.

pretation of the whole affects the interpretation of the parts also called downward causation or bifurcation controlled by external variables. But there is a difference. In the case of the gestalt interpretation of the smiling face, all the parts are present at the same time, and the viewer can choose either the whole face or eye as the figure and the rest as the background. If the viewer selects one of the pairs of eyes as the figure they appear to be smiling in the context of the smiling face and angry in the context of the angry face. But in the case of the witch's speech the soldier has to choose an interpretation of the sentence *On it sits a dog* without any access to the context from which it should have its interpretation. The decisive clue to how the sentence should be considered is uttered by the witch several sentences after the sentence in question.

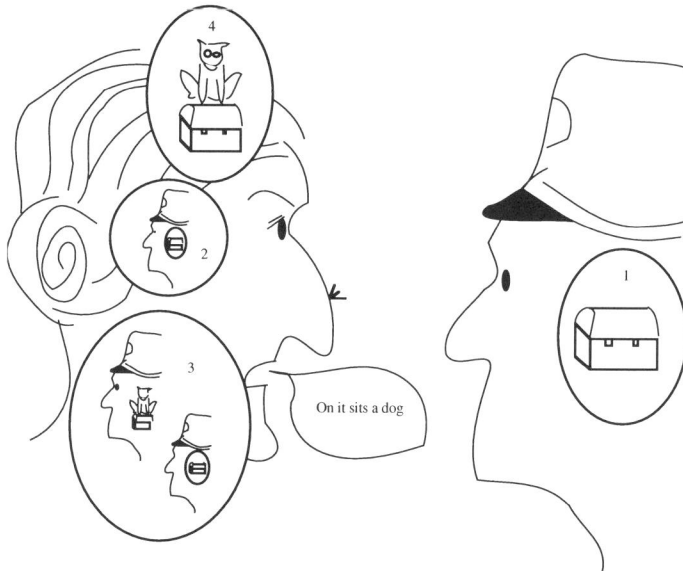

Fig. 6. The five conditions for the functionality of the utterance are illustrated by four balloons of thought. 1: the narrated mental space is accessible to the listener from the current situation. 1-2: the topics are accessible. 2 and 4: the predicate is new and informative. 3: the message is relevant (if he gets the information, he will be smiling, if not he will be sad). 4: the information is the whole truth about the topics.

The soldier probably makes the right interpretation (with *sits on* as the message) because he knows that they have a joint goal for their interaction, namely that she should inform him of how to get the money. And he has probably guessed that the money is in the chest. In this case it is obvious that if there is a dog sitting on the chest, it is relevant for the soldier to know, because then he has to remove it in order to get the money. In other words, he has anticipated the conclusion because he trusts the witch, he believes that the message of the current sentence aims at a later conclusion, and that the conclusion of her speech will be relevant in relation to his interests, which are to get money. We can call this downward causation, but also anticipated downward causation, determination from a later speech event (the conclusion) to an earlier speech event (the utterance and interpretation of *on it sits a dog*).

The whole case is illustrated by Fig. 6.

Anticipated downward causation

The interpretation of a text can be compared to an arch, which although constructed of many blocks allows many of them to hang in the air with no support underneath. An arch spans a wall opening by means of separate units (e.g., bricks or blocks) assembled into an upward curve that maintains stability through the mutual pressure of the load of the separate pieces. The vertical pressure from the weight of the load is converted into horizontal pressures by the wedge-shaped blocks and received by the piers flanking the opening.

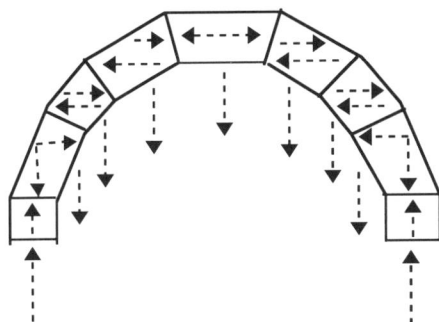

Fig. 7. The vertical pressure from the weight of the load is converted into horizontal pressure by the wedge-shaped blocks. Stability is maintained through the mutual pressure of the load of the separate pieces.

While an arch is being built, the wedge-shaped blocks will fall down until the keystone (the block at the top) is placed; consequently the blocks have to be supported by a scaffold, and when the keystone is placed, the scaffold can be removed. So the blocks support the keystone by forward causation, and the keystone stabilizes the blocks by downward causation.

The same is true every time a person communicates his or her thoughts by means of many sentences in a text. A sentence in the middle of a text is a precondition for the understanding of the subsequent conclusion, but on the other hand the middle sentence cannot be properly understood when its function in relation to the conclusion is not properly understood. The interpretation of the middle sentence hangs in the air until the conclusion is uttered.

What resembles the scaffold in 'in real time' communication is the fact that the listener trusts the relevance of a middle sentence, although this relevance is not apparent when it is heard. When hearing a middle sentence the listeners look forward to hearing the conclusion, at which time they will look back to the actual sentence and find the full interpretation.

In this way we can say that language users have 'a memory of the future'. Because communication is social cooperation with a joint goal, they can anticipate the meaning of the whole before it is uttered or understood and let it determine the interpretation of the earlier sentences.

This means that every sentence is governed by two principles of collaboration: The designators in the basis must not have a stronger formulation than necessary for recognition, and the predicates of the message must not have a weaker formulation than sufficient for relevance.

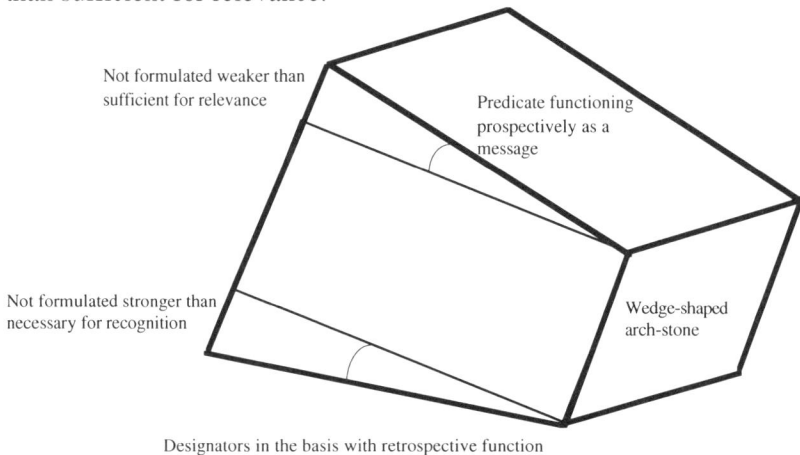

Fig. 8. The right angle between the two edges of the arch stone resembles the rules that the designators in the basis must not be formulated stronger than necessary for recognition, and the message weaker than sufficient for relevance.

The two principles regulating the strength of formulation of designators and predicators in relation to recognition and relevance govern the production and interpretation of every sentence in a text. The principles are like the angles on the wedge-shaped arch stones, which in a way enables all the stones in an arch to aim at the keystone. If the angles are not right, the arch will collapse, and if the strength of the base designator and the message predicator is not right, the text will collapse as a unit over time. All the sentences of a text aim at the same conclusion, the communication of which is the common goal of the joint action of the speaker and the listener.

This type of determination is of another type than both upward causation from the parts to the whole and downward causation from the whole to the parts; it is determination from a later goal to an earlier means, and I will propose to call this anticipated downward causation. The forces tying the parts of a temporal whole together are the participants' (speaker and listener) memory of the past and anticipation of the future in a communicative collaboration.

References

CLARK, H.H. 1996. *Using Language*. Cambridge: Cambridge University Press.

GRICE, H.P. 1967/1975. *Logic and Conversation*. In P. Cole & Jerry Morgan (eds.), *Syntax and Semantics, 3, Speech Acts*, Academic press.

MILLER, F.A. 1956. The magical number seven plus or minus two. Some limits on our capacity for information processing. *Psychol. Rev.* 63, 81-97.

NÆSS, A. 1963. *Filosofiens Historie I*. Copenhagen:Vintens Forlag.

PARTEE, B.H. 1984. *Compositionality*. In F. Landman & F. Veltman (eds.), *Varieties of Formal Semantics*. Dordrecht.

SEARLE, J.R. 1979. *Expression and Meaning*. Cambridge, Mass: Cambridge University Press.

SPERBER, D. & D. WILSON 1986. *Relevance*. Oxford: Blackwell.

TOGEBY, O. 1993. *PRAXT. Pragmatisk Tekstteori 1-2*. Aarhus: Aarhus University Press.

WITTGENSTEIN, L. 1953. *Philosophical Investigations*. Oxford: Basil Blackwell, Part II, XI.

12

Rule-based and Rule-generating Systems[1]

NIELS OLE FINNEMANN

1. Introduction

Until the 19th century scientists almost always assumed that, as a whole, the universe could be described as a uniform, completely rule-based and hence deterministic system. During the 19th century the notion emerged of the universe as a set of such systems, in part a consequence of the breakthrough of dynamic models in physics (e.g., statistical theories in thermodynamics (Boltzmann and Gibbs), biology (e.g., Darwin's theory of evolution) and other fields. Nature became dynamic and the natural dynamic included the evolution of new domains and levels. The origin of life was now seen as a first step in the evolution of a biological domain or level, and the later origin of human beings and mental processes were seen as a first step in the evolution of psychic, symbolic, social and cultural levels. The origin and evolution of these phenomena were now assumed to take place in physical nature (i.e. as processes within time and space) and no longer seen as fruits of a divine creational act or big bang at the very beginning of everything. The notion of the universe as a set of rule-based and layered systems has also been maintained in most 20th century theories (e.g., various kinds of functionalism and structuralism), eventually accompanied by theoretical reasoning on the relationships between the various systems and levels (e.g., psycho-physical parallelism, emergentism). Relationships which still seem to give rise to some highly intriguing questions on the connections and interactions between physical, biological and mental phenomena.

There is a good reason for this. If the universe as a whole is regarded as a single rule-based system, there is not much room for the idea of many distinct rule-based systems. And if the universe is regarded as a set of such distinct systems, it is not easy to see how there can be only one universe. If the relations between the vari-

---

1   This article is partly based on a presentation given at the symposium 'The emergence of codes and intentions as basis for signprocesses', Odense University, October 26-28, 1995.

ous systems (whether physical, biological or mental) are rule-based they cannot be distinct and autonomous, and if these relations are not rule-based one may wonder how they relate and how their autonomy can be maintained if they are all existing in the same universe of time and space.

There is a close relation between the notion of levels and the notion of downward causation. On the one hand, there cannot be anything like downward causation if levels are considered to be purely conceptual phenomena, while on the other hand one needs an idea of downward causation if levels are considered to be constituted as distinctive real processes in the world. A higher level process completely separate from and not interacting with lower level processes cannot be a process in the same universe as the lower level processes. Furthermore, without the effects of downward causation as one of the interactions there would be no reason to specify any higher level(s) in the first place. Without downward causation everything could be explained (except the existence of explanations) on the basis of lower level concepts alone.

It has been argued that higher level processes might constrain lower level processes without causing any effects.[2] It is not easy to see how this could be the case. If, for instance, we consider mental processes as higher level processes, it seems difficult to understand how an idea (a mental state) could act as a constraint on the neurophysiological system if the idea did not cause some neurophysiological processes. How this actually works is still completely unknown, but in any case it seems to function very well.

It has also been argued that there will always be an equivalent lower level description of the assumed higher level processes which causes the lower level effects. This would be very nice, since it would allow us to reach a real, unified theory of everything — and not only a unified physical theory. But so far there is no evidence that something like this is within reach of contemporary science. Partly this is due to the fact that even if a lower level manifestation of a higher level process exists, a fixed or invariant relationship between the two does not necessarily exist. I shall return to this theme later in the article.

The idea of downward causation presupposes the existence of separate but co-existing and interacting levels. There has to be an upper and a lower level and a connection which does not undermine the distinction. There can only be an upper level if the existence of processes on this level makes a difference for (i.e. causes an effect on) the processes on the lower level. Upper level phenomena have to be conceived of as autonomous actants able to cause effects on the lower level. Furthermore, the notion presupposes that the origin of the upper level can be explained as a (coincidental or rule-based) result of processes on the lower level.

---

2   See for instance Køppe, Emmeche and Stjernfelt in this volume.

The implications of these presuppositions (the existence of levels and the generic and interactional relation between them) are controversial in at least two respects:

1) Concerning the assumption of the existence of levels: if we assume the existence of an upper and a lower level (or even more levels), it follows that we do not consider the relationship between the levels as a completely deterministic relationship, since the assumption that the relation is deterministic implies that there is no way to distinguish a separate upper level. The upper level is always completely described by the lower level description. There would be nothing to add.

According to the tradition of modern science there is only one alternative left, namely to assume that the relationship between the levels is randomly variable. If so, there would be no relation to consider at all.

In this paper I will introduce another alternative: the relation is not completely random but variable, because the relations between levels are constrained by various sorts of redundancy functions stabilizing the higher level processes on the lower level scale and allowing interaction between the levels both as individual events and as repetitively occurring patterns.

That a relation between levels is variable indicates the following:

a)   That a given lower level process may be accompanied (eventually controlled or caused) by different higher level processes. There can be a number of different higher level causes for the same lower level effects. For instance, a machine (lower level system) may be a functional part in a number of different complex systems (higher level system). Hence, there can be more than one interpretation of such a machine. Take as a simple example the use of a given algorithm for a number of different purposes, or the number of possible codes for the interpretation of the same physical figure, e.g., two or more meanings of the same sequence of letters.

b)   That a higher level phenomenon may be manifested in different lower level processes. A goal (or a macrostate) may be achieved by means of a number of different procedures, tools or machines (or microstates). Take as a simple example the number of possible physiological variations in the pronunciation of the same sounds or a word (e.g., variations due to gender, age, dialect, sociolect, etc.) or the number of possible molecular microstates corresponding to one macrostate.

2) Concerning the generic relation between the levels (upward causation or emergence) and the assumption that upper level processes may cause effects on the lower level (downward causation): upward causation is controversial, since the notion implies that there is something in the effect which is not in the cause. However, after Darwin it is not easy to see how the idea of upward causation from simpler to more complex systems can be avoided. While there is something like

upward causation from simple to complex organisms inherited in Darwinism, there is no idea of downward causation: the notion of natural selection does not refer to the existence of a selector controlling development from above. In Darwinism selection takes place as a result of a blind process and not as the result of intentionally controlled intervention. But since Darwinism implies that the human mind and intentionality is understood as results of evolution, it follows that the process of upwards causation leads to the evolution of phenomena capable of exerting downward causation insofar as the human mind takes part in the further evolutionary process. This may take place in many different ways, one of these being the invention and production of tools, artifacts and symbols.

For those who deny the validity of the notion of downward causation a main question is whether, for instance, symbols, technologies, tools and artificially produced machines can be described with the same conceptual apparatus as the one used to describe the physical and chemical conditions for the emergence of these phenomena, i.e. without reference to human intentionality or similar notions for mental phenomena.

In this paper it will be argued that there cannot be a physical theory of the universe if there is not the capacity to create symbols in the same universe. The existence of theories presupposes the existence of symbols. It will also be argued that no symbol or mental process can be defined only according to physical criteria, insofar as the notion 'physical criteria' denotes the conceptual framework of contemporary physics. Furthermore, it will be argued that the assumptions of there being only one universe and of us being a part of this universe ourselves both because of our bodies (whether conceived of as physical or biological), and because of our minds, imply that we need to accept the following notions.

I   The notion of distinct levels. If the mind has no independent existence relative to the physical processes there is no room for the existence of *a theory* of physical processes as distinct from the physical processes.

II   The notion of coexistence and interrelations between different levels, since without such interrelations there would be more than one universe or there would be no descriptions within the universe.

III The notion of the emergence of and interaction between levels. The need for the notion of emergence follows from the fact that we cannot trace the existence of biological and mental processes as far back in time as the existence of observable physical processes. If biological and mental processes are generated within the physical universe, they are necessarily interrelated parts of this universe.

Now, one may ask how such things as organisms or mental processes might at the same time be regarded as generated from a former purely physical universe and as phenomena which possess certain kinds of autonomy including a capacity to cause effects on the lower, physical level. In the following I shall argue that the question cannot be answered within the conceptual framework of nature as a set of rule-based systems — and that the inclusion of mental processes in the idea of nature presupposes the idea of what will be denoted as rule-generative systems.

There are two basic and interconnected ideas. The first is that redundancy provides the basis for a transition from individual events which develop by chance or by choice into repetitive occurrences which allow a structure or pattern to acquire new functions or meanings and thereby also allow a change of rules or the establishment of a new rule. The second is that redundant patterns which serve as a means to stabilize a system on the lower level may do so while at the same time being utilized for various and changing functions and/or meanings on the higher level.

For these reasons redundancy provides a means of both stabilization and change as well as a means of interrelation and interaction between different levels in a system and between different systems.

The point of departure for this discussion will be taken in two symbol systems based on redundancy. The first example will be the computer and the second will be ordinary language. In both cases I will argue that the stability of these systems (which are both defined by the existence/presence of human intentions) is provided by means of — differently organized — redundancy functions. It will be shown that the use of various kinds of redundancy both allows the maintenance of systems in unstable micro- or macro-states, the suspension of previous rules, under-determination and over-determination as well as the generation/emergence/creation of new rules more or less independent of previous rules.

Since the notion of redundancy is both controversial as such and often avoided, I shall discuss the concept (as defined in Claude Shannon's mathematical theory of information and in the semiotic framework of J.J. Greimas) and give a more general definition in which the redundancy functions are seen as a means to overcome instability due to noisy conditions and even more important and less recognized also as a way to allow new rules to be generated, but at the cost of a rule-based stability, determination and predictability.

Finally, I will discuss some of the possible wider implications for the study of cultural and social systems — in which there will always be various kinds of noise (whether from the underlying levels and/or from the occurrence of individual variations) and address the question of downward causation from psychical (intentional) systems to physical and biological systems.

2. The rules in the computer

Although the computer is often seen as a rule-based machine — and as an paradigmatic model of the notion of rule-based systems — a closer look at the functioning of this machine gives an excellent demonstration of the limitations of this very notion while at the same time demonstrating that the use of redundancy functions is necessary for the physical processing of the symbolic (and hence mental and intentional) content in the machine.

In the case of computers the shortcoming of the notion of a rule-based system is directly related to the fact that the symbolic rules which are to be processed in the machine have to be represented and processed as a string of bits which can be manipulated on the level of the individual bits and hence completely independently of the formal rule itself (cf. Finnemann 1994). This may be difficult to do. Normally another program is needed to do it, and it may often give absurd consequences, but the important thing is that *is* possible to do, since this means that the previous states in the computer do not determine the later states in any compulsory way.[3] Automatically performed (rule-based) processes in the computer are the result of a deliberately composed sequence of steps which we choose to run automatically for the sake of our own convenience. The rules which control the data processing can only do so as a result of a process in which they are themselves manifested and processed in exactly the same way as any other kind of data.

Consequently, it is always possible to intervene in and change/modify the system of rules from the lower level of the bits. Since this can be done deliberately and bit by bit, there are no invariant restrictions on the character of such modifications. Rules can be suspended or varied, or their functions can be changed independently of the content of the rule and on a level beneath that of the rule itself. It is not only possible to change or modify any previous rule, it is also possible to feed completely new rules into the system if only they are manifested in the binary alphabet.

In this way the computer illustrates how a completely deterministic process on the higher level (of symbolic formalism) is processed in a system in which there are only random and optional relations between single and discrete states on the lower (physical) level, which is the level of the actual operations.

---

3   As originally shown by Turing, there will not always be a rule for the next step in a universal computing machine. He therefore described the machine as both an automatic calculating machine and a choice machine. There is no difference between these machines; there is a difference between situations in which the instruction for the next step is already defined and situations in which the next step is chosen deliberately. Since the instructions are never a part of the definition of the machine they can always be deliberately chosen.

One of the main points here is that the level of 'physical operation' and execution is always the level of binary digits allowing us to go from an interface directly to this level and manipulate any formal procedure according to our intentions.

It should be obvious from this — albeit brief — description that the formal rules used to perform the organization of the binary sequences do not guarantee the stability of the system, since they can be modified, varied, suspended or ascribed new functions, and so forth. Of course, we have all seen that the violation of formal procedures may cause the machine to go into a closed loop or freeze. We do need rules to stabilize our operations, but we do not always need the very same rules. And even if the machines freeze, we are able to restart and continue.

What we have here is a system in which the rules are processed in the same time, space and physical form as the phenomena (data, substance ...) being ruled. The rules are manifested as an integrated part of the ruled phenomena, on a par with them, implying that there are systems in which the rules can be changed, modified, suspended or ascribed new functions during the processes, whether influenced by any component part of the system or from lower level phenomena (noisy physical substance) or according to new intended or unintended external inputs. The computer is a machine in which physical and mechanical determination is restricted to a single move from one state to another on the level of the bits.

As a consequence of this it seems necessary to introduce a concept of what I will label rule-generative systems, which are different from rule-based systems.

Rule-based systems can be defined as systems in which the processes are governed by a set of previously given rules (given from the outside of the system and inaccessible from within the ruled system). The rules govern the system and guarantee the stability and existence of the system.

In contrast, rule-generative systems can be defined as systems in which the rules are the result of processes within the system and hence open to influence both from other processes in the same systems as well from higher or lower levels and the surroundings. Such systems are to some extent, but not completely, governed by the rules, which are themselves open to modification, change and suspension.

In such systems the rules are neither able to provide the stability nor to explain the interactional relations between the levels. Hence we need to explain how stability and interaction across levels can exist in these systems.

3. Redundancy as a means to stabilize noisy systems

To my knowledge the question of redundancy as a means to stabilize noisy systems was first addressed by Shannon (Shannon 1949), who tried to find a mathematical method to determine whether a received bit — let's say an /1/ — was actually an intended part of the message sent or whether it was changed from an /0/

as a result of the influence of noise during the transmission. Shannon's answer to the question was that it would be possible to solve the problem by adding a control code to the message sent. By means of this additional coding it would be possible to correct the received message, eliminating the noise resulting from the transmission. The additional code should be a distinct part of message, but it should have no impact upon the meaning of the message. For this reason he described the method as 'combating noise' by increasing the redundancy in the message.

Shannon uses the notion of redundancy in a rather vague and loosely defined way about any recurring patterns of no importance to the meaning or structure of the symbolic expression, and he is not very concerned with the various different forms of redundancy. However, such different forms can be identified, even in his own original paper, in which we can find several types of redundant structures which are distinct in respect to structure and/or function.

To the vague and general definition of redundancy as repetitively occurring, superfluous structures/patterns which are of no importance for the content of the message, we can add the following 4 definitions used — although not explicitly defined — in Shannon's paper:

1   Redundancy defined as repetitively manifested patterns/forms which are determined by the symbol system used: The idea is that certain parts of a message are determined by the rules of the symbol system in which the message is manifested, while other (and distinct) parts are deliberately chosen to represent the distinct meaning of the individual message. In this case redundancy is defined as the parts determined by the general system and opposed to the patterns/units which represent the distinct parts — which are assumed to represent the content — of the individual message.

2   Redundancy defined as possible but unused patterns/forms allowed by the symbol system: In this case it is not the manifested parts determined by the symbol system, which are seen as redundant, but the set of possible alternative, unused choices allowed by a given symbol system. Redundancy is still defined in contrast to the individual message, but this is now contrasted to other possible messages.

3   Redundancy defined as the statistically determined repetitively occurring patterns without regard to both the content and the rules of the symbol system itself. In this case redundancy is defined completely independent of the symbol system and the meaning.

4   Finally redundancy is defined as formal control codes which are added to the message during transmission and removed when the control procedures are performed.

If the classification is structured according to the relation to meaning we get the following definitions:

TYPE I: *Redundancy defined as opposed to meaning.*

(a)   Repetitive patterns without any meaning/function. Meaning is seen as related to the whole message, including rules necessary for the interpretation.

(b)   Patterns belonging to the system (invariants/constants). Meaning is seen as the new information and defined as the part of the message which is distinct from the (rule-governed) parts belonging to the rule structure of the symbol system.

(c)   The amount of possible alternatives to a specific message in a given language. Meaning is seen as the actually selected new information as in b).

TYPE II: *Redundancy defined as independent of meaning.*
      Recurrent patterns (statistically defined) in the whole message, whether representing the system or the specific information/meaning.

TYPE III: *Redundancy defined as formally defined meaning* — added for the purpose of 'combating noise'.

In this case redundancy is defined as calculated information added to a message to verify the legitimacy of each symbol — contrary to the possible, unintended occurrence of the same physical form as noise. Meaning (= the calculated, redundant information), is calculated by interpreting a given sequence of notation units as a formal expression (i.e., ascribing a formally defined semantic content according to which the legitimacy of the individual units can be verified by comparing with the ascribed 'values' of other units). Redundancy of this type is only redundant at the semantic level of the original message, since it is a specific sequence which has to be added to the message transmitted (instead of being eliminated) and is necessary for the verification. It forms a distinct or specific part of the transmitted message. In this respect it equals information.

Rather than going into further detail and explaining why Shannon needed all of these different notions, I shall concentrate on why he needed a notion of redundancy at all. The basic reason for this can be found by considering the character of noise as it reveals itself in the identification of notational units.

There are three aspects of noise involved. First we need to be able to identify notational units as distinct to the background. Notational units are always manifested in one substance or another. Second we need to be able to identify notational units as distinct compared to other units (in the same or related notational systems) and third as the most complicated aspect: we also need to be able to identify a notational unit as a legitimate (intended) unit compared to the possible but unintended occurrence of the same physical form.

Although Shannon was only concerned with physical noise in mechanical transmission systems, the basic question (how it is possible to distinguish between a physical unit/form which is intended as a symbolic unit from an physically identical form which is not intended as such) has to be solved in one way or another in any symbol system. The reason for this is that we can only use physical forms as symbolic units if these forms can also exist/occur without being symbolic units — whether the forms are provided by nature without any human intervention or by means of the latter. While the first and second aspects can always be solved by specifying certain physical criteria for the physical form of the individual units, there is no way to solve the third aspect by means of such physical criteria. This is why there cannot be a mechanical theory of symbol systems and of meaning.

Since Shannon's main purpose was to find methods to increase the capacity of the transmission channels, he was primarily concerned with methods to eliminate the redundant parts of the messages and hence reduce the amount of signals used to transfer the messages. What he found was that it was actually possible to reduce the amount of redundancy in the original message by means of various — primarily statistical — methods, but since these reductions made the transmission more vulnerable to noise (especially of type III), he also found that he could only eliminate one kind of redundancy (statistically defined) by introducing another (however more economical) kind, namely the formally defined control codes.

As one of the most interesting implications of his work we can state, first, that redundancy in one form or another seems to be necessary to maintain the stability of the symbol system on the basic level of physical manifestation, and, second, that redundancy on one level can to some extent be substituted for redundancy on another level. For instance, eliminating redundancy type II is only possible by adding redundancy type III, i.e. by substituting semantically defined redundancy for statistically defined redundancy — the latter being defined at the level of notation units.

Since redundancy type III is defined in a formal semantics, it can be defined independent of the semantic content of the message. In other words, it can be added before and eliminated after the transmission, without influencing the content of the message at all. In this case the formal procedure is neither part of the syntax of the message nor of the semantics, but of the computational syntax used to stabilize the message during transmission. Since any message can be stabilized by means of a number of different redundancy structures, it follows that a given message can have many physically different manifestations. There is no passage from the physical manifestation to the meaning which does not involve knowledge of codes to distinguish physical patterns which are noisy from redundant patterns in which meaning is always incorporated.

Conclusions concerning Shannon

(1)   Some kinds of redundancy are always needed to communicate messages —
       even in the case of physically precise (unambiguous) expressions. The basic
       necessity stems from the fact that any physical form which can be used as a
       symbol/notation unit (as information) can always exist as a mere physical
       form (as noise).

(2)   It is possible to substitute formally defined redundancy on the semantic level
       for (statistically) defined redundancy on the notational/physical level. The
       (economical and effective) point is that the former can be shorter than the
       latter. The theoretical point is that the stability of the whole system can be
       obtained in different ways — on different levels. Since a substitution of this
       kind is always possible, it follows that a given level can be modified both
       with and without effects on other levels. A new pattern may be generated
       without any impact (on the meaning or function of the system) at the time of
       formation, but it may be ascribed a function at a later time or a previous
       function may be changed into another or fade away. Changes may take
       place with as well as without impact on the content/function.

Although Shannon demonstrates some of the complexities involved in the notion
of redundancy, he is mainly concerned with the opposition between repetitive
structures on the one hand and singular occurrences on the other. Consequently,
he sometimes considers repetitive patterns as redundant and sometimes as part of
the rule structure of the symbol system, but always opposed to the singular occurrences which he considers as the distinct part representing the distinct meaning of
the expression. In short, if there is a repeatable pattern there is a kind of redundancy, and if there is an individual event there is meaning.

   It is probably no coincidence that this is quite contrary to the definition of redundancy by Greimas and Courtés (Greimas and Courtés 1979/1982), who are
concerned with the function of redundancy in ordinary languages, since it is well
known that repetitive patterns are often used as a means to express meaning in
linguistic messages. As a result, Greimas and Courtes' definition of redundancy is
opposite to that of Shannon's in that they define redundancy (or recursive patterns) as patterns of some — not yet theoretically defined — importance to the internal organization of meaning.

   The opposition between these two concepts of redundancy brings us directly to
the core of the difference between rule-based systems and rule-generating systems
based on redundancy functions. If as assumed both by Shannon and Greimas and
Courtés we are always dealing with rule-based systems, we are forced to define

redundancy in one of these mutually inconsistent ways. In one of the cases (that of Shannon), any kind of repetitively occurring pattern can be redundant, regardless of whether the repetition is completely superfluous or follows from the rules of the symbol system. If this is so, there is no way to explain how the use of repetitive patterns may take part in the expression of the content. In the other case (that of Greimas & Courtés) it is possible to specify the meaning of repetitive structures, while it is not possible to take into account the occurrences of individual events since the meaning is related to the repetitively occurring patterns. Yet at the same time the two concepts taken together show that meaning can both be manifested as repetitive patterns and as unique manifestations.

What we need is a concept of systems in which there are no *invariant* borders between individual occurrences, repetitive patterns without meaning, repetitive patterns which may have meaning and repetitive patterns necessary for the organization and structure of the expression.

It is no coincidence that both Shannon and Greimas/Courtés are actually in agreement when it comes to the question of how we can distinguish between regularly manifested occurrences which are redundant (and hence assumed superfluous) and those which are parts of the syntactical rules of the symbolic system (and hence assumed necessary). The only difference between these manifestations is the difference between patterns which have a regulative function and patterns which do not have any such function. What they both need, however, is to establish the possible connections between the individual events and the repetition of such events as redundant or eventually as part of the meaning and/or as functional rules. However, this is only possible to do if it is acknowledged that there are systems in which the function of a pattern may be variable.

4. Individual events, redundancy and the generation of new rules in language

I shall now demonstrate the existence of such relations by means of a linguistic example which will show how new codes or rules can be generated in systems independently of pre-existing rules by utilizing individual occurrences and redundancy functions.

The example is taken from a recent innovation in everyday Danish concerning a group of compounds which some years ago were changed — rather suddenly — to a new form as listed below:

New form

Børneren	for	Børne-haven	(kindergarten, nursery school)
Døgneren	for	Døgn-kiosken	(24-hour service kiosk)
Fritteren	for	Fritids-institutionen	(youth recreation center)

Trykkeren   for   Fjern-betjeningen   (remote-control unit)

There is a rule of reduction in this, and we can describe it by saying that a weak ending is substituted for the second part of some compounds. This is not a general rule in ordinary Danish and it is only applied to a limited group of compounds, namely compounds referring to central — new — institutions in daily family life in Denmark from the 1970s onwards.

Hence the conditions and restrictions for the use of the rule are extra-linguistic and not rule-based but based on the familiarity of the compounds in daily life (which is a case of redundancy). But the rule is not only based on — social — redundancy (familiarity), the content of the rule is also related to linguistic redundancy since it is a rule that reduces superfluous parts of the manifested expression.

Maybe one should also take into account that the compounds, except that of 'børnehaven', refer to quite new — and previously not yet culturally internalized — institutions, making the language usage in the area less stabilized.

We do not know the empirical details of this development, but we do know that there is an origin — a first case. Somebody spoke one of the new words for the first time (presumably the word 'børneren' — maybe coined by a five- or six-year-old girl or boy) on some particular occasion. Since it was an innovation, a new way to speak of something well known, we can furthermore assume that the articulation of familiarity was actually a part of the message (new meaning) contained in the new form in the first manifestation (hidden message: listen, I don't need to say 'børnehaven'. You know what I mean when I say 'børneren'). If so, the first manifestation of the new form is part of a specific meaning, as is often the case in ordinary language. The following steps are more unusual, since most linguistic innovations of this kind normally fade away very quickly. In this case, however, not only does the new form spread among a limited group — it spreads all over the country. The new form is repeated again and again and becomes familiar and commonly used as ordinary language, while the specific meaning in the first case (that the institution has now become so familiar that we don't need the whole word) fades away, which at the same time opens up for the use of the new form as a paradigmatic — regulative — form which can be used as a rule for similar innovations.

Familiarity — redundancy — is both a condition for first use of the word and for its acceptance and dispersion into larger groups, as well as for the application of the same pattern onto other words. It is the general precondition for the change as well as for the selection of the range of application.

The example can be regarded as a general paradigm, which may be called the mechanism or the principle for generating rules in redundant systems.

The mechanism is a process developing through 3 steps:

(1)   The first manifestation of a new form or pattern, or introducing a new way to speak of something which at the time has become familiar: for example, as an expression of the new information that it has become familiar (i.e. the new form represents a new meaning). There are also cases in which existing forms are used in new constellations (such as syllables, for instance, are used to form new words).

(2)   The acceptance of the new expression, i.e. repetitive use of the first manifestation, changing it from being new information to being an established custom — implying acceptance of the familiarity. This will normally take place in a smaller group and then — in some cases — it will spread. The most interesting cases being those which actually spread throughout the whole linguistic culture, that is, forms which can be used in public.

(3)   The spread of the use of the pattern as established custom and the use of the custom as a rule applied to — a set of — other compounds, in this case compounds representing central institutions in a newly changed way of daily life (Danish welfare society anno 1970 and onward).

Redundancy as a mechanism for variation in language is in use on all levels: notational, syllabic, syntactic, semantic including stylistic variance. Syntactical structure for instance can be described as a redundancy structure. In ordinary Danish a rich variety of meanings are expressed in the same syntactical scheme as most main clauses are manifested in the very same syntactical structure (while subordinate clauses are expressed in a slightly different scheme). This is quite contrary to the relation between syntax and semantics in formal systems in which semantical differences are often manifested in different syntactical expressions. The scheme of linguistic clauses allows a number of variations on the syntactical level. Some of these variations are optional in some cases, but not in others. Some variations may change the meaning, (i.e.: they are chosen to manifest a specific meaning) some will not (they may be chosen deliberately without impact on the meaning). The possible variations in the level of syntax is both dependent on the overall scheme and the allowed variations of the scheme, and on semantical choices. According to the circumstances — familiarity for instance — some parts of the scheme can even be left out. The syntactical scheme provides an important means of stabilization of meaning by the help of a range of possible utilizations and variations, or otherwise framed: it is one of the variable axis in the overall linguistic system.

   This is one of the reasons why I see ordinary language as based on redundancy,[4] and redundancy as a precondition or resource for generating meanings as well as new rules.

---

4   Concerning the concept of redundancy, it is always a phenomenon presupposing an observing and interpreting mind for which something can be redundant, implying that redundancy is also always relative to something more distinctive. That is: as a difference which in some respect is minor to another. Hence one might conclude that if there is distinct meaning there is also redundancy of some kind. It should also

Another — but connected — reason would be the existence of over- and under-determination, interferences between rules and the lack of rules for regulating relationships between overlapping rules and so forth — phenomena often described as marginal — expressed for instance in the phrase: no rule without an exception. Itself a 'rule' which can be applied to a very high degree in linguistic matters.

Redundant patterns on a given level can be used in different ways:

I   As a means to stabilize a level relative to another level, e.g.: syllables to stabilize the use of letters, or syntactical forms to stabilize meaning on the semantic level etc.

II   As a repertoire of forms from which new varieties can be created (pattern deviation).

III   As a repertoire of forms which can be taken into use — to express a new meaning or new aspects of meaning, or to ascribe a new regulative function.

In my view this is an obvious demonstration of the basic mechanism in redundancy-based symbol systems, such as linguistic and computational ones (while formal symbol systems are rule-based). I don't think it proves that language as such is not a rule-based system but is based on redundancy structures of this type. However, that the latter is the case is strongly supported by the fact that it provides a reasonable way to understand the development of language since it allows a development from first manifestations by way of repetitive manifestations to the generation of rules. How could language have developed in any other way? We still have a problem concerning the explanation of the natural origin of the human capacity to create symbols. But this is the only mystery left, while those arguing for the priority and pre-existence of linguistic rules also owe us a reasonable explanation of the origin of these rules.

However, it should be stressed that redundant systems do allow the formation of rules as a means of stabilization. But the point is that describing language (and other symbol systems) as based on redundancy implies that the establishment of rules is seen as part of the usage, including its acceptance, i.e. that the formation of rules is an integrated part of the use — contrary to describing language as a rule-based system, in which the rules are supposed to be given as invariants, somehow given from the outside.

In a broader perspective we could say that one of the main reasons that language has to be based on redundancy is inherited from the role of language as a mediator between senders and receivers who are not — and cannot be — fully synchronized with each other. One could also ask: why communicate at all if they

---

be noted that the only difference between a redundant pattern and a 'structure' is the function of the recurrent pattern: if redundant it might have no function at all, except that of the potential functions in the past or in the future, while »structures« means patterns which actually have an organizing function.

were synchronized beforehand? Redundancy provides a means to coordinate or adjust unsynchronized systems.

Instead of going further into this I shall now give a general definition of the concept of redundant systems, stressing the generative potential, which is often overlooked if not totally excluded (as is the case, for instance, in Shannon's use of the concept).

Redundancy ordinarily denotes the repetitive occurrence of patterns which have no function or meaning, and hence patterns which could just as well be left out: that is, passive, more or less irrational phenomenon. In contrast, it can be shown that redundant structures have important functions and are used for many purposes not only in ordinary language, but also in computers and in any other known uses of physical patterns as carriers of symbolic content. The basic reason for this is that systems based on the use of redundancy possess a set of mechanisms for semantic variation which cannot be found in strictly rule-based systems. This set of mechanisms basically consists in four axes of variation, as specified in the following points:

Redundant systems: four axes of variation

1) An axis constituted around the establishment of forms in a substance. The axis of variation of physical form as legitimate physical form — relative to the substance (new forms, variation of existing forms), for instance: the level of basic notation (in symbol systems using notations) whether alphabetical, binary notation or other forms. On this axis substance does matter in some way or another. In some cases new forms can be established by legitimating former — noisy — varieties as independent forms. The ultimate limit for establishing new forms is given in the physical substance used, and/or in a set of more or less well-defined physical and/or constitutional criteria for legitimate forms in a given system, one of the main points being that new forms can be legitimated as such, with or without a specific content or function.

2) An axis constituted around the establishment of compositions of elementary forms. The axis of variation of structural relations between legitimate forms or patterns. The levels of constellations in syllables and syntax in language, the level of the ascii-codes and algorithms in computers.

3) An axis constituted around variations in the strength of an articulation. The first axis of variation on the level of semantic content: The level of weakness-strength of a given content expressed. This 'more or less strong' type of variation is well known from the various speech acts (assertive, directive etc.). Variation on this axis can be both continuous and discrete in ordinary language (oral).[5] Such

---

5   Some linguists tend to define this axis as purely oppositional (binary oppositions), namely as the difference between marked and unmarked articulations. But I see no reason to exclude a continuous scale of variation.

variations are not expressed (but presupposed) in written manifestations, whereas only discrete variation (according to selection on a scale) is possible in computers. However, discrete variations can be approximated to nearby continuous variations, at least to the human sense organs.

4) An axis constituted around variations in semantic functions. The second axis of variation on the level of semantic content:

- a change in the content or modality of a given form (different from a change in the semantic strength);
- the transition from a first manifestation as a legitimate form with a new meaning, to the repetitive use of the new form — either with a change of meaning or in regulative function;
- a change in the content of the form from new meaning to conventional rule (e.g.: syntactically stored content).

The basic principle is that variation on one axis in some, but not all cases, implies variations on other axes and that rules are not necessary for the regulation of the relations between levels. The stability of the system is in some cases based on the stability on one level while there are variations on another, in other cases the stability is established in the mutual relationship between coexisting levels. Consequently, there can be many free variations in the forms on the lower level (as is the case on the notational level in written language, which allows us to use a great number of different physical manifestations of the 'same' letter while other physical variations represent the letter changing into another letter or the dissolution of the letter) as well as on the higher levels and in the interrelationships between levels.

5. Downward causation in rule-based systems?

If adhering to the notion of downward causation as suggested by Kim (Kim 1992: 120) implies 'that you are apparently committed to the consequence that these "higher-level" mental events and processes cause lower-level physical laws to be violated', defending this position seems difficult. To my knowledge at least, the notion of physical laws (contrary for instance to juridical and many other social and cultural laws) has always and has only been used as a notion of the relations and structures in the world which cannot be violated by any human being.

Thus, there are very strong logical reasons not to adhere to ideas which violate physical laws. The only question is, which laws? Those of Newton? Of modern thermodynamics? of relativity? of quantum mechanics? Or in other words: how can we reconcile ourselves with the notion of physical laws if these laws have no element whatsoever capable of explaining the origin and development of biological and mental domains in nature? Wouldn't it be reasonable to say that a theory of nature should take into account all the known natural phenomena — including for instance the existence of physicists who make theories on this very nature — as argued by Fink (Fink 1990: 20 ff.)? In my view, it would be a reasonable demand. Therefore, I have some difficulty with regard to the possible character of the basic physical laws assumed to determine the lower level physical processes.

Since I am not a physicist, I am not concerned with describing physical processes, but since I accept the idea that mental processes take place in the same universe as physical ones, I strongly need a physical theory which actually leaves room for, or at least allows, the origin and development of biological and mental processes in this universe. Unfortunately, it seems that no such theory is available for the time being. One may ask whether this is only a question of some missing links within the existing conceptual framework or whether a change of theoretical assumptions is needed, since the various physical theories seem to share the idea that biological and mental phenomena can either be derived in a mechanical way or do not have any place in the natural world at all.

The interesting thing here is not that a physicist may subscribe to any of these alternatives, but that it is of no importance to the physical theory whether he sticks to the former or the latter. This is apparently due to physicists' inclination to believe in the idea of a causally closed physical universe, which means that a physical theory cannot include any aspect which refers to the existence of non-physical phenomena such as biological and mental ones. If such phenomena are accepted, it is as peripheral phenomena which cannot be allowed to have any impact on — the understanding of — the physical universe.

We know the roots of this concept of nature very well. It was created as the foundational basis for modern physics in the 15th and 16th century. We also know that it formed the basis for the modern secular world view, according to which physical nature could be described according to a set of universal, mechanical principles. By means of these principles it was possible to overcome two main obstacles. First, that the natural laws on earth were the same as those of the whole universe. Second, that phenomena should not be explained as results of magical forces intervening in natural processes. Together these principles formed the basis for the idea that a secular description of nature was possible. But in spite of these great achievements there was also a price to be paid, since the whole model implied the exclusion of the human mind and language from this very nature. This of course became a main obstacle — and a question that remains unsolved — in later philosophy, in that mind and language (of course, I am inclined to say) need to be integrated into the very idea of a secular nature. The nature in which we actually live as constellations of molecules, chemical and biological processes with minds and languages.

Although language and mind were left outside there was also, as in Paradise, a snake *in* the modern secular concept of nature. While nature was conceived of as consisting of physical matter organized by invariant natural laws, the laws themselves were seen as immaterial and as given from the outside of the system — as created by God in the very beginning — and created as invariant laws acting upon nature, but themselves existing beyond time and space.

While the idea of nature as a system governed by a set of universal laws has played a major role in the modern process of secularization, it is itself rooted in religion. It is no coincidence that the religious basis was clearly articulated in the works of the founders of modern physics as well as in the works of later physicists and philosophers, at least until the first decades of this century. However, since the notion of God was identified with the notion of universal laws and with the notion of truth (as was the case in deism), there was no need to refer directly to the former when describing and defining the laws, except to explain how the actual world-machine was selected among the infinitely many possible machines — as Newton does in a letter 'to the reverend Dr. Richard Bentley, at the Bishop of Worcester's House on Park Street, Westminster':

The same Power, whether natural or supernatural, ... placed the Sun in the Center of the fix primary Planets, ... and therefore had this Cause been a blind one, without Contrivance or Design, the Sun would have been a Body of the same kind with Saturn and Jupiter, and the Earth, that is, without Light and Heat. Why there is one Body in our System qualified to give Light and Heat to all the rest, I know no Reason, but because the Author of the System thought it convenient; and why there is but one Body of this Kind I know no Reason, but because one was sufficient to warm and enlighten all the Rest.

(Letters from Newton to Bentley, Newton: *Opera Omnia*: IV: 430. The letter is dated Dec. 10, 1692, first printed 1756).

Given the idea that nature is a mechanical machine, it is impossible to explain the function of this particular machine purely on the basis of mechanical causation, since mechanical principles are not only blind, but also allow an infinite number of possible machines to exist.

The Newtonian reference to the idea of a divine Author demonstrates that he is actually presupposing a very strong kind of downward causation, but one that is restricted to take place once and forever as a great creational act in the very beginning — at a time when only the word existed according to the Bible. In this way modern physics evolved on the basis of the idea of downward causation initiated by a divine creator and explicated in the idea of natural laws which constituted the describable world as a causally closed physical universe. Nature was given top down. Given such laws, man could study Nature bottom up.

If, on the other hand, the selection of the specific machine is seen as a pure coincidence (and not as the result of the action of an Author/design), there is no way to maintain that the result of such first coincidences should be a rule-based machine at all. We may stick to the idea, but we have no obvious reason to claim that it is axiomatically true or to deny that the laws may also have evolved as regularities in the same time and space as the phenomena ruled.

There are some strong arguments which may explain why the notion of transcendentally given rules has not only survived in physics, but has spread into many other disciplines as well. The most important might be that we are almost always interested in knowledge which can be used in more than one case, implying that we are interested in recurring or recursive processes, even if nature as a whole develops irreversibly and hence never repeats its own former states — as is described in modern physics.

The idea of nature as one overall rule-based system is based on a monotheistic idea, but what about the notion of the universe as a set of such distinct systems? Should it be conceived of as a kind of polytheism? Or is it only a momentary idea waiting for someone to find the rules for regulating the relation between such systems?

Few, if any, seem to believe that modern science should have shifted from a monotheistic to a polytheistic foundation. The second option seems to be more widely accepted, mainly because of the philosophical principle of continuity. The idea of the existence of distinct, separate and autonomous systems seems to violate the idea that there is only one universe — and hence the basic principles of science.

It is possible to accept the basic idea of continuity, that there is only one universe, without accepting the existence of only one option: that the continuity can only be guaranteed by the existence of a set of universal rules or laws established from the very beginning as the result of a divine creational act. On the contrary, this option is based on a questionable identification of truth and law. Another option is that continuity in time and space could also be seen as a continuity of substance allowing a variety of changing relationships between substance and form as well as individual events to take place. Individual events and phenomena are found in many areas, in quantum mechanics, in biology and in human affairs — why not then in our theories about these phenomena?

I admit that many phenomena which at first sight seem to be individual or unique events, later prove to be instances of rule-based processes. I don't think we should rule out this experience, nor is there any reason to rule out the existence of some unique and unrepeatable phenomena in the world — individual life for instance, or various cultural phenomena. Maybe even physics, as some physicists have speculated, is a case of individual events which in some cases form the basis for a kind of 'habit formation' which eventually evolves into stronger 'natural laws' as a late (even if only measured in nanoseconds or less) and strongly stabilizing result.

Among the reasons to accept the notion of downward causation one might count the difficulty in describing or explaining the effects of human activity on nature without this notion. If we are not prepared to accept that in some cases mental processes may be necessary causal forces in nature, there is no reason to care about what we can do, what we actually do, and what we cannot or should not do. How, for instance, would it be possible to describe such artifacts as mechanical machines without any reference to the human motives manifested in the selection and organization of the physical matter and energy used? One might wonder whether anyone can imagine that these machines would be around if there were no causation from the human mind to the physical surroundings. Pure mechanical causation won't suffice, regardless of whether it is tried on the level of atoms and molecules or on a higher or lower level of physical organization.[6]

However, the notion of downward causation is often rejected because of its troubling implications. The notion is in conflict both with the Cartesian separation between mind and matter, and later with materialism, because it is assumed that it violates the notion of a causally closed physical universe:

> Downward causation prima facie implies the failure of causal closure at the lower level, and the in-principle impossibility of a complete theory of the lower level phenomena in their own terms. Can we seriously think that biological theories must include references to mental phenomena as causal agents?   *Kim 1995: 193-94*

Maybe not, but nonetheless I will try to be serious in my claim that biological theories must include references to mental phenomena as causal agents. The first part of the argument is simple. Since human beings are biological there is no way to eliminate our own mental processes and capacities from biology.

Accordingly, references to mental activities as causal agents are implied in evolutionary theories describing how we influence natural selection in various ways. We are able to decide to kill each other and other biological entities and execute such decisions — as well as to alter a huge number of species. Nowadays it seems that we have broadened the range for such effects to a new and unforeseeable scope, as we are now able to manipulate nature on the genetic level, while the lower limit — the bottom line — of such manipulations fades away since even in this area the basic components seem to be constituted as complex processes performed in time and space.

Much of this may be explained away, as if we always act in the same (predetermined) way regardless of whether we are aware of it or as if intentionality can only work on the basis of causality. In such cases we might say that this is only

---

6   Any artifact can always be described both as artifact and as pure physical phenomenon (for instance as a constellation of molecules or electrons, etc.). While the former description will need to include an intentional aspect (as for instance function), the latter will not, since it can only refer to mechanical relationships. Take, for example, a roof. While the artifactual description will refer to its function (to give shelter), which defines the roof as roof, the physical description will refer to the physical matter (a constellation of molecules of various kinds), the location of this constellation relative to the surroundings and so on, but never to its function as a shelter for a living organism. On the other hand, one may ask how it is possible to identify some molecules as belonging to a roof on a purely physical basis.

downward causation in a very limited and restricted way, meaning that this kind of action does not change the basic components and laws of the phenomena. This may be true. The only question is how we can detect the lower limits of mentally caused intervention. As we know from modern science, the basic units of Newtonian physics were not, as assumed, indivisible units. Nowadays we are able to split the atom, but not to describe a new invariant lower level. On the contrary, inside the atoms the distinction between matter and energy seems to fade away as a distinction between clearly separable phenomena. But there is still some substance, and it remains to be shown that this substance can always, and only, be defined by a specific quantifiable form — as has been assumed since the rise of modern science.

In the 20th century the notion that substance is defined by quantifiable form has been abandoned in various points of view and replaced by the notion of amorphous substances and autonomous forms and structures — possibly self-regulating structures able to produce innovations on the basis of pre-existing rules. However, it seems to be worth considering whether this is only one of the first steps towards overcoming the untenable identification of substance with — quantifiable — form which formed the axiomatic basis of Newtonian physics. But a first step only, since it leaves us plenty of forms and structures but no continuity in nature. The various theories of autonomous or self-dependent forms do not explain how the forms themselves (and new levels) come into existence and how they relate to the substances they form and in which they are forms. The next step might be to acknowledge that the relations between substances and forms may not always be invariant relations. If so, we might describe one of the conceptual lines in the history of modern science as the development from the notion of universal rules ruling the whole universe as if it were a static universe via the notion of dynamic rules of evolution and change, and on to the notion of a world in which the rules themselves might be changeable. From laws of a static universe via laws of possible change and on to the possible change of laws processed in the secular world.

We can find such changes of laws many places: in societies, cultures and biology and even in Einstein's theories, as he claims that light, for instance, is emitted as particles according to the laws of collision but spreads as waves according to the quite different set of laws for interference. Similarly, we may ask whether the transition between the laws of energy and of matter in the famous equation $e = mc^2$ could take place if it does not take time.

The only thing lacking is the recognition that even such changes of laws need to be understood as processes which themselves take place in time and space — whether accessible to human intervention or not. In such cases continuity is detectable in time and space, albeit only on the level of substances.

Once it is recognized that the notion of universal, transcendentally given natural laws in modern science is a specific instance of the notion of downward causation, it becomes possible to discuss whether it should now be removed from physical theory, but even so the question remains whether it can be removed from biological, psychological and cultural theories and whether it has any importance for the understanding of rule-generative systems.

6. Downward causation in rule-generating systems?

A definite answer to this question may not yet be in sight, which means that at present we are only able to reflect on the proper framing of this question. To this end I will take my point of departure in the relation between the notion of physical and mental states. In contemporary functionalist terms there is only a minor difference between these notions, and the difference is treated as a matter of the area of application — in different but otherwise amorphous substances. Models of physical states are transferred and used as models of mental states and vice versa. The domains are considered parallel coexisting levels.

However, this cannot be true since mental states — such as those caused by perceptual experiences, for instance — need to be stable in time independent of their surroundings. In other words, a mental state can only exist as an invariant unity over time, implying that a mental state is necessarily related to at least two different physical states. Instantaneous perception at a certain moment cannot take place at all. Since we know that perceptual inputs only come in a continuously flowing physical process, the question is how stable perceptual impressions — and in a broader framework, how mental states — can exist.

While, to my knowledge, we have no idea of how to explain the very origin of perceptual capacities and the human capacity to create symbols, we are able to state that these phenomena presuppose a capacity to 'store' signals coming in time as if the sequentially processed signals represented a simultaneously manifested state. And although we have only a rough picture of how perceptual impressions and mental content are incorporated in the neurophysiological system, we are forced to say that the mental states are manifested in the underlying neurophysiological processes in a way which implies that some processes in time on the lower level are utilized as (or cause) perceptual and symbolic content which does not vary according to the same time-scale. If it did there would only be chaotic impressions disappearing as soon as they appear.

The existence of mental phenomena presupposes that the underlying neurophysiological processes are organized and utilized according to a temporal dimension which is not implied in the description of these processes as purely neurophysiological/chemical and electrical processes. Therefore, we cannot exclude the possibility that a kind of downward causation may actually be involved. Mental processes may not change the neurophysiological system, but they certainly have impact on the actual processes performed in this system and may actually influence the functioning of the brain and the entire neurophysiological system.

We can demonstrate another aspect of the symbolic/representational capacity of the mind by comparing the mind to one of the most sublime of all known mechanical devices, the computer. While it seems impossible to deny that human beings possess the capacity to create various kinds of symbols and symbol systems including various kinds of notational systems, we know for sure that the computer cannot create its own notational system. While the human mind possesses the capacity to create a number of notation systems, the computer has no such property. The notational system has to be built into it by its human creators.

A comparison between the human brain and the computer is of course only possible because of their basic differences. There may also be differences concerning the depth of downward causation in the two systems. In the case of the computer we can say that the hardware of the computer is not changed or open for changes from the level of the software processed. In this case we know this is because the machine is built in a way which allows it to receive a specific kind of input manifested in a physically well-defined notational system. There is a bottom level for changes within the system. If the message is sent in another — stronger — voltage, this all changes. The limits to lower level changes are given as threshold values which cannot be transgressed without the system breaking down.

Concerning the mind, we know that we can create various representational systems even if we do not know how they are incorporated. The variety of legitimate input signals also seems to be much greater than in the case of computers, in which there are only two legitimate and discrete signals. While the computer is always digital, the mind might also be able to utilize analogic brain processes and hence to exploit a wider range of processes. Furthermore, we can say that if the neurophysiological system is a kind of an informational system — and that biological phenomena are defined by their genetic code — then there is no hardware involved in the definition at all. If there are only codes in some substance, there is also a way to disturb — and eventually change — the codes.

It seems worthwhile to pursue the idea that the neurophysiological system and the mind interrelate as different axes in a redundancy-based system, and that we cannot rule out the possible existence of downward causation in biological and mental systems. Meanwhile, it may finally be possible to dismiss the specific form of downward causation — the notion of eternally invariant and transcendentally given natural laws — which has previously been in use in the history of modern science.

References

BECKERMANN, A., FLOHR, H. & KIM, J. 1992. *Emergence or Reduction? Essays on the Prospects of Nonreductive Physicalism*. Berlin: de Gruyter.

FINK, H. 1990. Naturens enhed og videnskabernes. In Fink & Hastrup (eds.), *Tanken om Enhed i Videnskabernes*. Aarhus: Aarhus University Press.

FINNEMANN, N.O. 1994. *Tanke, Sprog og Maskine — en Teoretisk Anlayse af Computerens Symbolske Egenskaber*. Copenhagen: Akademisk Forlag. Translated by Gary L. Puckering (forthcoming): *Thought, Sign and Machine — The Computer Reconsidered*.

GREIMAS, A.J. & COURTÉS, J. 1979/1982. *Semiotics and Language. An Analytical Dictionary*. Bloomington: Indiana University Press. French original: *Semiotique. Dictionnaire raisonné de la théorie du langage*.

KIM, J. 1992. 'Downward causation' in Emergentism and Nonreductive Physicalism. In Beckermann, Flohr & Kim (eds.), 119-38.

KIM, J. 1995. Mental Causation in Searle's 'Biological Naturalism'. *Philosophy and Phenomenological Research* LV(1): 189-94.

NEWTON, I. 1729, 1782. *Opera Omnia*. Reprint edited by F. Cajoris, Berkeley 1946. (Letters from Newton to Bentley in Newton: *Opera Omnia*, 1782, IV: 429-42.)

SEARLE, J.R. 1995. Consciousness, the brain and the connection principle: A reply. *Philosophy and Phenomenological Research* 55(1): 217-32.

SHANNON, C.E. & W. WEAWER 1949. *The Mathematical Theory of Communication*. Urbana: University of Illinois Press, 1969.

SHANNON, C.E. 1951. Prediction and entropy in printed English. *Bell Syst. Tech. J.* 30, 50-64.

Part V
Philosophy

13

Making Sense of Downward Causation

JAEGWON KIM

Abstract

The idea of downward causation is central to emergentism, for the obvious reason that for emergent properties to play any causal/explanatory role they must be capable of causally influencing processes at lower levels. However, suspicions of potential circularity and conceptual incoherence have long surrounded this idea — for how could properties or phenomena have causal effects on the very processes that make their emergence possible and without which they could not even exist? This paper examines various conceptual/philosophical issues involved in this question, distinguishing unproblematic cases of downward causation from those that are problematic, i.e. those that involve 'synchronous reflective downward causation'. Finally, the paper offers a conceptual interpretation of downward causation.

1.

The idea of 'downward causation' implies vertical directionality, and this requires an ordering relation that generates an 'upward' direction and a 'downward' direction. This in turn suggests a hierarchically arranged system of domains that can give a precise and determinate meaning to the talk of something being located at a 'higher' or 'lower' or the 'same' position in relation to another item. As is familiar to everyone, positions on such a hierarchy are standardly referred to as 'levels', or sometimes 'orders'. We now encounter talk of 'levels' everywhere — as in 'level of description', 'level of explanation', 'level of organization', 'level of complexity', 'level of analysis', and the like. These 'levels' idioms now thoroughly permeate not only writings about science, including of course philosophy of science, but also the primary scientific literature of many fields (in particular, the biological and psychological/cognitive sciences, and various fields of social science). It is no accident that this phenomenon has coincided with what appears to be a strong return ('re-emergence', as one might say) of emergentism — if not all of its classic early doctrines but at least its characteristic concepts and slogans.

The emergentists of the early 20th century were among the first to articulate what may be called 'the layered model' of the world, although a general view of this kind is independent of the emergentist approach and has been espoused by those who are opposed to emergentism.[1] In fact, a model of this kind provides an essential scheme for the formulation of the debate between emergentism and the positions opposed to it — in particular, reductionism. Thus, the model itself is neutral as regards the emergentist/reductionist controversy. In any case, according to the layered model, nature is stratified into levels, from lower to higher, from the basic to the constructed and evolved, from the simplest to the more complex. All objects and phenomena are to have each a unique place in this ordered hierarchy. Most early emergentists, such as Samuel Alexander and C. Lloyd Morgan, viewed this hierarchy to have evolved historically: In the beginning there were only basic bits of matter — or only a spacetime framework, as Alexander maintained — and as time passed, these have evolved into increasingly more complex structures — atoms, molecules, cells, organisms, higher organisms with consciousness and mentality, social groups, and so on. Contemporary interest in emergence and the hierarchical model lies not in this kind of overarching quasi-scientific evolutionary history of the world, but rather in what it says about the synchronic structure of the world — how things and phenomena at different levels hang together at any given time, or over limited stretches of time. We want to know whether, and how, the emergentist ideas can help us in understanding the interlevel relationships between items belonging to the adjacent levels on this hierarchy, and ultimately how everything is related to the items at the bottom physical level (or, if an ultimate bottom level does not exist, what we take to be the lowest known level at a given time).

The layered model gives rise to many interesting questions: for example, how are these levels to be selected and characterized? Is there indeed a single unique hierarchy of levels that encompasses all of nature or does this need to be contextualized or relativized in certain ways? Does a single linear ladder-like structure suffice, or is a branching tree-like structure more appropriate? Exactly what ordering relations generate the hierarchical structure (that is, what exactly do 'higher' and 'lower' mean)? But these questions go beyond the scope of this paper. We will

---

1   See, e.g., Paul Oppenheim and Hilary Putnam, 'Unity of Science as a Working Hypothesis', in *Minnesota Studies in Philosophy of Science*, vol. 2, ed. Herbert Feigl, Michael Scriven, and Grover Maxwell (Minneapolis: University of Minnesota Press, 1958). As the title of the paper suggests, Oppenheim and Putnam advocate a strong form of physical reductionism, a doctrine that is diametrically opposed to emergentism.

work here with the fairly standard, intuitive notion of levels that I believe we all share.[2] This will not significantly affect the discussion to follow.

Although, as one would expect, there has been no universal agreement among the emergentists, the central doctrines of emergentism are well known. For our present purposes, we may take them to be comprised of the following claims:

(1)   Emergence of complex higher-level entities: Higher-level systems are gener-
       ated from the coming together of lower-level entities in new configurational
       (structural) relations.

Thus, higher-level entities are structures constituted by lower-level entities. We may note that structures may embed other structures, and that this is a cumulative process that can generate increasingly more complex systems. Exactly what sorts of relations can configure lower-level entities into a system with sufficient structural integrity and stability to qualify it as an entity in its own right? This is a complex and difficult question that is for empirical science to answer, with different answers for different domains, and it must be set aside for our present purposes. In any case, claim (1) is by no means special to emergentism; for its role is only to exclude physically 'alien' entities, such as Cartesian immaterial souls, the entelechies of neo-vitalism, elan vital, and the like. So it is unsurprising that the claim is completely at home with physical reductionism (what the early emergentists called 'mechanism'), the view that all things and phenomena are physical and are explainable and predictable ultimately in terms of fundamental physical laws.

A characteristically emergentist doctrine makes its appearance in the idea that some of the properties and behaviors of these complex entities, though physically grounded, can, in an important sense, be nonphysical, and belong outside the basic physical domain. The following three propositions unpack this idea.

(2)   Emergence of higher-level properties: All properties of higher-level entities
       arise out of the properties and relations that characterize their constituent
       parts. Some of these properties are 'emergent', while the rest are merely
       'resultant'.

Instead of the expression 'arise out of', expressions like 'supervene on' and 'are consequential upon' could have been used.[3] The idea is that when appropriate lower-level conditions are realized in a complex system (that is, the parts that constitute the system come to be configured in a certain relational structure), it will necessarily manifest a certain higher-level property, and, moreover, that no higher-level property can appear unless appropriate lower-level conditions are present.

2   For an informative discussion of the issues in this area see William C. Wimsatt, 'Reductionism, Levels of Organization, and the Mind-Body Problem', in *Consciousness and the Brain*, ed. Gordon G. Globus, Grover Maxwell, and Irwin Savodnik (New York & London: Plenum Press, 1976).
3   On the concepts of supervenience see my 'Supervenience as a Philosophical Concept', reprinted in *Supervenience and Mind* (Cambridge: Cambridge University Press, 1993).

Thus, 'arise out of' and 'supervene' are neutral with respect to the emergent/resultant distinction: both emergent and resultant properties of a whole supervene on, or arise out of, its microstructural, or micro-based, properties.

For emergentism, the distinction between properties that are emergent and those that are merely resultant is of central importance. For emergentism to be a viable doctrine, this distinction must itself be a viable one, and moreover it must be the case that there in fact is a significant class of properties that are emergent according to the distinction. How is the distinction characterized? For this purpose the emergentists standardly invoke the concepts of predictability and explainability.

(3)   The unpredictability of emergent properties: Emergent properties are not predictable even from the most exhaustive information concerning their 'basal conditions' — that is, it is not possible to infer or calculate what emergent properties (if any) a higher-level system will exhibit on the basis of a complete knowledge of the properties and behaviors of lower-level entities and the structural relations that configure them. In contrast, resultant properties are predictable from lower-level information.

(4)   The unexplainability/irreducibility of emergent properties: Emergent properties, unlike those that are merely resultant, are neither explainable in terms of, nor reducible to, their basal conditions.

I believe it is possible to give unity to these claims on the basis of an appropriate analysis of reduction. More specifically, on a certain conception of reduction, if we identify emergent properties with irreducible properties, it is possible to explain why emergent properties are neither explainable nor predictable on the basis of the conditions from which they emerge, whereas nonemergent (or resultant) properties are amenable to such explanations and predictions.[4]

Our main concern in this paper, however, lies with the issue of what emergent properties, after having emerged, can do — that is, make their own special contributions to the ongoing processes of the world. It is obviously very important to the emergentists that emergent properties can be active participants in causal processes involving the systems to which they belong. None perhaps understood this better than Samuel Alexander, a leading British emergentist early in this century, who made the following pointedly apt comment on epiphenomenalism, the position that mental properties are wholly lacking in causal powers:

[Epiphenomenalism] supposes something to exist in nature which has nothing to do, no purpose to serve, a species of noblesse which depends on the work of its inferiors, but is kept for show and might as well, and undoubtedly would in time be abolished.[5]

---

4   See for details my 'Explanation, Prediction, and Reduction in Emergentism', forthcoming in a special issue of *Intellectica* on emergentism.

5   *Space, Time, and Deity*, vol. 2 (London: Macmillan, 1927), p. 8.

If talk of emergent properties is to have any meaning, emergent properties must be causally effective properties, with powers to affect the course of events in which they are involved. In what ways, then, can emergent properties manifest their causal powers?

This is where the idea of 'downward causation' enters the scene. But when we view the situation with the layered model in mind, we see that three kinds of inter- or intra-level causation are possible: (i) same-level causation, (ii) downward causation, and (iii) upward causation. Same-level causation, as the expression suggests, involves causal transactions between properties at the same level — including cases in which one emergent property causes another emergent property to be instantiated. Downward causation occurs when a higher-level property, which may be an emergent property, causes the instantiation of a lower-level property; similarly, upward causation involves the causation of a higher-level property by a lower-level property.[6] I believe that, for the emergentist,[7] there is good reason to believe that downward causation is fundamental and of crucial importance in understanding all causation involving higher-level properties. For it can be shown that both upward and same-level causation presupposes the possibility of downward causation.

Here is a quick argument that shows why this is so. Suppose that a property M, at a certain level L, causes another property M^+, at level $L + 1$. Assume that M^+ emerges, or results, from a property, P, at level L. Note that as a higher-level property, M must have a lower-level base from which it emerges or results (this follows from claim (2) above). Now we immediately see a tension in this situation when we ask: 'What is responsible for this occurrence of M^+? What explains M^+'s presence on this occasion?' For in this picture there appear to be two competing answers: First, M^+ is there because, as initially assumed, M caused it; second, M^+ is there because its lower-level base P has been realized. Given the presence of its base P, M^+ must of necessity be instantiated, no matter what other conditions may have preceded it; P alone suffices to guarantee and explain M^+'s occurrence on this occasion, and without P, or an appropriate alternative base, M^+ could not have occurred. This apparently puts M's claim to have caused M^+ in jeopardy. I believe that the only coherent description of the situation that respects M's causal claim is this: M caused M^+ by causing its base condition P. But M's causation of P is an instance of same-level causation. This shows that upward causation entails same-level causation; that is, upward causation is possible only if same-level causation is possible.

6   We will often speak of one property causing another property. But, strictly speaking, causation is a relation not between properties but between instantiations of properties, or property instances, and talk of causation between properties should be understood accordingly.

7   As I have argued elsewhere, this holds for certain positions other than emergentism, e.g., the view that higher properties supervene on lower properties, and the view that higher properties are realized by lower properties.

As an example, consider this: physical/mechanical work on a piece of marble (M) causes the marble to become a beautiful sculpture (M^+). But the beauty of the sculpture presumably emerges from the physical properties (P — shape, color, texture, size, etc.) of the marble piece. Notice how natural, and in fact unavoidable, it is to say that the physical work on the marble caused it to become a beautiful sculpture by causing it to have these ('beauty-making') physical properties. This is an instance of same-level causation. Another example: a bee sting causes a sharp pain. But pain emerges from a certain neural condition N (say, C-fiber excitation). I believe that we want to say, and must say, that the bee sting caused the pain by causing N (the firing of C-fibers). This again is same-level causation.

An exactly similar argument will show that same-level causation presupposes downward causation. Briefly, this can be shown as follows: Suppose M causes P, where M and P are both at level L. But P arises out of a set of properties P^- at level L - 1. When we ponder the question how P gets to be instantiated on this occasion, we will again come to the conclusion that M caused P to be instantiated on this occasion by causing P^-, its base condition. But M's causation of P^- is downward causation. This completes the argument.

These considerations give strong support to the following general principle, which we may call 'the principle of downward causation':

- [The principle of downward causation] To cause any property (except those at the very bottom level) to be instantiated, you must cause the base conditions from which that property arises (either as an emergent or as a resultant).

This principle vindicates the importance most emergentists have attached to downward causation, but quite apart from that, it is an interesting result in itself. It shows downward causation to be essential to all higher-level causation; without it, no higher-level properties can be causally effective.

2.

Even the early emergentists were explicit on the importance of downward causation, although it is unlikely that they were influenced by anything like the argument of the preceding section. The following statement by C. Lloyd Morgan is typical:

Now what emerges at any given level affords an instance of what I speak of as a new kind of relatedness of which there are no instances at lower levels ... But when some new kind of relatedness is supervenient (say at the level of life), the way in which the physical events which are involved run their course is different in virtue of its presence — different from what it would have been if life had been absent.[8]

Compare this with what the noted neurophysiologist Roger Sperry, a tireless contemporary advocate of emergentism, says:

... the conscious subjective properties in our present view are interpreted to have causal potency in regulating the course of brain events; that is, the mental forces or properties exert a regulative control influence in brain physiology.[9]

Both Morgan and Sperry are saying that life and consciousness, emergent properties out of physicochemical and neural properties respectively, have a causal influence on the flow of events at the lower levels, levels from which they emerge. That of course is downward causation.

The appearance of an emergent property signals, for the emergentists, a genuine change, a significant evolutionary step, in the history of the world, and this requires emergent properties to be genuine properties with causal powers of their own. They are supposed to represent novel additions to the ontology of the world, and this could be so only if they bring with them genuinely new causal powers; that is, they must be capable of making novel causal contributions that go beyond the causal powers of their lower-level basal conditions.

But how do emergent properties manage to exercise their novel causal powers? According to the argument presented in the preceding section, they can do so only by causally influencing events and phenomena at lower-levels — that is, through downward causation. That was what we called the principle of downward causation. But is downward causation possible? The idea of downward causation has struck some thinkers as incoherent, and it is difficult to deny that there is an air of paradox about the concept: higher-level properties arise out of lower-level conditions, and without the presence of these in suitable configurations, they could not even be there. So how could these higher-level properties causally influence and alter the conditions from which they arise? Is it coherent to suppose that the presence of X is entirely responsible for the occurrence of Y (so Y's very existence is dependent on X) and yet Y somehow manages to exercise a causal influence on X? I believe a train of thoughts like this is in the back of the suspicions surrounding the idea of downward causation. But if downward causation is incoherent, that alone will cause serious damage to emergentism. For the principle of downward causation directly implies that if emergent properties have no downward causal powers, they can have no causal powers at all, and this means that emergent phenomena would just turn out to be epiphenomena, a prospect that would have severely distressed Alexander, Morgan, and Sperry.

---

8   *Emergent Evolution* (London: Williams & Norgate, 1927), pp. 15-16. Emphasis added.
9   'Mental Phenomena as Causal Determinants in Brain Function', in *Consciousness and the Brain*, ed. Globus, Maxwell, and Savodnik, p. 165.

But we need to analyze whether the kind of intuitive train of thoughts in the preceding paragraph against downward causation has any real merit. For cases in which higher-level entities and their properties prima facie causally influence lower-level entities and their properties seem legion. My typewriter has a mass of 10 kilograms. If it is dropped out the window of my second floor office, it will crash on the paved sidewalk, causing myriads of molecules of all sorts to violently fly away in every which direction. In fact, even before it hits the ground, it cuts a rapid downward swath through the air molecules, causing them to swirl away in all sorts of ways. Now if anything is a higher-level macro-object, typewriters surely are. And this cannot be a case in which the 'real' causal process occurs at the micro-level, between the micro-constituents of the typewriter and air molecules, for the simple reason that no micro-constituent, in fact no proper part, of this typewriter has a mass of 10 kilograms. There is no question that my typewriter, in virtue of having this mass, has a set of causal powers that none of its micro-constituents have; the causal powers this property represents cannot be reduced to the causal powers of micro-constituents of its bearers. Emergentists of course would not consider mass an emergent property; they would say that the mass of an object is a resultant property, a property that is merely 'additive or subtractive'. But this simple-minded example suffices to show that there can be nothing strange or incoherent in the idea of downward causation as such — the idea that complex systems, in virtue of their macro-level properties, can cause changes at lower-levels.

However, the idea of downward causation advocated by some emergentists appears to be stronger and more complex than what is suggested by our simple example. Consider again what Sperry says:

The subjective mental phenomena are conceived to influence and govern the flow of nerve impulse traffic by virtue of their encompassing emergent properties. Individual nerve impulses and other excitatory components of a cerebral activity pattern are simply carried along or shunted this way and that by the prevailing overall dynamics of the whole active process (in principle — just as drops of water are carried along by a local eddy in a stream or the way the molecules and atoms of a wheel are carried along when it rolls down hill, regardless of whether the individual molecules and atoms happen to like it or not).[10]

Sperry has used these and other similar analogies elsewhere; in particular, the wheel analogy seems to have been one of his favorites. What is distinctive about this form of downward causation seems to be this: Some activity or event involving a whole W is a cause of, or has a causal influence on, events involving its own micro-constituents. We may call this reflexive downward causation, to distinguish it from the more mundane nonreflexive kind, involved in the example of the falling typewriter above, in which an event involving a whole causes events involving lower-level entities that are not part of it.

10 'A Modified Concept of Consciousness', *Psychological Review* 76 (1969): 532-36.

For Sperry (and perhaps others), downward reflexive causation is not all that is involved in a situation in which an emergent exercises its causal powers. There is also an upward determination. The paragraph quoted above from Sperry continues as follows:

Obviously, it also works the other way around, that is, the conscious properties of cerebral patterns are directly dependent on the action of the component neural elements. Thus, a mutual interdependence is recognized between the sustaining physico-chemical processes and the enveloping conscious qualities. The neurophysiology, in other words, controls the mental effects, and the mental properties in turn control the neurophysiology.[11]

After all, an eddy is there because the individual water molecules constituting it are swirling around in circular motion; in fact, an eddy is nothing but these water molecules engaged in this pattern of motion. Take away the water molecules, and you have taken away the eddy — there won't be a disembodied eddy still swirling around without any water molecules! Thus, reflexive downward causation is combined with upward determination. When each and every molecule in a puddle of water begins to move in an appropriate way — and only then — will there be an eddy of water. But in spite of this, says Sperry, it remains true that the eddy is moving the molecules around 'whether they like it or not'.

Thus, reflexive downward causation is combined with upward determination. Schematically, the situation looks like this: a whole, W, has a certain emergent property, M; W is constituted by parts, a_1, ..., a_n, and there are properties P_1, ..., P_n respectively of a_1, ..., a_n and a certain relation R holding for the a_is. The following two claims make explicit what Sperry appears to have in mind (I do not want to rule out other inequivalent interpretations of Sperry):

(i)   [Downward causation] W's having property M at t causes some a_j to have P_j at t; but

(ii)   [Upward determination] each a_i's having P_i at t and R holding for the a_is at t together determine W to have M (or W's having M depends wholly on, or is wholly constituted by, the a_is having the P_is respectively and being related by R).

The question is whether or not it is possible, or coherent, to hold both (i) and (ii). Some may have noticed that (i) apparently involves simultaneous causation — both the cause and its effect occur at the same time. Whether or not simultaneous or instantaneous causation is possible — that is, whether causation always requires a time gap between cause and effect — is a long-standing issue in metaphysics and philosophy of science. I believe, however, that in the present context it is not productive to focus on this aspect of Sperry's claims; if necessary, we may substitute the 'dependency' or 'determination' idioms for the causal idiom. I think

11 Ibid.

all that Sperry wants to say can be captured by saying, for example, that the whole's having M at t is responsible for, and explains, its parts having certain properties. We may note that, in the last quoted passage, Sperry speaks of 'mutual interdependence' between the properties of the whole and those of its parts. Dependence, in a broad sense, is what is important to him; causation in any of its specific philosophical senses would not have interested him.

3.

As I said, downward causation as such presents us with no special problems; but what Sperry wants (also there is a hint of this in the quotation from Lloyd Morgan above) is the reflexive variety of downward causation, and it is this that we want to understand. How is it possible for the whole to causally affect its constituent parts on which its very existence and nature depend? If causation or determination is transitive, doesn't this ultimately imply a kind of self-causation, or self-determination — an apparent absurdity? (The individual water molecules swirling in a circular motion together cause the eddy to occur, but, says Sperry, the eddy causes the water molecules to move around just this way. If causation is transitive, as it is standardly supposed to be, doesn't this mean that the motion of the water molecules causes itself?)

Let us see if we can make coherent sense of reflexive downward causation. We can distinguish between two cases, the first of which is merely a restatement of the problem as set forth earlier:

- Case 1. At a certain time t, the whole W has emergent property M, where M emerges from the following configuration of conditions: W has a complete decomposition into parts $a_1, ..., a_n$; each a_i has property P_i; and relation R holds for the sequence $a_1, ..., a_n$. For some a_j, W's having M at t causes a_j to have P_j at t.

Note that time t is fixed throughout, and both the downward causation and upward emergence (or determination) hold for states or conditions occurring at the same time. We may, therefore, call this 'synchronic reflexive downward causation'. A whole has a certain emergent property, M, at a given time, t, and the fact that this property emerges at t is dependent on its having a certain micro-configuration at t, and this includes a given part of it, a_j, having P_j at t. That is, unless a_j had P_j at t, W could not have had its emergent property M at t (we may assume, without prejudice, that no alternative emergence base would have been available). Given this, it makes one feel uncomfortable, to say the least, to be told also that this instance of a_j is caused to have P_j at that very time, t, by the whole's having M at t.

But what exactly is the source of this discomfort? Why does this picture seem in some way circular and unreal? Moreover, what is it about causal circularity that makes it unacceptable? One possible explanation, something I find plausible myself, is that we tacitly subscribe to a metaphysical principle like the following:

- For an object, x, to exercise, at time t, the causal/determinative powers it has in virtue of having property P, x must already possess P at t. When x is being caused to acquire P at t, it does not already possess P at t and is not capable of exercising the causal/determinative powers inherent in P.

If a name is wanted, we may call this 'the causal-power actuality principle'. The reader will have noticed that this principle has been stated in terms of an object 'acquiring' property P at a time. In Case 1 above, we said that the whole, W, causes one of its proper parts, a_j, to 'have' P. It seems clear that if there is real downward causation, from W's having M to a_j's having P_j, this 'have' is properly understood as 'acquiring'. For if a_j already has P_j at t, what role can W's having M at t (or anything else) play in causing it to have P_j at t? Obviously, none. It would be stretching things too far to say 'Well, maybe it is helping a_j from losing P_j at t' or something of the sort. That would be entirely ad hoc and lacking in any independent motivation.

The incoherence involved in Case 1, therefore, can be seen to arise as follows: the assumption that W's having M at t causes a_j to have P_j at t implies, via the causal-power actuality principle, that a_j does not already possess P_j at t. But if a_j does not already possess P_j at t, it follows, again via the causal-power actuality principle, that a_j cannot, at t, exercise its determinative power in bringing about the emergence of M for W at t. That is, the emergence base of W's having M at t disappears, and hence W cannot have M at t. The Case 1 story, therefore, collapses.

I believe that if you are prepared to bite the bullet and reject the causal-power actuality principle, and live with causal circularity (perhaps even celebrate it in the name of 'mutual causal interdependence'), then Case 1 could serve as a model of downward causation for you. Speaking for myself, I think there is a good deal of plausibility in the principle that says that for properties to exercise their causal/determinative powers they must actually be possessed by objects at the time; it cannot be that the objects are in the process of acquiring them at that time. So let's try a different model.

- Case 2. As before, W has emergent property M at t, and a_j has P_j at t. We now consider the causal effects of W's having M at t on a_j at a later time t + Δt. Suppose, then, that W's having M at t causes a_j to have (or acquire) Q at t + Δt.

This, therefore, is a case of diachronic downward causation. It is still reflexive in that a whole causes one of its micro-constituents to change in a certain way.

Notice, however, that the mysteriousness of causal reflexivity seems to have entirely vanished. The reason is obvious: the time delay between the putative cause and effect removes the potential circularity, and the causal-power actuality principle is not violated. W's having M at t causes a_j to have Q at $t + \Delta t$. But a_j's having Q at $t + \Delta t$ is not part of the basal conditions out of which M emerges in W at t; so there can be no problem of viciously circular reciprocal causation/ determination.

This becomes particularly clear if we consider the situation under the four-dimensional (or 'time-slice') view of persisting things. On this view, W's having M at t turns into W at t having M — that is, the time slice of W at t having M. Let us use '[x, t]' to refer to the time slice of x at t (if t is an instant, [x, t] is a temporal cross-section). Diachronic downward causation, then, turns into this: [W, t] having M causes $[a_j, t + \Delta t]$ to have Q. It is clear that $[a_j, t + \Delta t]$ is not a constituent of [W, t], and that this gets rid of the hint of reflexivity present in Case 2. Under the time-slice conception, therefore, Case 2 is no longer a case of reflexive downward causation.

Examples falling under Case 2 are everywhere. I fall off the ladder and break my arm. I start walking toward the kitchen for a drink of water and ten seconds later, all my limbs and organs have been displaced from my study to the kitchen. Sperry's bird flies into the blue yonder, and all of the bird's cells and molecules, too, have gone yonder. It doesn't seem to me that these cases present us with any special mysteries rooted in self-reflexivity. For consider Sperry's bird: for simplicity, consider the five parts of this bird, its head, torso, two wings, and the tail. For the bird to move from point p_1 to point p_2 is for its five parts (together, attached to each other) to move from p_1 to p_2. The whole bird is at p_1 at t_1 and moving in a certain direction, and this causes, let us suppose, its tail to be at p_2 at t_2. There is nothing mysterious or incoherent about this. The cause, namely the bird's being at p_1 at t_1 and moving in a certain way includes its tail's being at p_1 at t_1 and moving in a certain way. But that's quite all right: we expect an object's state at a given time to be one of the causal factors that determine its being in another state at a later time.

We must conclude then that of the two types of reflexive downward causation, the diachronic variety poses no special problem, but that the synchronic kind is problematic, and it is doubtful that we can give it a coherent sense. This may well be due to its violation of what I called the causal-power actuality principle, but quite apart from any broad metaphysical principle that might help explain it, one cannot escape the feeling that there is something incoherent (perhaps, a form of causal circularity) about this variety of downward causation.

4.

Sperry appears to think that the case of the flying bird we have just considered and similar cases such as the rolling wheel and the swirling water eddy are paradigmatic cases of downward causation, and that the downward causal influence of consciousness on neural processes from which it emerges is to be understood on this model.

What we have seen, however, is that Sperry's examples, when understood as cases of synchronic reflexive downward causation, are difficult to make sense of and are almost certainly incoherent. In contrast, when they are taken as cases of diachronic reflexive downward causation, from properties of a whole to properties of its constituent parts at a later time, they appear to be free of metaphysical difficulties. But, for this very reason, they do not seem to constitute a metaphysically or scientifically distinctive variety of causation with potentials for significant new applications and therefore deserving of special methodological attention.

Emergentists like C. Lloyd Morgan will likely point out that the Sperry-style cases do not involve downward causation by emergent properties, since the motion of the bird as a whole is the same kind of event as the motion of its constituent parts. The properties implicated in causal relations in these cases are one and the same, namely motion, and this shows that these cases simply are not cases of emergent causation, whether downward or upward. It would seem, then, that contrary to what Sperry seems to suggest, emergent downward causation should not be identified with causation from properties of the whole to properties of its parts. The latter may still be a species of the former; as I said, however, it may be a highly special case of no great philosophical or scientific interest.

Let us, then, consider consciousness: the downward causal influence of consciousness on neurophysiological processes. Here again we may consider two varieties, synchronic reflexive downward causation and its diachronic counterpart. Can my awareness of pain at a given time causally influence its basal neural process (C-fiber excitation, say) at the very same time? I believe that we encounter here exactly the same difficulties that we saw in Sperry's examples of the water eddy and the like (taken as cases of synchronic downward causation). All these cases present to us a metaphysically incoherent picture, and I do not believe that classical emergentists, like Alexander, Morgan, and C.D. Broad, would necessarily have wanted it. Nor do I see why Sperry himself, as an emergentist, should need it; if there was a deeper reason, rooted in his larger philosophical picture of the world, for favoring synchronic downward causation, I fail to fathom it.

No doubt this takes out of action the variety of downward causation that prima facie might have looked to some emergentists particularly interesting and intriguing, and promising as a new methodological tool in understanding certain specially complex and puzzling aspects of the natural world, in particular the causal role of consciousness. But promise is one thing, reality is another. A new concept, if it is going to be useful as an explanatory paradigm, must itself make sense. I believe the concept of synchronic emergent downward causation fails this test. This leaves diachronic downward causation as the only survivor — up to this point, at any rate.

And one might say that that is all that emergentists need — the diachronic causal influence of emergent phenomena on lower-level phenomena, phenomena of the kinds out of which they have emerged. Consciousness, having emerged from biological phenomena and ultimately from basic physicochemical phenomena, can influence, and has influenced, these lower-level phenomena. Humans, as conscious cognizers and agents, have created new breeds of animals and new varieties of food plants, have built bridges and cities, have split the atom, and have sent spacecraft to the moon and Mars. Isn't this enough to give a raison d'etre — an indispensable causal/explanatory role — to higher-level mental/cognitive properties?

But the problem is that even this apparently unproblematic variety of downward causation has been beset with philosophical difficulties. In my view, the difficulties essentially boil down to the following single argument. If an emergent, M, emerges from basal conditions C, why can't C displace M as a cause of any putative effect of M? Why doesn't C do all the work in bringing about the putative effect of M and suffice as an explanation of why the effect occurred?[12] This is not the place to rehearse the argument in detail; I will sketch it in rough outlines. As you may recall, I earlier argued that any upward causation or same-level causation of effect P by cause M presupposes M's causation of P's lower-level base, P⁻ (it is supposed that P is a higher-level property with a lower-level base; P may or may not be an emergent property in the narrow sense). But if this is a case of downward emergent causation, M itself must be a higher-level property with an emergent base, M⁻. Now we are faced with the possibility that M⁻ may well preempt M's status as a cause of P⁻. For if causation is understood as nomological (law-based) sufficiency, M⁻, as M's emergence base, is nomologically sufficient for it, and M, as P⁻'s cause, is nomologically sufficient for P⁻. Hence, M⁻ is nomologically sufficient for P⁻ and hence qualifies as its cause. The same conclusion follows if causation is understood in terms of counterfactuals — roughly, as a condition

12 I first raised this question in my "Downward Causation' in Emergentism and Nonreductive Physicalism', in *Emergence or Reduction?*, ed. Ansgar Beckermann, Hans Flohr, and Jaegwon Kim (Berlin: de Gruyter, 1992). The argument can be generalized to the supervenience and realization views of the mind-body relation. For further discussion see my *Philosophy of Mind* (Boulder, CO: Westview Press, 1996), chs. 6 and 9; and *Mind in a Physical World* (forthcoming). See also Timothy O'Connor, 'Emergent Properties', *American Philosophical Quarterly* 31 (1994): 91-104, for an attempt to counter the argument.

without which the effect would not have occurred. Moreover, it is not possible to view the situation as involving a causal chain from M⁻ to P⁻ with M as an intermediate causal link. The reason is that the emergence relation from M⁻ to M cannot properly be viewed as causal.[13] This appears to make the emergent property M otiose and dispensable as a cause of P⁻; it seems that we can explain the occurrence of P⁻ simply in terms of M⁻, without invoking M at all. If M is to be retained as a cause of P⁻, or of P, a positive argument has to be provided, and we don't see one. In my opinion, this simple argument has not so far been overcome by an effective counter-argument.

If higher-level property M can, in some appropriate sense, be reduced to its lower-level base, M⁻, M's causal status can be restored.[14] But if M is emergent, this is precisely what cannot be done: emergence is defined, at least in part, in terms of irreducibility. That is, emergent properties, by definition, are not reducible to their underlying lower-level bases. The tentative conclusion, therefore, isn't encouraging for the emergentists: If emergent properties exist, they are causally, and hence explanatorily, inert and hence largely useless for theoretical scientific purposes.

If these considerations are correct, higher-level properties can serve as causes in downward causal relations only if they are reducible to lower-level properties.[15] The paradox is that if they are so reducible, they are not really 'higher-level' any longer. If they are reducible to properties at level L, they, too, must belong to L. Does this make the idea of downward causation useless? Not necessarily. One way to save downward causation might be to construe it conceptually. That is, the hierarchical levels that this idea suggests would be interpreted as levels of concepts and descriptions, levels in our conceptual/linguistic apparatus (that is, levels in our systems of representation), rather than levels of properties and entities in the world. We can then speak of downward causation when a cause is conceptualized or described in terms of concepts that are at a higher level in relation to the concepts in which its effect is described. But the very same cause may be representable in lower-level concepts and languages as well, and that a single causal relation may be describable in different languages. (The ideal of completed physics holds that every event in the world, without exception, has a full physical descrip-

13 C. Lloyd Morgan explicitly denies that emergence is a form of causation, in *Emergent Evolution*, p. 28.
14 See for more details my 'The Mind-Body Problem: Taking Stock After 40 Years' (forthcoming in *Philosophical Perspectives*, 1997).
15 Here I must enter some caveats. As the reader may recall, I earlier claimed that there is no special problem of downward causation, citing such examples as my typewriter crashing on the pavement of the sidewalk. Cases like this are not cases of downward causation that most emergentists have in mind, for like Sperry's example of the flying bird they don't seem to involve genuine 'higher-level' properties. Moreover, I believe that complex systems can bring new causal powers into the world, powers that cannot be identified with causal powers of more basic, simpler systems. It is, however, a debatable question whether these new causal powers coincide with 'emergent' properties as standardly conceived. I would like to restrict the argument in the text to consciousness and other standard examples of emergent properties. For further discussion, see my 'Explanation, Prediction, and Reduction in Emergentism' (forthcoming in *Intellectica*), 'Does the Problem of Mental Causation Generalize?', the *Proceedings of the Aristotelian Society* 97 (1997): 281-97, and *Mind in a Physical World* (forthcoming).

tion, and that every causal relation is ultimately representable at the physical level.)

This approach will not save downward causation in an objective sense; genuine downward causation does requires levels of entities and phenomena in the objective world, for the simple reason that causation is a relation between events in the world, not between concepts or descriptions. However, the approach may well be sufficient for saving downward causal explanation; explaining, after all, is an epistemic activity that takes place on a conceptual plane — that is, within theories and systems of concepts, and explanations are cognitive/conceptual products. And successful scientific explanations are an essential part of our scientific knowledge. The suggestion is that we think of a downward causal explanation as one in which the explanatory premises (the explanans) are formulated in a higher-level language or theory in relation to the language in which the explanandum (the phenomenon to be explained) is represented. Such interlevel explanations — explanations that bring out relationships between phenomena conceptualized at different levels — may provide us with valuable explanatory insights that are not obtainable from those couched exclusively in one language. Moreover, the conceptual approach to downward causation brings with it another interesting and important benefit, and it is this: it makes the 'levels' talk and downward causal explanations entirely consistent with reductionist metaphysical physicalism. The world out there is a wholly physical world; however, this need not prevent us from describing and explaining it at different conceptual levels or in different languages. It can be argued that downward causal explanation is all we need or should want.

These are tantalizing thoughts but more work needs to be done. To mention some of the questions that must be addressed: Exactly what does 'levels' mean for concepts and languages? What makes a given group of concepts, or a given language, 'higher' or 'lower' in relation to another group of concepts or languages? In particular, can we explain these concepts without presupposing objective levels in the real world? Would divorcing downward causal explanation from objective downward causation deprive such explanation of objective significance? What exactly are the explanatory insights to be gained from downward causal explanations as construed in this approach? And, most importantly, what is the scientific significance of downward causal explanations (no matter how they are construed philosophically)? These are interesting questions. But we must set them aside for another occasion.

Acknowledgments

In preparing the present version of this paper I benefited from comments and suggestions from the participants in the workshop seminar on downward causation in Aarhus, Denmark, May, 1997. H.H. Pattee's written comments received after the seminar were also thought-provoking and helpful. I am grateful to the organizers of the seminar — Niels Ole Finnemann, Peter Bøgh Andersen, and Claus Emmeche — for their hospitality and support.

References

ALEXANDER, S. 1927. *Space, Time, and Deity,* vol. 2. London: Macmillan.

BECKERMANN, A., H. FLOHR & J. KIM (eds.). 1992. *Emergence or Reduction?* Berlin: de Gruyter.

GLOBUS, G.G., G. MAXWELL & I. SAVODNIK (eds.). 1976. *Consciousness and the Brain.* New York & London: Plenum Press.

KIM, J. 1992. 'Downward Causation' in emergentism and nonreductive physicalism. In Beckermann, Flohr & Kim (1992).

KIM, J. 1993. Supervenience as a philosophical concept. Reprinted in *Supervenience and Mind.* Cambridge: Cambridge University Press.

KIM, J. 1996. *Philosophy of Mind.* Boulder, Colo: Westview Press.

KIM, J. 1997a. Does the problem of mental causation generalize? In the *Proceedings of the Aristotelian Society 97,* 281-97.

KIM, J. 1997b. The mind-body problem: Taking stock after 40 years. *Philosophical Perspectives* 11.

KIM, J. Forthcoming a. *Explanation, Prediction, and Reduction in Emergentism.* Forthcoming in a special issue of Intellectica on emergentism.

KIM, J. Forthcoming b. Mind in a physical world.

MORGAN, G. LLOYD 1927. *Emergent Evolution.* London: Williams & Norgate.

O'CONNOR, T. 1994. Emergent properties. *American Philosophical Quarterly 31:* 91-104.

OPPENHEIM, P. & H. PUTNAM 1958. Unity of science as a working hypothesis. In Herbert Feigl, Michael Scriven & Grover Maxwell (eds.), *Minnesota Studies in Philosophy of Science, vol. 2.* Minneapolis: University of Minnesota Press.

SPERRY, R.W. 1969. A modified concept of consciousness. *Psychological Review 76:* 532-36.

SPERRY, R.W. 1976. Mental phenomena as causal determinants in brain function. In Globus, Maxwell & Savodnik (1976).

WIMSATT, W.C. 1976. Reductionism, levels of organization, and the mind-body problem. In Globus, Maxwell & Savodnik (1976).

14

Emergence[1]

MARK H. BICKHARD WITH DONALD T. CAMPBELL[2]

Abstract

Accounting for emergence has proven to be extraordinarily difficult, so much so that whether or not genuine emergence exists seems still in doubt. I argue that this difficulty is primarily due to an assumption of a false and inappropriate metaphysics in analyses of emergence. In particular, common assumptions of various kinds of substance metaphysics make the notion of causally efficacious emergence seriously problematic, if not impossible. There are, however, many problems with substance metaphysics — arguably fatal problems — and an alternative process metaphysics makes causally efficacious emergence much more natural.

Introduction

Consider a kitchen table. A table appears to be an entity in its own right — large, with a particular shape, solid, capable of supporting smaller objects, and so on. But we also assume that it is made of molecules, and, in turn, atoms, and, in further turn, various subatomic particles. Perhaps the *only* physical reality is the swarm of quarks, gluons, and electrons that make up the table, and all of the other properties, of solidity, shape, and so on, are no more than manifestations of the interactions among those particles. Perhaps the properties of the table, and even the existence of a distinct object that we call a table, are all just *epiphenomenal* to the fundamental particle interactions.

1   Deepest thanks are due to Wayne Christensen, John Collier, Norm Melchert, and, most especially, Cliff Hooker, for comments on earlier drafts, and to the Henry R. Luce Foundation for support to Mark Bickhard during the preparation of this paper.
2   This paper was to have been written jointly with Don Campbell. His tragic death on May 6, 1996, occurred before we had been able to do much planning for the paper. As a result, this is undoubtedly a very different paper than if Don and I had written it together, and, undoubtedly, not as good a paper. Nevertheless, I believe it maintains at least the spirit of what we had discussed. Clearly, all errors are mine alone.

This is epiphenomenality in the sense of an appearance being false about underlying reality, such as the apparent motion of objects when watching a movie, when all that is 'really' happening is a rapid succession of still pictures that happen to be sufficiently similar to each other to give an impression, a strictly false impression, of objects and people and caused motion. Perhaps being solid, for example, is mere appearance, merely epiphenomenal in this sense, from the level of the fundamental particles.

Most of us would prefer that our experiences of tables not be false, not be merely epiphenomenal. It would be a strange world in which virtually all of our experiences were in fact false to reality. The issues become even more focused and interesting, however, when we consider not just tables, but living things, and things with minds — animals and people — and, most especially, our own mind. The supposed lessons from science are just as strong about plants, animals, and minds, as about tables. It would be a strange person indeed who would feel satisfaction in the conviction that his or her own mind did not really exist, but was merely an epiphenomenal manifestation of fundamental particle interactions.

We would like for tables and their properties to be real, as well as life and mind. But our best science suggests strongly that the world is integrated, that there are not different sorts of substances or fluids for every new kind of phenomena. We have learned that fire is not a substance *phlogiston*, heat is not a substance *caloric*, life is not due to *vital fluid*, and very few philosophers or scientists today are substance dualists about mind compared to matter. Instead, these phenomena are understood as the result — the natural result — of processes involving atoms and molecules that are familiar from other kinds of phenomena. Fire, heat, life, and so on, and, presumably, mind, are integrated with the rest of the natural world. Naturalism about the world is clearly the best bet. But, so long as naturalism seems to suggest that the only real reality is basic particles, the apparent dilemma remains.

Perhaps phenomena such as life and mind are somehow *emergent* out of lower level particles and processes. Perhaps they only exist insofar as those lower level particles and processes exist and occur, but they nevertheless have a reality of their own that comes into being, that emerges, when certain patterns or quantities or some other threshold criterion is satisfied. And, furthermore, perhaps, the reality they have *makes a difference*.

It is of little satisfaction if mind proves to be real in the sense of involving properties that genuinely exist, if those mental properties nevertheless have no causal power in the world, if they merely float along the basic particle interactions for the ride, but make no difference themselves. We all know in our own experience that mind, whatever it is, exists, but it would also be nice if our impressions of being able to make decisions and do things in the world are not themselves just epiphenomenal (Heil & Mele 1993). So, for emergence to do what we would want it to do, we need not only emergent instances of properties, but the emergence of properties or entities or processes that have genuine causal powers.

It has proven remarkably difficult to make good on these intuitions of emergence. The inexorable reality of quantum particles keeps grabbing all of the causal powers, leaving nothing for purported emergents. Perhaps we must simply accept this apparent lesson of contemporary science — that we ourselves are mere epiphenomena.

I will be arguing that genuine emergence does exist, and that the difficulties encountered in trying to make sense of it have been exacerbated by the presupposition of a false metaphysics — a metaphysics of substances (particles) and properties. There are good reasons to abandon such a metaphysical framework, and to substitute a process metaphysics. In this alternative process metaphysical framework, the possibility of emergence, including genuine causally efficacious emergence, is found to be trivial — the in-principle mystery of emergence is dissolved. Accounting for any *particular* emergence, however, such as that of mind, remains a deep, complex, and difficult problem.

The intuition of emergence is that of novel causal powers coming into being at specific levels of ontology (Beckermann, Flohr & Kim 1992; Beckermann 1992b; Hooker 1979, 1981a, 1981b, 1981c, 1989). The causal powers of purported emergents are the focus of much concern (Campbell 1974b, 1990; Kim 1992a, 1993b), but the criteria of novelty and the notion of levels are also of importance and interest (Wimsatt 1976a, 1976b). I will have a few things to say about each of them, and begin with novelty.

Novelty

The novelty of emergents, or potential emergents, can be construed with respect to time or with respect to ontology (Stephan 1992). Emergents in time — in history or evolution or cosmology, for example — are simply the first occurrences of whatever the emergent is claimed to be. Emergence in ontology is the stronger concept, and refers to something new coming into being with each instance of some level or pattern of lower level constituents. The two construals are closely related in that, on naturalistic accounts, temporal emergents would be the first instances of particular ontological emergents; conversely, an ontological emergent would be a temporal emergent the first time an instance appeared.

The emergence of novelty *per se*, at least in the sense of novel properties, seems uninterestingly trivial. There was presumably a first time for the cosmological emergence of an instance of the shape 'rectangle' or the configuration of one thing being 'above' something else. Among other requirements, these had to await the 'emergence' of entities out of the original superhot fields of the Big

Bang, and, for the relationship of 'above', presumably the aggregation of a mass with a significant gravitational field so that the directions of 'up' and 'down' would be determined. But the simplicity with which such a criterion of novel property emergence can be met seems to render it almost nugatory, and, correspondingly, novelty is generally considered to be a weak necessary criterion with little intrinsic interest.

If we turn the novelty criterion around, however, and consider it not just a requirement to be able to account for *something* new — anything — coming into being, but, rather, consider that most everything we are scientifically interested in did *not* exist at the moment of the Big Bang, and, therefore, that most everything we are scientifically interested in had to emerge since that time, novel emergence can become a very powerful negative criterion. In particular, any purported model of X — for any phenomena X — that cannot account for the historical and onto-logical emergence of X since the Big Bang is thereby at best incomplete. More importantly, any model of X that makes the emergence of X impossible is thereby refuted. This holds even if we ignore any issues regarding the causal status of X, though, of course, in most cases of scientific interest, X presumably will have *some* causal status.

Contemporary models of cognitive representation, for example, generally begin with some set of representational atoms, each with its own representational content, and attempt to account for all representation as various combinations of these atoms. But such models cannot, in principle, account for the emergence of the representational atoms themselves. The attempts to account for representation (combinations) already presupposes representations (atoms). There are rejoinders to such a claim, of course, and the issues are not trivial, but this characterization of the current scene is at least prima facie correct, and I argue that it is in fact deeply correct of symbol models, causal models, information models, current functional models, and connectionist models alike (Bickhard 1993; Bickhard & Terveen 1995). If so, this inability *in-principle* to account for the emergence of representation refutes these models of representation.

In any case, this characterization of current models of representation *could* well be correct, and that is all that I need at this moment to illustrate the potential power of emergence, even of just novelty, as a principle by which theories and models can be evaluated. Any theory of X must be at least consistent with the emergence of X or else it commits a non-naturalism of cosmology. If X cannot have historically emerged, then either it existed from the beginning or it was non-naturally introduced. Our best current science tells us that nothing familiar existed from the beginning, and that nothing was non-naturalistically introduced. Consistency with the possibility of emergence, then, is a scientifically necessary requirement — given contemporary science — as well as a powerful metaphysical requirement, for any model of any phenomena.

Causality

But this is 'just' a requirement to be able to account for the novel emergence of X, because there was a time at which X did not exist. If X supposedly has any causal powers of its own, then accounting for X must account not only for its cosmological and ontological novelty, but also for those emergent causal powers. This has been the focus of most of the concern about what emergence is and whether it exists or not — can genuine, and genuinely novel, causal powers emerge?

Emergence presupposes a notion of levels. The universe at its origin was a superhot flux of quantum fields; everything since then is the result of condensation, symmetry breaking, and organization out of that original flux, sometimes with clear hierarchical *levels* of organization. Quark excitations stabilize in combination with other such excitations into nucleons, which combine with electrons to form atoms, which combine chemically to form molecules, which combine gravitationally to form planets or, in derivative chemical ways, to form rocks, water, cats, humans, and, presumably, minds. This hierarchy of levels is one of the inspirations for the intuition of emergence: maybe *everything* has arisen in at least a generally similar way. Note that successively higher levels often require successively lower temperatures to emerge.

Downward Causation. If causal powers do emerge, then, within the framework of any reasonable naturalism, any causal consequences of those higher level emergent powers will themselves involve constituent levels of matter, or at least constituent levels of organizations of quantum processes. That is, *any* consequences of emergent causality will affect lower levels, constituent levels, of pattern and organization as well as the level at which the emergence occurs. More concisely, causal emergence implies downward causation (Campbell 1974b, 1990; Hooker 1979, 1981a, 1981b, 1981c; Kim 1992a). Since 'interesting' emergence involves causal emergence, and causal emergence implies downward causation, downward causation becomes a strong criterion for genuine causal emergence and for interesting emergence more generally.[3]

Levels? Emergence involves higher levels, but what constitutes the difference between higher and lower? What counts as a level? These questions lead in several directions, one of which I will focus on in particular.

Note first, however, that the paradigmatic hierarchy of ever higher levels traces progressively lower temperatures of emergence and stability. Each level 'condenses' out of lower levels with weaker forces, and, therefore, are stable and

---

3   Kim (this volume) argues that at least some versions of downward causation are conceptually coherent,
     but that, of course, leaves open the questions of whether or not the phenomenon is metaphysically or
     physically possible.

persistent in time only at lower temperatures. For at least some levels, such a differentiation of energy regimes in which stability is possible might seem to be definitive of the levels, though not necessarily of the particular kinds of emergents at those levels.

This temperature differentiation of emergence levels, however, ultimately proves unsatisfactory. 'Higher' levels might exhibit stability in the same temperature regime as constituent levels, such as for strictly mechanical machinery, or even manifest stability at higher energy levels. If, for example, an organism can protect itself against high temperatures, perhaps with perspiration and the production of heat shock molecules, the whole organism may remain viable at ambient temperatures at which isolated proteins would denature.

The strong intuition about the nature of levels remains that of ontological inclusiveness: higher levels include lower levels as constituents — regardless of the energy realms for stability. Later I will argue that even this seemingly most basic sense of levels is flawed.

A Logical Point. Emergence seems prima facie to be in conflict with naturalism. Higher levels of organization or constituency would seem to have whatever properties they have solely in virtue of those constituents and the relationships among them. If there were anything emergent beyond that, it could not be causally efficacious on pain of violating the completeness of the account of the physical world at those lower levels. One powerful way of putting this is to point out a problem: If the lower level includes everything that is physically — causally — relevant, then higher level emergence can be causally efficacious only at the cost of violating the causal closure of the physical world (Kim 1993a, 1993b). Such a result seems wildly non-naturalistic and something to be resisted. But if causal emergence yields such a result, then perhaps causal emergence too should be resisted.[4]

On the other hand, there are certainly laws of regularity of causal efficacy that 'emerge' at higher levels of pattern or organization — e.g., atomic stability and chemical valence (Hooker 1981c, 1989) — that cannot be deduced from lower level laws alone. The *pattern* or *organization* of the constituents, minimally, is also required. One aspect of the issue of what counts as higher and what belongs to lower, then, focuses on such patterns and organizations. They constitute initial and boundary conditions with respect to lower level laws, and they are necessary to be able to account for higher level causal properties (Hooker 1981c, 1989; Küppers 1992). Should they be included as part of the *lower* level, in which case

---

4   British emergentists had a kind of organizational conception of what counted as lower, and still wanted
    to claim that something else could be emergent at the higher level (Beckermann, 1992a, 1992b;
    McLaughlin, 1992; Stephan, 1992; Stöckler, 1991). The emergent property supposedly came into being
    with particular organizations of constituents, but it was in-principle not derivable from lower level con-
    siderations. Such emergence was itself presumed to be part of the physical laws of the universe: under
    such and such organizational or patterns conditions, this new causal property comes into being. This
    position may constitute a physicalism, but it violates the non-ad-hoc-ness of naturalism.

we again face the consequence that any resultant causal properties will be counted as *not* emergent? Or should they be counted as constituting (part of?) the *higher* level, in which case novel causal properties clearly *do* emerge (van Gulick 1992)?

In part this is a stipulative difference, and our preferential stipulation will depend on how strong or weak a notion of emergence we wish to consider (Beckermann 1992a; Emmeche, Køppe, Stjernfelt, this volume; Horgan 1993a; Hoyningen-Huene 1992, 1994; McLaughlin 1992; O'Conner 1994; Stephan 1992; Stöckler 1991).[5] Within the perspective developed to this point, our choice of which seemingly arbitrary stipulation to make — whether to count pattern as higher level or as included in the lower level — might depend most reasonably on what is at stake. Neither choice violates naturalism; countenancing emergence, however — counting pattern as 'higher' — fits our naive intuitions and shields the causal efficacy of, for example, emergent mind, which most of us would probably appreciate. So, perhaps the best of all possibilities is to accept a conception of emergence that accepts causal-property resultants of organization as of higher level, and, therefore, emergent: we retain naturalism, emergence, and the causal reality of, among other considerations, mind.[6]

5   There is an epistemological view of emergence that depends on higher level properties not being deriv-
    able from lower level considerations, as a distinct issue from that of whether or not the higher level
    properties are determined by lower level properties and relations (Hoyningen-Huene, 1992). In such a
    view, chaotic systems provide a clear kind of (epistemic) emergence in that their course over time is not
    calculable in-principle, even though it is completely determined. Among other consequences, this im-
    plies that it may not be determinable which of two or more different attractors a given system is or will
    be in because the attractors themselves or (inclusive) their basins of attraction may be chaotically mixed
    and not separable in any physically realistic sense (e.g., Newman, 1996). I find this to be an interesting
    conception of emergence, but it is not the one at issue in this paper. I am concerned with issues of onto-
    logical and physical emergence, not only epistemological unpredictability (Hooker, 1979, 1981a).
6   This would likely be considered to be too weak a notion of emergence by some — the British emergen-
    tists, for example. But the point of the concept of emergence is to differentiate novel causal powers.
    Causal powers that are in principle not derivable from lower causality and initial and boundary condi-
    tions would certainly be a kind of emergence — though likely an empty kind, and certainly an ad-hoc
    kind — but it is difficult to find a reasonable argument that this should be held as the only notion of
    emergence. Conversely, the point of reduction, at least in the sciences, is to reduce the number of onto-
    logical kinds necessary to understand the world, without necessarily prejudicing, and certainly without
    necessarily rejecting, the reality of at least some aggregations of instances of those kinds. Hooker, for
    example, distinguishes between ontological reality, which is a reality of ontological kinds, and physical
    reality, which can include aggregations of instances of those kinds. Ontological reduction can, in this
    view, occur without eliminating the physical reality of those aggregations: atoms, molecules, living be-
    ings, and, presumably, minds can well be physically real in this view, even though ontological reduc-
    tion may show that the only ontological kinds are of sub-atomic particles (Hooker, 1979, 1981a,
    1981b, 1981c). That is, ontological reduction of X does not necessarily carry the implication of the
    elimination of the reality of X.
    The key point would seem to be that of the existence of genuine emergent causal powers. If it were held
    that higher level physical systems might 'exist', but that their causal consequences were strictly a result
    of the working out of the causal powers of the fundamental particles that constituted them, then that
    physical existence might seem unacceptably pale and unsatisfying as a notion of emergence. This stance
    depends on a strong distinction between causal consequences and causal powers, because it is clear that
    differing organizations of particles will have, in general, differing causal consequences. So the issue is
    whether or not there are emergent causal powers, whatever those might be. The assumption that this dis-
    tinction between causal consequences and causal powers makes sense, in turn, depends on the assump-
    tion that there exists something that bears those genuine causal powers — distinct from mere causal

Ultimate reality: microcausation?

But is the situation that simple? It seems reasonable within its own framework, but, even accepting emergence as the result, for example, of organizational boundary conditions on the manifestations of lower level laws, there nevertheless remains a strong seduction toward the conclusion that all *real* causality occurs only at the ultimate level of physical reality, presumably some class of fundamental particles (Kim 1989, 1990, 1991, 1992b, 1993a, 1993b; Klee 1984). In this view, the 'merely' stipulative distinction between whether to count organization as part of higher or lower levels may usefully diagnose issues concerning relatively higher and lower levels where all levels under consideration are higher with respect to ultimate micro-levels, but it does not even address considerations that might privilege that ultimate micro-level itself above all other levels.

It may be the case that particular consequences in the world depend on initial and boundary configurations, patterns, and organizations of fundamental particles, but, it might seem, all genuine causality occurs, and *only* occurs, at this ultimate level of particle mechanics. However much it may be the case that the *outcome* of causality depends on the patterns in which it works its causal *consequences*, nevertheless the only causal *powers* extant are those of these basic particles. So, all other lawful regularities, at whatever level of 'emergence', are really just supervenient on and epiphenomenal with respect to that basic level. Of course it is necessary to take into account the space-time configurations within which basic particle mechanics plays out its causal dance, but the only genuine causality is in the interactions among those particles. Causal *consequences* may depend on higher level patterns, but the only causal *powers* are those of fundamental particles.

This is prima facie an extremely attractive picture. Its conceptual attractiveness is not diminished at all by the recognition that particular kinds of initial or boundary conditions can reliably yield particular kinds of regularities of consequences, and that these can look like emergents. All that *follows* from the view of ultimate reality being ultimate microcausation; it is not in contradiction to it. So, no matter the analysis of the distinction between relatively higher and lower levels, and no matter the semantic choices made about what counts as higher and what as lower, this view remains as a continual deflator of pretensions of emergence. What might appear to be emergence is really just basic, very micro-, particles interacting with each other.

---

consequences. Fundamental particles are the obvious candidate for these bearers of ultimate causality. It is to this set of issues regarding causal powers that I now turn in the main text.

Fields. But, such particles are not all there is. There are also fields, and, in particular, quantum fields. Quantum field theory yields a very different picture than that of micro-particle mechanics. Quantum fields yield non-local interactions, such as result in the Pauli exclusion principle. Note in contrast that, in the particle picture, all causality is itself atomized to the very local points of particle to particle encounters. Quantum field theory yields a continuum of never ending activity, of process, even in a vacuum (Aitchison 1985; Bickhard, in preparation-c; Brown & Harré 1988; Saunders & Brown 1991). The background is not one of nothing happening except geodesic motion and local particle encounters — of an inert stage for particle mechanics — but, rather, a background of seething continuous creation and annihilation of quantum excitations of the field with various symmetries, therefore conservations, constraining the interrelationships within this activity. Ontology is not atomized to particles on a space and time stage, and cause is not atomized to points of particle encounters.[7]

In fact, *there are no particles.* Quantum field theory yields the conclusion that everything is quantum field processes (Brown & Harré 1988; Davies 1984; Weinberg 1977, 1995, 1996; Saunders & Brown 1991). What appear to be particles are the consequences of the quantization of field excitatory activity, which is no more a particle than is the quantization of the number of waves in a vibrating guitar string.

To illustrate the 'reality' of this continuum of non-particle field processes, consider what is known as the Casimir effect. Two conducting plates held close together in a vacuum will inhibit the 'virtual' excitations between the plates because the waves of those excitations will be constrained by the physical distance between the plates. There is no such inhibition of the foam of virtual creations outside of that gap. Therefore vacuum activity between the plates will be less than outside of the gap, and this results in a difference of pressure exerted on those plates. The net effect is a force pushing the plates toward each other, which has been experimentally verified (Aitchison 1985; Sciama 1991; Weinberg 1995). Note that this force does not involve any particles; instead it is the result of that *continuum* of vacuum activity that is so unlike the atomization of substance and cause in the standard view.

Quantum field theory eliminates the localization and atomization of substance into particles, the localization and atomization of cause into particle encounters, and the localization and atomization of levels of systems into objects. *Everything*

---

7   Notions of causality must be re-examined both in the context of quantum field theory and of emergent causality. One interesting proposal, though not fully adapted to field theory, is Collier (1997). Pattee (this volume) would eliminate the notion except in an agent centered sense. Inquiring about *the* cause of something makes false presuppositions in most complex circumstances — there can be multiple necessary and sufficient complexes of process involved. It would still seem, however, that a distinction needs to be made between phenomena that are accidentally related and those that are more deeply related, however complex, and that 'cause' is often used to mark that distinction.

is organizations of quantum processes (van Gulick 1993); causality is constraints on that quantum field activity, such as those that yield momentum or energy conservation (Aitchison & Hey 1989; Bickhard, in preparation-c; Kaku 1993; Ryder 1985; Nakahara 1992; Sudbery 1986; Weinberg 1995).

In this view, everything is organization of process. There is no ultimate level of 'real' particles on which everything else is supervenient, and with respect to which everything else is epiphenomenal. So that seduction is eliminated. The ultimate level of micro-particle micro-causation does not exist.

It might seem that the micro-causation argument against emergence could simply be recast with respect to quantum fields instead of particles: the only reality is quantum fields, and everything else is epiphenomenal to that. The first part of this point is correct: everything is quantum field processes. But the critical point is that quantum field processes have no existence independent of configuration of process: quantum fields *are* process and can *only* exist in various patterns. Those patterns will be of many different physical and temporal scales, but they are all equally patterns of quantum field process. Therefore, there is no 'bottoming out' level in quantum field theory — it is *patterns* of process all the way down, *and* all the way up.[8]

Consequently, there is no rationale for delegitimating larger scale, hierarchical, patterns of process — such as will constitute living things, minds, and so on. That is, quantum field theory is an antidote to the seduction of including all patterns in the 'supervenience base', and, therefore, not counting properties that are dependent on perhaps complex patterns as constituting any kind of emergence. The point of quantum field theory in this discussion is to eliminate the temptation to devalue pattern so that pattern does not support emergence. In quantum field theory, pattern is *everything* because there is no level at which something unique and bottoming out, e.g., particles, can be found.[9] It is, therefore, at best incomplete to say that everything is quantum fields: everything is *organizations* of quantum field processes — at many different scales and hierarchical complexities. Micro- and macro- alike *are* such organizations.

This resurrects the possibility of choosing to consider manifestations of organizational boundary conditions as of higher level, thereby resurrecting a naturalized

8   Furthermore, there is no scale above which quantum effects can be ignored, and, therefore, below which it might seem processes can be privileged as a reduction base: non-classical quantum effects can occur at *any* scale — superconductivity, for example. Still further, quantum processes *per se* cannot be privileged as a base for classical processes because there are no classical processes *per se* — there are no classical processes other than (emergents of) organizations of quantum processes.

9   Particles are precisely such a 'bottoming out' of organization because particles have no internal organization. That, in fact, is definitive of particles. This lack of internal organization, in turn, ensures sharp boundaries: any non-sharp boundary would require some sort of organization internal to that boundary. Together, lack of internal organization and sharp boundaries (whether extensionless or not) yield point level localisms of causal influence and constraint. This set of properties forms a metaphysical package, and the entire package is rejected in a quantum field perspective: there is no bottoming out; there are no sharp boundaries; and (almost) nothing is local.

emergence. More correctly, the recognition that everything is organization of process — just at differing scales and with differing hierarchical organizations — makes the choice to consider pattern and organization as of lower level, and thus to render properties of those patterns and organizations as epiphenomenal, a choice that renders *everything* epiphenomenal because there is no level at which anything is other than an organization of quantum field process, including even the smallest scale quantum fluctuations. The choice between countenancing organizational emergence and not countenancing it, then, is no longer arbitrary: to reject this form of emergence is to eliminate any level of non-epiphenomenality. That would seem to be a *reductio ad absurdum* of that position.

In particular, in quantum field theory (or any process metaphysics), there is no basis for excluding pattern from supporting emergence because everything is equally pattern, including higher level things such as minds. Minds cannot be 'merely' epiphenomenal unless *everything* is taken to be epiphenomenal[10] because there is nothing else that can be privileged in the metaphysics other than pattern, and there is no inherent reason to privilege any particular scale of such pattern over any other.[11]

But the consequences of shifting to a quantum field view ramify more densely and more distantly than emergence per se, and at least some of those further consequences need to be examined lest we *implicitly* presuppose a micro-atomization ontology even while *explicitly* rejecting it.

Supervenience

Notions of supervenience are attempts to distill the intuition that higher level properties depend on lower level properties. No change at the higher level without a concomitant change at the lower is the motto. There are importantly different varieties of attempts at explication of this intuition, but the issues that I want to focus on seem to be in common at least to both weak and strong supervenience (Kim 1990).

---

10 Assuming that minds can be understood naturalistically as organizations of particular kinds of processes. (A process model of mind, of course, can be expected to be quite complex.)

11 It is arguable, incidentally, that the 'basic particle' reduction picture is not just factually false, but it is also logically incoherent. For example, if the particles have no extension, then a field view is forced in order to account for particle interactions, since the probability of such particles ever actually hitting each other is zero. If particles have finite extension, however, then they pose problems of compressibility, velocity of transmission of force through their diameter, extreme difficulty in explaining differing kinds of interactions (gravity, electricity, etc.), and so on. If a move is made to a combination of particles and fields (the typical contemporary semi-sophisticated view), then all of the basic issues are already granted anyway in the granting of fields at all. Any field view destroys the seduction into a micro-particle reduction because configurational and organizational properties make differences in causal power, not just in the working out of lower order causal power. There are no particles, but, even if there were, so long as fields are granted at all, the microreduction motivation fails — and a strict particle view is not only factually false but conceptually incoherent as well. (It is worth pointing out that Special Relativity plus conservation of energy forces a field physics, and, thus, a field metaphysics.)

The lower level of a supervenience dependency, the supervenience base, must include both lower level constituents and relationships between them.[12] 'Sphere' is not supervenient on two hemispheres that are physically distant from each other, but would be supervenient on precisely the same constituents if they were in the proper physical relationship with each other (Baker 1993). A supervenience base, however, does not include any relations external to the unit or system being considered. The property of being the longest pencil in the box, for example, is not supervenient on the molecules and internal relations that make up that pencil (Teller 1992). By adding a new longer pencil to the box, the original pencil ceases to have that property, yet nothing of the supervenience base has changed.

The property of being the longest pencil in a box is not of great independent interest, but there are other properties that are of deep importance that are similarly externally relational. Global quantum field constraints, such as the exclusion principle or a conservation constraint applying across spatially separated parts of a quantum system, are externally relational — they are not local.

The property of being in thermodynamic equilibrium is relational to the environment, and so, consequently, is the property of being a far-from-equilibrium system. Necessarily open systems are those that are inherently far-from-equilibrium, and, therefore, require constant or at least intermittent interaction with an environment to be able to exist over time — otherwise they move to equilibrium and the far-from-equilibrium system ceases to exist. This implies that far-from-equilibrium systems, and all of the properties that they have qua far-from-equilibrium systems, are externally relational and, therefore, cannot be supervenient in the standard sense.[13] A flame, for example, is not supervenient: its existence is dependent on its environment (adequate oxygen, not too low a temperature, and so on) as well as on its own 'constituents' per se. Furthermore, its supposed supervenience base is constantly changing, and any supposed micro-particle base is similarly in constant flux. The only persistence that constitutes the persistence of the flame is a persistence of an organization of process, not of the constituents that undergo that process. That organization of process, in turn, can be persistent only if appropriate transactions with the environment are possible and do in fact continue, such as inflows of oxygen and fuel vapor and outflows of combustion products. Conversely, if the constituents of a flame at a particular point in time were frozen — literally — then the supervenience base would remain the same, but there would no longer be a flame. Other even more important examples of far-from-equi-

---

12 Though it is not clear what is supposed to bear those internal relations. The syntactic assimilation of relations to properties as all being 'just' N-adic predicates for varying Ns seems to have obscured the metaphysical problems that relations pose to any substance-property metaphysics (Olson, 1987).

13 It is already clear that causally relevant properties are not necessarily local, and, therefore, not necessarily supervenient (Burge, 1989, 1993; LePore & Loewer, 1987, 1989; van Gulick, 1989). The point here is an extension of that to the existence of certain kinds of systems — in particular, of far-from-equilibrium systems. For other discussions of inadequacies of the concept of supervenience, see Collier (1988) and Horgan (1993a, 1993b).

librium systems, and, therefore, of the limitations of the supervenience explications, are living things and minds.

The supervenience intuition seems strong: higher levels depend on lower levels. But far-from-equilibrium systems constitute counterexamples to any presumed general applicability of supervenience as currently explicated. What is the source of the problem? Supervenience is explicated in terms of entities — particles — and properties (Kim 1989, 1990, 1993b). This is basically an Aristotelian metaphysics, and is an inadequate metaphysics for relationships and process, most especially open process. 'Entities' that are organizations of underlying far-from-equilibrium process are not supervenient so long as supervenience discounts external relations, and so long as it counts lower level constituents as part of the supervenience base. Flames, waves, vortexes — none are supervenient on underlying constituents. They are more like knots or twists in an underlying flow — nothing remains persistent other than the organization of the knot itself. They are topological entities, not substantive entities.[14]

Living cells may contain structures that are in equilibrium stability, at least on relatively short time scales, but remaining alive requires continuous maintenance of far-from-equilibrium conditions, and, therefore, continuous flow and exchange with the environment. 'Living', then, is not a supervenient property: it is externally relational, and it requires a continuous flow of constituents. I argue that normativity, from functional normativity (functional — dysfunctional) to representational normativity (true — false) (Bickhard 1993) and on up through rationality (Bickhard, forthcoming) and ethics (Bickhard, in preparation-a), is dependent on far-from-equilibrium systems properties. If this is so, or even if it is plausible, then the stakes involved in overlooking the inability of constituent and property based explications of supervenience to apply to far-from-equilibrium systems are quite serious.

The sense in which *everything* is organization of quantum process, then, is even deeper than might at first appear. A first temptation in understanding 'organization of process' is a constancy of constituents — particles — engaged in some motions and interactions; perhaps particles running around each other to form an atom. But far more important are organizations of process that have no constituents, or certainly no unchanging constituents. The organization is every-

---

14 And quantum field theory requires that all entities are topological entities, not substance entities. Topological entities are defined in terms of what classes of shapes can and cannot be continuously deformed into each other without breaking or tearing anything. A surface with one hole in it, for example, can be smoothly deformed into a teacup, but a surface with one hole in it cannot be smoothly deformed into a surface with two holes in it — something has to tear. Similarly, a sphere cannot be smoothly deformed into a torus (doughnut), and a simple loop cannot be smoothly deformed into a simple overhand knot (with the ends joined). Such considerations at the level of vacuum processes have proven to be central to quantum field theory (Atiyah, 1987, 1991; Dijkgraaf & Witten, 1990; L. Kaufmann, 1991; Weinberg, 1996; Witten, 1988, 1989). Clearly they are important at a macro-level: a flow with a vortex in it is causally different from a flow with no vortex.

thing; the constituents either do not exist or are not part of the supervenience base. Quantum field theory suggests that there are no constituents in the classical sense at any level. There are only certain wave properties that are maintained in the flux of quantum vacuum activity, like a soliton wave in water, but for which the vacuum takes the place of water. What we normally consider as constituents, as particles or entities, are persistences of instances of organizations of underlying quantum process: they are topological. If those persistences are due to equilibrium stabilities, then we have classical paradigm cases such as atoms for which it is easy to overlook that quantum field nature, thus process nature, of even the electrons and quarks. If those persistences are far-from-equilibrium system persistences, then we must look elsewhere than equilibrium to understand such persistence, and the relevance of external relations is directly manifest; the basic reality of the *organization* of process, relatively independent of whatever engages in that process, is more likely to be forced on us.

The dependence of higher on lower, then, remains. But the explication of supervenience as attempts to capture that dependence must relinquish the conception of the supervenience base as involving particular constituents and their internal relations. The *types* of the instances of lower level process patterns involved may be important — e.g., oxygen rather than nitrogen for a flame — but the dependence on the identities cannot remain. Furthermore, dependence cannot be simply mereological even with that modification: among other reasons, the necessity of external relationships must be accommodated. A vortex in a flow cannot exist if the flow itself does not exist.

Note that this view not only eliminates the localization and atomization of substance (substance disappears) and causality (point-localized particle encounters), but also of entities. Waves do not have definite boundaries; neither do flames, vortexes, and so on. A thorough and deep de-localization and de-atomization is required. We do not have an acceptable and well understood metaphysics of this sort.

In this view, the *possibility* of emergence, even causally efficacious emergence, is — at least in principle — trivial. There is no mystery, no non-naturalism. Everything is process organization, and, therefore, every causal property is a property of process organization. Higher levels and lower levels alike are levels of the organization of process. There cannot be the temptation, therefore, to privilege the constituents at the lower level, or even at some ultimate level, because there are no particles, and even lower level instances of process organizations may be in constant flux. It's pattern and organization all the way down.[15] So a higher level causal emergent is just as legitimate as a lower level causal emergent.

---

15 There exist, of course, questions about the nature of the vacuum processes which are (hierarchically) organized at so many different scales. That nature is largely unknown (Atiyah, 1991; Bickhard, in prepara-

Accounting for the emergence and causal efficacy of any particular kind of phenomena, of course, can still be of enormous difficulty and complexity,[16] but the impossibility in principle of any such emergence that a substance metaphysics yields (no new substances can emerge within a substance metaphysics, only combinations or blends of the basic substances can occur) is eliminated. At least in principle, in this view, the possibility of causally efficacious emergence is trivial, though the specifics of any particular emergence may well not be.

Reduction and anti-reduction

A particle and property metaphysics tempts us to think that the only real causality is found at the micro-particle level. If so, then anything that is a resultant of those particle interactions working their way within some initial or boundary condition constraints is most fundamentally due to those particle causal powers and particle interactions. Everything else is epiphenomenal to that, and can be eliminatively reduced to it — perhaps with the caveat of the cognitive limitations of human beings to handle the complexities required. In this cognitive view, higher levels are necessary considerations only because of their relative cognitive simplicity for humans, not for any metaphysical or even physical reasons.

Common sorts of rejections of such eliminative reductionist conclusions include the claim of multiple realizability of the higher level in the lower level and of cross-cutting kinds from higher to lower. The central point in such objections to eliminative reduction is that higher properties (or kinds) cannot always be eliminated in favor of lower properties (or kinds) because there can be multiple ways — perhaps unbounded or infinite numbers of ways — in which the higher level can be realized in the lower. The necessary correspondences between higher properties (kinds) and lower, then, do not hold. There are an unbounded number of ways to physically construct a computer, and therefore being a computer cannot be defined in terms of any of them.

The disputes in this area turn on what counts as a property or kind, in particular whether or not disjunctions of properties or kinds are themselves legitimate properties or kinds, on the nature of laws, and the relationship among laws, properties, and kinds, and so on (Burge 1989, 1993; Fodor 1981; Kim 1989, 1990, 1992b, 1993b; van Gulick 1989). If, for example, potentially unbounded disjunctions of

---

tion-c; Brown & Harré, 1988; Misner, Thorne, Wheeler, 1973; Saunders & Brown, 1991). But continuity, non-locality, and virtual excitations, for example, compel that that nature is not particle-like.

16 We now have some idea, for example, of the nature of the emergence of life, though it is enormously complex. The nature of mind is still quite elusive. Mind is the last mystery that still resists naturalism. This chapter attempts to block arguments against the metaphysical acceptability of the notion of emergence, but it does not present any model of the emergence of any particular phenomena. My own contributions to a model of mental phenomena can be found elsewhere (e.g., Bickhard, 1992, 1993, in press, forthcoming, in preparation-a).

kinds are legitimate kinds, then what it is to be a computer can be defined in terms of the disjunction of all of the physically possible ways that one could be realized.

So long, however, as the temptation remains to grant ultimate reality only to an ultimate micro-particle level of reality, it seems that the issue regarding reduction is foregone. Metaphysically everything is either *at* the micro-particle level, or else it is epiphenomenal and reducible to that level. Human cognitive limitations may require consideration of higher level epiphenomena because they are simpler, but they have no more metaphysical reality than that.

In the quantum process view, however, issues of multiple realizability and cross-cutting kinds still exist, but they exist as issues of what sorts of organizations of what sorts of process organization instances will yield particular emergent properties. Computers can be silicon, vacuum tubes, fluidic, even mechanical (though they tend to be rather slow), so long as certain organizational relationships are realized. This is the same point as is made within a particle view, except that there is no temptation to eliminate everything above the level of fundamental particles — there aren't any. The organizational properties that constitute something as a computer are just as legitimate as those that constitute something as an atom or cell or brain. The special properties that emerge with each of these need to be accounted for — a decidedly non-trivial task — but there is no need to fend off possible eliminative reduction to fundamental particles. Even within a particle view, the organizational properties cannot be ignored. But in a process view, such organizational properties (perhaps richly hierarchical) are *all that there is*. There is no more basic or fundamental reality.

The emergence of properties and entities

Because everything is organization of process, every causally efficacious property is a property of organization of process.[17] The possibility of causally efficacious property emergence, therefore, is assured. But what about entities? Particles have been eliminated, so entities cannot simply be combinations of particles. But how do we get to entities from properties and process organizations?

Paradigm entities are stable instances of organizations of underlying process, such as atoms or animals. There are two kinds of such stability: 1) equilibrium or energy well stability, and 2) open process, far-from-equilibrium, stability.[18] Energy

17 The British emergentists notwithstanding, the scientific use of the concept of emergence fits quite well with this notion of emergence in organization, rather than some sort of emergence beyond anything non-ad-hoc attributable to organization (e.g., Anderson & Stein, 1984; Bechtel & Richardson, 1992; Broschart, 1996; Careri, 1984; Chapman & Agre, 1986; Cherian & Troxell, 1995; Maes, 1992; Tucker, Hirsh-Pasek, Hollich, this volume).
18 There is also a form of persistence of *types* of process organization that is the result of *instances* of that organizational type causing, or at least increasing the probability of, the creation of more instances of that organizational type, such as in auto-catalysis or reproduction. I will not address these here (Bickhard, 1993; Bickhard & Campbell in preparation). Complex hierarchies will tend to be hierarchies

well stabilities are those process patterns that would require energy input to destabilize them. They exist, or would exist, at thermodynamic equilibrium. So long as the ambient energy is not sufficient to destabilize them, to disrupt their cohesion (Collier 1988, 1995), they will tend to persist. Atoms are a paradigm example.

Necessarily open system stability, in contrast, cannot exist at equilibrium. Necessarily open systems are inherently far from equilibrium and cease to exist if they approach equilibrium. But approach equilibrium they inexorably will, unless there are continuous exchanges with the environment that maintain the critical far-from-equilibrium conditions. The stability of far-from-equilibrium systems, then, depends on the stability of those conditions in the environment and relations to the environment that maintain the necessary far-from-equilibrium conditions. In some cases, all such conditions of stability are in the environment per se, and the system stability is completely dependent on that environment. A far-from-equilibrium system in which chemical solutions continuously flow into a container, for example, can exhibit fascinating properties (such as self-organization), but the stability of any such system is captured in the reservoirs and pumps for the chemical solutions, not the open system per se.

A flame, in contrast, contributes to its own stability. It generates above-combustion-threshold temperatures, and, in an atmosphere and gravitational field, that yields convective inflow of oxygen and outflow of combustion products. The heat also releases fuel vapor from the substrate, such as a piece of wood. The flame makes no contribution to the general availability of oxygen or fuel (though that

---

of various levels of relatively stable organizations of process — atoms, molecules, cells, organisms, and so on. There is no requirement that all such kinds of stability in a hierarchy be of the same form, though once far-from-equilibrium stabilities occur, all higher levels will inherit far-from-equilibrium properties. Atoms and molecules (most of them), for example, will constitute energy well stabilities within dissipative (far-from-equilibrium) organisms, while far-from-equilibrium organisms will be constitutive of higher level far-from-equilibrium species, ecosystems, and the biosphere (Bickhard & Campbell, in preparation). Clearly, the particular properties emergent in any particular organization of underlying process will depend not just on the *abstract* organization of processes that yields that emergence — the organization that constitutes the phenomenon or entity in question. Those emergent properties will also depend on the kinds of lower level stabilities and lower level emergents that participate in those constitutive processes. Atomic stability emerges in certain organizations of process among electrons, protons, and neutrons; atomic stability is not possible with constituents of atoms themselves (you cannot build atoms out of atoms), though a different kind of stability — molecular stability — sometimes is possible. Similarly, it makes a crucial difference whether the participants in a flame or an organism process are oxygen or helium: stability is possible in the first case, but not the second. Emergent properties, including stabilities, therefore, are usually dependent on most or all of the lower level hierarchy of levels of process. Exceptions to such hierarchical dependence, such as the claims of functionalism that functional properties are independent of realization, are the exception (and even the claims of functionalism can be challenged). Furthermore, there will often not be a clean differentiation of levels that is consistent across all portions of a process hierarchy. The hierarchy of organ, tissue, cell, molecule, and so on that is characteristic of a heart or kidney, for example, interacts at an equivalent level in most animals with the process of oxygen transport, in which most of those intermediate levels are missing — there is no tissue or organ level above hemoglobin. Similarly, large scale oxygen cycles or water cycles interact in the biosphere in crucial ways with multi-levelled cell-organism-ecosystem hierarchies, but, again, with most of the levels missing. Levels crossing is ubiquitous (Lemke, this volume). Accounting for emergents in terms of hierarchies of lower level process, clearly, can be very complex.

might be disputed in the case of a fire storm), but it does contribute to the temperature requirement and to the local availability of oxygen and fuel and the dispersal of waste. I call such systems *self-maintenant* systems — they contribute to their own maintenance.

Consider now a far-from-equilibrium system with the following general property: it has more than one way of being self-maintenant, and it can shift between or among available ways with at least some degree of appropriateness to what environmental conditions require. A bacterium, for example, might keep swimming if things are getting better, and tumble for a moment if they are not (Campbell 1990). In conditions of 'getting better', keep swimming; in conditions of 'getting worse', randomize direction. Note that the switching between forms of contribution to self-maintenance requires some signal from the environment that can be used as an indication of which form is currently appropriate. I call such systems *recursively* self-maintenant — they tend to maintain (with respect to variations in the environment) their own condition of being self-maintenant (in those environments).

I now want to offer some extremely inspissated outlines of how this framework might be able to account for some normative emergences.

Note that a self-maintenant system either succeeds in maintaining system stability or it does not. If it does, the system remains stable in the world, and its causal consequences continue. If it does not, then the system ceases to exist, and its causal consequences qua that system cease. If the match flame has gone out, then the paper will not burn. The flame, then, serves a function (actually several) relative to the maintenance of the flame itself. And it makes a causal difference, an asymmetric difference, in the world whether or not that function is well served or not served. The difference between the flame existing or not existing is obvious; the asymmetry derives from the persistence of the relevant emergent properties if it continues, and the cessation of those emergent properties if it ceases. The asymmetry, then, derives from the asymmetry between the existence of open system emergents and the non-existence of those emergents — from the basic asymmetry between far-from-equilibrium and equilibrium.

I claim that this is the general form in which function, and dysfunction, emerge. Function is contribution to self-maintenance, and is relative to the far-from-equilibrium system whose maintenance is in focus (Bickhard 1993, in preparation-a).

Note also that a *recursively* self-maintenant system could be wrong in its switching from one manner of self-maintenance to another. In particular, such a shift of process involves an implicit anticipation of subsequent self-maintenant interactions with the environment, but the environment may or may not cooperate. If the environment 'misbehaves', if things are actually getting worse for the bacterium in spite of continued swimming that is supposed to make things better, then that implicit anticipation has been falsified. Furthermore, the system may be able to detect such a falsification: tumbling may be triggered yet again. In a more complicated system, perhaps a higher level signal (perhaps generated internally to the bacterium)[19] could indicate falsification even while the signal to switch from swimming to tumbling remains with the swimming. Any such higher level error signal (higher than the signal for switching from swimming to tumbling — e.g., a signal that the swimming-tumbling detector is being fooled by saccharin instead of sugar) would have to be a surrogate or vicariant for overall system stability in order for the 'error' to be a functionally genuine error for the system (Campbell 1974a). But even the existence of such an error detector would do the bacterium no good unless that signal could in turn control or trigger some *further* self-maintaining process. It might, for example, shift to an entirely different set of interactive strategies for self-maintenance, or, in a much more complex system, such error signals may guide learning, not just subsequent behavior.

My basic point, however, is that such implicit anticipations, and their potential falsification in and of and by the system itself, constitutes an emergence of truth value in the system itself. Truth value is one of the criteria, and a crucial and very difficult criterion to meet, for the emergence of representation. I argue, in fact, that such truth-valued anticipations constitute the most primitive form of emergent representation, out of which all other representation is differentiated and derived (Bickhard 1993, in preparation-b).

I have barely outlined these two claims of normative emergence, of function and of representation; I have not offered anything like an adequate argument for these particular emergents *here*. My point, however, is illustrative, not conclusive. My point is to illustrate a prima facie not-implausible possibility. Note that, in these models, function and representation emerge as properties of certain kinds of open, far-from-equilibrium, systems. That is, they emerge in certain kinds of organization of process. The possibility of their emergence, therefore, and of their causally efficacious emergence, is not precluded. Not precluded, of course, is not the same as 'accounted for'. That requires the full arguments not presented here. But, for them to be not metaphysically precluded is already a large step beyond the intricate impossibilities yielded by standard particle and property metaphysics. As mentioned at the beginning of this paper, requiring that a model of X not preclude the emergence of X already rejects every model of representation[20] (and function; Bickhard, in preparation-b) available in the contemporary literature.

---

19   The illustration leaves the realm of biological reality here. I haven't bothered to find out if any actual bacterium is capable of this. My point is more general, and this is illustration.

20   — and of all other forms of normativity as well.

Emergent causality

Some conceptions of emergence would have it that any property that is in-principle derivable from the internal constituents and relations of an entity would not be eligible to be considered emergent (McLaughlin 1992; Kim 1989,1991). I have argued that there are deep problems with this view. First, much of its appeal comes from an underlying assumption of a basic level of reality consisting of fundamental particles. On this assumption, the temptation is strong to conclude that everything that is ultimately real is at this fundamental particle level, and everything else is epiphenomenally supervenient on it. This particle assumption, however, is false: there are no particles. Instead, special relativity forces a field physics, and, therefore, metaphysics, and quantum field theory forces a field view in which the fields are continuously in process. There are no particles engaged in this process. It is more akin to spontaneous vibrations of an intrinsically oscillatory medium. The 'particleness' arises from a quantization of that oscillatory activity, akin to the quantization of a vibrating guitar string. This activity is inherently and necessarily organized; it is not definable independently of some patterning or organization. That is, organization is not something superimposed on a more basic level of reality; it is a necessary aspect of *all* reality. So, delegitimating process organization as a potential locus of emergence renders *all* reality epiphenomenal, because there is no reality that is not constituted as process organization.

Furthermore, the propagation of properties of such activity, and the constraints on that propagation, are, in many respects, non-local — such as the Pauli exclusion principle, or EPR phenomena. Such non-locality is yet another blow to an assumption of a strict particle, thus strictly local, metaphysics.

Conceptually integrating such process conceptions, with the continuity of process and non-locality that they involve, undermines related notions such as micro-reduction and supervenience. Supervenience, for example, is defined in terms of constituent particles and relations. It cannot handle external relations. But many critical phenomena, and important kinds of entities, are far-from-equilibrium, thus necessarily open, thus cannot be modelled without taking into account the external relations that maintain such far-from-equilibrium conditions, and the non-constancy of constituents that is involved in those open transactions. Examples include flames, living beings, and, arguably, minds. This critical importance of external relations at macro-levels is in addition to the inherent involvement of non-local, external, relations at the quantum field level.

My conclusion is that, since everything is equally patterns of underlying process, macro-organizations of such process are equally valid as physically real as are micro-organizations of such process. Furthermore, since internal and external relations of process are all that there is, then process organization is a valid candidate to be constitutive of emergents, instead of, for example, being neglected as part of the supervenience base. That is, higher levels are higher levels of organization of process relative to lowers levels of organization of process, and properties that derive from such higher levels are valid candidates for being emergent.

But, clearly not *all* such properties of higher level pattern will be emergent. All that I have done to this point is to propose and defend the position that such higher levels of process organization cannot simply be dismissed as grounding emergence — cannot simply be relegated to a non-emergence-candidate supervenience base, for example. So, the question remains if anything can be said about what sorts of process organizations do, or might, yield emergence.

Clearly, every particular kind of emergence will require its own particular model, so the question is whether anything interesting can be said more generally. This question focuses attention on the conceptions of what emergence is that were mentioned earlier — in particular, on novelty and causality. (Much of the ensuing discussion has focused on what counts, or what should count, as 'higher level'.) Novelty *per se*, as discussed, is not problematic: every new organization instantiates the higher level property of having that organization. Causality, however, is crucial, and, I argue, criterial. Emergence that is non-trivial is emergent causality — the emergence of novel causal properties.

So the question of what could support emergence becomes a question of what could support novel causal properties. As mentioned, any emergent causality will, assuming a naturalistic closure and integration of causality, necessarily involve downward causality. Downward causality, then, can serve as an additional, related, criterion for emergent causality.

What can be said about process organizations that yield emergent causality — likely indicated by, among other phenomena, downward causation? There is one major divide in kinds of process organizations that is strongly relevant to this question: the distinction between linear and non-linear process and interaction. Linear process yields consequences that are simply the additive sum of the influences of the lower level consequences. Such summative consequences are characteristic, for example, of simple aggregations of constituents (Christensen, Colliers & Hooker, in preparation; Wimsatt 1976a, 1986). Emergence has, from its historical beginning, been taken to be in contrast to such summations (Beckermann 1992a, 1992b; McLaughlin 1992; Stephan 1992; Stöckler 1991).

So, non-linearity is crucial to causal emergence (Christensen, Collier, & Hooker, in preparation; Küppers 1992). Note that far-from-equilibrium systems are intrinsically non-linear. But non-linearity is not limited to far-from-equilibrium systems. The forces that hold together a kite, and thus produce, among other things, the property of lift in a wind, are non-linear. In fact, cohesion in general is a manifestation of non-linearity (Collier 1988 1995). But non-linearity is also not limited to energy well stabilities of entities. Phase shifts of all kinds, such as freezing, explosions, magnetization, and so on also manifest non-linearity. As such, they make at least the first cut for being candidates for emergence.

Just as being the longest pencil in the box is a marginal example of an external relation property, while being a far-from-equilibrium system is an example that is not marginal, it is to be expected that there will be marginal cases of emergence as well as centrally important kinds. Marginal cases can nevertheless be important to conceptual understanding, but I am concerned here with broad a characterization of conditions for emergence. Non-linearity provides a first major cut, but is it the case that *every* instance of non-linearity is an instance of emergence?

By definition, every instance of non-linearity is an instance whose causal properties cannot be derived aggregatively from lower level consequences. In that sense, every instance of non-linearity is an instance of emergence. But there is a further set of important distinctions to be made, one that either demarcates central classes of emergents, or that might by some be taken to be criterial for emergence (again, we encounter a semantic arbitrariness). This further set of distinctions is in terms of the kinds of downward causations that result.

For example, without attempting to be exhaustive, we can find the following kinds of downward causation. Consequences outside of a system that are non-linear with respect to the lower levels of the system, but that nevertheless influence lower level external processes would constitute a downward causation — this is among the weakest kinds. Disturbances in air flow around a kite might be an example. Constraints *internal* to a system that are non-linear consequences of the organization of the system would be a more powerful case. System stability, whether of energy well or far-from-equilibrium form, would be examples.

Non-linear constraints *internal* to the *constituents* of a system — that is, one level down from the previous constraints mentioned — would be a still more powerful case. Here, in fact, we find some of the most interesting kinds of emergence. The processes internal to cells, for example, are strongly constrained by the overall processes of the organism (Moreno & Umerez, this volume). Such 'meta-internal' downward causations can extend even to the existence of complex molecules that would not exist otherwise. The influence of surroundings on the internal processes of a computer chip (van Gulick 1989) would be another example.

Still another kind of downward causation involves constraints on the *generative* processes — sources of constructive variation — as well as the activities per se, of lower levels. The easiest examples here are biological. Changes in the organization of an ecosystem, for example, can alter the selection pressures on the constituent organisms. Similarly, but at a much larger scale, alterations in the earth's biosphere can change the selections, and, at least indirectly, the variations, with respect to the species and ecosystems at constituent levels. In such instances, we find a causation, and a downward causation, via selection (Campbell 1990). Such downward causation via selection is among the strongest kinds of emergent causation.

Conclusion

The intuition that genuine causally efficacious emergence occurs — of mind, for example, especially yours or mine — is very strong. But serious difficulties have been encountered in trying to account for the mere possibility of any such emergence. I suggest that these difficulties are due to an inadequate and, according to our best current science, false metaphysical framework that is presupposed in attempting those accounts. Within a more acceptable process metaphysics, the mere possibility of emergence is trivial, and the hard work of creating good models of actual emergents can proceed.

References

AITCHISON, I.J. R. 1985. Nothing's Plenty: The vacuum in modern quantum field theory. *Contemporary Physics* 26(4), 333-91.

AITCHISON, I.J.R., HEY, A.J.G. 1989. *Gauge Theories in Particle Physics*. Adam Hilger.

ANDERSON, P.W., STEIN, D.L. 1984. Broken Symmetry, Emergent Properties, Dissipative Structures, Life and Its Origin: Are They Related? In P. W. Anderson (ed.), *Basic Notions of Condensed Matter Physics*. Benjamin/Cummings, 262-85.

ATIYAH, M. 1987. *Michael Atiyah Collected Works. Vol. 5: Gauge Theories*. Oxford: Oxford University Press.

ATIYAH, M. 1991. Topology of the Vacuum. In S. Saunders & H. R. Brown (eds.), *The Philosophy of Vacuum*. Oxford: Oxford University Press, 275-78.

BAKER, L.R. 1993. Metaphysics and Mental Causation. In J. Heil & A. Mele (eds.), *Mental Causation*. Oxford: Oxford University Press, 75-95.

BECHTEL, W., RICHARDSON, R. C. 1992. Emergent Phenomena and Complex Systems. In A. Beckermann, H. Flohr & J. Kim (eds.), *Emergence or Reduction? Essays on the Prospects of Nonreductive Physicalism*. Berlin: de Gruyter, 257-88.

BECKERMANN, A. 1992a. Introduction — Reductive and Nonreductive Physicalism. In A. Beckermann, H. Flohr & J. Kim (eds.), *Emergence or Reduction? Essays on the Prospects of Nonreductive Physicalism*. Berlin: de Gruyter, 1-21.

BECKERMANN, A. 1992b. Supervenience, Emergence, and Reduction. In A. Beckermann, H. Flohr, J. Kim (eds.), *Emergence or Reduction? Essays on the Prospects of Nonreductive Physicalis*. Berlin: de Gruyter, 94-118.

BECKERMANN, A., FLOHR, H. & KIM, J. 1992. *Emergence or Reduction? Essays on the Prospects of Nonreductive Physicalism*. Berlin: de Gruyter.

BICKHARD, M.H. 1992. How Does the Environment Affect the Person? In L. T. Winegar & J. Valsiner (eds.), *Children's Development within Social Context: Metatheory and Theory*. Hillsdale, N.J.: Erlbaum, 63-92.

BICKHARD, M.H. 1993. Representational Content in Humans and Machines. *Journal of Experimental and Theoretical Artificial Intelligence* 5, 285-333.

BICKHARD, M.H. Forthcoming. Critical Principles: On the Negative Side of Rationality. In Herfel, W. & Hooker, C.A. (eds.), *Beyond Ruling Reason: Non-formal Approaches to Rationality*.

BICKHARD, M.H. In preparation-a. *The Whole Person: Toward a Naturalism of Persons*. Cambridge, Mass.: Harvard University Press.

BICKHARD, M.H. In preparation-b. Interaction and Representation.

BICKHARD, M.H. In preparation-c. Variations in Variation and Selection: The Ubiquity of the Variation-and-Selective-Retention Ratchet in Emergent Organizational Complexity. Part II: Quantum Field Theory.

BICKHARD, M.H. In press. Levels of Representationality. *Journal of Experimental and Theoretical Artificial Intelligence*.

BICKHARD, M.H. & CAMPBELL, D.T. In preparation. Variations in Variation and Selection: The Ubiquity of the Variation-and-Selective-Retention Ratchet in Emergent Organizational Complexity.

BICKHARD, M.H. & TERVEEN, L. 1995. *Foundational Issues in Artificial Intelligence and Cognitive Science — Impasse and Solution*. Amsterdam: Elsevier Scientific.

BROSCHART, J. 1996. A Geometrical Model of the Emergence of Case Relations. Presented at the *Conference on Functionalism and Formalism*, University of Wisconsin: Milwaukee, Wisconsin, April 1996.

BROWN, H.R., & HARRÉ, R. 1988. *Philosophical foundations of quantum field theory*. Oxford: Oxford University Press.

BURGE, T. 1989. Individuation and Causation in Psychology. *Pacific Philosophical Quarterly* 70, 303-22.

BURGE, T. 1993. Mind-Body Causation and Explanatory Practice. In J. Heil & A. Mele (eds.), *Mental Causation*. Oxford: Oxford University Press, 97-120.

CAMPBELL, D.T. 1974a. Evolutionary Epistemology. In P. A. Schilpp (ed.), *The Philosophy of Karl Popper*. LaSalle, Ill.: Open Court, 413-63.

CAMPBELL, D.T. 1974b. 'Downward Causation' in Hierarchically Organized Biological Systems. In F. J. Ayala & T. Dobzhansky (eds.), *Studies in the Philosophy of Biology*. Berkeley, Cal.: University of California Press, 179-86.

CAMPBELL, D.T. 1990. Levels of Organization, Downward Causation, and the Selection-Theory Approach to Evolutionary Epistemology. In G. Greenberg & E. Tobach (eds.), *Theories of the Evolution of Knowing*. Hillsdale, N.J.: Erlbaum, 1-17.

CARERI, G. 1984. *Order and Disorder in Matter*. Benjamin/Cummings.

CHAPMAN, D. & AGRE, P. 1986. Abstract reasoning as emergent from concrete activity. In M. P. Georgeff & A. L. Lansky (eds.), *Reasoning about Actions and Plans, Proceedings of the 1986 Workshop*. San Francisco: Morgan Kaufmann, 411-24.

CHERIAN, S. & TROXELL, W.O. 1995. Intelligent behavior in machines emerging from a collection of interactive control structures. *Computational Intelligence* 11(4), 565-92. Cambridge, Mass. and Oxford: Blackwell.

COLLIER, J. 1988. Supervenience and Reduction in Biological Hierarchies. In M. Matthen & B. Linsky (eds.), *Philosophy and Biology: Canadian Journal of Philosophy*, suppl. 14, 209-34.

COLLIER, J.D. 1995. Emergence in Natural Hierarchies.

COLLIER, J.D. 1997. Causation is the Transfer of Information. In H. Sankey (ed.), *Causation and Natural Laws*. Dordrecht: Kluwer.

CHRISTENSEN, W.D., J.D. COLLIER & C.A. HOOKER. In preparation. Autonomy, Anticipation, Adaptation: Towards an epistemics-relevant analysis.

DAVIES, P.C.W. 1984. Particles Do Not Exist. In S.M. Christensen (ed.), *Quantum Theory of Gravity*. Adam Hilger, 66-77.

DIJKGRAAF, R. & WITTEN, E. 1990. Topological Gauge Theories and Group Cohomology. *Commun. Math. Phys.* 129, 393-429.

FODOR, J.A. 1981. Special Sciences. In J. Fodor *RePresentations*. Cambridge, Mass.: MIT Press, 127-45.

HEIL, J. & A. MELE. 1993. *Mental Causation*. Oxford University Press.

HOOKER, C.A. 1979. Critical Notice. R. M. Yoshida: Reduction in the Physical Sciences. *Dialogue* 18(1), 81-99.

HOOKER, C.A. 1981a. Towards a General Theory of Reduction. Part I: Historical and Scientific Setting. *Dialogue* 20, 38-59.

HOOKER, C.A. 1981b. Towards a General Theory of Reduction. Part II: Identity and Reduction. *Dialogue* 20, 201-36.

HOOKER, C.A. 1981c. Towards a General Theory of Reduction. Part III: Cross-Categorial Reduction. *Dialogue,* 20, 496-529.

HOOKER, C.A. 1989. Evolutionary Epistemology and Naturalist Realism. In K. Hahlweg, C. A. Hooker (eds.), *Issues in Evolutionary Epistemology*. New York: State University of New York, 101-50.

HORGAN, T. 1993a. From Supervenience to Superdupervenience: Meeting the Demands of a Material World. *Mind* 102(408), 555-86.

HORGAN, T. 1993b. Nonreductive Materialism and the Explanatory Autonomy of Psychology. In S. J. Wagner & R. Warner (eds.), *Naturalism: A critical appraisal*. Notre Dame, Ind.: University of Notre Dame Press, 295-320.

HOYNINGEN-HUENE, P. 1992. On the Way to a Theory of Antireductionist Arguments. In A. Beckermann, H. Flohr & J. Kim (eds.), *Emergence or Reduction? Essays on the Prospects of Nonreductive Physicalism*. Berlin: de Gruyter, 289-301.

HOYNINGEN-HUENE, P. 1994. Zu Emergenz, Mikro- und Makro-determination./On Emergence, Micro-determination, and Macro-determination. In W. Lübbe (ed.), *Kausalität und Zurechnung*. Berlin: de Gruyter.

KAKU, M. 1993. *Quantum Field Theory*. Oxford: Oxford University Press.

KAUFFMAN, L.H. 1991. *Knots and Physics*. Singapore: World Scientific.

KIM, J. 1989. The Myth of Nonreductive Materialism. *Proceedings and Addresses of the American Philosophical Association* 63, 31-47.

KIM, J. 1990. Supervenience as a Philosophical Concept. *Metaphilosophy* 21(1-2), 1-27.

KIM, J. 1991. Epiphenomenal and Supervenient Causation. In D.M. Rosenthal (ed.), *The Nature of Mind*. Oxford: Oxford University Press, 257-65.

KIM, J. 1992a. 'Downward Causation' in Emergentism and Non-reductive Physicalism. In A. Beckermann, H. Flohr & J. Kim (eds.), *Emergence or Reduction? Essays on the Prospects of Nonreductive Physicalism*. Berlin: de Gruyter, 119-38.

KIM, J. 1992b. Multiple Realization and the Metaphysics of Reduction. *Philosophy and Phenomenological Research* 52, 1-26.

KIM, J. 1993a. *Supervenience and Mind*. Cambridge: Cambridge University Press.

KIM, J. 1993b. The Non-Reductivist's Troubles with Mental Causation. In J. Heil & A. Mele (eds.), *Mental Causation*. Oxford: Oxford University Press, 189-210.

KLEE, R.L. 1984. Micro-Determinism and Concepts of Emergence. *Philosophy of Science* 51, 44-63.

KÜPPERS, B.-O. 1992. Understanding Complexity. In A. Beckermann, H. Flohr & J. Kim (eds.), *Emergence or Reduction? Essays on the Prospects of Nonreductive Physicalism*. Berlin: Walter de Gruyter, 241-56.

LEPORE, E. & B. LOEWER 1987. Mind Matters. *Journal of Philosophy, 84*, 630-642.

LEPORE, E. & B. LOEWER 1989. More on Making Mind Matter. *Philosophical Topics,* 17(1), 175-91.

MAES, P. 1992. Learning Behavior Networks from Experience. In F.J. Varela & P. Bourgine (eds.) *Toward A Practice of Autonomous Systems*. Cambridge, Mass.: MIT Press, 48-57.

MCLAUGHLIN, B.P. 1992. The Rise and Fall of British Emergentism. In A. Beckermann, H. Flohr & J. Kim (eds.), *Emergence or Reduction? Essays on the Prospects of Nonreductive Physicalism*. Berlin: de Gruyter, 49-93.

MISNER, C.W., K.S. THORNE & J.A. WHEELER 1973. *Gravitation*. Freeman.

NAKAHARA, M. 1992. *Geometry, Topology, and Physics*. Institute of Physics Publishing.

NEWMAN, D.V. 1996. Emergence and Strange Attractors. *Philosophy of Science* 63(2), 245-61.

O'CONNER, T. 1994. Emergent Properties. *American Philosophical Quarterly* 31(2), 91-104.

OLSON, K.R. 1987. *An Essay on Facts*. Stanford, Cal.: Center for the Study of Language and Information.

RYDER, L.H. 1985. *Quantum Field Theory*. Cambridge: Cambridge University Press.

SAUNDERS, S. & BROWN, H.R. 1991. *The Philosophy of Vacuum*. Oxford: Oxford University Press.

SCIAMA, D.W. 1991. The Physical Significance of the Vacuum State of a Quantum Field. In S. Saunders & H.R. Brown (ed.), *The Philosophy of Vacuum*. Oxford: Oxford University Press, 137-58.

STEPHAN, A. 1992. Emergence — A Systematic View on its Historical Facets. In A. Beckermann, H. Flohr & J. Kim (eds.), *Emergence or Reduction? Essays on the Prospects of Nonreductive Physicalism*. Berlin: de Gruyter, 25-48.

STÖCKLER, M. 1991. A Short History of Emergence and Reductionism. In E. Agazzi (ed.), *The Problem of Reductionism in Science*. Dordrecht: Kluwer, 71-90.

SUDBERY, A. 1986. *Quantum Mechanics and the Particles of Nature*. Cambridge: Cambridge University Press.

TELLER, P. 1992. A Contemporary Look at Emergence. In A. Beckermann, H. Flohr & J. Kim (eds.), *Emergence or Reduction? Essays on the Prospects of Nonreductive Physicalism*. Berlin: de Gruyter, 139-53.

VAN GULICK, R. 1989. Metaphysical Arguments for Internalism and Why They Don't Work. In S. Silvers (ed.), *Rerepresentation*. Dordrecht: Kluwer, 151-59.

VAN GULICK, R. 1992. Nonreductive Materialism and the Nature of Intertheoretical Constraint. In A. Beckermann, H. Flohr & J. Kim (eds.), *Emergence or Reduction? Essays on the Prospects of Nonreductive Physicalism*. Berlin: de Gruyter, 157-79.

VAN GULICK, R. 1993. Who's in Charge Here? And Who's Doing All the Work? In J. Heil
    & A. Mele (eds.) *Mental Causation*. Oxford: Oxford University Press, 233-56.
WEINBERG, S. 1977. The Search for Unity, Notes for a History of Quantum Field Theory.
    Daedalus 106(4), 17-35.
WEINBERG, S. 1995. *The Quantum Theory of Fields. Vol. 1. Foundations*. Cambridge.
WEINBERG, S. 1996. *The Quantum Theory of Fields. Vol. II Modern Applications*.
    Cambridge.
WIMSATT, W.C. 1976a. Reductionism, levels of organization, and the mind-body problem.
    In G. Globus, G. Maxwell & I. Savodnik (eds.), *Consciousness and the Brain*. Plenum.
WIMSATT, W.C. 1976b. Reductive Explanation: A functional account. In R.S. Cohen,
    C.A. Hooker, A.C. Michalos & J. Van Evra (eds.), *PSA-1974*. Boston Studies in the
    Philosophy of Science. Dordrecht: Reidel, vol. 32, 671-710.
WIMSATT, W.C. 1986. Forms of Aggregativity. In A. Donogan, A.N. Perovich & M.V.
    Wedin (eds.), *Human Nature and Natural Knowledge*. Dordrecht: Reidel, 259-91.
WITTEN, E. 1988. Topological Quantum Field Theory. *Communications in Mathematical
    Physics* 117, 353-86.
WITTEN, E. 1989. Quantum Field Theory and the Jones Polynomial. *Communications in
    Mathematical Physics* 121(3), 351-99.

Contributors

ANDERSEN, PETER BØGH
Department of Information and Media Science, University of Aarhus. Niels Juels gade 84, DK-8200 Aarhus N, Denmark.

BICKHARD, MARK H.
Department of Philosophy, 15 University Drive, Lehigh University, Bethlehem, Pa. 18015, USA.

†CAMPBELL, DONALD T.

CHRISTIANSEN, PEDER VOETMANN
Department of Studies in Mathematics and Physics and their Functions in Education, Research and Applications. Roskilde University Center. P.o. box 260, DK-4000 Roskilde, Denmark.

EMMECHE, CLAUS
Niels Bohr Institute, University of Copenhagen, Blegdamsvej 17, DK-2100 Copenhagen Ø, Denmark.

FINNEMANN, NIELS OLE
Department of Information and Media Science, University of Aarhus, Niels Juels gade 84, DK-8200 Aarhus N, Denmark.

GOLINKOFF, ROBERTA M.
Department of Educational Studies, University of Delaware, Willard Hall, Newark, Del. 19716, USA.

HIRSH-PASEK, KATHY
Department of Psychology, Faculty of the Cognitive Psychology Division, Temple University, Philadelphia, Pennsylvania, Pa. 19122, USA.

HOLLICH, GEORGE
Department of Psychology, Faculty of the Cognitive Psychology Division, Temple University, Philadelphia, Pennsylvania, Pa. 19122, USA.

KIM, JAEGWON
Department of Philosophy, Brown University, Providence, R.I. 02912, USA.

KRUSE, TOVE ELISABETH
Department of History and Social Conditions, Roskilde University Center. P.o. box 260, DK-4000 Roskilde, Denmark.

KØPPE, SIMO
Psychological Laboratory, University of Copenhagen, Njalsgade 94, DK-2300 Copenhagen S, Denmark.

LEMKE, JAY L.
Brooklyn College School of Education, City University of New York, Brooklyn, New York 11210, USA.

MORENO, ALVARO
Department of Logic & Philosophy of Science, University of the Basque Country, 1249, E-20080 Donostia (San Sebastian), Spain.

NIÑO EL-HANI, CHARBEL
Institute of Biology, Research Group on History, Philosophy, and the Teaching of Biological Sciences, Federal University of Bahia, Brazil.

PATTEE, H. H.
Department of Systems Science, State University of New York at Binghamton, Binghamton, N.Y. 13901, USA.

PEREIRA, ANTONIO MARCOS
Institute of Biology, Research Group on History, Philosophy, and the Teaching of Biological Sciences, Federal University of Bahia, Brazil.

STJERNFELT, FREDERIK
Department of Comparative Literature, University of Copenhagen, Njalsgade 80, DK-2300 Copenhagen S, Denmark

TOGEBY, OLE
Department of Nordic Languages and Literature, University of Aarhus, Niels Juels gade 84, DK-8200 Aarhus N, Denmark.

TUCKER, MICHAEL L.
State University of New York at Buffalo, Buffalo, N.Y. 14260, USA.

UMEREZ, JON
Department of Logic & Philosophy of Science, University of the Basque Country, 1249, E-20080 Donostia (San Sebastian), Spain.

Author Index